KT-379-926

VINOPOLIS
CITY OF WINE

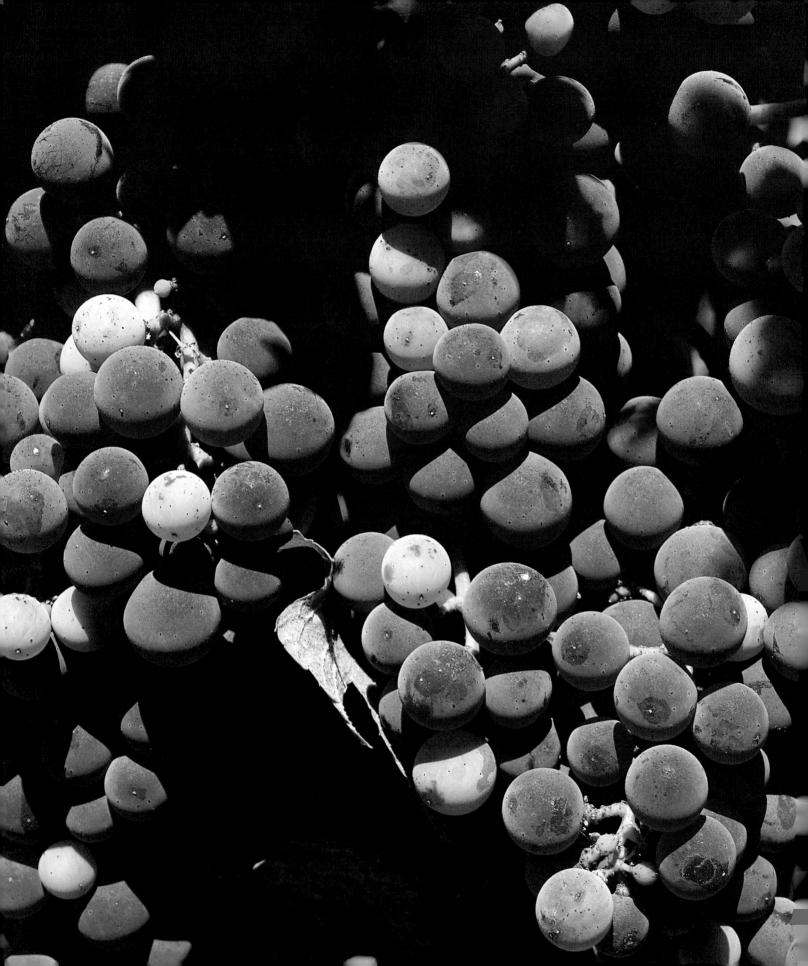

VINOPOLIS

WORLD WINE GUIDE

Your Personal Wine Odyssey

Oz Clarke

WEBSTERS

LITTLE, BROWN AND COMPANY

BOSTON NEW YORK LONDON

Created and designed for Wineworld London plc by
Websters International Publishers Limited,
Axe and Bottle Court,
70 Newcomen Street,
London SE1 1YT

First published in 1999

Copyright © 1999 Websters International Publishers
Text copyright ©1999 Oz Clarke
Grape Personalities and their captions; cartoons; and map artwork
© 1999 Wineworld London
Portions of the text contained in this book were originally
published as *Book of Wine* by Websters for J Sainsbury plc.

All rights reserved. No part of this work may be reproduced or utilized
in any form by any means, electronic or mechanical, including
photocopying, recording or by any information storage and retrieval
system, without the prior written permission of the publishers.

A CIP catalogue for this book is available from the British Library
ISBN 1-870604-25-3 hbk/0-316-85200-7 pbk

Colour separations by Technographics PTE Ltd, Singapore
Printed and bound in Hong Kong by Dai Nippon Printing

Acknowledgements

Thanks are due to the following for their help with the *Vinopolis World
Wine Guide*: Bob Campbell MW; Huon Hooke; James Lawther MW;
Angela Lloyd; Dan McCarthy; David Moore; Stuart Pigott; Norm Roby;
Victor de la Serna; Steven Spurrier; Phillip Williamson; Claire Harcup;
Fiona Holman; Nigel O'Gorman; Michael Johnson (Ceramics) Ltd for
supplying the Riedel glasses on pp.40-1; Screwpull for providing the
corkscrew on p.41; the wine merchants who supplied bottles for pp.36-7;
and the producers who provided the wine labels used throughout the book.

Thanks are also due to the creators, staff and investors who made
Vinopolis, City of Wine, and this book, possible in the first place.

Full picture credits can be found on p.271.

Credits

Editor Anne Lawrance
Wine Editor Margaret Rand
Art Editor Emma Skidmore
Photography Mick Rock/Cephas Picture Library
Vinopolis Identity Lewis Moberly
Grape Personalities Paul Schofield/New Division
Cartoons Penny Sobr/New Division
Map Illustrator Timothy Slade
Indexer Naomi Good
Proofreader John Malam
Production Kâren Smith
Publishers Adrian Webster (Websters)
        Tony Hodges (Wineworld)

Photograph captions:
Page 2 *Merlot grapes ripening*
Page 6 *Montana's Brancott Estate vineyards, Marlborough, New Zealand*
Page 9 *Veuve Clicquot Champagne*

The more you explore... the more you taste... the more you enjoy...

Contents

Introduction

We have a motto at Vinopolis. The more you explore, the more you taste, the more you enjoy. And this truly sums up my life in the world of wine, which means I feel I have found a second home in the wonderful vaulted chambers that make up the Vinopolis experience. I have always believed that the world of wine is a vast, endlessly fascinating world in which I have happily careered about for most of my adult life. Except that now, instead of having to dash around from one corner of the globe to another, from one wine style to another, from reds to whites, pinks to sparklers, old world grandees to New World tyros – now, it's all here, all under one magnificent roof – wine, as it was yesterday, as it is now, and as it will be tomorrow.

And Vinopolis couldn't be coming to fruition at a better time. We stand astride two centuries. The 20th century, which is the most thrilling, radical century wine has seen, and the 21st century, which promises to make bad wine extinct, to make good wine available to all and great wine available to many, and to do so by utilizing methods that combine sensitive, post-technological Ruritanian simplicity with technological wizardry that few of us yet comprehend.

As the 20th century dawned, wine was appreciated on two levels. Most inhabitants of countries that produced wine drank it as a simple beverage. As for the precise provenance of the wine, the age of the vines, the grape variety, its suitability for aging – please! Life was hard enough without troubling oneself with such irrelevancies. And then there was a tiny élite of connoisseurs whose very lives seemed to revolve around the quality of what they ate and drank. Whatever fine wine existed was drunk ceremoniously by such people, mainly members of the upper reaches of society, determined to protect their exclusive domain from any encroachment by lesser mortals – people such as us, for whom wine appreciation represented not a symbol of élitism but a simple desire to share fully in life's pleasures.

That was 100 years ago. The winds of social change that were to transform society were just beginning to stir. Within these 100 years, the world would become dominated by democratic systems of government, and equality of opportunity would be their rallying cry. Wine appreciation too has become democratized – classless, affordable, available to all. But for this to happen, wine itself had to change and this is exactly what has happened. Apart from a few enduring classics, the majority of wines that we drink today would be unrecognizable to the wine drinkers of 100 years ago.

It is reasonable to assume that a few of the great reds of Burgundy and Bordeaux of 1900 would taste similar to those of today – after all, the vineyards are the same, the grape varieties are the same. It is reasonable to assume that some of the best old Spanish sherries and the finest vintage ports would not have changed much. Or perhaps the great German Rhine wines, the intensely sweet wines of Sauternes in France or Tokaji in Hungary – surely these march on peerless and changeless through the decades?

Yet I'm pretty sure that even these bulwarks of ancient glory have changed out of all recognition. So much more is now known about how to bring a vineyard's crop to optimal ripeness year after year. The scientific details of a grape's sugar levels, its acid, tannin, colour and probable wine flavour can now be minutely calculated whilst the grape is still on the vine. Is this better than trusting to the sixth sense of a grower who understands the vagaries of every leaf and berry on his land and whose family has done so for generations? In one year out of ten perhaps not. But in nine years out of ten, surely.

And so much more is known about how to transform those grapes into wine. Indeed, it is fair to say that every component part that makes up the modern winery has been researched or invented during the 20th century, and most of it during the last quarter of the century.

So what does the 21st century hold? Greater scientific control, greater homogenization of production techniques and flavour? Yes, it does. But before we start fretting about the awful possibility

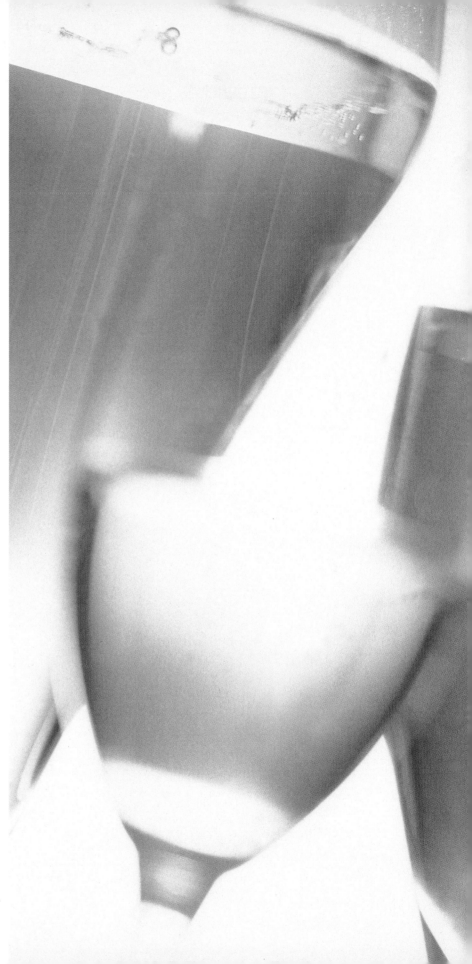

of all wine dumbing down to the flavour level equivalent of a global fast food chain, let's look at the positive points. What 20th century progress has done is to make it possible to produce attractive drinkable wine anywhere in the world. It is understandable that traditionalists worry about loss of individuality in their favourite wines, but they needn't. Modern methods offer an empowerment of modern vineyard owners and winemakers to achieve the most characterful, most individual results from their grapes. Traditionalists worried about the loss of so-called 'terroir' – an expression of place evident in the taste of the wine – should rejoice that it is at last possible to maximize the flavours of their favourite wines because modern knowledge allows grape growers and winemakers a range of decisions that will enable them to make wines with flavours either ancient or modern from the same field of vines.

And what of the vast majority of the world's vineyards that never have produced wines with any discernible 'sense of place'? Modern knowledge will allow them to discover whether or not they do possess hidden treasures. And what about the new vineyards, planted on land that has never borne a crop of grapes? Again our knowledge will allow star vineyards to burst into our consciousness. Names that do not exist now will be extolled in ten, 20, 50 and 100 years' time.

All of this, the past right back to ancient time, and the future, as far forward as our fertile imaginations will let us see, Vinopolis aims to show you. And in this complete guide I take you into greater detail – again giving due reverence to all the great old traditions of wine and all the established areas of the world. But I also take you forward, up and away, to the new countries, to new grape varieties and the superstars of the future who confidently rub shoulders with the great figures of the past. Above all, I try to impart to you the thrill and excitement of the world of wine – as it was, as it is and as it will be.

PART ONE **Exploring Wine**

The Story of Wine

WINE LEGENDS

We can't be sure about the exact origins of wine but numerous legends abound. Noah is often credited with being the first winemaker. The ninth chapter of Genesis describes how he planted a vineyard, 'drank of the wine and was drunken; and he was uncovered within his tent'.

Another popular legend ascribes the discovery of wine to the court of a semi-mythical Persian king, Jamsheed. A jar of grapes set aside for eating later in the year had started to froth and give off a pungent aroma. It was deemed unfit for consumption. A young woman from Jamsheed's harem, intent on taking her own life by drinking this 'poison', instead stumbled upon the joys of wine.

Wine is as old as civilization – probably older – while the vine itself is rooted deeply in prehistory. There was at least one species, *Vitis sezannesis*, growing in Tertiary times – just a mere 60 million years ago. I don't expect that *sezannesis* ever turned into wine – not on purpose, anyway – but aeons later its descendant *Vitis silvestris* surely did (and still does in Bosnia-Herzegovina where it is called the Iosnica). By the Quaternary era – around 8000 BC – the European vine *Vitis vinifera* (from which nearly all the world's wines are now made) had come on the scene. The Transcaucasian region, home today to the Georgians and Armenians, is one of *Vitis vinifera's* native lands and is believed to have been the place where grapes were first harvested to be made into wine some 7000 years ago.

The original metamorphosis of grapes into wine was almost certainly a happy accident. Indeed, it would have been almost impossible for Neolithic people not to notice how the flavour and effect of their wild grapes, *Vitis silvestris*, changed when the juice began to run and ferment. The result – however unpalatable to today's tutored taste – must have cheered the chill of cave-dwelling at the onset of pre-central heating winter. By the time people were gathering into cities in the rich lands of the Near East, wine was well established as a privilege of the wealthy. Paintings and sculptures show that both Egypt and China were making and drinking it around 3000 BC, but we know much more about the wines of Ancient Greece. They were so richly concentrated that they were drunk diluted: two parts wine to five of water. And they were syrupy sweet – yet with a sting of salt or a reek of resin, leached from

An amphora, used to transport wine and other liquid goods throughout the Roman Empire.

casks washed out in sea-water or from amphorae lined with pitch-pine. Through trading, the Greeks spread their vine and wine knowledge around the Mediterranean – to the benefit of the world's wine drinkers ever since.

THE ROMANS

By the middle of the 1st century BC, vineyards criss-crossed the Italian landscape from southernmost Sicily to the Alpine foothills and wine was both an everyday beverage and a major export. More importantly, as the Empire gained ground, so did the grape. In all their newly won territories the Romans established vineyards – climate permitting (and even if it didn't look promising they persevered, as in the Mosel region of Germany, where they used straw fires, between the vines, to combat autumn frosts). Today, Europe's traditional wine regions – Bordeaux and Burgundy, Rioja and Rhine, Loire and Languedoc, to name a handful – can all claim to have had Roman foundations.

Most of Rome's wine – whether made at home or in the provinces – was a somewhat plebeian tipple: tart and tough, for quaffing young before it turned to vinegar. Often its taste was softened by the addition of honey, herbs or spices – which also acted as preservatives. But not the top-notch wines. These, we must suppose, were noble creations, aged for a decade or more: the legendary Falernian – according to Pliny the Elder, so fiery it would catch light from a spark – reached its prime at 20 years yet would happily survive 100. The Romans' ability to age wine – in wooden casks and then in earthenware or glass amphorae (sealed with pitch or plaster) – represented a significant development in winemaking. But it was short-lived, doomed to disappear with the Empire.

THE CHURCH

Since the art of amphora-making was lost and wine could no longer be matured in 'bottle', quality suffered. But that aside, the Dark Ages were not as murky, in wine terms, as they might have been. In fact, the thrusting barbarians – ever thirsty – not only maintained existing vineyards but also extended them, as in Burgundy where Germanic settlers cleared the forests and replanted with vines. But throughout medieval times, the guardian of Western culture and civilization – Rome's legacy – was the Church; so for 1000 years, Western Europe's wine heritage was largely nurtured by the monasteries. They were expert agriculturalists able to study and develop vine and wine sciences; they were also powerful landowners whose expansionist policies often involved acquiring established vineyards or planting new ones. The monks produced wine for sacramental purposes, for their own use and for sale; along with other farm produce, it was a source of income. In the absence of storage know-how, the wines themselves were mostly light and fresh – ripe for quick consumption.

CORKS AND BOTTLES

The role of the Church declined in the 16th century with the Reformation – at least in northern Europe – but this did not convulse the wine world half as much as the discovery of the usefulness of corks a century later. For the first time since the Roman era, wine could now be stored and aged in bottle. Throughout the Middle Ages, it had been kept in cask which presented a dual handicap: first, too long in wood could rob a wine of all its fruit and flavour; second, once the cask was broached the wine inevitably deteriorated unless it was drunk within a few days. The bottle, with its much smaller capacity, solved the former problem by providing a neutral, non-porous material that allowed wine to age in a different, subtler way. And it also removed the latter problem by providing

A Benedictine cellarer sampling his monastery's wares – from a 13th century manuscript.

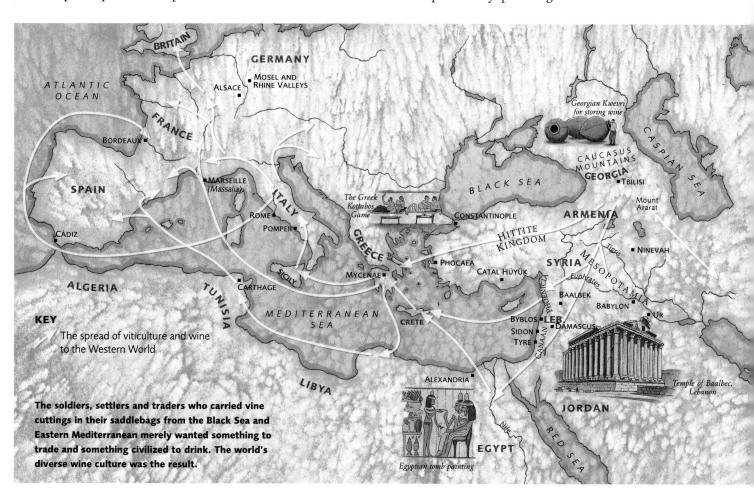

The soldiers, settlers and traders who carried vine cuttings in their saddlebags from the Black Sea and Eastern Mediterranean merely wanted something to trade and something civilized to drink. The world's diverse wine culture was the result.

KEY

The spread of viticulture and wine to the Western World

sealed containers of a much more manageable size for a single session's drinking.

However, the cork-and-bottle revolution was not an instant success: bottles were initially so bulbous that they would only stand upright, which meant the corks eventually dried out and let in air. But, by the mid-1700s, longer, flat-sided bottles were designed which would lie down, their corks kept moist by contact with the wine. Winemaking now took on a new dimension. It became worthwhile for a winemaker to try to excel; wines from distinct plots of land could be compared for their qualities, and the most exciting could be classified and separated from run-of-the-mill wines. Today's great names of Bordeaux, Burgundy and the Rhine first began to be noticed.

THE PHYLLOXERA CRISIS

In the early 19th century, Europe seemed one massive vineyard. And *Vitis vinifera* had emigrated – thanks to explorers, colonists and missionaries. It went to Latin America with the Spaniards, to South Africa with the French Huguenots and to Australia with the British. Could anything halt its triumphal progress?

Yes, phylloxera could, and it did. *Phylloxera vastratrix* is an aphid which feeds on and destroys vinifera roots. It came from North America in the 1860s, and by the turn of the century had destroyed all of Europe's vineyards and most of the rest of the world's as well. The solution, grafting vinifera on to American root-stocks – the phylloxera-resistant *Vitis riparia* – was exhausting and expensive. The most immediate effect in Europe was that only the best sites were replanted and the total area under vines shrank dramatically. Elsewhere the havoc was comparable and vineyard acreage is only now expanding to old original sites destroyed almost a century ago.

THE 20TH CENTURY

And what of wine today? It is a long step from the heavy-hearted replanting of barely economic hillsides a hundred years ago to the laden shelves of today's wine stores. In only a few generations wine has undergone changes as far-reaching as any in its history. How has it happened?

The early decades of the century were not auspicious. Prohibition in the United States between 1920 and 1933 did not stop the populace from drinking wine or any other sort of alcohol, but it did kick quality out of the window. The point of wine became its alcoholic content, not its flavour. In 1919 New Zealand only narrowly avoided voting in Prohibition. Post-war economic depression throughout the West could well have stifled the wine revolution; and yet in the late 1960s and 1970s there was the biggest change of all: the introduction of temperature-controlled winemaking.

By the apparently simple trick of cooling the fermentation and subsequently keeping the wine cool, winemakers in hot climates such as Australia found they could make wine of a standard never before dreamt of and at a price affordable by everybody. The cold revolution started in the New World and in the 1980s spread to the Old; at the same time the classic grape varieties of the Old World were taking root all over the New. But far from seeing a homogenization of wine styles, we are seeing the birth of new national and regional traditions. As never before, wine, in the Psalmist's words, 'maketh glad the heart of man'.

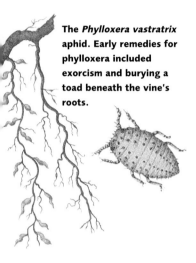

The *Phylloxera vastratrix* aphid. Early remedies for phylloxera included exorcism and burying a toad beneath the vine's roots.

WINE AND HEALTH

Imagine a world without antiseptics or antibiotics – a world where even the smallest cut was likely to become infected, and where even the water for washing wounds was likely to be dirty. In such a situation, wine, if available, was safer for both drinking and cleansing purposes: the Jewish Talmud recommends wine as 'the foremost of all medicines', and the Greek physician Hippocrates (c. 450 BC) stressed its importance as a medicine and general antiseptic, not to mention its importance as part of a balanced diet. The great 2nd-century Roman physician Galen recommended wine for disinfecting wounds, and many medicines were decoctions of herbs and spices in wine, or, later on, spirits.

In more recent times, research has shown that moderate consumption of wine, especially red wine, can reduce the risk of coronary heart disease, the scourge of the 20th century. The phenolics in red wine appear to reduce the amount of cholesterol in the arteries, making moderate wine consumption a healthier option than total abstinence. The golden rule, however, is not to overdo it.

Growing the Grapes

Anyone planting grapes to make wine must ask him or herself two questions. What will the natural conditions (geography, geology, soil, climate) of my vineyard allow me to achieve? What do I, as a winemaker, want to achieve? Winemakers in the world's classic vineyard areas have developed their wine styles over the centuries by endlessly asking and answering these questions.

A grape variety is chosen primarily for its ripening qualities: its ability to ripen at all in cooler areas, like Germany, or its ability to resist overripening in hot areas, like the Mediterranean. Different grape varieties react differently to soil and climate; their interaction results in an infinite number of possibilities.

SOIL

Views on the importance of soil vary according to where you are in the world. Europeans tend to lay more stress on soil than growers in the New World. Drainage is crucial: well-drained soil is warmer and so advances ripening; gravel, sand and loam are warm. Clay is poorly drained and cold and so holds back ripening; chalk is in between. Less well-drained soils can be useful in areas that get hot and dry. Many grape varieties favour particular sorts of soil – successful combinations of vines and soils include Cabernet Sauvignon on the gravel of the Médoc in Bordeaux, Riesling on the slate of Germany's Mosel region and Chardonnay on the chalk of Champagne in north-eastern France.

CLIMATE

Too little rain means not enough juice. Too much rain, however, is far worse. Rainstorms just before the vintage will swell the grapes and dilute the juice: quantity rises and quality plummets.

Obviously heat is essential to ripen grapes – good wine can only really be produced at latitudes of between 30 and 50°N and 30 and 40°S. Cool climates (like Champagne) need early-ripening varieties (like Chardonnay): the later-ripening Sémillon, for example, would never ripen at all in such conditions. The ideal is a match of grape and climate that will produce a long, even ripening and an optimum balance of sugar and acidity; this is what makes for finesse in wine.

SITING THE VINEYARD

The point at which this perfect balance is achieved is the 'margin': the place where it is almost too cold to make that particular wine. So fine red Burgundy, at its best the epitome of finesse, walks a climatic tightrope between success and disaster. The best growers of the New World have looked at the unpredictability of red Burgundy and taken note: when they plant Pinot Noir it is in regions that are cool, but not as riskily cool as the Côte d'Or. Their wines are good but, taking fewer risks, seldom hit such heights.

Pruning Cabernet Sauvignon vines in the vineyards of Château Léoville-Barton, St-Julien, Bordeaux on a frosty morning in early January. In winter, vines become dormant and, as well as pruning, now is the time for manuring and ploughing. The last job of winter is to take cuttings for grafting on to rootstocks. In a few months' time, as temperatures rise, the vines will awaken and start to bud; protection from frost is important at this stage. The grower will also be kept busy spraying the vines against insects and diseases, and controlling the weeds.

During summer, vines will flower, fruit will set and excessive vegetation is trimmed back to allow plenty of light and air to reach the developing grapes. Early autumn sees the preparation of equipment in the winery and then comes the great day – out go the troops of pickers, the tractors or the giant harvesting machines (this one is at work in Montana's Brancott Estate vineyards, Marlborough, New Zealand) to pluck the fruits of another year's labour.

The warmest spots in a cold region can be found by planting on a south-, east- or west-facing slope (in the northern hemisphere). Slopes get more sun than flat land and are less subject to frost. Forests and mountains can protect from the prevailing wind, and keep off the rain. Proximity to water also promotes a warmer climate. The coolest spots in a warm region can be found by seeking higher altitudes.

TERROIR

This much-misunderstood term is best translated as the precise combination of soil, climate and exposure that characterizes each vineyard. No two vineyards, therefore, have identical terroir. The concept of terroir lies behind much European vineyard classification, and the value of specific vineyard siting is gaining ground in the New World.

PLANTING THE VINEYARD

Even once the grower has selected the spot and the grape variety (in parts of Europe, Burgundy's Côte d'Or for example, there may not be much choice about the latter), he must decide which clone or clones will be best. The rootstock must be selected, and in matching clone with rootstock with soil and climate there are even more permutations to be reckoned with. The grower must decide how far apart to plant the vines, and in what directions the rows should run. Running rows up and down the slope, or across, will have different effects in terms of sun on the grapes and canopy, and air circulation: it all depends on the local conditions. Another vital question is how densely to plant the vines, because more closely planted vineyards have a lower yield per vine – an important quality consideration.

TENDING THE VINEYARD

Pruning, training and canopy management (see box on p.245) are all directed at obtaining the optimum-sized crop (as many grapes as the vine can bring to full ripeness in a particular climate and soil) of intensely flavoured grapes. Obtaining maximum ripeness within a given yield is also an important consideration. In a cool climate on poor soil the vine can ripen fewer grapes than in a warm climate on deep, rich soil, so here the grower needs to prune harder to reduce the number of fruiting buds. Vines are then trained so that they bear their grapes in the most suitable position: partially exposed to the sun so that they'll ripen; with good air circulation so that they won't rot; high enough off the ground to avoid frost, or low enough to benefit from heat stored in the soil.

Organic and biodynamic viticulture are the reactions of the 1990s to the chemical herbicides and fertilizers of the 1970s and 1980s. Organic viticulture means using only natural products in the vineyard; biodynamic viticulture goes further, and uses herbal preparations, applied in homeopathic quantities, according to the phases of the moon.

Grape Varieties

My glass is filled with a dark purple fluid with a savage scent of smoke, plums and spices. It is wine. My glass is filled with pale, sharp liquid, puckering to my tongue. That's also wine. And my glass is filled with something honeyed, gently golden and soothing ... or perhaps pale brick-red, redolent of mint, blackcurrant and eucalyptus. These, too, are wine. Yet if you were to pull wine grapes off the vine and chew them, they would taste much like any other black or white grape but with thicker skin and more pips. For these grapes come from a single species among many – *Vitis vinifera*, whose character is only properly expressed through the conversion of its juice, by yeast action on its sugars, into wine.

VITIS VINIFERA

The *Vitis vinifera* makes all the decent wine in the world. There are at least 5000 varieties of *Vitis vinifera*, of which only about 100 are important for wine, and perhaps only 20 or 30 of these have more than local relevance.

THE STAR VARIETIES

These are the most influential varieties in the wine world today.

REDS

Cabernet Sauvignon The great, all-purpose, omnipresent red wine grape of the world, easy to grow and with an unstoppable personality. It's the backbone of most great red Bordeaux, and can be equally stylish in, for example, Australia, California and Italy. Dark and tannic when young, great Cabernet wines can need a few years to soften, the fruit becoming sweet and perfumed, with a fragrance of cedarwood, eucalyptus or mint mingling magically

Noble of line, firm of backbone, *Le Colonel Cabernet Sauvignon* has led his troops from Bordeaux to elegant conquest of the world's vineyards.

with the fruit. Simpler Cabernets can be cedary and plummy within two or three years of the vintage. Oak-aging rounds out the fruit and adds a seductive vanilla flavour. The Bordeaux paradigm is a blend of varying proportions of Cabernet Sauvignon, Cabernet Franc and Merlot, with smaller additions of Malbec and Petit Verdot; elsewhere varietal Cabernet Sauvignon is more common, though a small admixture of something else, usually Merlot, can help to smooth out Cabernet's sometimes raw edges.

Gamay Inseparably linked with Beaujolais, where it produces some of the most gluggable light red in the world. Beaujolais Nouveau is bottled within weeks of the harvest; other Beaujolais, including the age-worthy Cru wines are given a less hurried start to life. Elsewhere in France and in Switzerland Gamay is often blended.

Rosalee Grenache, that sturdy Spanish gypsy, revels in the sun from Avignon to Australia, and blends in well on her travels.

Grenache Noir A Mediterranean variety widespread throughout southern France and (as Garnacha) Spain which has spread from there to California and Australia. In the New World it is often used as bulk wine, though Rhône Rangers (see p.200) in California have discovered its quality, as have producers in Australia's Barossa Valley. In France it reaches its apogee in Châteauneuf-du-Pape where it is the major component of the blend, bringing spicy, chewy strawberry and herby flavours. It produces wonderful juicy wines in Spain – its most characterful incarnation is in Priorato, Catalonia.

Malbec A minority grape in the red Bordeaux blend, it comes into its own in Argentina and Cahors in South-West France. It generally tastes plummy and rustic, but in Argentina and Chile it

A simple, happy fellow is *Georges Gamay*. He is the essence of Beaujolais: a fruity picnic companion on a summer's day, sprawling amongst the flowers, juice dripping down his chin.

Miguel Malbec, the elegant cowboy, owes his darkness to grandfather Michel in Old Cahors, but his fruity smile to the Argentinian sun.

achieves wonderful damson depth and alluring floral perfume.

Merlot Red wine without tears. That's the reason Merlot has vaulted from being merely Bordeaux's red wine support act, well behind Cabernet Sauvignon in terms of class, to become the darling of the 1990s. It is able to claim some seriousness and pedigree – as in the great Bordeaux wines of Pomerol and St-Émilion – but it can also make wine of a fat, juicy character with luscious flavours of blackcurrant, black cherry, plum and mint which can be glugged back almost as soon as the juice has squirted from the press. Chile is the leader here with California in hot pursuit.

Nebbiolo This variety is spreading only slowly from its homeland in north-west Italy, where it makes Barolo and Barbaresco, though it's starting to pop up in California. Its name derives from the Italian for fog, *nebbia*, because it ripens late when the hills are shrouded in autumn mists. Young Barolo and Barbaresco have awesome tannin and acidity and fleeting raspberry, roses and black cherry aromas underlaid by flavours of mint, licorice and tar that become complex with age.

Pinot Noir At its best, Pinot Noir makes hauntingly beautiful wine. But it's far less forgiving to grow and vinify than Cabernet Sauvignon, and until recently Burgundy was the only source of great Pinot – and then only if you were lucky with the vintage and the winemaker. Well, red Burgundy is still erratic. But the good news is that winemakers in certain parts of New Zealand, California, Australia, Chile and Germany have cracked its secrets. Rarely deep in colour, Pinot Noir nonetheless possesses a wonderful fruit quality when young – raspberry, strawberry, cherry or plum – that becomes more exotic with age, the plums turning to figs and pine, and the richness of chocolate mingling perilously with truffles and well-hung game.

The *Marchese di Sangiovese* has poor relations across Italy, but in Tuscany his breeding shows. A new-formed friendship with Colonel Cabernet may mellow his tough charms.

Sangiovese Though widely planted in Italy, Sangiovese reaches its greatest heights in central Tuscany. Yet all Sangiovese is not equal: there are umpteen different clones, and it was often the inferior, high-yielding ones that were planted in the late 1960s and 1970s. The current replanting in Chianti Classico, Brunello di Montalcino and Vino Nobile di Montepulciano is being done with more care. The wines are well structured, often highly acidic, slightly spicy with a farmyard character, with tobacco, bitter cherry, herb and raisin flavours. Simple wines are pale, lively and cherryish; top ones develop great complexity. California is now working its magic on this grape and Argentina is flexing its muscles.

Syrah/Shiraz Syrah so far produces world-class wine in only two countries. In France its heartland is Hermitage and Côte-Rôtie in the Rhône Valley, a mere 270 hectares (670 acres) of steeply terraced vineyards producing hardly enough wine to make more than a very rarefied reputation. In Australia, as Shiraz, it produces some remarkable reds. And wherever Syrah appears it trumpets a proud and wilful personality based on a majestic depth of fruit – all blackberry and damson, loganberry and plum – some quite strong tannin, and some tangy smoke, but also a warm creamy aftertaste and a promise of chocolate. It

Manly *Omar Shiraz* is a travelling player with two star turns. As 'Syrah' he raises the roof on the slopes of the Rhône and his 'Shiraz' plays to a rapturous reception Down Under.

Maxine Merlot teamed up elegantly with Colonel Cabernet in her French youth, but now she's the cowgirl of the vines and we fall for her soft, fleshy charms the world over.

Nero Nebbiolo stands proud, dark and brooding on his Piedmont terraces. He takes time to know and demands respect, from old Italian rivals and cosmopolitan visitors alike.

A prince among grapes, *Le Duc de Pinot Noir* proudly shows his Burgundian pedigree: elegant, fragrant, but temperamental if left too long in the foreign sun.

is these characteristics that have made Syrah increasingly popular throughout the south of France. California is turning out some superb southern-Rhône-like blends; and some exciting examples are now appearing from South Africa, Chile, Argentina and Italy.

Tempranillo This is Spain's best-quality native red grape and it can make wonderful red wine, with wild strawberry, vanilla, sometimes blackcurrant and spicy, tobaccoey flavours. It is important in many different regions – Rioja, Penedés (as Ull de Llebre or Ojo de Liebre), Ribera del Duero (as Tinto Fino or Tinta del Pais), La Mancha and Valdepeñas (as Cencibel), Navarra, Somontano, Utiel-Requena and Toro (as Tinto de Toro). It's also found in Portugal, especially in the Douro and Dão (as Tinto Roriz or Aragonez). Wines can be deliciously fruity for drinking young, but Tempranillo also matures well, and its flavours blend happily with oak. There are now plantings of Tempranillo in California as well as Argentina, too.

One pays respects to the Spanish ambassador, *Pedro Tempranillo*; one dines at his Rioja estate, and sups approvingly his dry, scented red wine. One does not mention that oaky, vanilla nose or his age, ever.

Despite his Italian ancestry, big *Zak Zinfandel* is California's very own star. At his best he's as fruity as they come; but let us pass over his pink period.

Zinfandel California has made Zinfandel its own, and it was only in the early 1990s that it was conclusively proved to be the same as the far less widely grown Primitivo of southern Italy. Zinfandel makes all styles of wine, from sweetish rosés for early drinking to dark, strapping reds. The best examples are sturdy, berryish wines with plenty of flavour but little subtlety. They will age in bottle for several years. Zinfandel can also be found a little in Australia and South Africa.

WHITES

Chardonnay I'm always getting asked, 'When will the world tire of Chardonnay?' And I reply 'Not in my lifetime'. For the vast majority of wine drinkers the Chardonnay revolution has only just begun, and to many people good dry white wine simply equals Chardonnay. And that's that. Although a relatively neutral variety

At her peak, *Charmaine Chardonnay* attracted admirers worldwide to her Burgundian court, but now she has spread her buttery, citrus favours so widely, some think she hails from the New World.

if left alone, the grape can ripen in almost any conditions, and is found in virtually every winemaking country in the world, developing a subtle graduation of flavours going from the sharp apple core greenness of Chardonnay grown in cold climates, through the exciting, bone-dry yet succulent flavours of white Burgundy, to the rich, tropical fruit versions that Australian winemakers have spread throughout the world – Australia and California have virtually created their reputations on great viscous, almost syrupy, tropical fruit and spice-flavoured Chardonnays. The use of oak for fermenting and aging helps explain the multitude of different flavours of which this grape is capable, often giving a marvellous round, nutty richness to otherwise savoury, dry wines.

Chenin Blanc This versatile great white wine grape, sadly underrated, makes a full range of styles from sparkling to still, dry to sweet, with flavours of green apples, lemons, melons, nuts and chalk to apricots, peach, honey and marzipan. The top wines keep almost indefinitely, reaching a marvellously honeyed and minerally maturity. It's most at home in the Loire Valley in France, where

Charlie Chenin Blanc is the David Bowie of wines. He can be dry, sweet or sparkling but, the older he gets, the more of a honey he becomes.

She smells almost sweet, but then she is dry. She sounds German, but is French. Perfect with smoked salmon or dim sum. Set aside cultural questions: just say *Yum Yum*.

is it also called Pineau de la Loire. South Africa has long used Chenin (also known as Steen) for easy-drinking, dryish whites through botrytized desserts to modern barrel-fermented versions. California, with a few exceptions, only employs it as a useful blender, while New Zealand and Australia have produced good varietal examples.

Gewürztraminer 'Gewürz' means spice, and this variety has a characteristic aroma and flavour of musky roses and lychees, although it is exotic rather than strictly spicy. It reaches its peak in France's Alsace region; nowhere else approaches the same quality, although northern Italy, Germany and Austria can produce distinctive flowery, grapy wines and New Zealand and Chilean examples can be tropical, refreshing and often marginally off-dry. Gewürztraminer at its best is intensely aromatic, with peachy, floral complexity and relatively high alcohol content. Acidity can be low: in hot years and in hot climates the wine can turn flabby. Alsace Gewurztraminer is generally fermented dry, but the Vendange Tardive and Sélection de Grains Nobles wines are unctuous, luscious, waxy rich wines with even higher alcohol levels and variable sweetness.

Muscat Not one grape but a whole family, of which some are better than others – but all give wine of an intoxicating grapiness and generally low acidity. Some have black grapes, some white. Muscat Blanc à Petits Grains has the most finesse, Muscat of Alexandria and Muscat Ottonel are coarser and Muscat Hamburg is the least well regarded, being generally better as a table grape. Muscat can make all styles of wine from light and dry (Alsace) through light, sweet and fortified (Beaumes-de-Venise or Rivesaltes), heavier and sweeter (Moscato de Valencia) to the very dark, rich and old fortified Muscats of North-East Victoria,

Maurice Muscat may be 'petit', but boy is he fruity. The grapiest of grapes, he brings a smile to everyone's lips and wins laurels for his sweet disposition.

Australia. In Italy it is used for sweet *passito* styles made from dried grapes, and for light, sweetish spumante. Sweet Muscats are also made in Greece, South Africa, California and Eastern Europe and all are for drinking young.

Pipo Pinot Grigio is as fresh as a Venetian gigolo, but his Alsatian cousin, *Pierre Pinot Gris*, has the luscious charm of a cherub.

Pinot Gris/Pinot Grigio At its finest in Alsace, Pinot Gris achieves levels of concentrated spiciness not found elsewhere. It can be dry, semi-sweet or very sweet, and examples from Grand Cru vineyards will improve in bottle for ten years or more. In Germany (as Ruländer) it is generally more earthy and flowery. Italian Pinot Grigios are light and should be drunk young. It is also found in New Zealand and in Oregon in the United States.

Riesling This grape (which is not the same as the inferior Laski Riesling a.k.a. Olasz Riesling, Welschriesling or Riesling Italico) used to be synonymous with the cool vineyard regions of Germany's Rhine and Mosel Valleys, with Alsace and with parts of Austria.

Maximillian von Riesling is an unhappy grape, noble but misunderstood. Racy and elegant (when most expect bland or cloying), will he ever find true love beyond the connoisseur?

It still does produce marvellous wines here, peach-perfumed and with an ability to hold on to piercing acidity, even at high ripeness levels, and in lusciously sweet wines, so long as the ripening period has been warm and gradual rather than broiling and rushed. As the wines age, a flavour perhaps of slate, perhaps of petrol/kerosene develops. In Australia the style is totally different but just as successful: here the flavours are of toast and lime, with the toastiness developing as the wines mature for perhaps a decade or more. In

California it is taken less seriously. Italian examples are generally light, though top growers produce wines with good depth.

Sauvignon Blanc A grape of intense, sometimes shocking flavours – most notably lean, vivid gooseberry, nettles, citrus fruits and asparagus. Sauvignon first came to attention as the grape used for Sancerre, a bone-dry Loire white. The grape, however, is not as easy to grow as Chardonnay and its flavours are not so adaptable. It is highly successful when picked not too ripe, fermented cool in stainless steel, and bottled early. This is the Sancerre model followed (some would say with even greater success than in the Loire) in New Zealand, where its gooseberry flavours can be even more assertive. Sauvignon also lends itself to fermentation in barrel and aging in new oak. This is the model of the Graves region of Bordeaux, although generally here Sémillon is blended in with Sauvignon to good effect. The acidity that is Sauvignon's great strength should remain, but there should be a dried apricot kind of fruit and a spicy, biscuity softness from the oak. Sauvignon is also a crucial ingredient in the great sweet wines of Sauternes and Barsac from Bordeaux, and in sweet wines from the United States, South Africa, Australia and New Zealand.

Sémillon/Semillon The large-berried and thin-skinned Sémillon grape is grown extensively throughout the world, but only in France and certain parts of Australia does it make great white wines. In hot climates, high-yielding Sémillon produces characterless or overblown, fat wine. But treated correctly (picked ripe, and with low yields), it makes deliciously lemony dry whites, particularly in France, and richer, waxier wines in Australia, especially in the hot Hunter Valley. Top Australian Semillons are full, toasty and age wonderfully to acquire a majestic richness and high viscosity, with a butterscotch or beeswax character. When blended with Sauvignon, Sémillon is responsible for the great sweet wines of Sauternes and Barsac. Sémillon's thin skin is particularly susceptible to the ravages of the noble rot fungus *Botrytis cinerea*, which concentrates the sugar in the grape, raises its potential alcohol and bestows an unmistakable honeyed character on the wine. Such wines acquire a deep burnt-toffee colour and honeyed layers of nutty butterscotch as they age. Much dry white, too, in and around Bordeaux is based on a blend of Sémillon and Sauvignon Blanc.

Viognier Gloriously apricot-scented wine which used to be confined to just two small ACs, Condrieu and Château Grillet, in France's northern Rhône Valley. Now, however, it is grown more widely in the south of France and California and to some extent in Australia. All should be drunk young, though sweeter styles (an old tradition which is currently being revived) might prove to age better. Quality does tend to vary: some of the wines are overcropped and underpowered.

Serena Sauvignon Blanc switches effortlessly from dry as a bone, sometimes austere, in her Loire homeland to fruity and fragrant in southern climes.

Buxom Sarah Sémillon is much misunderstood. In Australia it's worth the wait to get to know her, and in Bordeaux she's an absolute sweetie.

Violet Viognier was a rare flower, her apricot cheeks and floral perfume found only in the northern Rhône. Now she bestows her charms abroad, will her magic fade?

Muscat Blanc à Petits Grains (white Muscat with small berries) is one of about 200 different branches of the Muscat family and makes the finest wines.

The Art of the Winemaker

Wine would 'happen' whether we wanted it to or not. As ripe grapes split, and the juice runs, so it comes in contact with naturally occurring yeasts in the vineyard. The result is wine – of a sort. But the creation of the individual flavours we find attractive is much more complex, and the winemaker has to make choices at every stage of the process, according to the style and quality he or she wants.

RED WINE

The grapes are rushed from the vineyard with as little delay as possible: everything that happens from the moment of picking affects the final quality of the wine. For the finest quality, the grapes must be healthy and at optimum ripeness. Unhealthy grapes are left unpicked or discarded in the vineyard or at the winery.

When black grapes arrive at the winery, they are crushed and destemmed prior to fermentation. The resulting mush of flesh, skins and juice (called the 'must') is then pumped into a fermentation vat.

Red wine is usually fermented in stainless steel or cement tanks; huge open wooden vats are also used. The winemaker may rely on the wild yeasts present in the cellar to start the fermentation or, as is common in the New World, he may inhibit wild yeast growth with a combination of cool temperatures and sulphur dioxide and then initiate fermentation with a pure yeast culture.

Red wine is fermented at a higher temperature than white because other qualities (colour and tannin, mostly) are needed in the wine. Temperatures ranging from 18-35°C (64-95°F) are usual. This range of temperature is crucial to the style of wine produced. If the temperature gets too hot, however, the yeasts can malfunction and the wine can taste stewed. For a light red wine, the juice and skins may be separated after a day or two; more usually, the skins stay with the juice until the fermentation is over.

After fermentation comes pressing. The new wine will be run off into vats, or into new oak barrels. Now comes the secondary, or malolactic, fermentation. During this process, vital for most red wines, bacteria convert the sharp malic (green apple) acid – naturally present in the grape – into mild lactic (milk) acid. This helps to make the wine more stable. If the new wine is left to itself, the malolactic fermentation will happen naturally as the cellar warms up in the spring after the harvest; or the winemaker can inoculate the wine with malolactic bacteria.

The length of time for which a wine is to be aged, and whether in vat or barrel, depends on what sort of wine is wanted – a wine for drinking young or one for laying down in bottle – and also on the characteristics of that particular wine. New oak barriques of 225 litres (50 gallons) in size are one of the most fashionable things a winery can have. Oak imparts tannin to the wine, but also a buttery vanilla flavour, and the newer the oak, the more forceful its impact. It needs careful handling so as not to totally overpower the wine.

As the new wine sits in barrel after fermentation, the lees (dead yeast cells and other solids in suspension) sink to the bottom; the first task is to rack the wine, which simply means running it off its lees. Such racking may be done several times a year as the wine ages. Even after racking, there may be some solids still in suspension in the wine. These are removed by fining. Egg whites are one of the agents traditionally used for fining

Grapes are very nearly an all-in-one winemaking kit. The colour of red wine comes from the grape skins, not the juice, which in virtually all wine grapes is colourless. Tannin, found in red wines, comes from the skin and pips (seeds). The trace compounds that give wine its flavour are located just under the skin. Millions of wild yeast cells settle on the surface of a ripe grape. These are quite weak, however, and other yeasts come into play during fermentation. The grape juice contains sugar, which is turned into alcohol by the action of yeast during fermentation. It also contains acids which are crucial to the flavour and longevity of the wine.

CARBONIC MACERATION

One time grapes are not crushed is when carbonic maceration is to be used. This process produces a red wine with maximum fruit and minimum tannin – think of Beaujolais Nouveau and that lovely light bubblegum taste. The wine produced won't last long, but who cares? It won't need to. For carbonic maceration, whole bunches of grapes are put into tanks filled with carbon dioxide. The grapes undergo an intracellular fermentation which produces some alcohol, plenty of aroma and deep colour, but not much tannin. As the grapes burst, their juice mingles with that of the crushed grapes and completes fermentation in the normal way.

The second year *chai* (cellar) at Château Margaux in Bordeaux. The upright barriques are awaiting the new vintage from the first year *chai*.

red wine. Isinglass (derived from fish) can also be used for both red and white; Bentonite (a sort of clay) is used for whites only. These pass through the wine collecting solids on their way, and sink to the bottom, without leaving traces in the wine. Fining must be done with care to avoid removing flavour.

Finally, filtering will remove any trace of cloudiness. Again, the danger is that this process can strip flavour and character from the wine along with the undesirable elements.

ROSÉ WINE

There are two main methods of making pink wine. The most obvious is to blend white wine with a little red, but that isn't legal in the European Union (EU) except for in the Champagne region of France. The other main method is to take red grapes, begin fermenting them on their skins as if red wine were the aim and when it deepens to the shade required, run it off its skins and leave it to finish fermenting without them.

WHITE WINE

Unlike red wine, white wine is fermented without the skins; so on arrival at the winery the grapes are destemmed, crushed and then pressed.

Wooden vats, small new oak barriques and tanks made of fibreglass, cement or stainless steel are all used for fermentation. The fermentation temperature should be kept lower than for reds – 10-25°C (50-77°F) is normal for white wines – to preserve freshness and aroma. All modern fermentation tanks have automatic cooling systems so there's no danger of overheating. Fermentation lasts roughly four to six weeks: the lower the temperature, the slower the fermentation. White wines, particularly Chardonnay, are sometimes fermented in new oak barriques. Doing this gives all the advantages of aging the wine in new oak –

ABOVE TOP During the fermentation of red wine, the skins rise to the surface and form a cap. The winemaker must pump the wine up and over this in order to keep the wine in contact with the skins as well as to avoid bacteria forming on the cap.

ABOVE Two glasses of Chardonnay – the glass on the right has been fined or filtered.

Tastevins, or wine tasters, were used by winemakers for tasting the wine in their cellars. They were also used by merchants on purchasing expeditions. Although no longer a common sight, some Burgundian producers still use them.

those rich, buttery flavours – as well as integrating the flavours better.

Malolactic fermentation, so crucial for reds, is frequently prevented in whites, especially in hot climates, to preserve a sharper, more tangy acidity. The same process of racking, fining and filtering, described earlier for red wine, is then implemented. An additional method for white wine is cold stabilization: chilling the wine to -5°C (18°F) or so to precipitate out any solids.

SWEET WINE

Sweet whites occur naturally when the sugar in the grape is not fully transformed into alcohol during fermentation. The grapes must be infected with noble rot (*Botrytis cinerea*) which dehydrates them and concentrates the sugar levels; or they must be picked and left to shrivel, as for Vin Santo in Italy; or they must be made from late-harvested grapes that are not infected with noble rot. Icewine (Eiswein) is late-harvested wine made by picking and pressing the grapes while they are frozen, thus concentrating sweetness and flavour. Cheap sweet wines are made by adding sweet unfermented must to finished wine.

SPARKLING WINE

Sparkling wine results from a second fermentation under pressure, so that the carbon dioxide gas produced can't escape until the wine is poured into the glass – whereupon it froths. The Champagne method, which creates all the great

sparklers, creates this fermentation inside the bottle by the addition of yeast and sugar to the base wine. It is difficult (requiring expert removal of yeast deposits), expensive and incomparably delicious. Alternatives include bottle fermentation – where the second fermentation takes place inside a bottle, but the wine is then filtered and transferred under pressure to another bottle. In the *cuve close*/tank method/Charmat method (all different names for the same thing) the second fermentation takes place in bulk tanks. The cheapest method of all is simple carbonation, where gas is pumped into the wine under pressure.

FORTIFIED WINE

These are made as for reds or whites, with the difference that grape spirit is added – either during fermentation in order to stop it and leave residual sweetness in the wine, or afterwards when the wine has fermented out to dryness.

BLENDING AND BOTTLING THE WINE

Blending sounds like a dirty word: something that only happens to the cheapest of wines. But call it 'selection' and it sounds better. The point is that every single vat and barrel of wine has the potential to be slightly different from its neighbour. The blender's task, whether the wine is a commercial brand or a Grand Cru Burgundy, is to select the best lots and put them together in the best way possible, while ruthlessly declassifying the rest.

This is the moment when the winemaker's work is finally complete. He must select the right moment for the wine to be bottled: too early, and it will not reach its full potential; too late, and it will already have lost its freshness. Some wines do all their aging in the cellar, and once bottled are ready to drink immediately; others benefit from some time in bottle. Some wines are designed to age for many years in bottle before reaching their peak. The precise period for which they should age, however, will depend on many factors, including the quality and style of the vintage and the winemaking decisions taken by the producer.

CHAPTALIZATION AND ACIDIFICATION

In an ideal world all the grapes would be perfectly ripe every year. In the real world a cold summer may mean underripe grapes, or a hot climate may mean grapes that lack acidity. Both situations can be corrected by the winemaker.

CHAPTALIZATION is the process of adding sugar to the must. It increases the alcohol in the final wine; none should be left unfermented. There are strict legal controls on how much sugar may be added.

ACIDIFICATION is the process of adding tartaric acid; it usually happens only in hot climates. In the EU it is illegal to chaptalize and acidify the same wine; but chaptalization is routine in most of northern Europe, and acidification is equally routine in many parts of, say, Australia.

FLYING WINEMAKERS

A term coined in the 1980s for what was then a new phenomenon: highly trained and technological young winemakers, often Australian, who began arriving in underperforming regions and turning out fresh, fruity wines where only dross had existed before.

So far so good: this is New World winemaking in all its temperature-controlled, hygienic glory, being applied to regions that had the potential but not the know-how. Sometimes it begins with something as simple as washing out all the pipes with water at the end of each day; sometimes it involves new vine varieties or new pruning and training systems.

It can be controversial, too. Winemakers who jet in for short periods can be too quick to impose a formula: flying winemaker wines, so the criticism goes, all taste alike.

Even if that criticism could sometimes have been justified in the early days, it can't now. Winemakers like Hugh Ryman, Jacques Lurton, Kym Milne, Michel Rolland and Peter Bright, who between them make wine in most of the globe, certainly have a personal style, but they are not formula winemakers; they want wines that reflect the terroir. If wine styles at the cheapest end are becoming homogenized this is as much a result of our disinclination to pay a proper price for more individual, characterful wines. And at the very least, they taste a great deal better than before.

A winemaker checking on the progress of his fermenting Merlot in tank.

Great People of Wine

There are many people, past and present, who have shaped the face of wine over the years. In fact, there are hundreds of people who by rights should have a place in wine's hall of fame – here are just some of them.

Bacchus was the common name in Ancient Rome for the classical god of wine whose name is still richly associated with wine. The Greeks called him Dionysus. The son of the god Zeus and mortal Semele, he wandered through Egypt, Syria, Asia and India, teaching the inhabitants the cultivation of the vine and the elements of civilization. According to Roman literature he was followed by crowds of women, the Bacchae, who are represented in ancient art as being in the grip of madness or frenzy. The festivals established by the Greeks for his worship took on an increasingly wild character as time went on – the word bacchanal came to mean any form of drunken revelry. Bacchus in classical myth is at once a lawgiver and bringer of peace, and a dangerous and unpredictable figure.

A statue of Bacchus, the god of wine, from the grounds of Château Mouton-Rothschild in Bordeaux, France.

Dom Pérignon (1639-1715) was the most famous winemaking monk of all and is regarded as the 'father' of Champagne (see p.85).

DOM PERIGNON

Pliny the Elder (AD 23-79) was an immensely prolific Roman writer. The only work which survives, however, is his *Natural History* written in 37 volumes. Book 14 is devoted to wine, Book 17 to viticulture, and Book 23 to wine as medicine. Along with a great deal of practical information, much of it apparently gained from wide independent research, he emphasizes the importance of locality and soil in wine quality; he puts less stress on grape variety. Pliny also ranks the wines of the day in order of quality, putting Falernian (see p.12) first.

Monastic orders for nearly 1300 years owned most of the best vineyard land in Europe. The Benedictines and Cistercians were the most active in viticulture, not only keeping it alive in the desolation that followed the fall of the Roman Empire in the West and the Barbarian invasions, but also proving the most entrepreneurial and scientific of landowners. They experimented with grape varieties and soils, insisting on the Riesling grape for vineyards all over Germany, and mapping the complex patterns of soil and flavour that characterize Burgundy's Côte d'Or; they kept meticulous records of weather and were experts on drainage. Vineyards were planted and tended from Portugal in the west to Hungary and beyond in the east, until the French Revolution of 1789 and the reign of Napoleon brought about the dissolution of monastic life.

Jean-Antoine Chaptal (1756-1832) was a chemist and, as Napoleon's Minister of the Interior, an administrator of genius. Wine quality had gone to pieces after the revolution, and adulteration and fraud was rife; Chaptal was determined to bring the producers to their senses. His book *Trait Sur La Vigne* (1801) was his bestselling attempt to convince winemakers of the benefits of scientific advance, but his name is more associated nowadays with chaptalization, the technique of adding sugar to must in order to raise the alcohol level (see box on p.24).

Louis Pasteur (1822-95) laid the foundations of the modern science of winemaking through his work on fermentation and microbiology. Before Pasteur, the transformation of sugar into alcohol and carbon dioxide was though to be spontaneous; he demonstrated that it was produced by the action of yeast on sugar. His discovery of the different micro-organisms that cause wine maladies went a great way towards improving overall quality; the technique of heating wine (or indeed milk) to kill such organisms is called pasteurization after him.

Jules Guyot was a 19th century French scientist who gave his name to the Guyot system of vine pruning which has been adopted in many parts of the wine world. 'Single Guyot' training involves leaving one long cane on the vine, with six to ten buds on it (in Europe the precise number may be limited by appellation laws), plus a shorter spur with two buds, one of which will become the following year's cane. 'Double Guyot', the system used widely in Bordeaux, involves leaving two canes and two spurs.

André Simon (1877-1970) was hugely influential in disseminating knowledge and appreciation of fine wine and food. He came to Britain from his native France as the agent for Pommery Champagne and soon found himself sharing his remarkable knowledge of wine in a series of pioneering lectures written for the newly formed Wine Trade Club. He went on to set up the Wine and Food Society (now the International Wine and Food Society), of which there are now 150 branches worldwide, and thousands of members. The most notable of his 104 books is the three-volume *History of the Wine Trade in England*; in 1964 he wrote *The Wines, Vineyards and Vignerons of Australia* – preceding most people's interest in the wines of that country by 20 years.

Baron le Roy de Boiseaumarié (1890-1967), a leading proprietor in Châteauneuf-du-Pape in the southern Rhône, laid the foundations of the appellation contrôlée laws of France, and thus for the equivalent laws of every other country that has followed France's system. In 1923 he produced the results of his research into the suitability of his native soil for each of the 13 grape varieties grown there; he also outlined the pruning and winemaking techniques, the level of ripeness of the grapes and the maximum crop. His work was combined with that of Joseph

Capus, member of the Chamber of Deputies for the Gironde and professor of agriculture at Cadillac, who in 1927 succeeded in getting a law passed that restricted the grape varieties that could be used in any region to those 'hallowed by local, loyal and established custom': inferior newcomers were thus banned.

Albert Julius Winkler (1894-1989) and **Maynard Amerine** (1911-98), scientists at the University of California at Davis, worked together on a system of classifying the climates of wine regions according to heat summation. They assumed a growing season from 1 April to 31 October and calculated the number of 'degree days' based on the amount that average mean temperatures during that period exceed 10°C (this being the minimum temperature necessary for vine growth). They divided California into five regions, from Region I, the coolest, to Region V, the hottest. Their system is widely used as a guide to which varieties to plant in which parts of the state.

André Tchelistcheff (1901-94) was born in Moscow, studied enology and viticulture in France and then moved to California, where his work at Beaulieu Vineyard in the Napa Valley laid the foundations of the modern California wine industry. He was a pioneer of temperature-controlled fermentation, understood how to control the malolactic fermentation, and developed frost prevention techniques in the vineyard, such as heaters and wind machines. Vine diseases were another field of enquiry, and he stressed the vital importance of cellar hygiene. He worked widely as a consultant to other winemakers in California, and was made a Chevalier de l'Ordre du Mérite Agricole by the French government in 1954.

Baron Philippe de Rothschild (1902-88) established the principle of château bottling in Bordeaux. This is now the rule for almost all the wine of the region, and certainly all that bears the name of a significant property, but when Baron Philippe inherited Château Mouton-Rothschild

Baron Philippe de Rothschild died in 1988 after 65 years of managing Château Mouton-Rothschild. The 1987 vintage, his last, was dedicated to him and his likeness appears at the top of the label.

Robert Mondavi (above left) and Len Evans (above right) whose work in California and Australia respectively has brought New World wines to the fore.

wine industry. He left his family winery, Charles Krug, after a dispute with his brother Peter, and in 1966 set up his own winery in the Napa Valley. Here he developed the concept of varietal wines, did pioneering work with different sorts of oak barrels and took on the great wines of Europe on their own terms. He became an unofficial spokesman for the Napa and for wine as a whole, crusading against the neo-prohibitionists of the late 1980s and promoting wine as part of a civilized lifestyle, which he continues to do.

Max Schubert (1915-94) was Australia's most original winemaker, a maverick who believed – and proved – that Australia could make red wine as great and long-lived as that of the finest Bordeaux. A trip to Bordeaux in 1949 showed him that Cabernet Sauvignon and small new French oak barrels were vital parts of the equation; the only problem he faced back in Australia was the almost complete absence of both. So he experimented instead with Shiraz and American oak; and thus was born Grange Hermitage, now Australia's most famous and prestigious red wine. At the time, however, the Australian taste was for fortified wines, and Schubert's employers, Penfolds, initially disliked the results of his work and told him to stop making it. Luckily for us – and luckily for all Australian winemakers inspired by the example of Grange – he ignored them until they saw the light.

Michael Broadbent MW (b.1927) was the pioneer of modern wine auctions. He originally trained as an architect before deciding that he preferred wine, and joined auctioneers Christie, Manson & Wood in 1966; Christie's had at that stage held no wine auctions since the war. Broadbent set about combing the cellars of the stately homes of England for wines which their owners either didn't know were there, or didn't know what to do with; his erudition and scholarly approach attracted wine buyers worldwide and helped to create today's vigorous investment market for fine wine. He is also the author of a number of seminal books, including *The Great*

in 1922 it was usual for even the finest châteaux to sell their wine to the négociants, or merchants, and leave it to them to mature and bottle it. Baron Philippe rightly believed that to do so was to lose control of quality. His other achievements included the promotion of Mouton-Rothschild to First Growth status in 1973, after many years of lobbying. Mouton-Rothschild is the only château to have been promoted.

Professor Emile Peynaud (b.1912) changed the face of winemaking in Bordeaux. He worked with the great Jean Ribéreau-Gayon at Bordeaux University's Institut d'Oenologie and was professor of enology there; as a teacher he inspired a generation of winemakers with his insistence on clean, hygienic winemaking and ripe, healthy grapes, concepts that had been by no means widespread before his time. He also acted as consultant winemaker to many Bordeaux châteaux, and was instrumental in persuading them of the value of attention to detail at all stages of the winemaking process. From him they learnt control of the malolactic fermentation, better control of fermentation temperatures, and that the best thing to put in dirty old wooden barrels was not wine but geraniums.

Robert Mondavi (b.1913) was the leader and, in many ways, the inventor of the modern California

Vintage Wine Book, with its tasting notes on wines going back to the 18th century.

Len Evans (b.1930), winemaker extraordinaire, persuaded Australians to love table wine, and thus forced the pace of development in that country. Born in Wales, he arrived in Australia in 1955. In 1965 he became director of the Australian Wine Bureau and set about promoting the joys of good wine to a nation whose principal interest was in its alcohol content. He succeeded so well that a red wine boom overtook Australia in the late 1960s. Evans set up as a wine producer himself in New South Wales's Hunter Valley, a career which took him on a roller-coaster of success and disaster. As one of Australia's leading wine show judges, he continues to wield formidable influence over the development of styles and quality.

Marchese Piero Antinori (b.1938) of Tuscany, together with his enologist **Giacomo Tachis**, changed the direction of Italian wine. In 1966, when Antinori took over his family firm, Italian wine was just about at its nadir of quality and reputation. Antinori and Tachis's innovation was to ignore the wine law and make wines of superlative quality using grape blends and winemaking techniques not permitted for DOC wines; Tignanello, a Sangiovese-based red aged in French oak barriques, and Sassicaia, a blend of Cabernet Sauvignon and Cabernet Franc made by Antinori's cousin Mario Incisa della Rochetta with Tachis, were the first of a new breed of vini da tavola. They were soon dubbed super-Tuscans, spawned hundreds of imitators and led the revival of modern Italian wine. The law has now been changed to accommodate them.

Hugh Johnson (b.1939) is almost certainly the most successful and widely read wine author of all times whose bestselling books (which include *The World Atlas of Wine*, *Wine*, *The Story of Wine* and *Hugh Johnson's Pocket Wine Book*) have steered millions of readers in many languages to an understanding and appreciation of their subject. He succeeded André Simon as editor of *Wine & Food* magazine, is a director of Château Latour in Bordeaux and a founder of the Royal Tokaji Wine Company in Hungary.

Richard Smart (b.1945) is at the forefront of work on canopy management, the term used to describe pruning and training techniques designed to improve grape ripeness, yield and health. Canopy management is most needed where vines are naturally ultra-vigorous and prefer to produce masses of leaves and shoots rather than concentrating on ripening their grapes; this is the case in many parts of the New World. In New Zealand excess vine vigour was a major limiting factor in wine quality until Smart's work showed ways of dealing with it. The widespread adoption of his techniques has greatly improved wine quality. (See also box on p.245.)

Robert Parker (b.1947) is a hugely influential wine critic whose palate moves markets internationally and persuades winemakers to change the style of their wines (although none of them would ever admit it). He practised as a lawyer before starting his newsletter, *The Wine Advocate*, in 1978, and made his mark by praising the quality of the 1982 vintage in Bordeaux when other US critics dismissed it as being too soft and unlikely to age; he was proved right and his reputation was made. Now his tasting notes and his marks out of 100 (based on the US high school system of marking) can send prices soaring or plummeting. Château owners in Bordeaux try to wait for his published comments on their wines before setting their prices, and his taste for rich, lush reds has helped to establish the dominance of that style worldwide.

DECANTER'S HALL OF FAME

Wine magazine *Decanter* pays tribute to key people in the wine world with a yearly award. The winners are:

1999 **Jancis Robinson MW** *UK*

1998 **Angelo Gaja** *Italy*

1997 **Len Evans OBE** *Australia*

1996 **Georg Riedel** *Austria*

1995 **Hugh Johnson** *UK*

1994 **May-Elaine de Lencquesaing** *Bordeaux, France*

1993 **Michael Broadbent MW** *UK*

1992 **André Tchelistcheff** *California, US*

1991 **José Ignacio Domecq** *Jerez, Spain*

1990 **Professor Emile Peynaud** *Bordeaux, France*

1989 **Robert Mondavi** *California, US*

1988 **Max Schubert** *Australia*

1987 **Alexis Lichine** *Bordeaux, France*

1986 **Marchese Piero Antinori** *Italy*

1985 **Laura and Corinne Mentzelopoulos** *Bordeaux, France*

1984 **Serge Hochar**, *Lebanon*

Italian winemaker Marchese Piero Antinori with a selection of his top wines.

PART TWO **Enjoying Wine**

How to Taste Wine

Anyone can open a bottle of wine and enjoy it without knowing the first thing about it. But, like music or painting, you'll get a million times more out of it if you learn even just a little. And enjoyment, to my mind, is what wine is all about.

FLAVOUR

If I gave you a cup of tea and a cup of coffee, could you tell me which was which? Sure you could. If I asked you to shut your eyes and then gave you a slice of beef and a chunk of cheese, would you have any trouble saying which was which? Or a tomato, a peach and a plum? Of course not. You could easily taste the difference between all these. Well, believe it or not, the flavour differences in wine are just as marked – and you can tell them apart if you set your mind to it.

It's true that with wine most people haven't built up the memory bank of good, bad and indifferent which we take for granted with our basic food and drink. But it can be built up – in two ways. First, by following the simple procedures of wine-tasting which I'll outline in just a moment. And second, by thinking as you drink. Many of the strongest tastes in wine are very common – apples, blackcurrants, strawberries, peaches, cherries, lemons; others are more surprising and maybe more fanciful – guavas and lychees, yoghurt, coal smoke, nettles and petrol. You'll find all these words in this book and they're used because wine has no language of its own. It borrows its vocabulary from what our senses of sight, feel, smell and taste have already experienced in other areas of our lives.

APPEARANCE

Let's look at the wine first. Apart from the pleasure to be gained from the splashy pink-red of a new Beaujolais, the cascade of bubbles and froth in a glass of Champagne, or the burnished sunset gold of an old Sauternes, it is also the first test as to whether or not the wine is healthy. Unless it is an old wine that has thrown a sediment, it shouldn't be hazy or milky. Check the colour by part-filling your glass, then tilt it above a white surface – a napkin, tablecloth, your host's shirt.

The colour of a wine is a major clue to its age, and the age of a wine is a major clue to its flavour. White wine can range in colour from a pale, almost greeny, white to a full rich gold. Now, the pale greeny-white ones are likely to have a tangy flavour – a sharper, greener flavour; whereas the gold ones are more likely to taste golden – richer, rounder, riper. The pale ones will come from cool areas of the world, in general; whereas the golden ones will come from warmer areas where the grapes ripen more.

Very young red wines have a pink to purple spectrum in their 'red' – a young Beaujolais Nouveau will have a bright, fresh, pinky-red kind of colour, and the flavour is going to be all youthful vibrancy, all freshness. Mature wines have a gradually encroaching orange from the edge – the meniscus – of the wine, and the red itself will be lightening to something between orange and brown. The red of a nine-year-old Reserva wine from Rioja in Spain, for example, will have lost all its fresh youthfulness, becoming bricky-red, orangy-brown with a mature flavour.

SMELL

To get the most out of the 'nose' of a wine, swirl the glass very gently in a circular motion so that the wine laps about the bowl. If you're worried about spilling it all over the carpet, remember,

The first thing to do when you're tasting a wine is to look at it. Take the glass by the stem, and look at the colour against a white background. You can see whether the wine is clear or hazy (it's unlikely to be the latter), and you can get some clues as to the character of the wine.

Swirl the wine around in the glass to release the aromas from the surface of the wine upwards.

gently does it; you're not trying to imitate the whirlpool effect in a jacuzzi, only to disturb the wine so that the volatile aroma elements get agitated and rise up from the surface. It's just the same principle as, say, rubbing some herbs or flower petals between your hands to smell them better. Smells are volatile and escape into the atmosphere. You want to catch them in the top of your glass as they escape.

Now put your nose into the mouth of the glass and take a good healthy, steady sniff – don't snort as though you're in the critical stages of a catarrh bout, but don't be too dainty about it either. And, as aroma rises up into your nasal cavity, register the first thoughts that come into your head. It may be a simple smell like apples. It may be something rich like honey or rough like tar. But whatever you smell, just register it, and soon you'll be building up a new memory bank which will enable you to recognize wines, and to compare bottles long since drunk with the one you have in front of you. One more thing. Some wines really don't smell of anything much at all. So register that too, and buy something else next time. And now. Shall we taste?

FAULTS IN WINE

Unfortunately, some wines do have faults. If you order a bottle of wine in a restaurant and find that it is affected by one of the following – send it back. You can't send back a wine simply because it isn't to your taste but you are entitled to a replacement for anything that is obviously faulty. A good restaurant won't quibble – it can, in turn, send the bottle back to its supplier for a replacement or refund.

Here are the four common faults to watch out for:

OXIDIZED Too much contact with air can harm a wine. This can happen in the fermentation tank, in the barrel, or in the bottle. In a red wine, it manifests itself as a kind of musty mushroom flavour. In a white wine, it starts with a raisiny flatness and can go on to a drab, bad sherry kind of flavour. In bad cases the colour of both reds and whites can go brown.

SULPHUR Sulphur is an important antioxidant used in winemaking. But, applied over-enthusiastically, it can ruin the taste of a wine. It may manifest itself as the acrid stench of a recently struck match, or it may be a dank sourness and taste of mothballs in the heart of the wine.

VINEGAR Wine begins to go vinegary when acetic bacteria attack it, either in the fermentation tank or as a result of infection in the storage barrel.

CORKED This doesn't mean that bits of cork have crumbled into your wine. That's annoying, but perfectly harmless, and it doesn't mean your wine is corked. A corked or corky wine is one where the cork has become contaminated, often with the compound Trichloranisole, or TCA. Statistically between two and five per cent of corks are affected in this way, and the cork industry is busy seeking solutions. The use of plastic corks is one such. Corked wine has a horrible dank, mouldy smell and taste.

TASTE

Right – up with that glass and take a good mouthful, and concentrate very hard for a moment. You can taste the wine, can't you? But where is the 'taste' occurring? The wine is in your mouth, sure, rolling around your tongue, but the real tasting is happening not on your tongue but in your nasal cavity again. The tongue simply registers saltiness, sweetness, bitterness and acidity. Everything else – the difference between a plum and a peach, between chicken and cheese – is registered by those 'volatile aroma elements' rising up into the nasal cavity.

Where the mouth is important is for checking out acidity and toughness. All wines have acidity, it's getting it in balance that matters. Fruit without acidity is very boring: think of the difference between a cool-climate Cox's Orange Pippin and a hot-country Golden Delicious. In all wines, sweet or dry, there must be acidity, and your mouth will tell you when it's just right, or when it's too sharp from underripe grapes. Some grapes naturally produce more acidity than others; the soil and the climate are other factors determining acidity. But acidity must be balanced by sweetness or alcohol or 'extract' (the solids in wine, including minerals and glycerol).

Most red wines have some element of toughness too. This comes from tannin in the grape skins, pips and stalks. Tannin is the same bitter element you get in strong tea which furs your gums and tongue. But without it no decent red wine could age or develop any of the deep exciting flavours that make it special. Too little tannin and the wine seems flat and feeble, too much and it strikes you as harsh and raw. Young wines which need more age will probably have a lot of acid and tannin, and be difficult to taste. Many modern winemakers aim to produce wines with soft tannins, not harsh, astringent ones.

Take a mouthful of wine and breathe through it so that the air can release flavours in the wine. Then swallow it and breathe out through your nose. All aromas, flavours and perfumes are registered and transferred to the brain from the nasal cavity.

THE TASTE OF OAK

Wines that have been matured, or even fermented, in oak have an unmistakable flavour. An oaked Chardonnay, for example, will have a creamy, buttery, vanilla flavour to it. There will be a small touch of cinnamon spice as well. These are the classic flavours of oak maturing for a red wine as well as for a white. If the oak is dominant, you may get the sappy smell of a timber yard when you sniff the wine: this is generally a sign that the producer has overdone things. As always in wine, balance is crucial.

The final element is the aftertaste. If you are 'tasting' rather than drinking the wine, you'll spit your mouthful out and then ponder the flavour a moment to see what develops. But let's assume you're drinking it at table. Just take a moment to concentrate on what flavour remains after you've swallowed. Good wines have a lovely lingering finish which often seems to get better after the wine has been spat out or swallowed. Unready young wines – which will be good – also have this delicious finish to make up for being tough in the mouth. And good length – a wine that goes on and on in the mouth even after you've swallowed it or spat it out – is a sign of quality.

How do you tell if a wine will benefit from aging? Practice is the only answer. It can take time to learn the difference between a wine that is going through a closed stage and one that will never improve with age – but it's worth the effort.

Spit out your mouthful and take a moment or two to consider all the elements and flavours of the wine. Are they all in balance? Is the combination pleasing? Does the wine have good length?

The Taste of the Grape

The taste of wine is intimately bound up with grape variety. Here are some of the classic flavours, as well as some more bizarre nuances.

RED

CABERNET SAUVIGNON Dark, tannic, blackcurrants, cedar, lead pencils, mint, tobacco, dark chocolate.

GAMAY Strawberries, peach, pepper.

GRENACHE NOIR Toffee, blackberries, spice.

MALBEC Plums, spice, earth.

MERLOT Soft blackcurrants, plums, mint, roses, honey, raisins, rich fruitcake.

NEBBIOLO Dark, dense, very tannic, prunes, raisins, tobacco, tar, hung game, chocolate, roses, violets.

PINOT NOIR Fragrant, silky, strawberries, black cherries, plums, raspberries, game, licorice, autumnal undergrowth.

SANGIOVESE Black bitter cherries, plums, herbs, raisins, tobacco, tea.

SYRAH/SHIRAZ Rich, deep-coloured, tannic, cloves, black pepper, loganberries, redcurrants, blackcurrants, blackberries, raspberries, plums, herbs, tar, smoke, game, licorice, toffee.

TEMPRANILLO Strawberries, vanilla, sometimes blackcurrants, pepper.

ZINFANDEL When made as a red wine, berries, spice.

WHITE

CHARDONNAY From apples, citrus fruits, tropical fruits through to full, spicy oak, butter, cream, wax, vanilla, toast and grilled nuts.

CHENIN BLANC Very dry to sweet: green apples, minerals, lemons, melons, nuts, chalk; to apricots, peaches, angelica, honey, marzipan.

GEWÜRZTRAMINER Fairly dry through to sweet; spice, tropical fruits, freshly ground pepper and Nivea. Lychees are the most characteristic aroma.

MUSCAT Dry to very sweet, and grapy; orange peel, treacle, raisins, toffee.

PINOT GRIS Spice; in richer examples, honey, raisins, mushrooms, earth.

RIESLING Very dry to very sweet: steely edge, slate, apple; to lime, petrol, raisins, even honey, musky, tropical fruits.

SAUVIGNON BLANC Very dry to very sweet: lean green flavours, crisp, vivid gooseberry, nettles, citrus fruits, asparagus, smoky, herbal, elderflower; going to raisins, honey and nectarines (mainly when blended with Sémillon and aged in oak) though still with an acid edge.

SÉMILLON Dry to very sweet: green apple, lemons, lanolin, wax, herbs; to cream, honey, nuts, peaches and sometimes custard.

VIOGNIER Full, dry, zesty lemon acidity, apricot, marshmallows, mayflower blossom, cinnamon spice.

Finding the Wine You Want

An influx of new countries and new climates into the serious wine league has meant that the old list of classic wine styles – Bordeaux, Burgundy, Sancerre, Mosel Riesling, Champagne – is no longer much of a guide to choosing a wine. So I've divided modern wine into 15 categories by style, to help you explore.

WHITE WINES

❶ Unoaked, neutral dry whites Most Italian whites made from Trebbiano and Garganega come into this category; so does a lot of wine made from Muscadet and Sylvaner. Believe me, there are plenty of times when you just want freshness in a wine. Think of a plate of shellfish, and a salt wind blowing in from the sea ...

❷ Unoaked, fruity dry whites Not all Chardonnay and Sémillon is oaked, believe it or not. The south of France, Chile and Australia produce good unoaked examples. Whites from Italy, Spain and Portugal also fit here. Not all are wines to drink young. Unoaked top-quality Chablis will need a few years to round out.

❹ Rich, oaky dry whites The New World style of Chardonnay, as created by Australia: it's ripe, upfront and dripping with round, ripe apricot and peach fruit, sweetened and spiced up by new oak. It's utterly approachable and easy to drink. Spain, Tuscany and the south of France can also do it. Toasty Australian Semillons also hit the spot.

❻ Aromatic, grassy dry whites Principally Sauvignon Blanc from New Zealand, the Loire and, increasingly, Chile, South Africa, Hungary and the south of France.

❼ Medium-sweet whites These include demi-sec Vouvray, fine German Kabinett and Spätlese, Vendange Tardive from Alsace and Riesling from the US.

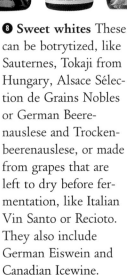

❸ Elegant, oaky dry whites Think of oaked white Graves, or some Premier or Grand Cru Chablis; there's also Blanc Fumé and oaked Sauvignon Blanc. And, of course, white Burgundy, all nuts and oatmealy-ripe fruit. Some New World producers make Chardonnay like this, too.

❺ Aromatic, flowery or spicy dry whites Alsace is top of the list here, for its Gewürztraminer, Muscat, Pinot Gris and Riesling. Austrian Riesling and some wines from southern Germany are made like this as are certain Hungarian whites. New World Riesling fits here, too.

❽ Sweet whites These can be botrytized, like Sauternes, Tokaji from Hungary, Alsace Sélection de Grains Nobles or German Beerenauslese and Trockenbeerenauslese, or made from grapes that are left to dry before fermentation, like Italian Vin Santo or Recioto. They also include German Eiswein and Canadian Icewine.

ROSÉ WINES

❾ A lot of rosés, especially those from Portugal, are medium-sweet, but there are good dry ones from the south of France, Spain and elsewhere.

RED WINES

❿ Light, low-tannin reds These range from Beaujolais Nouveau at the lightest end, along with other reds made by carbonic maceration, through

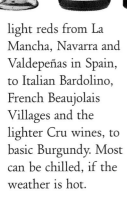

light reds from La Mancha, Navarra and Valdepeñas in Spain, to Italian Bardolino, French Beaujolais Villages and the lighter Cru wines, to basic Burgundy. Most can be chilled, if the weather is hot.

MEDIUM

⓫ Medium-weight reds If you want elegance, go for village Burgundy, red Loires and reds from New Zealand and Washington State; also California and Oregon Pinot Noir and most Chianti. Basic Bordeaux will be more rustic and German reds softer. Warmer climate medium-weight reds include south-western French reds like Cahors and

Madiran; South African Pinotage, most California Zinfandel, many southern French vins de pays, most Côtes du Rhône and reds from much of Spain and Portugal. Most Australian Shiraz also fits into this category: ripe, almost sweet and sinfully easy to enjoy.

⓬ Spicy blockbusters These are warm climate heavyweights full of the spicy flavours of plums and earth and oak. Zinfandel, Grenache and Shiraz from California and Australia come into this category, as do top Rhônes and Syrahs from elsewhere, and top Barolos and Barberas.

⓭ Elegance on a grand scale Take classic proportions, add more weight, more concentration and more refinement, and this is the result. Classed Growth red Bordeaux, plus top Cabernets from California and Australia, are the benchmark. Top Italian Cabernets and Sangioveses, top Riojas, and Grand Cru red Burgundies also fit here.

SPARKLING WINES

⓮ Champagne sets the style for white and rosé fizz, but looka-likes from Australia, California and New Zealand can be just as good and cheaper. Australia's sparkling red Shiraz is a style found nowhere else; not even Germany, which makes red sparklers but makes them very sweet.

FORTIFIED WINES

⓯ These can be sweet, dry or in between, and some are even comparatively light-weight. The lightest and driest are fino and manzanilla sherries; dry amontillado and oloroso sherries are richer and heavier. Tawny and Colheita ports are medium-weight and fairly sweet; vintage ports are much sweeter and richer. (These distinctions usually apply, too, to New World fortifieds in the same styles.) Madeira, too, comes in grades of sweetness and weight, from Sercial right up to Malmsey. The Muscat *vins doux naturels* from the south of France are fairly light and fairly sweet; the red Grenache-based ones are heavier. The most intense fortifieds of all are Liqueur Muscats and Tokays from North-East Victoria in Australia.

Buying and Storing Wine

You don't have to own a country house in order to lay down wine and build up a cellar. All you have to do is buy some wine in advance so you don't have to rush out to your local store every time you fancy a glass or two, and then have somewhere suitable to keep it. If you've got a cellar to keep it in – marvellous. If not, look around for a suitable nook – like a cupboard under the stairs or a disused fireplace – that is relatively dark, quiet, vibration-free and cool. That's all there is to it.

WHERE TO BUY WINE

Buying wine of all sorts is now easier than it's ever been. You can pick bottles of all qualities, from basic and everyday through to very fine indeed, off the shelf in wine merchants up and down the land; and whether you visit a supermarket, a wine warehouse or a wine merchant depends on what you want.

If you'd like some advice – on what a particular wine tastes like, or what food it will go with, or when to drink it – your best bet is to seek out an independent merchant. You may pay a little more per bottle, but you get to pick their brains in the process. Many do mail order, which means you have to buy at least one mixed case, but if you don't mind the financial outlay this can offer the best of both worlds in terms of convenience and advice.

However, there's not a lot of point in expecting advice in a high street chain, and even less in a supermarket. You might be lucky in a high street chain, and find a manager who knows his stock, but not many do. Most of the chains boast of how thoroughly they train their staff, but sadly it seldom shows. However, prices and choice are generally good.

Wine warehouses are much the same in those respects, although they often have bottles of selected wines open for tasting, in which case you can judge for yourself. The main difference between wine warehouses and other chains is that at a warehouse you have to buy by the case, which can be mixed.

Auctions should be treated with caution. Yes, there are bargains to be had, but bear in mind that many merchants take the opportunity of getting rid of duff stock at auction. You also have no guarantee that the wine has been well stored, and if you find it's faulty you have little chance of redress.

Some fine wines, notably red Bordeaux, can be bought en primeur (see box on p.57) – that is, in the spring after the vintage. You can then take delivery of the wine about 18 months later. It's a way of obtaining scarce wines, but don't assume you'll pay less. And only go to a reliable merchant. How do you know if a merchant is reliable? The best test is if they are well established, have dealt in en primeur wines for many years, and have a reputation to lose.

LOOKING AFTER WINE

Make sure you store your wine at the proper temperature. This should ideally be at approximately 10°C (50°F). Stable temperatures in the area of 15-20°C (60-70°F) should not damage it, but may mean that it ages faster. Temperatures above 20°C (70°F) are not good for wine. And wine should never be allowed to freeze.

Consistency in temperature is crucial so the loft and the garage – freezing in winter, boiling in

HOW TO ASSESS MATURITY

Accept that laying down wine means that a lot of it will be drunk a little too early or a little too late. Judging the peak of development of a wine is often easier once the wine has passed it. If you have a whole case or more of a wine, open one bottle at the beginning of its estimated period of maturity. That way you can judge how fast it's maturing.

CREATING A CELLAR

Creating a cellar isn't difficult. Here are a few important dos and don'ts.

DO

✔ *Buy wine for short-term storage as well as wine for aging in the longer term.*

✔ *Buy the sort of wine you drink anyway – and that goes with the type of food you like to cook.*

✔ *Buy wine in a variety of styles, so that you have something for every occasion.*

✔ *Be cautious to begin with. You don't have to fill your cellar in one go: wait for good offers and good vintages.*

✔ *Shop around and find a wine merchant that you trust.*

✔ *Read the newspaper columns and keep up to date with vintages and producers.*

✔ *Buy a single bottle of a wine before splashing out on a case, to see if you like it.*

✔ *Use your cellar to explore your tastes in wine. Buy interesting-looking bottles whenever they take your fancy, and try them at leisure.*

✔ *If you want to, ask a wine merchant to fill your cellar for you, to a certain budget. But it's less fun.*

✔ *If you can afford it, consider buying double your requirements of some long-term wines, like vintage port or red Bordeaux. Keep the wine until it is mature, then sell half to fund new purchases. This was the traditional way of making your cellar pay for itself – but it doesn't work so well in these days of erratic wine values, so only buy wine in this way if you can afford to lose money.*

✔ *Look warily at wine merchants' special offers. Sometimes a merchant has overbought of a good but unfashionable wine; more often he is having trouble shifting an off-vintage.*

DON'T

✘ *Buy large amounts of styles of wine that you seldom drink – even if it has been the vintage of the century.*

✘ *Buy more than you are likely to need, unless you are trying to fund your cellar this way. Wine does not live forever and can decline rapidly once it is past its best.*

✘ *Be pressurized by a wine merchant into buying too much, or more expensive wine than you've budgeted for, on the grounds that this will be the only chance to buy. It seldom is.*

✘ *Miss the boat, on the other hand, with certain wines that are always in short supply.*

✘ *Mind making mistakes.*

Keep a cellar book to record purchases in. Make a tasting note every time you open a bottle, to help you to remember what it was like.

---

summer – are not recommended. More gradual seasonal changes should not be a problem. Special temperature-controlled wine cabinets, or even purpose-built cellars (which are dug underneath a house) are available, but are expensive. Look in specialist magazines for advertisements for these. Investigate cheaper options, like lining a convenient closet with insulation to maintain an even temperature.

Keep your wines somewhere dark and free from vibration. Light can adversely affect white and sparkling wines, in particular. If you have to store your wine in a bright spot, keep the bottles in their original boxes or drape a blanket over the top to protect them.

Store the wine on its side to keep the corks moist: if the cork dries out, it will shrink and let air in. Either buy a wine rack or use an old cardboard box – ideally one used for spirits with the bottle divisions still inside because the card used for these is stronger. If your house is very dry, buy a humidifier to stop corks drying out and shrinking.

Finally, it's perfectly possible to rent storage space in merchants' cellars, and you can often organize this through the merchant from whom you bought the wine. But this is only feasible for seriously fine wine you want to keep for several years – you can't just run down on Saturday night to grab a couple of bottles.

Serving Wine

A piece of advice: don't take it too seriously. Young wines can undergo a fair amount of battering and still come up smiling. You can serve a red wine too cold, or a white wine too warm, and still enjoy it. But there are a few factors that can make wine more fun and the flavours more delicious.

GLASSES

Wine does taste better out of the right glasses. However, you *can* get by with just two sorts of wine glass: the classic red, which is fine for all sorts of table wine, and port and sherry, and the Champagne flute (see glasses below marked ★). It is the shape of the glass that is most important: it must have a reasonable stem to hold it by, and a generous bowl curving in towards the top. This shape has two advantages; when you swirl the glass round, all the smell gets concentrated in the top – and you don't spill wine all over the place.

And for both these reasons, don't fill the glass more than half full.

OPENING THE BOTTLE

Put your corkscrew into the centre of the cork, give it a good twist around until it's right in, then simply pull it out. Tight corks can often be loosened if you run hot water over the bottle neck to expand the glass. If the cork is loose and falls in, just push it right in and don't worry about it.

Opening sparkling wine is a serious business – always make sure that you point the cork away from people. Remove the foil, loosen the wire, hold the wire and cork firmly and then twist the bottle. If the wine froths, hold the bottle at 45 degrees and have a glass at the ready (tilt it slightly and pour the wine down the side of the glass to ensure the bubbles don't froth over the top of the glass).

TEMPERATURE

Whites, rosés and sparkling wines are best chilled – they taste fresher and it emphasizes their acidity. I'd give Chardonnay an hour in the refrigerator; a Sauvignon, a Riesling or a rosé wine two hours or more. Don't overchill older wines – one hour is quite enough. A light, fruity red can even be chilled for an hour too. Full-bodied reds are usually better at a cool room temperature; over-heated wines often taste flabby and uninteresting.

Port is drunk in small measures, hence the modest capacity of the classic port glass.

This elegant glass is designed to bring out all the crispness of a fino or manzanilla sherry.

White wine doesn't need to breathe as much as red so the classic white wine glass has a smaller bowl.

★ The classic red wine glass has a generous bowl that shows off the wine's colour and bouquet.

Red Burgundy needs a glass with a wider bowl and more tapering sides to maximize its perfume.

AIRING AND DECANTING

Opening young to middle-aged red wines an hour before serving makes very little difference. The surface area of wine in contact with air in the bottle neck is too tiny to be significant. Decanting is different, because sloshing the wine from bottle to decanter mixes it up thoroughly with the air. The only wines that really need to be decanted are those that have thrown a sediment. Ideally, you need to stand the bottle upright for a day or two to let the sediment settle. Draw the cork gently. As you tip the bottle, shine a bright light through from underneath, so that you can see the sediment as you pour, all in one steady movement. Stop pouring when you see the sediment approaching the bottle neck. I would decant a mature wine only just before serving. Elderly wines often fade rapidly and an hour in the decanter could kill off what little fruit they had.

Look for a corkscrew with a generous helix – one that you can slide a matchstick up and down. This stops the corkscrew tearing the heart out of the cork.

Red Bordeaux needs contact with air for its complexities of flavour and bouquet to show.

★ This narrow Champagne flute preserves the bubbles in the wine and keeps it fizzy longer.

Serving Wine with Food

There are some basic rules: red wine with red meat, white wine with fish and white meat. These still largely apply, but happily they are not binding. The people who laid down the rules had never thought of drinking wine with Chinese food, for example.

Here are the other main points to remember:

• Match not only the flavour of the wine to the flavour of the food, but the intensity of flavour and weight or body of the wine as well. A heavy, alcoholic wine will not suit a delicate dish.

• Try to match the acidity of a dish to the acidity of the wine. Acid flavours like lemon or tomato need acidity in the wine.

• Richness in a dish can either be cut through, with an acidic wine, or matched with a rich one. Either way, the wine should be full in flavour so as not to taste lean and mean.

• Consider sweetness when pairing wines with food. Sweet food makes dry wine taste lean and acidic.

• If a dish has sauce, then the flavours of the sauce should be taken into account.

• Red wine is traditionally drunk with cheese, but white is generally better (especially with blue cheese, although port with Stilton is traditional).

• Pastry dulls the palate, softening the flavours of the other ingredients with it. Go for a more subtle wine than you might otherwise have chosen.

• Contrary to the old adage that white wine should be served with fish, the red grapes Pinot Noir and Gamay can go with certain types of fish, such as salmon and red mullet.

• There is a great deal of sense in the old rule of white wine before red, young wine before old and light before heavy. The palate adjusts more easily to wines served in this order.

The final arbiter is your own palate. If you like a glass of Chardonnay with your venison, then go ahead and enjoy it!

Vintages

Bordeaux Varies from region to region: a great year for Sauternes is not necessarily great in the Médoc.

	98	97	96	95	94	93	90	89	88	86	85
Northern Haut-Médoc (inc. St-Estèphe, Pauillac, St-Julien)	7○	7○	9○	8○	7○	6◐	9◐	9◐	8◐	9○	8○
Southern Haut-Médoc (inc. Margaux, Listrac, Moulis)	7○	6○	8○	8○	6○	6◐	9◐	8◐	7◐	8○	8●
St-Émilion, Pomerol	8○	7○	7○	8○	7○	6◐	9◐	9◐	8◐	7●	9○
Graves, Pessac-Léognan (R)	8○	7○	8○	8○	7○	6◐	8◐	8◐	8◐	7●	8○
Dry Graves, Pessac-Léognan (W)	9○	5○	8○	8◐	9○	5●	9◐	8◐	9●	6◐	7○
Sauternes	7○	9○	9○	7○	6○	4◐	10◐	9○	9○	9◐	6●

Burgundy Hugely variable – it's best to look at the producer's name before the vintage rating.

	98	97	96	95	94	93	92	91	90	89	88
Chablis	7○	7○	10○	8◐	6●	6●	7●	6◐	9●	8◐	8○
Côte de Beaune (W)	7○	8○	9○	9○	7○	6◐	9○	6●	8●	9○	8○
Côte de Beaune (R)	8○	8○	9○	8○	5○	8○	6●	7◐	10○	8●	8●
Côte de Nuits (R)	8○	8○	9○	8○	6○	9○	6●	7○	10○	8●	8○
Beaujolais Crus	8○	7○	8○	9◐	7●	8●	5○	9●	6◐	7◐	8○

Champagne Vintage wines are only released in very good years.

	98	96	95	90	89	88	86	85	83	82	81
Vintage Champagne	8○	9○	7○	9◐	8●	9◐	7●	9◐	7●	9◐	8●

Rhône Reds from the northern Rhône, based on Syrah, take to aging well but only a minority of southern Rhône reds are made for long aging, and most whites should be drunk young.

	98	97	96	95	94	93	92	91	90	89	88
Côte-Rôtie	8○	7○	7○	8○	7○	4●	6◐	9◐	7○	8◐	9○
Hermitage (R)	8○	7○	8○	8○	7○	3●	6◐	8○	10○	9○	9○
Hermitage (W)	8○	7○	9○	8○	7○	5●	7◐	9◐	9○	8○	9●
Cornas, St-Joseph	8○	7○	7○	8○	8○	4●	6◐	8○	9○	8○	9○
Châteauneuf-du-Pape (R)	9○	6○	6○	8○	7○	6◐	5●	5●	9○	10○	9●
Condrieu	8◐	7○	9◐	8●	8◐	5◐	7◐	9◐	8◐	9◐	

Loire Muscadet and Sauvignon are best in cooler years; hot years suit the sweet wines and the reds.

	98	97	96	95	94	93	92	91	90	89	88
Muscadet	7○	8●	8◐	8◐							
Savennières	7○	9○	8○	8○	6○	7○	6○	5●	9○	9○	8○
Sweet Anjou/Vouvray	6○	9○	9○	9○	8○	6○	5○	4●	9○	10○	8○
Central Vineyards Sancerre, Pouilly-Fumé	7○	9○	8●	9○	7○	7○	6●	7○	8●	8◐	9○
Bourgueil, Chinon Saumur-Champigny	7○	8○	10○	8◐	5◐	6◐	5●	4●	10◐	8○	8●

Alsace Only wines from the 50 Grand Cru vineyards and the best *lieux-dits*, Vendange Tardive (VT) wines and botrytized Sélection de Grains Nobles should be aged more than two to four years.

	98	97	96	95	94	93	92	91	90	89	88
Riesling (esp. Grand Cru)	8○	9○	8○	9○	6◐	6◐	5●	6●	9●	10●	9●
VT, Sélection de Grains Nobles	8○	9○	7○	8○	9◐	5◐	5◐	4●	9○	10◐	8○

Italy As winemaking methods can differ within the same DOCs, ratings can only be approximate.

	98	97	96	95	94	93	92	91	90	89	88
Barolo, Barbaresco	9○	10○	9○	8○	6○	7○	5○	6◐	10◐	9○	8○
Barbera	9○	9◐	7◐	8○	6●	7●	6●	7◐	10●	9●	8◐
Amarone, Recioto, Ripasso	7○	10○	7○	10○	7○	8○	5●	5●	10○	9○	8●
Chianti Riserva (*Classico, Rufina*), Carmignano Riserva	7○	10○	8○	9○	7○	8○	5●	7●	10●	6●	9●
Vino Nobile di Montepulciano	8○	10○	8○	8○	7○	7○	5●	7●	10●	6●	9●
Brunello di Montalcino	9○	10○	8○	9○	8○	8○	4●	8○	10◐	8●	9○

A GUIDE

The term 'vintage' simply refers to the year in which the wine was harvested. Most wines these days bear a vintage date, but vintage guides are only relevant to the top five or ten per cent of any country's produce. The majority of wine we drink is simple, everyday stuff designed for quick consumption.

Warmer spots – southern Europe, California, South America and mainland Australia – are more consistent weatherwise. But often their best vintages are the cooler ones. Cooler places – New Zealand, Tasmania, New York State and northern Europe – are more variable.

And yet within this overview some estates will produce good wine in a poor year, and vice versa. As a rule of thumb you're likely to get a better wine by choosing one from a great winemaker in a second-rate year than the other way round.

Spain A relatively even climate. Only a few wines need further bottle aging.

	98	97	96	95	94	93	92	91	90	89	88
Rioja (R)	6○	8○	8○	9○	5●	6◑	7○	7◑	8●	4◑	4●
Ribera del Duero	7○	6○	9○	8○	9○	4◑	6●	8○	8●	7◑	6●
Penedés (R)	7○	7○	8○	7○	8◑	7◑	6◑	8●	8●	6◑	8●
Penedés, Conca de Barberá (W)	7○	7○	8○	7○	7●	6●	6●	7○	8◐	6◐	8◐

Portugal Vintage port is only declared in exceptionally good years.

	95	94	92	91	87	85	83	80	77	75	70
Vintage port	8○	10○	9○	8○	7◑	9○	8◑	7◑	9◑	5◑	8●

Germany A Kabinett needs five years in bottle, a Spätlese rather more and the top Beerenauslese (BA) and Trockenbeerenauslese (TBA) will live for decades. Simple QbAs need no further aging.

	98	97	96	95	94	93	92	91	90	89	88
MOSEL-SAAR-RUWER											
QbA, Kabinett, Spätlese	8○	8○	7○	9○	8◑	9○	7●	6◑	10○	7●	9○
Auslese, BA, TBA	7○	9○	8○	9○	9○	9○	7○	6◑	10○	8○	9○
RHINE											
QbA, Kabinett, Spätlese	8○	9○	8○	7○	7◑	8○	9○	6◑	10◑	7●	8●
Auslese, BA, TBA	7○	9○	8○	7○	9○	8○	8◑	6◑	9○	9●	8○
PFALZ											
Riesling Spätlese	8○	9○	8○	5○	7◑	8○	9○	6◑	10○	9○	8●
Grauburgunder/ Weissburgunder Auslese	8○	10○	8○	6●	7●	9◑	8●	5◑	10●	9●	8●

United States There can be enormous climatic variation, but most wines are made for early drinking.

	98	97	96	95	94	93	92	91	90	89	88
NAPA VALLEY											
Cabernet- or Merlot-based	9○	8○	7○	8○	8○	7◑	8◑	8○	9○	6●	6●
SONOMA COUNTY											
Cabernet- or Merlot-based	8○	7○	6○	8○	8○	7◑	8◑	8○	9○	8●	7●
NAPA/SONOMA											
Chardonnay	7○	8○	7○	8◑	9○	7●	8●	7◑	9●	5○	8◐
CARNEROS/RUSSIAN RIVER											
Pinot Noir	9○	8○	8○	8○	9○	7◑	8●	9●	8●	8◐	7◐
OREGON											
Pinot Noir	9○	5○	6○	5◑	9○	7●	9●	8●	9●	8◐	8◐
WASHINGTON STATE											
Cabernet- or Merlot-based	8○	8○	8○	7○	9○	7◑	9○	8◑	7●	9●	7◐

Australia Most wines are made to be drunk young.

	98	97	96	95	94	93	92	91	90	89	88
NEW SOUTH WALES											
Hunter Valley Semillon (premium unoaked)	9○	7○	8○	9○	7○	7◑	6◑	9○	6●	8◑	3●
SOUTH AUSTRALIA											
Barossa/Clare – Shiraz	8○	9○	9○	8○	10○	6◑	6◑	8●	8●	5●	7●
Coonawarra Cabernet	9○	8○	9○	5◑	8○	7◑	7◑	9○	10●	5●	8●
Clare/Eden Valley Riesling	10○	10○	9○	8○	8○	6●	7●	8●	8●	4◑	8●
VICTORIA											
Cabernet Sauvignon	8○	9○	5○	7◑	8○	7●	6●	9○	8●	4●	8●
WESTERN AUSTRALIA											
Cabernet Sauvignon	6○	8○	10○	8○	8○	9◑	6◑	9●	8●	8●	6●

New Zealand Only the best have serious cellaring potential.

	98	97	96	95	94	93	92	91	90	89	88
Hawkes Bay Cabernet Sauvignon	10○	7○	8○	7○	9◑	7○	6●	9●	7◑	10●	8◐
Martinborough Pinot Noir	9○	7○	9○	6◑	9◑	7●	7●	9●	6◐	9○	5○
Marlborough Sauvignon Blanc	7◑	8◑	9◑	5◑	9◑	8◐	7◐	9◐	8◐	9○	7○

South Africa Only the occasional Chardonnay, Cabernet Sauvignon or Shiraz should be aged.

	98	97	96	95	94	93	92	91	90	89	87
Cabernet-Sauvignon-based	8○	9○	5◑	9○	8○	6●	8●	8●	7●	8●	7●
Pinotage	8○	8○	6◑	9○	8○	7◑	8●	9●	7●	9○	7●
Shiraz	8○	7○	7○	9○	8○	7◑	8●	7◑	7○	8●	7◑
Chardonnay	7○	9◑	7●	7●	6◑	8◑					

KEY

Numerals 1-10 represent an overall rating for each year.

○ needs more time
◑ ready but will improve
● at peak
◐ fading or tired

Laying Down Wine

The point at which a wine reaches its peak depends on a number of factors: grape(s), winemaking techniques and site are all important. It can be tricky deciding when a bottle is ready, so here's a guide to when to drink wines from the classic grape varieties. When I say that a wine will keep, I mean that it will improve in bottle, developing depth and complexity. Some wines, especially fortified wines, will keep in bottle without developing further. The vast majority of wines today are designed to be drinkable upon release.

RED GRAPE VARIETIES

Cabernet Sauvignon Top Classed Growth red Bordeaux from the Médoc will need ten years to mature, and will last for another ten. California Cabernet from the Napa Valley will age for up to 12 years and can be drunk from five. Some top Italian Cabernets may take ten years to reach their peak. The best Australian Cabernets can last up to 25 years but can be enjoyed from five years onwards, and Spanish Cabernet from Torres or Jean León in Penedés will live for ten years or more, as will top Chilean examples.

Merlot In Bordeaux, most top Pomerols and St-Émilions will mature and fade more quickly than similar quality wines from the Cabernet Sauvignon-dominated Médoc. US and Italian Merlots are made for drinking young although a few serious wines will last eight to 12 years.

Nebbiolo This Italian star is one of the most long-lived of all red grapes. Much Barolo is

drinkable from six years, but will keep for 12-15; Barbaresco is slightly less long-lived. Basic Nebbiolo should be drunk within five to seven years.

Pinot Noir Simple Burgundy is best young, though top wines can last 20 years or more. Some California and Oregon Pinot is showing cellaring potential. Pinot Noir from New Zealand and Australia should usually be drunk within three years.

Sangiovese The very top Tuscan wines can be drunk between five and ten years after the vintage, though certain wines (Flaccianello della Pieve, Tignanello, Sassicaia, Le Pergole Torte) need longer. Most Chianti can be drunk on release, though good Riservas may improve further. California Sangioveses can be drunk young.

Syrah/Shiraz Syrah (alias Shiraz in Australia) can be very long-lived. It can also be used to make soft, early-drinking wine. The weightier northern Rhône wines need between five and eight years to come round, and will live for more. Southern Rhônes are less long-lived, although the most concentrated Châteauneuf-du-Papes need ten years to mature and last for 15 to 20. Most Australian Shiraz is meant to be drunk within three years but top old vine Shiraz from the Barossa can improve for ten years or more.

Tempranillo Most Spanish reds are drinkable upon release; exceptions include Ribera del Duero wines, which can need five or six years to mature after release, and can live for ten or 12.

MATURITY CHARTS

Maturity charts can only be a forecast of how you might expect a typical wine from one of the best producers of a region to perform. In each chart, the curving line and the coloured bands indicate at what point a wine is *ready* to drink, at its *peak* or *fading*. The bottom line is calibrated in years. If you like to drink wines very young, you may consider a wine ready before the chart says; conversely, if you like mature wines, you may want to add a few years to each assessment.

1990 Médoc Cru Classé – a sensational year, both ripe and long-lived.

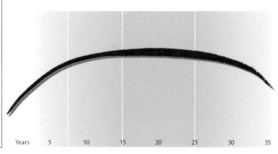

Years　5　10　15　20　25　30　35

1990 Barolo – a superb year in Piedmont, but patience is needed for the tannins to soften.

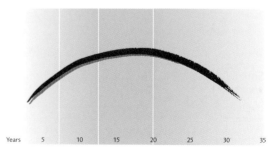

Years　5　10　15　20　25　30　35

WHITE GRAPE VARIETIES

Chardonnay Most Chardonnay is for early drinking. Exceptions include Premiers and Grands Crus from Chablis or the Côte d'Or, which can last ten years or more. Non-vintage Champagne is generally better with a further six months in bottle, and vintage versions should always be good for a decade. US Chardonnays for aging – for up to eight years – generally come from Carneros, Sonoma, California's South Central Coast and Washington. In Italy, only the best barrel-fermented wines will age up to five years or, in exceptional cases, eight to ten. In Australia, premium wines from warm regions such as the Hunter and Barossa Valleys can last up to five years. Wines from cooler areas like the Yarra Valley and Margaret River may see out a decade.

Chenin Blanc In most parts of the world, Chenin Blanc is made to be drunk young although it does have enormous aging ability. In France, the Loire dry Chenins that can and should be aged include those from Vouvray, Jasnières and Savennières – the latter can last for decades. Sweet wines for aging come from Vouvray, Anjou, Montlouis, Coteaux de L'Aubance, Coteaux du Layon, Bonnezeaux and Quarts de Chaume. They can taste quite light in youth but can be cellared for 50 years or more. In California, some Chalone Chenin Blancs can age for eight to ten years.

Gewürztraminer Only Alsace Gewurztraminer can be aged and then only really Grand Cru or lieux-dits wines; they should be drunk within a decade. Vendange Tardive and Sélection de Grains Nobles wines will last up to 20 years or more. Simple Gewürztraminer will keep for up to seven years.

Riesling In Germany, a Kabinett from a good producer will need about five years to mature, and will continue to improve for up to another four. A Spätlese should last for ten years or more, an Auslese for 15 or more, and Beerenauslese, Trockenbeerenauslese and Eiswein

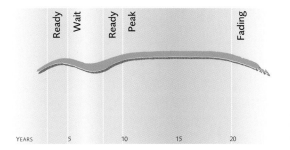

1995 Unoaked Hunter Valley Semillon – a vintage worth the wait.

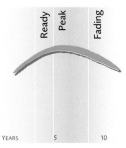

1995 Chablis Premier Cru – an excellent vintage for laying down.

should not be drunk for at least ten years and will improve in bottle for decades. The sweeter the wine, the longer its life. Top Australian examples from the Eden and Clare Valleys can live up to 20 years. Botrytized versions can live 15 years, but are also attractive from three to five. In Alsace, the best wines from good vintages will happily last for 15 years. A Vendange Tardive wine will last perhaps 20 years and a Sélection de Grains Nobles even longer. Top Austrian wines from the Wachau will also age for five years or more.

Sauvignon Blanc This is nearly always at its best young, or with at most a couple of years in bottle. In France, top Pouilly-Fumé and Sancerre can last for up to a decade. Only in Graves does Bordeaux really produce Sauvignon Blanc that ages well: non-Classed Growth châteaux should last four years; the top châteaux for longer. In the Haut-Médoc, Château Margaux's 100 per cent Sauvignon, Pavillon Blanc, can last for anything up to ten years.

Sémillon The only Sémillons to age come from the French regions of Sauternes and Graves (both blended with Sauvignon) and from Australia – but mostly only the unoaked versions. Lesser white Graves should last four years, but wines from the top châteaux can and do last much longer. The finest Sauternes need ten years to mature and can live for decades. Unoaked Australian Hunter Valley Semillon can live for up to 20 years.

PART THREE **The Wine Odyssey**

FRANCE

France has virtually every grape-growing condition you could ask for, from the chilly and desperate, to the torrid and broiling. As a result, many of the classic wine styles that newer winemaking countries try to copy were created here. Along with red Bordeaux and Champagne there is red Burgundy, still (just) the pinnacle of Pinot Noir performance. There is white Burgundy, made from the world's most popular grape, Chardonnay. Sauternes is one of the world's classic sweet white wines. The smoky reds of the Rhône Valley, the quick-maturing fruity wines of Beaujolais and the grassy Sauvignons of the Loire have all been copied throughout the world.

Yet wine in France has been shaped not just by geography and climate, but by history and culture. If you want to see the 1789 revolution almost in action, go and look at the vineyards of Burgundy, how they were wrested from the Church and have been divided and subdivided over succeeding generations. If you want to see the works of the 18th- and 19th-century aristocracy, go to the Médoc, where they built their châteaux and planted their vines within shouting distance of each other. The hot, harsh Rhône was a refuge of schismatic popes, and, more recently, the arid hills of the Midi have become a home from home for Australian-trained winemakers importing New World technology to the lands that nourished courtly love and medieval troubadours. Well, probably they whistle as they work.

Beaujolais is one of the last bastions of tradition in France but even here modernity is breaking through.

THE CLASSIFICATION SYSTEM

France's system of classifying wines has become the starting point for the wine law of almost every other country, even if some discard more than they keep. It is based on the concept of terroir; the terroir of a region, according to this way of thinking, is what makes it different from all other regions. Each region, therefore, should have its own grape varieties and own wine style. There are pros and cons to this.

It has certainly preserved a great variety of wines, made from a vast number of different vine varieties. New World countries, able to follow fashion in what they plant, have a poverty of resources in comparison. (They also have a far shorter history of winegrowing, of course.) On the other hand, it has helped to enshrine laziness and old-fashioned winemaking: it has been easy to say that a particular flavour comes from the terroir, when in fact it comes from dirty vats.

It is also important to realize that the French system of classification (and this applies to almost all others throughout the world) is not a guarantee of quality. The words 'Appellation d'Origine Contrôlée' mean that the wine comes from where it says it comes from. They don't say that it's good. Yes, AC wines have to pass a blind tasting, but see my objection above: it's all too easy to confuse tradition with terroir. It's only a minority of AC wines that are not worthy of their appellation but, nevertheless, remember that the best guide to quality is the name of the producer.

A few regions, notably Bordeaux, Burgundy, Champagne and Alsace, have classifications over and above the national one. These may well carry quality implications and I'll discuss this later.

Appellation d'Origine Contrôlée (AC) is the most tightly controlled of French categories. Producers may plant only listed varieties and take only a certain yield per hectare. Viticultural methods may also be stipulated, as may methods of winemaking – whether you're allowed to add sugar or acid. All wines must pass a tasting panel.

Vin Délimité de Qualité Supérieure (VDQS) is a shrinking category, because the policy is to promote these to AC when they're ready.

Vin de pays was introduced in 1968 to recognize simple country wines that had some regional character. Enterprising winemakers in the south have used it as a way of producing high-quality, modern wines from whatever grape varieties they please, without the constraints of AC rules.

Vin de table is the most basic wine, sold without indication of region, vintage or grape variety.

ENGLISH CHANNEL

BELGIUM

PARIS

N

SEINE

CHAMPAGNE

REIMS

PARIS

RENNES

LORRAINE

STRASBOURG

GERMANY

ALSACE

Moselle

Marne

Aube

Saône

Rhine

NANTES

TOURS

Mayenne

Sarthe

Loir

Seine

Yonne

BURGUNDY

DIJON

Doubs

Sèvre Nantaise

LOIRE VALLEY

Cher

Indre

Vienne

Sioul

JURA

Ain

GENEVA

SWITZERLAND

SAVOIE

Isère

LYON

ATLANTIC OCEAN

Gironde

Isle

Dordogne

Allier

Loire

RHÔNE VALLEY

A L P S

BORDEAUX

Lot

Rhône

Drôme

Durance

Var

BORDEAUX

SOUTH-WEST

Tarn

Gard

Hérault

Ardèche

NICE

BIARRITZ

TOULOUSE

Garonne

LANGUEDOC-ROUSSILLON

PROVENCE

P Y R E N E E S

Aude

MARSEILLE

MEDITERRANEAN
SEA

PERPIGNAN

SPAIN

WINE REGIONS OF FRANCE

- Champagne
- Lorraine
- Alsace
- Burgundy
- Jura
- Savoie
- Rhône Valley

- Provence
- Corsica
- Languedoc-Roussillon
- South-West
- Bordeaux
- Loire Valley

0 km   100
0 miles   50   100

CORSICA

Bordeaux

Bordeaux is different from all other French wine regions. It is bigger and more productive than most, and yields a greater variety of wines – red, dry white and sweet white. The red is probably the world's most famous: British wine lovers have long known it as claret, and it has lent its style to many Cabernet-Sauvignon-based wines produced elsewhere, from California to Coonawarra. Sauternes, too, was for a long time the archetypal sweet white wine.

These wines come not just from world-famous chateaux like Latour, Lafite and Yquem but from more humble properties too: the thousands of farmhouses that dot the regions of the Médoc, Graves, St-Émilion, Pomerol and Sauternes. Yet it is the river that is the heart of the region: the Gironde, formed by the confluence of the Dor-

dogne and the Garonne, both flowing from the heart of France to the Atlantic and passing, on their way, the quays of Bordeaux, from where, for centuries, ships have set out, laden with wine, bound for northern Europe and even America. No wonder Bordeaux is so cosmopolitan.

Look at the names of châteaux and négociants – Lynch-Bages, Léoville-Barton, Palmer, Nathaniel Johnston and Shröder & Schyler – and you get a potted history of the English, Irish, Scots and Dutch families who arrived in Bordeaux to set up trading companies (perhaps as early as the 17th century) and then started to grow vines. Many are still there. It was Dutch technology, too, that drained the marshlands that are now the vineyards of the Médoc. And for 300 years from 1152 Bordeaux belonged to the English crown, having

OPPOSITE **Château Margaux, one of Bordeaux's five Premiers Crus, produces one of the Médoc's greatest wines under the guidance of inspired winemaker Paul Pontallier.**

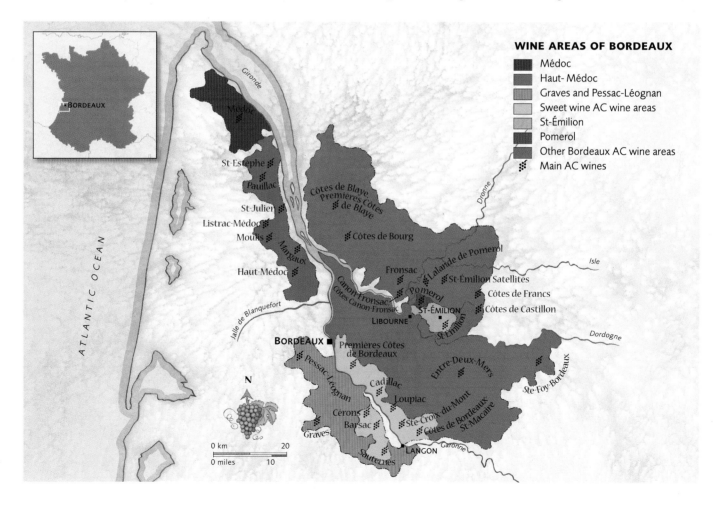

New oak barriques in the cellars of Château Cos d'Estournel, St-Estèphe. All great red Bordeaux is matured in a proportion of new oak, but only the most concentrated wines in the ripest years are given 100 per cent new oak.

formed part of the dowry of Eleanor of Aquitaine when she married Henry II of England: no wonder British wine drinkers still feel such an attachment to Bordeaux.

In those days, however, the wines were not the ones we know now. They came partly from the area around the city of Bordeaux itself, but even more from further up the Garonne and Dordogne rivers, from what are now Bergerac, Entre-Deux-Mers, Gaillac, even Cahors. It was only with the planting of the Médoc, after those 17th-century Dutch engineers had worked their magic, that the region began to take on the face we know today. Only then were most of the grand porticoed and turreted châteaux built; and it is with châteaux, above all, that Bordeaux is associated.

Not all Bordeaux châteaux are grand. Some are simple farmhouses of no pretension whatever. Yet the principle is the same: a château, in Bordeaux terms, is a single estate making its own wine. And that wine is a single grand vin bearing the château name, with perhaps a second wine with a different name. It is totally different from Burgundy where a producer will have small parcels of land in many appellations, and will make them all separately.

Variety in Bordeaux (and there is enormous variety: several thousand châteaux, each producing a wine different from that of its neighbours) comes from four factors: vine varieties, climate, soil, plus the personality of the château owner.

First, climate. The Gulf Stream, plus the Gironde estuary, help to keep frosts at bay (even so, it can still be a problem), and the presence of the Landes forest – thick pine woods stretching between the vineyards and sea – helps to absorb the force of Atlantic storms. But Bordeaux, in spite of its warm summers and mild autumns, is still a marginal climate in wine terms. It needs all the help given by the soil to ripen its red grapes.

The soils are also the determining factor in which grapes grow where. In the Médoc there are great ridges of gravel running alongside the river. Gravel is well drained and therefore fairly warm, which helps the late-ripening Cabernet Sauvignon to ripen. The Graves has plenty of gravel too; but there is cold clay in Pomerol (perfect for the early-ripening Merlot) and limestone in St-Émilion added to the equation. The soil can vary from yard to yard, from slope to crest of hill; and each château, just as it has its own pattern of soils, has its own particular proportions of each vine.

CLASSIFICATION

Bordeaux Rouge and **Blanc** are the basic appellations, covering the region's reds and whites.

'Now I like claret – whenever I can have claret, I must drink it. 'Tis the only palate affair that I am at all sensual in ...'

JOHN KEATS, LETTER, 18 FEBRUARY, 1819

Bordeaux Supérieur is red with a fraction more alcohol than basic Bordeaux and subject to a stiffer tasting panel.

Inside this framework, there are large areas – like the Médoc, Graves, St-Émilion, Entre-Deux-Mers – each of which has its own AC.

Bordeaux also has numerous classifications. In 1855 the leading châteaux of the Médoc were classified into five levels (see box on p.55), and with them was included one Graves property, Haut-Brion. Sauternes and Barsac were also classified at the same time. St-Émilion was first classified in 1955, and the Graves in 1959. Alone of Bordeaux's major regions, Pomerol has no classification and doesn't want one, thank you very much.

The famed gravel of the Médoc can clearly be seen in the vineyards of Château Langoa-Barton, St-Julien.

The Grapes

All red Bordeaux (with a few notable exceptions) is made from a blend of three and sometimes all five permitted red grape varieties.

CABERNET SAUVIGNON is the greatest of them all in the Médoc and Graves, where in good years it gives thrilling blackcurrant sweetness, and in lesser years a rather sharp, green-grassy rawness. That's why it needs that warm gravel soil to ripen.

CABERNET FRANC is lighter and less intense than Cabernet Sauvignon, and blended with it; although in St-Émilion, where there's less gravel and more limestone, it's normally an important partner in the blend along with Merlot.

MERLOT is the softest and plummiest of the lot, widely planted everywhere for its easy approachability, but treasured in Pomerol and St-Émilion for its ability to ripen to a wonderful structured spiciness. Merlot doesn't get any better than this.

PETIT VERDOT is added in small quantities for the colour and perfume it gives to the blend. It's late-ripening and in poor years might not make it at all, but its fans adore it.

MALBEC is plummy and rustic; sometimes added but not highly regarded in Bordeaux.

SAUVIGNON BLANC adds pungency and acidity to the white blend, both dry and sweet. It's never as pungent as in the Loire, but it's often bottled as a varietal.

SÉMILLON gives richness to the white blend. Susceptible to botrytis, it is the major player in Sauternes.

MUSCADELLE adds a grapy flavour and plenty of aroma to the Sauternes blend. It's added in small quantities – two or three per cent only.

The Médoc

The Médoc is divided into two halves: the half near the city of Bordeaux, the Haut-Médoc, is where all the greatest wines come from. The more remote half, the half stretching towards the mouth of the Gironde, is the home of altogether simpler wines. Either way, if your idea of the perfect wine region involves quaint farmhouses tucked into folds of the hills, and beaming, round-faced vignerons with tastevins tucked into the pockets of their blue overalls, then you will find the Médoc a severe disappointment. This is château country, where every side road winds past three or four, and every château looks out on to ranks of groomed vines.

The other thing about the Médoc is that it is rather flat. In fact it is very flat. Yes, there are hills, but none of them is steep enough to make you change gear, and quite a lot of them are so shallow that if the locals didn't proudly point them out you'd miss them altogether. Shallow or not, they are vital to the wine.

Gravel is the Médoc's secret weapon – it is this warm, well-drained gravel soil that is so suited to the Cabernet Sauvignon grape, and Cabernet Sauvignon is the most important part of the blend in most great Médoc wines. The gravel lies in ridges alongside the river, deposited there over millennia; and where it is deepest you will find the best vineyards. They say in the Médoc that to make great wine a vine needs to see the river; and it is true. In the dodgy vintages where not all the grapes ripen properly and the differences

The spectacular modern winery at Château Pichon-Longueville, Pauillac.

between the best vineyards and the rest really stand out, it is the vines on these gravel banks that show their quality.

Gravel is the main feature of the soil in four of the six smaller appellations (St-Estèphe, St-Julien, Pauillac and Margaux) that have been carved out of the whole in the Médoc and this is where the Classed Growth properties are concentrated. There are occasional Classed Growth châteaux elsewhere (Cantemerle, for example, which occupies a gravelly outcrop on otherwise inferior land, and has the appellation of Haut-Médoc) but not that many, and none of the absolutely top châteaux. Moulis' soil is pretty good and has gravel, and some star properties like Chasse-Spleen and Poujeaux, but Listrac is generally less well favoured and has more clay. So let's take a tour, and see what's what.

Margaux

The road through the grey industrial suburbs of Bordeaux is a pretty drab affair; it's hard to believe that you're within 15 minutes of the villages of Labarde, Cantenac and Margaux, source of some of the silkiest, most elegant red wine in France. Pauillac is more impressive, St-Julien more classically consistent, but Margaux at its best has a fascinating, teasing brilliance. Château Margaux is its epitome, with a flavour of violets and a texture of silk. The turreted Château Palmer makes magical wine, and Rauzan-Ségla, d'Angludet, the moated d'Issan, Monbrison, La Gurgue, Ferrière and Labégorce-Zédé all show what can be done. Sadly, not all Margaux châteaux are as good. It has more underperforming Classed Growths than any other Médoc appellation, but the good news is that one by one they seem to be picking up. Sometimes a change of the generation in charge can work wonders.

St-Julien

There isn't much to St-Julien in terms of volume. It's the smallest of the main Médoc communes – but it is concentrated quality, with over 75 per cent of its vineyards belonging to Classed Growths. Beychevelle, to the south, with its

THE 1855 CLASSIFICATION OF THE MÉDOC

In 1855 the wine brokers of Bordeaux classified the leading châteaux of the Médoc into five levels, and included with them one Graves property, Haut-Brion. They based their classification on the market price of the wines. The only time it has been changed since was when Baron Philippe de Rothschild, after years of lobbying, managed to get Mouton-Rothschild promoted to First Growth; it had previously been a Second.

FIRST GROWTHS
(Premiers Crus)
Lafite-Rothschild, Pauillac; Latour, Pauillac; Margaux, Margaux; Mouton-Rothschild, Pauillac (since 1973); Haut-Brion, Pessac-Léognan.

SECOND GROWTHS
(Deuxièmes Crus)
Rauzan-Ségla, Margaux; Rauzan-Gassies, Margaux; Léoville-Las-Cases, St-Julien; Léoville-Poyferré, St-Julien; Léoville-Barton, St-Julien; Durfort-Vivens, Margaux; Lascombes, Margaux; Gruaud-Larose, St-Julien; Brane-Cantenac, Margaux; Pichon-Longueville, Pauillac; Pichon-Longueville-Lalande, Pauillac; Ducru-Beaucaillou, St-Julien; Cos d'Estournel, St-Estèphe; Montrose, St-Estèphe.

THIRD GROWTHS
(Troisièmes Crus)
Giscours, Margaux; Kirwan, Margaux; d'Issan, Margaux; Lagrange, St-Julien; Langoa-Barton, St-Julien; Malescot-St-Exupéry, Margaux; Cantenac-Brown, Margaux; Palmer, Margaux; La Lagune, Haut-Médoc; Desmirail, Margaux; Calon-Ségur, St-Estèphe; Ferrière, Margaux; Marquis d'Alesme-Becker, Margaux; Boyd-Cantenac, Margaux.

FOURTH GROWTHS
(Quatrièmes Crus)
St-Pierre, St-Julien; Branaire-Ducru, St-Julien; Talbot, St-Julien; Duhart-Milon-Rothschild, Pauillac; Pouget, Margaux; La Tour-Carnet, Haut-Médoc; Lafon-Rochet, St-Estèphe; Beychevelle, St-Julien; Prieuré-Lichine, Margaux; Marquis-de-Terme, Margaux.

FIFTH GROWTHS
(Cinquièmes Crus)
Pontet-Canet, Pauillac; Batailley, Pauillac; Grand-Puy-Lacoste, Pauillac; Grand-Puy-Ducasse, Pauillac; Haut-Batailley, Pauillac; Lynch-Bages, Pauillac; Lynch-Moussas, Pauillac; Dauzac, Margaux; d'Armailhac, Pauillac (formerly known as Mouton-Baronne-Philippe); du Tertre, Margaux; Haut-Bages-Libéral, Pauillac; Pédesclaux, Pauillac; Belgrave, Haut-Médoc; Camensac, Haut-Médoc; Cos-Labory, St-Estèphe; Clerc-Milon-Rothschild, Pauillac; Croizet-Bages, Pauillac; Cantemerle, Haut-Medoc.

Below this classification there is another, of Crus Bourgeois, or middle-class growths. This is somewhat differently organized; properties pay to belong to a Syndicat and then obey certain rules on winemaking. The châteaux are classified as Crus Bourgeois Exceptionnels, Crus Grands Bourgeois and Cru Bourgeois; there are some 300 of them.

A classically elegant Pauillac produced under the guidance of the charismatic Madame de Lencquesaing.

The tower of Château Latour, Pauillac, with the Gironde estuary beyond.

neighbour Branaire-Ducru, produces a wine which is soft, plummy even, but which develops a lovely, always gentle flavour. The greatest exponent of this style is Château Ducru-Beaucaillou, just north of Beychevelle. Its wine is so soft and rich it sometimes seems coated with honey – remarkable for a dry red wine – but as it ages it gradually begins to reveal the hallmark of great St-Julien, that penetrating, uplifting scent of cedar. Château Gruaud-Larose, just to the left as the road turns north past Ducru-Beaucaillou, is also very fine, but for me the heart of St-Julien lies in its northern vineyards, and in particular in the elegance of Léoville-Barton and the concentration of Léoville-Las-Cases.

Pauillac

This is the home of Cabernet Sauvignon, where most top vineyards have at least 70 per cent: there's a hefty shoulder of gravel that runs from the St-Julien border past the town of Pauillac to the little stream north of Château Lafite, which marks the end of the appellation. And we start with a bang, because on leaving St-Julien the first sight on the right is the round tower which marks the vineyards of Château Latour. Latour is Bordeaux's most imposing, longest-lasting wine, tough and dark to begin with yet slowly building to a rich blackcurrant, mint and cedar strength.

Yet right next door is Château Pichon-Longueville-Lalande, lush and succulent. There's

SECOND WINES

These are what is left when the finest lots have been selected for the grand vin, or main château wine. The lesser lots of wine will often include wine from younger vines, or from less favoured parts of the vineyard. Second wines are sold under a name that is different from, but generally related to, the château name, like Les Forts de Latour from Château Latour, or Dame de Montrose from Château Montrose. With careful selection and in a good vintage they can be excellent, and top second wines, especially Les Forts de Latour and Lafite's Carruades de Lafite, sell for very high prices. In poor vintages they are best treated with caution unless from particularly careful producers or from châteaux that made no grand vin at all in that vintage. From underperforming châteaux they are best avoided altogether. It is fashionable for châteaux to tell journalists that they have selected only a tiny proportion of their crop for the grand vin – some claim to use less than half, and to put most of the rest into their second wine. Some may even be telling the truth.

a lot more Merlot here, and some of the vines are actually in St-Julien. Opposite is Pichon-Longueville, denser and firmer in style; Lynch-Bages, nearer the town of Pauillac, is fat and juicy, but in time heady with cassis and mint. North of the town, Mouton-Rothschild makes astonishing rich, cedary wine like celestial pencil sharpenings, and Lafite makes something lighter and more elegant, but no less intense.

St-Estèphe

There's just one great gravel bank to come, and it stares you in the face as you pass Lafite and dip and climb to turn left in front of the pagoda towers of Cos d'Estournel, where the wine is classically proportioned and unfailingly refined. It's far and away the best in St-Estèphe, where Montrose, Lafon-Rochet, Cos-Labory, Calon-Ségur, de Pez, Meyney and Haut-Marbuzet are impressive, but not as good. Lesser St-Estèphes can be a bit tough, a bit muddy, reflecting the clinging dampness of clay after rain, and most vineyards need a fair bit of Merlot to add ripeness and body to their wines.

Moulis and Listrac

Suddenly the carpet of vines is gone. Scrub returns, and forest and pasture. This is because the gravel has been largely replaced by heavier clay soil. It is significant that in this area between Margaux and St-Julien there are no Classed Growths. Even so, Listrac can boast châteaux of the calibre of Clarke, Fourcas-Hosten and Fourcas-Dupré, and Moulis has Poujeaux, Maucaillou and Chasse-Spleen, the last of which makes wine which is consistently up to Classed Growth standards and charges Classed Growth prices.

Haut-Médoc

This is, confusingly, the more southerly part of the Médoc and the part that contains the six individual appellations we've just visited. It is 'haut' in the sense of being further upriver than the more northerly half. There are pockets of good terroir and even some Classed Growths, like La Lagune and Cantemerle. Cissac, Citran, Lamarque,

THE EN PRIMEUR CAMPAIGN

The châteaux of Bordeaux have devised an excellent method of selling all, or nearly all, their wine in one go: it's called the en primeur campaign. And for a few weeks every spring Bordeaux goes mad. Each château fixes an 'opening price' for its wine and sets about dealing with the merchants who are, in a good vintage, queuing up to buy. In a few feverish hours or days it can have sold everything and be counting its money; all it has to do now is mature the wine in its cellars for a further year or 18 months, bottle and ship it out.

Selling the wine so soon has pros and cons for the châteaux. Yes, they have a guaranteed sum for the wines. But if the vintage becomes ultra-fashionable prices will rise, and the château will see none of the extra: it will all go to the middlemen who play the market. Not that the châteaux mind: in a poor vintage when demand is sluggish, those same middlemen have to take the wine off their hands.

For the consumer, buying en primeur (via a wine merchant) can be a way of obtaining scarce wines. But you need to pick a reputable merchant (if the merchant goes bust before your wine is delivered you may have difficulty obtaining it) and while prices can rise they can also fall, and you won't necessarily get a bargain.

Sociando-Mallet, Bel-Orme-Tronquoy-de-Lalande and Beaumont all make good to excellent wine.

Médoc

This used to be called the Bas-Médoc until they got fed up with a name they felt was faintly derogatory, so now it's just Médoc. But it's the same place: the remote reaches of the Médoc, far from the city of Bordeaux and with none of the dry crunch of gravel underfoot which characterizes the best areas. Yet there are some very good wines coerced from this unpromising soil. Potensac is the best, and Patache d'Aux, La Tour-St-Bonnet, La Tour-de-By and La Tour-Haut-Caussan are all worth seeking out. The lesser wines, the most petit of petits châteaux – well, some are trying hard, and some are just going for volume, producing overpriced, underpowered red from vineyard yields that are far too high and that are beaten hands down, year after year, by ripe, supple Cabernets from the Pays d'Oc or Chile.

Super seconds are what you get when you combine ambitious château owners with a classification that was made in 1855 and hardly changed since. Super seconds are a way of recognizing that certain Second Growth châteaux are making wine far better than their peers, and perhaps even of First Growth standard. There's no formal list, but Pichon-Longueville-Lalande, Pichon-Longueville, Cos d'Estournel (Les Pagodes de Cos is their second wine), Léoville-Las-Cases and Ducru-Beaucaillou are all widely accepted to be super seconds. Léoville-Las-Cases virtually charges First Growth prices.

St-Émilion and Pomerol

The vineyards strung across the slopes and plateaux of the right bank of the Dordogne river, and centred on the sleepy little port of Libourne, manage to look totally different from those on the Médoc bank. The châteaux that dominate the Médoc landscape are absent here: yes, the properties still bear the title of château, but the houses in question are largely farmhouses. The people are different, too: they're less formal than the Médocains and more relaxed. It's an intensively cultivated region, more spread out than the long-limbed Médoc, with the result that properties can be spectacularly difficult to find: one road, and one vineyard, you rapidly discover, looks exactly like any other.

St-Émilion

This is the biggest area on the whole right bank. The thick carpet of vines begins just over a mile to the east of Libourne, and sweeps along the plateau almost engulfing the little Roman town of St-Émilion. St-Émilion lives by wine: the foundations of its steep, narrow streets and its crowded buildings are honeycombed with caves burrowed into the rock where, even today, wine is made and stored.

There are three types of vineyard in the appellation St-Émilion: the côtes, the graves and the sables. The town itself is the axis for the côtes vineyards, or those on the slopes. Most of St-Émilion's greatest wines come from these 140 hectares (350 acres), where the soil is a mix of limestone and clay.

The graves are less spectacular: flat or undulating fields spreading back across the plateau towards Libourne and Pomerol. Most is sand and clay soil; in spite of its name there is only one surge of gravel that runs through its two greatest vineyards, Figeac and Cheval Blanc.

The third area, the sables, is down by the river, where the wine is basic St-Émilion or at best Grand Cru, and is mostly undistinguished.

This relative lack of gravel explains why Cabernet Sauvignon is unimportant here: it just won't ripen. Merlot and Cabernet Franc take centre stage.

The best properties, as I've said, are concentrated on the côtes, where they produce a wonderful balance of fruit and toughness, sometimes succulent, juicy and gulpable, with a richness of honey and raisins and buttery fruitcake. Canon-La-Gaffelière, Pavie, Ausone, Arrosée and Angélus show this style to perfection. Sometimes they start more slowly, with a tighter structure, until a few years' aging coaxes out that honeyed richness. Magdelaine and Curé-Bon are like this. The two great châteaux of the graves, Figeac and Cheval Blanc are both

A horse-drawn plough turning the soil near the base of the vines at Château Magdelaine, St-Émilion. A few owners still use horses in the vineyards because, unlike tractors, they don't compact the soil.

powerful wines, less immediately honeyed and soft than most St-Émilions. The best of the rest are La Dominique and Corbin.

Of the simple sables properties Monbousquet is among the classiest. At their best these wines have a short youthful burst of sweet, buttery fruit, simple and soft. Teyssier is another name to look for. In the satellite appellations (St-Georges-St-Émilion and Puisseguin-St-Émilion, Montagne-St-Émilion and Lussac-St-Émilion) quality is patchy, but there are several châteaux, notably St-Georges and Calon, where the wines are as good as a Grand Cru St-Émilion.

Every year, the *ban de vendanges* (the official opening of the vintage) is declared from the top of the tower (far right) which overlooks St-Émilion.

MICRO WINES AND MACRO PRICES

Can a wine – any wine – be worth £1500/$2370 a bottle? That's £250/$395 a glass. And that's a lot of money. Imagine if you spilled it.

But this was the price paid by some lucky buyer for Le Pin 1982, back at the peak of the market in November 1997. And they were lucky to get it: only about 650 cases of Le Pin are made each year, and even the château's owner, Jacques Thienpont, only has one bottle and two double magnums of the 1982 vintage.

Le Pin is the most famous example of a new phenomenon in wine: micro wines. Others are La Mondotte, Le Dome and Valandraud. All are in St-Émilion or Pomerol, and all are tiny, just a hectare or two. The principle is that all vineyards have corners that are better than the rest: if you separate out the very best grapes and wines you can make a tiny quantity of something sensational.

These wines have soared to the top of the market for another reason, too: their opulent, concentrated flavours are in tune with fashion. Finesse and elegance are less fashionable than power; and some of these wines are aged in up to 150 per cent new oak. (That means putting it into 100 per cent new oak barriques, and then into new oak again after racking.)

The other thing is that they are mostly relatively recent inventions, and their long-term track record is unproven, either in the cellar or at auction.

Pétrus, however, is in a different mould. It was attracting superstar prices long before the micro wines popped up, and is managed by Christian Moueix, who is devoted to finesse in wines, not power. Pétrus, along with Cheval Blanc and the Médoc First Growths, is a blue chip investment wine. Other wines worldwide that have become investment wines include Domaine de la Romanée-Conti Burgundies, Grange from Australia and a handful of California Cabernets like Caymus Special Selection. Few, however, can match the prices of top Bordeaux.

This leading St-Émilion estate is right on the border with Pomerol and shares some of its characteristic richness while adding a unique touch of extra spice and fruit all of its own.

St Peter (Pétrus) holding the keys to heaven. He also makes an appearance on the château's label.

ST-ÉMILION CLASSIFICATION

Unlike the classification of the Médoc, this is supposed to be revised every ten years or so. The most recent revision was in 1997.

St-Émilion is the overall appellation for the region, for the simplest wines.

St-Émilion Grand Cru isn't as grand as it actually sounds: there are about 200 of these châteaux, and most are just simple wines for drinking young. If the phrase Grand Cru is ever going to mean anything serious in St-Émilion most of these ought to be demoted to basic St-Émilion.

Grand Cru Classé is where quality starts. There are just over 60 Grand Cru Classé châteaux. Some are very good indeed and ought to be promoted; many are still failing to thrill.

Premier Grand Cru Classé is the top of the St-Émilion tree. There are 13 of them, with Ausone and Cheval Blanc separated out as Class A wines and the rest Class B, as follows:

Class A Cheval Blanc; Ausone.

Class B Angélus; Beauséjour-Bécot; Beauséjour-Duffau-Lagarrosse; Belair; Canon; Clos Fourtet; Figeac; La Gaffelière; Magdelaine; Pavie; Trottevieille.

Pomerol

This is the back of beyond. It's a formless, charmless block of fields to the north-east of Libourne, which just happens to produce Merlot-based wines which have caught the imagination of the world. Fifty years ago nobody had heard of it; and the properties are tiny, usually only between five or ten hectares, and sometimes less.

But the wines are remarkable. Sometimes it's difficult to believe that they are merely red wines: they're buttery, honeyed, creamy, plummy – and then you find there's a taste of mint, of blackcurrant jam and chocolate. But there's also a hint of something minerally, a backbone without which the flavours might be almost too luscious.

Some of the properties in the west, like Clos René and de Sales, are on sandier soil, and these are quite absurdly rich and yummy almost as soon as they're made. Conversely, there are a few properties like Petit-Village and Beauregard over near St-Émilion, where the lighter soil and a sprinkling of Cabernet Sauvignon makes for a leaner, more Médoc-like style of wine.

But the heart of the matter is in the scarcely discernible swell heading north. Here iron and minerals underlie clay that is as thick as plum pudding, and here are the best properties of Pomerol, including Pétrus, Trotanoy, Lafleur, Lafleur-Pétrus, Gazin, Vieux-Château-Certan, Le Pin, Certan-de-May and Latour-à-Pomerol.

Lalande-de-Pomerol

A mini-Pomerol really, with a touch of Pomerol's easy style. Annereaux is a good bet, as are Les Hauts-Tuileries, Bertineau-St-Vincent and Lavaud-La-Maréchaude.

THE MERLOT STORY

When sufficiently ripe, rich and concentrated, Merlot gives what is nowadays the supremely fashionable style of Bordeaux. It is used in Pomerol almost exclusively, and is also the dominant grape in St-Émilion, and the mainstay of neighbouring Lalande-de-Pomerol. It thrives on the thick, impenetrable clay and reaches down, in the best sites, to a mineral- and iron-rich subsoil. Château Pétrus in Pomerol is in some years 100 per cent Merlot, and the world's most expensive red wine, fellow Pomerol Le Pin, is approximately 90 per cent Merlot. Think opulent fruit; think spicy, almost exotic complexity. Merlot of this concentration and this richness is shockingly easy to drink young; which is why it appeals to the new generation of wine drinkers weaned on supple, upfront New World reds that have no need to spend years in a cellar prior to drinking.

Graves and Pessac-Léognan

'Haut-Brion? Can't miss it. Just go past the builders' merchants, turn right at the hospital, past the housing estate and it's opposite the garage.' Okay, I'm making up the precise directions, but you get the point: Château Haut-Brion, one of the finest red wine properties in Bordeaux and indeed in the world, is in the middle of a suburb.

And it's not the only one. La Mission Haut-Brion is just down the road, so is Pape-Clément, and they're all hemmed in by houses. What the locals grow in their gardens I don't know, but this is some of the most valuable vineyard land in the world.

In the 18th century this was the main source of good red Bordeaux: it was conveniently near the city and port, while the Médoc was much more inaccessible. What's more, the terroir was good: deep, very gravelly soil which was ideal for producing the most favoured light red of the day.

The Graves, however, is more than just this. It stretches south for 56km (35 miles) along the left bank of the Garonne river, and from Martillac, a few miles south of Bordeaux, right down to past Langon, almost on the edge of the Gironde département, the soils are increasingly sand and clay. The Graves stretches right to the edge of the sweet wine regions of Cérons, Barsac and Sauternes, and in fact in these lower reaches one or two quite respectable sweet white wines are made. Since the Graves also has a name for dry whites, it can claim to be the only Bordeaux region that makes all three styles.

But not all of the Graves is equally good. In 1987 the most northerly communes were given

La Mission Haut-Brion once belonged to a religious order known as the Preachers of the Mission.

Haut-Brion produces a red wine which, over the last decade, has nearly always fully justified its exalted status. There is also a small amount of white.

their own appellation, Pessac-Léognan, so that technically is where Haut-Brion and the rest are. Once you get out of the suburbs it's some of the most attractive countryside in Bordeaux, less monotonous than the Médoc because less intensively planted with vines. Swathes of woodland are interspersed with vineyards, with the châteaux (and they're proper châteaux here; after all, they had the city of Bordeaux to keep up with) set well back from the road. Domaine de Chevalier is here, making good red and world-class white; so is richly flavoured de Fieuzal and long-aging Haut-Bailly. Cabernet Sauvignon is the main grape, with Cabernet Franc and Merlot to fill out the blend.

Go further south again and you leave Pessac-Léognan and enter the Graves proper, where the properties are less grand and the whole aspect less ambitious. Here the tobaccoey-cedary scent and minerally earthiness of great red Pessac-Léognan is replaced by a more simple plummy earthiness, attractively juicy when young but not needing or wanting to age in bottle for very long. It was also the site, until about 15 or 20 years ago, of some of the worst sins committed in the name of Graves.

These sins were white, off-dry and sulphury, and must have put entire generations completely off the idea of white Graves. But in came cold fermentation and new oak barriques, and hey presto! White Graves became ultra clean, ultra

Château de Fieuzal is one of the most up-to-date properties in the region and near the top of the tree for both reds and whites. The Sauvignon-based white of Château Couhins-Lurton is equally modern in style.

'To the Royal Oak Tavern, in Lumbard Street, where Alexander Broome the poet was, a merry and witty man, I believe, if he be not a little conceited, and here drank a sort of French wine, called Ho Bryan, that hath a good and most particular taste that I never met with.'

DIARY OF SAMUEL PEPYS, 10 APRIL, 1663

Statues and paintings of Bacchus crop up all over the place in France. This charming statue is the focal point of the entrance hall to the *chai* of Château Haut-Brion. Festivals such as the Bacchanalia of Roman times were held in his honour (see also p.26).

fresh wine with a good whack of new oak – sometimes too good a whack, in fact – and a new wine style was born.

The whites from Pessac-Léognan are still better, classier and have more complexity and higher prices too, but simple white Graves, made from Sauvignon Blanc and some Sémillon, is undeniably good value. But it's in the minority these days: the acreage of red vineyard outnumbers white by around two to one.

CLASSIFICATION

Graves is the basic appellation for both red and dry white wines.

Graves Supérieures covers medium to sweet whites, and they're supposed to have a slightly higher alcohol content: 12 degrees instead of 11 degrees.

Pessac-Léognan covers reds and whites in the northerly section.

The 1959 classification is as follows:

Red wines Bouscaut, Cadaujac; Haut-Bailly, Léognan; Carbonnieux, Léognan; Château de Chevalier, Léognan; Domaine de Chevalier, Léognan; de Fieuzal, Léognan; d'Olivier, Léognan; Malartic-Lagravière, Léognan; La Tour-Martillac, Martillac; Smith-Haut-Lafittte, Martillac; Haut-Brion, Pessac; La Mission Haut-Brion, Talence; Pape-Clément, Pessac; La Tour-Haut-Brion, Talence.

White wines Bouscaut, Cadaujac; Carbonnieux, Léognan; Domaine de Chevalier, Léognan; d'Olivier, Léognan; Malartic-Lagravière, Léognan; La Tour-Martillac, Martillac; Laville-Haut-Brion, Talence; Couhins-Lurton, Villenave d'Ornon; Couhins, Villenave d'Ornon; Haut-Brion, Pessac (added in 1960).

Sauternes

The time to visit Sauternes is in the autumn. This is when the leaves turn as golden as the wine and when the sun filters through the morning mists that rise where the cold river Ciron meets the warmer Garonne. It's when the pale golden stone of the châteaux becomes visible through the trees, and it's when the owners of those châteaux watch their grapes ceaselessly, waiting for them to rot.

But it has to be the right sort of rot. Only *Botrytis cinerea*, noble rot, will attack the Sémillon and Sauvignon Blanc grapes to produce the desired unctuous, spicy, honeyed flavour. First the healthy bloom on the grapes begins to crack, then they shrivel into ill-formed, slimy raisins.

The botrytis fungus feeds on the sugar and tartaric acid within the grape, and pierces the skins so that the grapes dehydrate, thus concentrating the sugar that is left. It also changes the chemical make-up of the juice to produce glycerol, which is why botrytized wines are so richly viscous.

But the botrytis arrives as and when it pleases. Sometimes (and these are the best years) it turns up early and blankets the vineyards with mould; in other years it may be late and patchy, or never arrive at all. In these years selection is the key to making decent Sauternes, and conscientious winemakers will send the pickers through the vineyards time after time, day after day, to pick only the botrytized grapes and leave the rest for another time. If there is no botrytis at

Château d'Yquem is often rated as the most sublime sweet wine in the world. Other top producers in the region include Climens, Guiraud and Rieussec.

CRYOEXTRACTION

Cryoextraction, in the late 1980s, looked as though it might be the saviour of Sauternes in wet vintages; in practice it is so expensive that only top châteaux can afford it.

It consists in essence of putting the newly picked grapes overnight in a giant refrigerator: a cold room specially installed for the purpose. Excess water on and in the grapes freezes, and when the grapes are pressed only the stickily sweet juice runs out.

It's great in theory, but it puts the already sky-high costs of producing Sauternes even higher; and it can't be a substitute for noble rot. Many châteaux are investing instead in strict selection in the vineyard and meticulous winemaking.

A basket of Sémillon grapes which have been affected by noble rot.

The Food of Bordeaux

THE FIRST THING you notice about the food of Bordeaux is that it is rather simple. And this makes sense: nothing partners a good, mature red Bordeaux better than roast meat, and if that comes in the form of steak frites, perhaps with the chips fried in duck or goose fat, you have the perfect dinner to round off a hard day's tasting. Pauillac is also a perfect match for tender lamb fed on the salt marshes.

In the autumn you may be offered *ceps*, big, fat mushrooms picked in quantity and sold on roadside stalls; restaurants will also serve oysters in season, harvested from the bay at Arcachon and served with small, spicy sausages. Arcachon is also a good place for shellfish; but in Bordeaux's city centre you can also find platters of *fruit de mers*, sea-fresh and crying out for a bottle of Sauvignon.

If you crave something more elaborate, try

lamproie à la bordelaise: lampreys (which are rich, meaty fish at the best of times) cooked in a sauce of shallots, red wine, garlic and parsley. It's delicious, but it's so rich I can only ever face it once every five years or so.

Come the autumn there's abundant game – pheasant, wild duck, woodcock, wood-pigeon, rabbit and hare – but if you want local cheese to finish off your red wine, forget it. Bordeaux, unusually for a wine region, has no decent cheese of its own. So it has adopted a couple. Mimolette, a dark orange, mature gouda, hard and served in thin slices, sets off red Bordeaux very well – and actually, it's not the easiest of wines to match with cheese. And whatever you do, don't try drinking it with Bordeaux's other adopted cheese, Roquefort. Roquefort comes from the Languedoc, but it's a perfect match with Sauternes. Not a cheap way of finishing a meal, I admit.

If you're set on having pudding you could try pouring some red Bordeaux over strawberries, or you could sample the macaroons made in St-Émilion. A *St-Émilion au chocolat* is a chocolate charlotte made with these macaroons, and exceedingly good it is too.

all then the wine will be made with overripe grapes: it will be sweet, but it will not have the endless fascination of Sauternes at its best. And if the weather doesn't oblige – if it is too cold, or too rainy – then there may be no Sauternes at all, and the châteaux will have to fall back on dry white wine to make a living. Some properties also grow some red grapes, for the same reason. Even in the best vintages, the yield from the grapes will be only a quarter or so of that regularly taken by Médoc châteaux of equivalent quality. So you could say Sauternes isn't expensive. On the contrary, it's cheap – well, relatively cheap.

When the grapes arrive at the winery they can be curiously unwilling to ferment. It's all that sugar: yeasts work only sluggishly in a very sweet solution. And when the alcohol gets to 13 or 14 degrees they give up altogether, leaving masses of residual sugar in the wine.

Young Sauternes is almost shockingly easy to drink; but it does improve with age, over seven or eight years or more. New oak barrels used to age the wine in the cellars add a creamy vanilla flavour to the apricot, honey and marzipan of the wine, so Sauternes doesn't have the sweetness of sugar from a packet: it's honey, as rich and satisfying as when spread on hot toast and butter.

There are five villages that make Sauternes: Sauternes itself, Barsac (which makes a slightly lighter style of wine and may call its wine either Sauternes or Barsac), Preignac, Fargues and Bommes. All have seen a massive revival since the early 1980s, with a string of good vintages from 1983 to 1990 encouraging investment.

The only appellations for the region are Sauternes or Barsac.

THE 1855 SAUTERNES CLASSIFICATION

The Sauternes classification was made in 1855, at the same time as the Médoc was being classified. Château d'Yquem, quite rightly, is put head and shoulders above the rest, as a First Great Growth; other leading châteaux are grouped underneath, as First and Second Growths.

First Great Growth (Premier Cru Supérieur) Yquem, Sauternes.

First Growths (Premiers Crus) La Tour-Blanche, Bommes; Lafaurie-Peyraguey, Bommes; Clos Haut-Peyraguey, Bommes; Rayne-Vigneau, Bommes; Suduiraut, Preignac; Coutet, Barsac; Climens, Barsac; Guiraud, Sauternes; Rieussec, Fargues; Rabaud-Promis, Bommes; Sigalas-Rabaud, Bommes.

Second Growths (Deuxièmes Crus) de Myrat, Barsac; Doisy-Daëne, Barsac; Doisy-Dubroca, Barsac; Doisy-Védrines, Barsac; d'Arche, Sauternes; Filhot, Sauternes; Broustet, Barsac; Nairac, Barsac; Caillou, Barsac; Suau, Barsac; de Malle, Preignac; Romer-du-Hayot, Fargues; Lamothe Despujols, Sauternes; Lamothe-Guignard, Sauternes.

This leading estate in Barsac has a reputation for rich, elegant wines with a light, lemony acidity that keeps them fresh.

CHÂTEAU d'YQUEM

This is the best, most concentrated, most complex and long-lived Sauternes of all. The medieval château stands at the highest point in the Sauternes vineyards, and the grapes are picked and the wine made with meticulous care: the pickers may be sent through the vines for up to 11 successive pickings in some years, and instructions are relayed to them from the press house even as they pick as to the sort of grapes that are needed. In years when the botrytis is most plentiful word might even come through to pick more unbotrytized grapes, to maintain the balance of the wine.

Botrytized wines have been made here for generations, but nobody knows who first dared to ferment the juice of these rotten grapes, and to taste the result. The 1810 cellar book at Yquem refers to 'triage', or successive selective pickings, but it is likely that it was common practice long before that. The château makes a dry white wine, Ygrec, which has great intensity and a full, toasty flavour. It's difficult to find, and expensive, though less expensive than Yquem itself.

These days Yquem is drunk with pudding, with Roquefort cheese or with *foie gras* (ambrosial combinations all), but according to 19th-century menus it was then also served with fish.

This bottle of 1794 Yquem was sold at auction in London in 1986 for £36,000/$57,000.

Other Bordeaux Regions

It's the starry châteaux of Bordeaux that make the news, but the region is big and varied enough to cater for anybody who wants the cedar and blackcurrant flavours of red Bordeaux without a massive price tag. It's worth bearing in mind that Bordeaux is not by its nature the most inexpensive wine region, and wines at rock bottom prices are likely to be rock bottom quality; but that being said, there's some good stuff to be had if you're prepared to track it down.

Entre-Deux-Mers

'Between two seas' is a bit of an exaggeration: between two rivers is more like it. Entre-Deux-Mers is the wedge of land at the confluence of the Dordogne and Garonne, and it's lovely mixed farming country. The appellation applies only to dry whites, and they're a pretty good buy, crisp and quite pungent. The juicy, slightly earthy reds of the region take the appellation of Bordeaux or Bordeaux Supérieur.

Premières Côtes de Bordeaux

Mostly earthy, rustic reds, not hugely exciting, though the odd property does better. They come from a sliver of land running down the right bank of the Garonne, and it's at the far southern end that the Premières Côtes spring their surprise: sweet wines from the appellations of Cadillac, Loupiac and Ste-Croix-du-Mont. In a good year these are like mini-Sauternes; much lighter, but with a nicely honeyed richness.

Cérons

Another mini-Sauternes, a tiny patch of land immediately north of Barsac, within the Graves area. The appellation is for sweet white, but given the risk of waiting for botrytis the growers tend to concentrate on reds and dry whites instead.

Bourg and Blaye

Bourg – or Côtes de Bourg, to give it its full name – is the better of these two appellations on the right bank of the Gironde, making quite solid, rustic reds with dry blackcurrant fruit and a whiff of cedar. Premières Côtes de Blaye reds may have a slightly cooked jamminess about them.

Fronsac and Canon-Fronsac

This really is a good place to look for classically proportioned red Bordeaux. Quality is uneven across the board, but the Pomerol négociant house of J-P Moueix has made some shrewd investments here, and the cleverest importers are cherry-picking the best wines.

Dordogne Outposts

On the right bank of the Dordogne the action is mostly red. Tucked between St-Émilion and Bergerac are the Côtes de Francs and the Côtes de Castillon, home to one or two good properties. The majority turn out light, simple reds, slightly earthy and with a touch of Merlot sweetness.

The Moulin du Haut-Benauge, in vineyards near Gornac in Entre-Deux-Mers. The region used to be an important cereal-growing area.

Burgundy

Burgundy is the name of the Grand Duchy which once covered much of eastern France. It was famous for all sorts of things – its lavish architecture, its patronage of the arts, its great monastic establishments. But Burgundy had something even more to offer – its inspiring cuisine and its remarkable wines. Today it is the home of the most subtle, silky, fascinating red wines in the world, and of whites that challenge Chardonnay-makers the world over to try to imitate their endless complexity.

It was the monasteries of Cluny and Cîteaux that developed many of Burgundy's vineyards. The Cistercians, rigorous in this as in all else, paid particular attention to the variations of soil and terroir on the Côte d'Or; to them can be attributed the idea of the Cru. They made what would nowadays be called microvinifications of different plots and demonstrated that different patches of vineyard produced wines of different flavours and characters; their detailed mapping of the Côte d'Or is the basis of today's vineyard boundaries.

Then, in 1789, came the French Revolution. The monasteries were dispossessed, and their vineyards sold to the highest bidders. In Bordeaux, the aristocratic château-owners ensured that their estates stayed in one piece from generation to generation; in more workaday Burgundy this did not happen, and as families intermarried and intermarried again down the years each inheritance was divided and subdivided. Until the Revolution, and even after, the 50-hectare (125-acre) Clos de Vougeot vineyard had one owner; now it has over 80. So a grower in Burgundy will own vines in a long list of different villages, and will vinify and bottle each of them separately. In Bordeaux a producer sells just one, or perhaps two wines under his estate name; in Burgundy he might sell ten or more.

This creates another layer of complexity in what is already a complex appellation system. To put it in perspective, let's remember that the Côte d'Or is a single, east-facing slope of land some 48km (30 miles) long, divided into the Côte

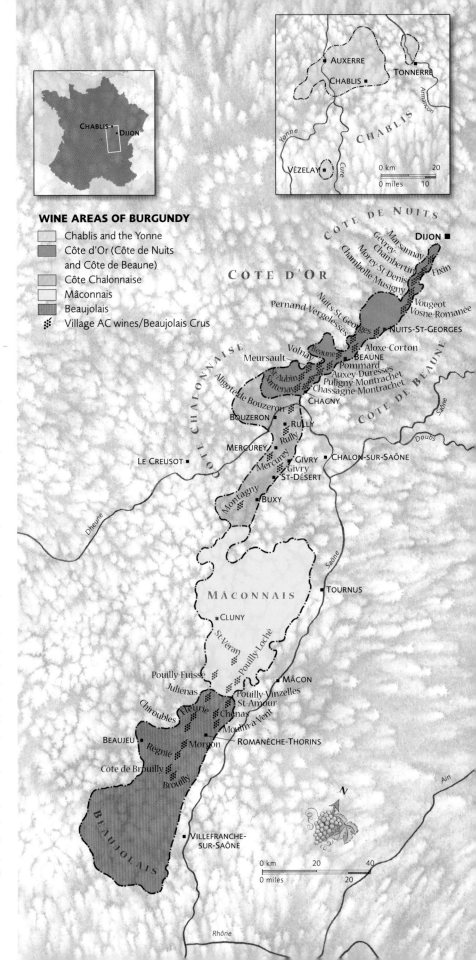

WINE AREAS OF BURGUNDY

- Chablis and the Yonne
- Côte d'Or (Côte de Nuits and Côte de Beaune)
- Côte Chalonnaise
- Mâconnais
- Beaujolais
- Village AC wines/Beaujolais Crus

de Nuits in the north and the Côte de Beaune in the south. It's scarcely a mile wide at its broadest point. Added to this is Chablis to the north. To the south are the Mâconnais, Côte Chalonnaise and Beaujolais. And in this space are crammed five different levels of vineyard classification.

CLASSIFICATION

In Burgundy, **general appellations** are the most basic, catch-all appellations: Bourgogne Rouge or Blanc; Bourgogne Aligoté, for whites made from that grape; and the inferior Bourgogne Passe-Tout-Grains, for blends of Pinot Noir and Gamay.

Regional appellations are slightly more specific: Chablis, for example, covers all the wines of that region that have no higher classification; Hautes-Côtes de Nuits and Hautes-Côtes de Beaune cover the backwaters of the Côte d'Or, the remote vineyards high in the hills beyond the main part of the Côte; and Côte de Beaune-Villages and Côte de Nuits-Villages mop up the wines of villages without their own appellations.

Village wines apply to the best villages along the Côte – Meursault, for example, or Volnay – which have their own appellations.

Premiers Crus are the next level up, for the second-best vineyards within each village. The wines state the name of the village and the vineyard, as in Meursault-Charmes.

Grands Crus are the top wines of Burgundy, the cream of the vineyards. They even dispense with the village name on the label: La Tâche, for example, a Grand Cru from the village of Vosne-Romanée, is known only by its vineyard name. Indeed, any village with a famous Grand Cru vineyard has long since annexed its name to form part of the village name: the village of Aloxe-Corton was plain Aloxe until it hijacked the name of its Grand Cru vineyard, Corton.

THE WINE TRADE

The fragmentation of the vineyards into the hands of numerous smallholders has had other effects, too. If you have only a couple of barrels of one wine and three of another and four of yet another, and you're a peasant farmer with few resources, you might well think it insufficiently lucrative to bottle them yourself and then find buyers. So what do you do? Why, you sell the lot to a négociant, or merchant.

Louis Jadot is a leading Burgundian négociant, producing wines of great authenticity.

BIODYNAMIC VITICULTURE

Is this the viticulture of the future, or is it an example of New Age battiness? Biodynamic viticulture is certainly as far removed as you can get from the industrial spray-everything-in-sight approach that threatened to take over the vineyards of Burgundy, like those of everywhere else, in the 1970s and early 1980s. It involves restoring the ecology and balance of the soil by the application of herbal and mineral preparations in homeopathic quantities, according to the times of the day and year and phases of the moon. It is based on the teachings of Rudolph Steiner. Yes, it sounds peculiar, but some very hard-headed winemakers – leading names in Burgundy like Lalou Bize-Leroy of Domaine Leroy and Anne-Claude Leflaive of Domaine Leflaive – swear that it has made their vines healthier.

The Grapes

Pinot Noir and Gamay are the red stars;
Chardonnay reigns supreme over the whites.

PINOT NOIR is the aristocrat of Burgundy, and a very temperamental one it is too. It reaches its peak on the Côte d'Or, but the northerly climate of Burgundy is only just warm enough for it, and in years when it doesn't ripen properly it can be green and acidic. Overcrop it and it loses its personality; vinify it carelessly and every one of your mistakes will show in the wine. Yet, when a careful grower on a good site is blessed with good weather then all is forgiven: the soft, red-fruits richness, turning to chocolate, cherries, plums and cream as it matures, with the texture of silk in the mouth, is one of the most beautiful flavours in wine.

GAMAY has no pretensions – its main purpose is to produce purple-fresh, gurgling, bright-eyed Beaujolais. Sometimes it tries to get a bit more serious, but if it isn't winking behind its solemn exterior there's no point to it.

Chardonnay

CHARDONNAY is the superstar of the white wine world, planted in every country that makes wine. It combines crisp, fresh flavours with a remarkable ability to be enriched by aging in oak barrels and in bottle. From the steely, taut attack of good Chablis through the musky apple softness of Mâcon, to the creamy, buttery, smoky, honeyed flavours of Meursault or Puligny-Montrachet, Burgundy produces Chardonnay in every conceivable form.

ALIGOTÉ is never planted on the best sites, though in Bouzeron it has an appellation to itself. It makes a tangy, lemon-sharp, sour-cream flavoured wine which at its best can age a few years.

The hill of Corton in the Côte de Beaune. The fragmentation of vineyards into numerous small plots is typical of Burgundy.

For years the négociant houses were the glossy, international face of Burgundy, while the growers kept their boots in the soil. The négociant premises dominate Beaune and Nuits-St-Georges, and their huge cellars and imposing reception rooms (compared with the simple farmhouses of most growers) tell you all you need to know about who held the balance of power in the market. They would buy sufficient quantities of wine from growers up and down the Côte to be able to blend commercial volumes of Pommard or Beaune, and sometimes it was good and sometimes it wasn't.

Latterly things have changed. Nowadays many of the best wines (not all, because standards have risen among the négociants, too) come from growers who make and bottle their own wine. These are the new superstars.

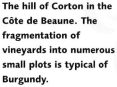

Méo-Camuzet's wines are heavily influenced by legendary winemaker Henri Jayer, showing the heady perfume and exhilarating fruit, enriched by oak, that top Burgundy is all about.

Chablis

The Grand Cru vineyards of Chablis are the most favourably sited; even in a difficult year they produce wine of character and individuality. Vaudésir is seen here in the foreground.

Chablis is one of the most famous white wines in the world – and yet it comes from a tiny spot on the map, just a collection of hillsides at the northern extremity of Burgundy where wine is made in the teeth of some of the most difficult weather conditions in France. No wonder the whole world has, at one time or another, wanted to imitate it.

Wanted but not succeeded. The name of Chablis has been grossly abused over the years, taken without permission by producers in the United States, Australia, Argentina, New Zealand and many other countries and used on wines that have no connection whatever with the real thing, save that they are white. Most aren't even made from Chardonnay.

These abuses are gradually coming to an end now, partly because non-EU countries are enacting laws against them and partly because the offending producers are realizing that it doesn't get them taken seriously. And so, worldwide, people are coming to know Chablis as it really is: steely, bone-dry, cool as flint and slow to reveal itself, but at its best aging for years in bottle.

It's like this because of the climate, and because of the soil. It's cold up here – only just warm enough most years to ripen the Chardonnay grapes, and with spring frosts a constant threat. Only in the last few decades, since the growers began using smudge pots (see box below) has there been much defence against the sort of savage frosts that can destroy the buds, and thus most of the crop.

Add to this unfriendly climate a limestone soil – Kimmeridgian limestone in the central part of the appellation, Portlandian limestone in those parts producing Petit Chablis – and you have a recipe for steely, acidic wine. (Limestone and chalk soils encourage acidity in wine.)

Yet curiously it can bring out the best in Chardonnay. Chardonnay is, after all, one of the world's most versatile grapes; and here it responds to the challenge by aging to a complex, minerally dry richness. Sounds like a contradiction in terms? That's what makes old Premier and Grand Cru Chablis so fascinating.

Even simple Chablis is generally best left for a year or two. When young it can be closed and taste frankly uninteresting – just aggressively dry and taut. Even top-class Grand Cru Chablis can be closed and ungiving in youth. The winemaking has a part to play here: traditionally the wine was made in big old oak vats which imparted no oak flavour to the wine; the nearest modern equivalent is stainless steel or cement although these do not give the contact with air that can add complexity. Stainless-steel-fermented Chablis has all the zing, the shocking green-fresh acidity which is a crucial component of the taste of simple modern Chablis. But a large number of producers use oak barriques and age the wine on its lees for the bigger wines of the Premier and Grand Cru vineyards: this imparts a vanilla richness and a nutty softness to the wine which marries well with the taut, sinewy acidity.

A newer idea is to put the wine through the malolactic fermentation (see p.22), which softens it and reduces that austere mineral attack, but to my mind this turns it into just another light Chardonnay, of which the world has a great many already. It seems to me that it's the slow-aging, minerally tautness of Chablis that makes it unique. But it's all a question of taste.

FROST CONTROL

Smudge pots, portable oil-burning stoves, are set at intervals between the rows of vines and left burning all night when frost threatens. Water sprinklers are a newer invention: they soak the vines in a spray of water which then freezes on to the young buds. As the air temperature drops below freezing, the ice remains at 0°C (32°F), thus protecting the buds from damage.

Harvesting Chardonnay grapes in the Grand Cru vineyard of Les Clos in the heart of Chablis.

The division in Chablis is over new oak; but like all divisions it can get a bit confusing. Even those who don't generally favour new oak for Chablis can be seduced by William Fèvre's Grand Crus; while Jean Durup's steely unoaked wines are the epitome of traditional Chablis.

CLASSIFICATION

In Chablis, it is the ability of the grapes to ripen in a disobliging climate that makes the difference between good and great wines.

Petit Chablis is hardly used nowadays, since the growers are generally able to use Chablis instead; it always denoted a lighter, slighter style of wine.

Chablis is the appellation for more than half of the region's production. Ideally this will be minerally and refreshing, but in cool years it can be rather taut and raw unless aged for several years.

Premiers Crus are more serious, though mixed in quality because various ordinary Chablis sites have been upgraded for reasons more to do with politics than quality. There are 40 different Premier Cru vineyard sites but they have been grouped together under 12 different names to simplify the matter: Beauroy, Côte de Léchet, Fourchaume, Les Fourneaux, Mélinots, Montée de Tonnerre, Montmains, Mont de Milieu, Les Vaillons, Vaucoupin, Vaudevey and Vosgros.

Grands Crus come only from a single sweep of hill directly north of the town of Chablis. A hundred hectares (250 acres) are shared by seven Grand Cru plots and there is a dramatic leap in quality between most Premiers Crus and the Grands Crus. A Grand Cru wine has weight, an intense penetrating rich personality which almost achieves the sumptuous glories of Corton-Charlemagne or Montrachet from the Côte de Beaune. But it's never quite as indulgent: that dry, reserved fruit so characteristic of Chablis is always there, even in the most impressive wines.

The seven Grand Crus are: Les Blanchots, Bougros, Les Clos, Les Grenouilles, Les Preuses, Valmur and Vaudésir.

Côte d'Or

It's just a hillside. That's all it is. Yet there has always been something special about this particular hillside. Is it called the Golden Slope because of the fiery gold of the vines at vintage time? Or because of the liquid gold the soil produces? Sometimes it seems a fancy based on a thousand disappointing bottles of 'fool's gold'. Whatever the reason, its best wines are gastronomic gold of a rare kind.

Côte de Nuits

There are two distinct parts to the Côte d'Or – the Côte de Nuits and the Côte de Beaune. Geographically the Côte de Nuits – the northern part, centred on the town of Nuits-St-Georges – begins in the Dijon suburbs. Driving out of Dijon you see it gradually turn from a slope of houses and patchy vines to a fully fledged wine region: a swathe of vines that runs all the way to Santenay and beyond.

In the 19km (12 miles) of the Côte de Nuits there are just 1400 hectares (3500 acres) of vines. To the east the flat, vineless Saône basin stretches for 80km (50 miles) to the Jura mountains. To the west, the steep ranked vines come to an exposed halt a mere few hundred yards from the road. All the important wine here is red. The best sites are east- or south-east-facing, and are a mix of infertile limestone, clay and marl. The wines have a strong, uncompromising flavour; they begin life tough and intense with the chewy, sour-sweet attack of damsons or plums eaten whole and not quite ripe. In seven to ten years, the rasping tannin seems to melt into the wine, leaving first the flavours of plum, damson and cherry in full flight. With time, those fruit flavours go deeper, sweeter, more cooked, chocolaty, toffee-rich, and are overlaid by scents of long-hung pheasant, dead leaves, mushrooms and leather. Great Burgundy has to be approached with imagination and time to spare.

THE WINES

The first wine village of the Côte, **Marsannay**, is almost on the fringes of suburban Dijon. It's more famous for rosé than red, but the red is very attractive, with some quite solid raspberry fruit.

Fixin, at the north of the Côte de Nuits, is on the solid, dark, sometimes rustic end of this spectrum of flavours.

Gevrey-Chambertin, however, represents the full glory of Burgundy. The most famous Grands Crus – Chambertin Clos de Bèze, Latricières-Chambertin and Chambertin itself – can be everything a red wine dares to be – weighty, muscular, yet full of chocolate and plums and prunes and game.

The picture among the simpler village wines is less rosy, and wines that should have some of the plummy, gamy fascination of their grander siblings are too often overproduced and pale. The vineyards spread remorselessly across the main road towards the railway; and with very few exceptions good vineyards don't do this. There is good village Gevrey made, but the best often comes from hillside vineyards between Gevrey and Brochon; vineyards to the south of Gevrey are mostly close-packed Grands and Premiers Crus.

Morey-St-Denis used to be obscure, and thus the source of good-value flavours that had some of the savoury fruit of Gevrey-Chambertin. Well, it's no longer obscure, and it went through a phase of overproduction. Its reputation now lies in the hands of some top-class growers, and there are some excellent wines to be had here, if you choose carefully. But they're no longer cheap.

Chambolle-Musigny should be the most fragrant of Burgundies – scents of roses and violets

OPPOSITE **Sunset over the vineyards of Meursault, the biggest and most popular white wine village in the Côte d'Or.**

1996 is an utterly seductive vintage; some time is needed for Grand Crus to mature.

'To Beaune; a range of hills to the right under vines, and a flat plain to the left, all open and too naked ... Stop at Nuits for intelligence concerning the vineyards of this country, so famous in France and indeed in all Europe; and examine the Clos de Vougeot, of 100 journaux, walled in, and belonging to a convent of Bernardine monks. When are we to find these fellows choosing badly?'

ARTHUR YOUNG, TRAVELS DURING THE YEARS 1787, 1788 AND 1789

really do mean something here. If a Chambolle-Musigny tastes solid and gooey, it has been over-sugared by a lazy producer; make a note of that producer's name and avoid his wine in the future.

Vougeot, the village, isn't that important, although they make a tiny amount of rather good white there. It is the walled vineyard of Clos de Vougeot which is world famous; all of it is Grand Cru, though by no means all is good enough to merit it. At its best it is a delicious, almost creamily soft, plummy wine. But there are too many owners here, too much demand for the wine, and too many shortcuts.

Flagey-Échézeaux sounds more like a sneeze than a wine village, but it is home to the Grands Crus of Échézeaux and Grands-Échézeaux – lovely fragrant, raspberry-rich wines. But not cheap.

Vosne-Romanée is both more famous and more expensive (even more expensive). It has a cluster of Grand Cru vineyards dominated by the estate of Domaine de la Romanée-Conti which can, when on form, make wines that transport Burgundy to even greater heights. They're as creamy as fresh *foie gras*, as savoury as roast beef straight from the oven, as sweet as plums and prunes. These are the Grands Crus of Richebourg, La Tâche and Romanée-Conti. Romanée-St-Vivant, for long an underperformer, is at last catching up with these top three. There is also a host of other good wines in Vosne-Romanée, in particular the Premiers Crus of aux Malconsorts, Les Beaux-Monts and Les Suchots – often savoury, sometimes burly with tannin, but full of fruit.

Nuits-St-Georges has no Grands Crus, but in the vineyards of Les Pruliers, aux Thorey, Les Vaucrains and Les St-Georges some excellent wine is made. It usually starts a bit tough, but

after a few years there's that wonderful mix of rich prunes, chocolate and smoke. The vineyards of Prémeaux are included in the same appellation.

Côte de Beaune

At the end of the Côte de Nuits the ridge of hillside dips a little, then recovers itself and sets off again. The slopes are gentler here, and the area is about double that of the Côte de Nuits, at 3000 hectares (7500 acres). Again, most of the wine is red, but here, where limestone breaks through, it's the whites that are the stars. The style of Corton-Charlemagne, Meursault-Charmes or Perrières, Montrachet or Chassagne-Montrachet can seem strange to a generation brought up on textbook-correct New World Chardonnay – it's too vegetal, particularly in Meursault, and the fruit isn't to the fore in the same way. But get your palate tuned in and you'll become addicted to these smoky, creamy flavours.

THE WINES

The Côte de Beaune begins in grand style with the hill of Corton and its tonsure of trees. Three villages share this hill and its red and white Grands Crus: Ladoix-Serrigny, Pernand-Vergelesses and Aloxe-Corton.

Ladoix is the first village and it has the smallest area of Grand Cru vineyards. They are its only claim to fame, since its village wine is hardly ever bottled under its own name.

Pernand-Vergelesses, when it's not making red Corton Grand Cru and white Corton-Charlemagne Grand Cru, makes some nice soft, raspberry fruit-pastille reds, and some dry, direct white. There's a little Aligoté here from old vines, and it's the best on the Côte d'Or.

Aloxe-Corton has the lion's share of the Corton hill, both for red Corton and white Corton-Charlemagne. The red should have a magically exciting blend of savoury richness and perfumed sweetness; the white should blast you with rich, impressive, buttery strength. But, as so often in Burgundy, there are too many owners and too many standards of quality. The whites, on the whole, are more consistent than the reds.

1993   1993

VOSNE-ROMANÉE
1er CRU - "LES SUCHOTS"
APPELLATION VOSNE-ROMANÉE 1er CRU CONTRÔLÉE

Domaine Robert ARNOUX
PROPRIÉTAIRE-VITICULTEUR À VOSNE-ROMANÉE (CÔTE-D'OR)
PRODUCT OF FRANCE

750 ml   MIS EN BOUTEILLE À LA PROPRIÉTÉ   13,5% vol.

PRODUCT OF FRANCE

1995
Richebourg
GRAND CRU

Domaine Anne Gros
Propriétaire - Viticulteur
A 21700 Vosne-Romanée

Premier Crus in Burgundy have to state the name of the commune in larger type than Grand Crus do. The Grand Cru label on the right just names the vineyard – Richebourg.

HOSPICES DE BEAUNE

The Hospices de Beaune, or Hôtel-Dieu, is Beaune's most famous historic building. It was founded in 1443 by Nicolas Rolin, Chancellor to Duke Philippe the Good of Burgundy (whose notable deeds included forbidding the growing of vines on land deemed unsuitable, and selling Joan of Arc to the English for 10,000 gold crowns). The Hospices cared for travellers, the poor and the sick, and was funded from the start by the sale of wine from its endowment of vineyards. Even today, when it is no longer used as a hospital, it is the site of an annual auction of wines, held on the third Sunday of each November.

The wines up for sale are those from the Hospices' own vineyards and the various cuvées, all sold in barrel and all from the new vintage, are named after the Hospices' benefactors, from Nicolas Rolin onwards. They are sold to the wine trade, usually to the négociant houses of Burgundy, and are then moved into the cellars of their new owners for maturation and bottling.

Prices at the auction are almost always higher than current market values would suggest. Why? Because charity auctions, whether of wines or of pictures or anything else, do tend to loosen purse strings. The PR attached to buying a particularly expensive lot is not lost on the hard-nosed merchants of Burgundy either. But even if the prices bear little resemblance to what the wines would normally fetch, the price movements – up a lot, up a little, even (rarely) down on the year before – do give an indication of how prices will go for the new vintage.

But the other reason people go to the Hospices' weekend is for the parties. Burgundy lets its hair down in no uncertain fashion: there are three huge feasts held; on Saturday night at Clos de Vougeot, on Sunday night in Beaune and on Monday lunchtime at the Paulée de Meursault, where the guests bring fine, old and interesting bottles with them for everyone else to taste. And nobody plans anything much for the evening.

The Hospices de Nuits also holds an auction of its wines every March, but it is a low-key affair and attracts far less attention.

The colourful glazed roof tiles of the Hospices are typical of the region and give a clue to the wealth of the medieval Burgundian court. This was one of the artistic centres of Europe.

Drouhin's Beaune Clos des Mouches has a reputation which far exceeds its Premier Cru status and is in much demand.

Savigny-lès-Beaune is a terrific village for Burgundy novices to start with. It makes light, beautifully perfumed wine, often with a touch of incense to its strawberry and redcurrant fruit; and it's relatively inexpensive. But as always with Burgundy, don't be seduced into buying the cheapest. Good growers know their worth. **Chorey-lès-Beaune** is another good source of not- too-expensive light red.

Beaune itself is not only the main town of Burgundy, full of restaurants and shops, but also the source of some reasonably priced and reasonably reliable red Burgundy. There are lots of Premier Cru vineyards – Les Grèves, Les Teurons, Les Cent Vignes, Clos des Mouches and Les Marconnets are worth looking out for – making soft wines full of redcurrant, raspberry and strawberry flavours, the tannins and acids holding it all in balance.

Pommard is strong, meaty stuff with fat, plummy fruit at its best; and in recent years it's been getting better. Just as well: its extreme popularity in the United States had proved its downfall, with the usual problems of overproduction.

Volnay is the opposite in style: light, ethereal red, with a beautiful cherry scent, grown on soil with a lot of chalk in it. Premiers Crus will have more structure, but should always be wonderfully fragrant.

Monthélie has only begun to attract attention in recent years, because its wines used to be sold as Côte de Beaune-Villages. They're full, earthy, chewy cherry reds which can be a good buy.

Auxey-Duresses is in a similar position: with a fair amount of red and white to its name, it used to shelter beneath the name of Meursault. Juicy reds with a rather spicy fruit and nutty whites of some stylishness are the ideal, and there are some very good growers.

Meursault is unique, wonderful wine. There's a little red, but the vast majority of these soft, rolling slopes are crowded with Chardonnay

The Food of Burgundy

RED BURGUNDY is made to go with rich sauces; it's perfect for beef stewed slowly and long with red wine, mushrooms and onions, and for rich game. And since this is fertile farmland filled with Charollais cattle, and since the frugality of the local farmers found a way of using up anything edible, these are precisely the sorts of dishes in which Burgundy abounds.

Charollais cattle produce beef, but not such fine, flavoursome beef as other breeds.

Not so good for plain roasting, in other words, but well suited to the stewpot, if accompanied there by a bottle of red Burgundy. (Any dish labelled *à la bourgiugnonne* will have a sauce of red wine, mushrooms, bacon and onions; and the red wine should be Burgundy.)

The chickens of Bresse are famous, too, and these are *poulets*, or young birds. Their pale and succulent flesh has a wonderfully intense flavour. Try them roasted or sautéed with cream. *Coq au vin* requires exactly that, a cockerel. For *poule au pot* you should correctly use an aged hen, stringy and too old for laying. Eggs get cooked in red wine as *oeufs en meurette*; the numbers of Burgundian recipes using red wine far outnumber those using white. Freshwater fish recipes using pike, crayfish and others often use white wine but can also use red; cream, as in so much Burgundian food, features heavily.

In fact, there's hardly a dish in Burgundy that won't do horrible things to your cholesterol levels. Snails come with garlic and butter, and every lunch and dinner ends with cheese, one of the richest of which even shares the name of Chambertin with one of the Côte's best red wines.

In Beaujolais charcuterie comes into its own: *jambon persillé* and a hundred different sausages, made with odds and ends of the pig and pungent with garlic, and all perfect with the Gamay grape, and perhaps a little mustard from Dijon at the northern end of the Côte de Nuits.

This part of France doesn't have a wealth of desserts and sweets but there are some local specialities. One of these is Dijon's *pain d'épice*, or spiced gingerbread, made with honey, ginger and cinnamon.

vines capable of producing some of the world's most gorgeously attractive dry white wines. The flavour is so soft, so creamy, so full of honey and oatmeal and peaches and cinnamon and nutmeg, that you would think it would take a grower who was either criminal or insane to mess it up by overproducing. Sadly, some do.

Blagny, in the hills above Meursault, makes reds under the village appellation. The whites are sold as Meursault-Blagny rather than Blagny.

Puligny-Montrachet is a quiet, low-profile village whose anonymous streets give little hint that they house the growers of a white wine more rare, more perfect than any other. Montrachet, and its fellow Grands Crus – Bâtard-Montrachet, Bienvenues-Bâtard-Montrachet and Chevalier-Montrachet – keep the superlatives flowing long after the last glowing mouthful is swallowed. The wine is dry, certainly, but only because it contains no sugar; everything else is a richness, a lusciousness, a succulence made of honey and butter, nuts and cream and glyceriny fruit. Yet whereas Meursault might be satisfied with this, Montrachet and its peers have something more – something mineral, something smoky even, coffee-bean smoky, crackling wood-fire smoky, incense smoky, all mingling in with perfumes, fruits and an impressively rich texture.

Luckily, below the Grands Crus, there is a good range of Premiers Crus of great personality and exciting flavours, in particular Le Cailleret, Les Combettes, Les Folatières and Les Referts. And there are straight village wines, which if from a good grower can be excellent. But the range of quality that goes out under the name of Puligny-Montrachet is far too great, and inexpensive wines are unlikely to be a bargain.

Chassagne-Montrachet village wines are not quite so widely seen, which is a good thing for quality as it means that slightly less overproduction goes on. At their best they have a lovely, broad, savoury flavour to match the warm buttery core of the wine. Chassagne also has a chunk of Montrachet, and two other Grands Crus, Bâtard-Montrachet and Criots-Bâtard-Montrachet. Nevertheless, Chassagne produces more red

than white, and from a good grower these are quite chunky, perfumed wines, often a good buy.

St-Aubin is hidden away beyond the old Paris road to the west, but makes nice, strawberry-fruited reds and good toasty, biscuity whites.

St-Romain, even further off the beaten track, is home to some fairly solid cherry-stone tasty reds and fresh flinty whites. **Santenay** makes some attractive jammy, savoury reds. Finally, **Maranges** is a fairly recent addition to the list of Burgundy appellations: three villages, Cheilly, Dezize and Sampigny, may hyphenate the name of Maranges with their own. The reds are soft and pleasant, the whites hardly ever seen.

The Hautes-Côtes

Up above the main strip of Côte vineyards, the land folds into valleys, and forest rises up the slopes. The vineyards, dotted about on south-facing slopes, make the wines of the **Hautes-Côtes de Nuits** and the **Hautes-Côtes de Beaune**. The Pinot struggles to ripen, and it is usually just pleasant, light and strawberryish. Chardonnay is the usual white variety, with a little Aligoté. Most are perfectly fresh but don't have the excitement of the Côte de Beaune whites.

1986 Beaune Premier Cru on sale at the Château de Meursault. International demand plus restricted production of the top wines combine to push prices ever higher.

The wine that those of us who love Burgundy dream about, from Domaine Leflaive, one of the most famous white Burgundy producers of them all.

Côte Chalonnaise

The Côte Chalonnaise has always had the reputation, if it has had any reputation at all, of being the halfway house between the Côte d'Or to the north, and the Mâconnais and Beaujolais to the south. This may be justified geographically, because the region is indeed crammed into the hills and valleys between the Côte de Beaune and the Mâconnais. But in terms of style the wines often have a greater similarity to the wines of Chablis and the Yonne far to the north than to the fat, broad whites of the Mâconnais or the round, plummy reds of the Côte de Beaune.

It's all a question of geography and climate. The Côte Chalonnaise is an extension of the Côte de Beaune, but whereas the latter benefits from a long, low, continuous south-east-facing slope, angling gently to the sun, this begins to drift away to the west just past Santenay, and what remains to the south is about as predictable and uniform as a porcelain pot smashed with a baseball bat. The whole area is twists and turns – hummocks, dells and dips, as forest, meadow and vine all fight for their place. So what finally happens is that when there is a suitable chunk of south-to-east-facing hillside, it is planted with vines, usually with forest above and pasture below. Limestone soils, in particular around Montagny and Rully, are planted mostly with white grapes; heavier clay soils, especially those at Mercurey and Givry, are planted primarily with red. These vineyards are often surprisingly high up, sometimes clearing 350 metres (1000ft), and the local microclimates are cooler and less favourable to grape ripening than the Côte d'Or. So what with irregular landscapes, high vineyards and uncertain summer and autumn warmth, the wines are light, occasionally sharp, rarely rich, but when from good producers, full of attractive, sometimes unexpected flavours.

The Wines

The grapes are those common to Burgundy as a whole; which is to say Chardonnay and Aligoté for the whites, Pinot Noir and Gamay for the reds. Aligoté and Gamay are very much minority grapes, although the Côte Chalonnaise can boast the best village for Aligoté in the whole of Burgundy: Bouzeron.

Bouzeron even has its own appellation for Aligoté, in the form of Bourgogne Aligoté de Bouzeron. Good growers here are able to boast of vines up to 100 years old, and it is these old vines that make the Aligoté special. It is pale in colour, with greenish highlights, sometimes with a tiny prickle still in the wine, and it has the clean-living but unctuous smell of buttermilk. Sniff a bit longer, because everything changes when you taste it. The buttermilk disappears, swept aside by a full but curiously neutral lemony freshness and a nip of pepper. It should mostly be drunk

The vineyards of Rully have come into their own as Côte d'Or prices have risen inexorably beyond many wine lovers' reach.

young and fresh, though the best can age surprisingly well.

Rully is just over the hill from Bouzeron, but the village is far more lively. It's a source of Crémant de Bourgogne, the sparkling wine which is made by the same method as Champagne and comes in pink or white versions. It's a pretty good and less expensive substitute for Champagne, having all the biscuity flavours plus a rather broader palate.

There are decent reds and whites made here too. The reds are rarely full in colour or body, and are best young; the whites are also light and unsuited to aging, with a soft edge and round, appley fruit. Some oak barrels find their way into the aging process, but preferably not too many: the wines just don't have the structure to cope with too much oak. Many of the vineyards have Premier Cru status, but it's honestly a bit ambitious to think that their wines have the quality of a Côte d'Or Premier Cru.

Mercurey has long been the most important village around here, so much so that an alternative name for the region is the région de Mercurey. Chalon itself is an old port on the river Saône to the east, but Mercurey is bang in the middle of the vineyards and produces more wine than all the other villages put together. It's nearly all red, though there is some white which is usually a bit flat-footed and ponderous. The red is better: rarely weighty, but with an intense strawberry fruitiness, balanced on one side by tannin and earthiness but finished with a lingering spicy scent of wood smoke. The best can age, too, which is not generally a characteristic of Côte Chalonnaise wines. As in Rully, there are Premiers Crus all over the place, but their wine is not noticeably better. It all depends on the talent and dedication of the producer.

Givry is also mainly a red wine village, with just a dribble of white. Some of the red is really good, sweeter fruited somehow than Mercurey, a little more cherry perfumed, rounder and smoother. It's straightforward, decent-quality red Burgundy.

Montagny makes only white wines under its own name; reds are sold as Bourgogne Rouge. All the white vineyards here qualify for Premier Cru status providing they reach 11.5 degrees of alcohol, and while you certainly shouldn't think of them as being the equivalent of, say, Premier Cru Meursault, some are really pretty good, with a bit of oak-aging to back up the full fruit and good acidity. Most go through the hands of the co-operative at Buxy which seems to be a pretty efficient organization.

Chardonnay grapes arriving at the co-operative at Buxy. Co-ops like these are the source of much inexpensive generic white Burgundy.

Lesser Burgundies, when from good producers like these, are an excellent alternative to the great wines of the Côte d'Or.

Mâconnais

Suddenly we're in the south. Just a glance at the roofs will tell you so: the cramped, grey tiles of northern France give way to warm Provençal orange. So it's not surprising that in the Mâconnais it's a little bit warmer than in the more northerly stretches of Burgundy, and there's less risk of a late frost wrecking the year's hopes.

There's another sight to look out for here, as well: the startling rock of Solutré, which thrusts like the prow of a battleship out above the little villages that produce Pouilly-Fuissé. It's an important prehistoric site: early hunters used to drive animals over the edge, which seems to be

neither the tidiest nor the most efficient way of securing lunch, but presumably they knew what they were doing.

Pouilly-Fuissé, at its best, is the finest white of the Mâconnais, but the region is much more than just Pouilly-Fuissé. We're still dealing with the same range of grapes as in the rest of Burgundy – white Chardonnay and Aligoté, red Pinot Noir and Gamay – but the styles are quite different. The reds are coarser, lacking the perfume and smoothness of the Côte d'Or and even Côte Chalonnaise reds, while the whites, even at the most basic level, have something fat and not quite dry about them: southern characteristics

The rock of Solutré dominates the vineyards of Pouilly-Fuissé. The quality of the wine here is pretty mixed.

from Burgundy grapes. Indeed, the vintage usually starts a week or so before that of the more northerly regions, and the vines bud earlier in the spring.

CLASSIFICATION

The basic appellation, **Mâcon**, is for red wines made from Gamay, and for white wines from Chardonnay.

Bourgogne Rouge is the appellation for Pinot-Noir-based reds – demonstrating that the appellation covers a multitude of styles throughout Burgundy. Bourgogne Rouge from the Mâconnais can be attractive, but it will be a world away from the basic wines of a top Côte d'Or grower.

Mâcon Supérieur is the same as plain Mâcon but with a degree more alcohol to its credit. That's supposed to indicate a riper, and therefore a better wine. Well. You'd be hard pushed to tell the difference.

Mâcon-Villages comes from one or more of the 43 best villages, and nearly all the whites of the region come under this banner. A few reds use it, too. The producers can, if they wish, hyphenate the name of their village with the name of Mâcon, as in Mâcon-Lugny or Mâcon-Viré, which are the best known. These wines are generally a bit better, and worth their higher price.

St-Véran is the appellation for white wine from eight villages surrounding Pouilly-Fuissé. The villagers reckoned that their wine was better than that of the rest of Mâcon, but the Pouilly-Fuissé producers certainly weren't going to share their name with anybody. So the appellation of St-Véran was the result. It can offer some pretty good wines too: full, soft and buttery at their best, although some can be slightly dull. It's good value for money on the whole.

Pouilly-Vinzelles and **Pouilly-Loché** are made in the villages of (you guessed it) Vinzelles and Loché. They're not dissimilar to St-Véran, though maybe a bit fuller, but at least they're not as expensive as Pouilly-Fuissé.

Pouilly-Fuissé is capable, without question,

Few Mâcon wines will have the weight to stand up to a good dish of Charollais beef – which is perhaps why this animal looks so confident.

of making the region's finest white wine. A tiny handful of producers do make lovely stuff, dripping with ripe, melon-juicy fruit, and swathed in coils of honey and spice, with a tight mineral core. They demand, and get, high prices. Unfortunately, however, the majority of the wines of the appellation are lumped together and made at the local co-operative, and a lot is sold under various merchants' labels. The price is still high, and the quality quite definitely isn't. My advice is to steer clear – only buy Pouilly-Fuissé from a top producer.

Jean-Jacques Vincent is one of the leading growers in Pouilly-Fuissé, producing rich, ripe, concentrated Chardonnay.

CO-OPERATIVES

Co-operatives dominate the whole of the Mâconnais. In general they've had a highly beneficial effect on quality. It all depends on whether the co-op has a strong or a weak director, one who is prepared to push through reform and modernization in the teeth of opposition from his own members (growers are as instinctively conservative as any other farmers), or one who shares their prejudices or isn't prepared to challenge the petty jealousies and in-fighting of the community. Ideally, single grower's wines are still the best, but many of the co-operatives do deliver the goods, for a reasonable price.

Beaujolais

This is the quintessential French wine region – the wine region of one's imagination, all tumbling hills and dales, sun-dappled farmyards with scratching hens and snoozing cats, and the hypnotic whiff of fermenting grapes coming from every shadowy cellar.

The granite hills above Lyon, the last splutter of the Massif Central before it declines into the flat, wide Saône Valley, are above all red wine slopes. There is a little rosé and some fairly good, stone-dry white, but when most people think of Beaujolais they think of red wine – or rather purple-pink, pink-red, foaming, gushing fruit-of-the-vine red wine. And it comes only from one grape – the Gamay. There's Gamay grown elsewhere in France, notably in the Loire and in the Ardèche, but it seldom has the bright, easy-breezy, unpretentious drink-me character of good Beaujolais. Beaujolais is not a wine to pontificate about or to lay down – it's there to drink, to enjoy.

Most of the time that's all there is to it. And a lot of the time, sadly, there isn't even that. Beaujolais, even basic Beaujolais, is no longer cheap enough to take quite so casually. At the same time most of it has lost its easy brightness, without acquiring anything else in the process. It's hard to find good simple Beaujolais these days – Beaujolais of the kind that makes you smile, that cries out to be poured from a jug into a tumbler and drunk with some *saucissons* and a hunk of bread still warm from the oven.

But the good news is that there is some very good wine from the top Crus. The Crus of Beaujolais are a group of ten villages in the north of the region with particularly good hillside sites. They make richer-flavoured wine, which can sometimes improve with age, providing you don't leave it undrunk for too long. We're talking about a couple of years at the most, usually. Simple Beaujolais should be drunk as soon as you can get your hands on it. And there's no better time to start than in November each year when Beaujolais Nouveau arrives.

BEAUJOLAIS NOUVEAU

Beaujolais Nouveau is simply the wine of the new vintage. There used to be a lot of razzmatazz attached to the race to get the first bottles to London, with cars, aeroplanes and motorbikes leaving speed limits in shreds behind them. Well, that's a thing of the past; and now that the first wines of each year arrive from Australia some time in the summer, even the thrill of drinking the first of the new vintage has lost its gloss. You used to be able to pretend you really were sitting in some French café, drinking wine straight from the press. Somehow you can't any longer. Hardly anybody notices the arrival of the first Beaujolais –

The Grapes

It's Gamay, Gamay, Gamay and just a little Chardonnay.

GAMAY NOIR À JUS BLANC is Gamay's full name and that white juice is all-important. It denotes the superiority of the true Gamay over all the other grapes that have been given the name over the years, many of them with red flesh – and no serious wine grape has red flesh. Gamay proper, the early-ripening Gamay Noir à Jus Blanc, has more affinity for the Beaujolais region and its granite soil than anywhere else on earth.

Lots of other countries have tried to produce red of the same style, but nobody ever seems to manage to do it consistently, even using carbonic maceration (see p.22), which is another of the things that makes Beaujolais special.

CHARDONNAY can be attractively minerally and light but there's not much white Beaujolais made.

Gamay

Known as the 'King of Beaujolais', Georges Duboeuf is responsible for over ten per cent of the wine produced in the region.

which is a shame, because when it's good it's just the thing to ward off a dank November day.

CLASSIFICATION

Beyond Beaujolais Nouveau there are three levels of Beaujolais.

Beaujolais and **Beaujolais Supérieur** count as simple Beaujolais (Supérieur simply means an extra degree of alcohol). It comes mostly from the villages in the flatter, sandier south of the region, and quite a lot is made as Nouveau.

Beaujolais-Villages comes from 39 villages with better, more granitic soil, mostly in the north of the region. Some is also released as Nouveau, and has a bit more substance than simple Nouveau, plus that rush of cherry, peardrops and peaches fruit.

Cru Beaujolais comes from the top ten villages, with the best hillside sites. There are differences between them, but what they have in common – the Gamay grape – is really more important than their differences. If you like one, you're certain to like them all – unless you've picked a wine from a poor producer.

The Ten Crus Beaujolais

Heading from south to north, these are as follows:

Brouilly is the largest Cru, making nicely balanced wine, full of fresh, almost peachy flavour, gentle and creamy when young. It matures quickly and is at its best about six months after the vintage.

Côte de Brouilly is the core of Brouilly, with slightly different soil. The lovely stream of fruit is very much the same as in Brouilly but it's a little fuller, and it doesn't peak quite so soon.

Regnié, the most recent of the Crus, was promoted in 1988. There's still a question mark over whether it's really as good as the others.

Morgon, on the other hand, can be really special. The wines begin life in a deeper, more exotic way, redolent of plums and cherries and herbs, but if you age them they develop a remarkable sumptuous warmth of chocolate and damsons. The best gain a flavour which is quite Burgundian, though it's not as good as really good Burgundy.

Harvested Gamay grapes at Juliénas, one of the ten Beaujolais Crus.

Chiroubles matches its name – chirpy, flirtatious wine that doesn't age well. Drink it young.

Fleurie is the most popular of the Cru wines, and consequently often the most expensive, but it's not automatically better than the others. It's juicy, crammed with the scent of flowers and ripe fruit, all apricots, cherries and chocolate.

Moulin-à-Vent isn't cheap either, but it's a different kind of wine. Far more serious than the others, and tannic and tough when young. You have to wait three or five years, perhaps longer, for it to turn into something surprisingly Burgundian, though not too grand to match good sausages and mash.

Chénas produces attractive, plummy wines which again need some age, though less than Moulin-à-Vent.

Juliénas has a lovely cherry and peach fruit but also a little more tannin and acidity than some of the others. It's not quite as expensive as some, either.

St-Amour has an appropriate name – it's all fruit and perfume. Drink it young and often.

Generic Burgundy Wines

Yes, I know I've said it before. I shall say it again, too, in the context of all sorts of other countries and regions. But in Burgundy, almost more than anywhere else, you should choose wine according to the reputation of the producer, not the appellation. And if it's true for the Premiers and Grands Crus it is just as true for basic Burgundy, the wines with the simplest regional appellations. Bourgogne Rouge or Blanc, for example, can come from anywhere in the region – so it might be from the least favoured spots in the Côte Chalonnaise or the Mâconnais. Equally, a Bourgogne Rouge or Blanc from a top-flight Côte d'Or grower with holdings in Volnay or Meursault might come from the land just adjoining a Premier Cru; or even from young vines that will make something much grander when they grow up. It's not difficult to see that whereas the first example will be clean but dull, the second will have vibrancy and style. The second may be getting on for twice the price of the first, but to be honest there is no point in buying the very cheapest Burgundy. Other countries, other regions, can do cheap wine better than Burgundy. And one other thing: when you're buying Beaujolais, remember that the best, most individual wines come from producers, be they growers or négociants, who are based in the region. It seldom comes from companies based in Beaune further north.

Having said that, let's take a look at which are the best bets among the basic appellations.

CLASSIFICATION

Rock bottom in Burgundy is **Bourgogne Grande Ordinaire**. It's so rock bottom that it's not seen that often any more. It can be red, white or rosé, and it's a great deal more ordinaire than it is grande. It comes from just about any old grapes on any old scraps of land not fit for cattle or corn. Gamay is the mainstay for the red, and it's usually pretty unattractive, acidic stuff. Pinot Noir is allowed, but I've had my say on cheap Pinot Noir and I won't labour the point. The red César and Tressot, two traditional northern grapes, are also allowed in the Yonne area to the north. The white is usually based on Aligoté, but cheap Aligoté is no more enthralling than cheap Pinot Noir.

Bourgogne Passe-Tout-Grains is almost always red, although in theory it can be rosé as well. It's a mixture of Gamay and Pinot Noir of which at least one third must be Pinot Noir. It's a way of using up all the odds and ends, and it can be perfectly nice when it's young. But in today's world, with utterly delicious wines readily available for low prices, Bourgogne Passe-Tout-Grains simply does not count as good value.

Bourgogne Aligoté I've touched on in various places. The best comes from Bouzeron in the Côte Chalonnaise, and here it's too good for kir, the traditional Burgundian mix of Aligoté and Crème de Cassis.

Bourgogne Blanc and **Bourgogne Rouge**, as mentioned above, can either be deadly dull, or they can offer some of the best value in Burgundy. A quick glance at the address on the label can be a clue to quality: for Bourgogne Blanc, an address in Puligny-Montrachet or Meursault is a good start, for Bourgogne Rouge, any of the top red wine villages. It's not infallible, but it's a start.

Other good Bourgogne Rouge comes from the villages of Epineuil, Irancy and Coulanges-les-Vineuses in the Yonne, around Chablis. It's cool up there and the reds are light, but they can be deliciously fresh and strawberryish, and they're not expensive. Conversely, in Beaujolais, it is in theory possible for the Cru villages to declassify their wine as Bourgogne Rouge, in which case it would be all Gamay. Personally I've never come across such a wine, but theoretically it is possible.

Crémant de Bourgogne is Burgundy's sparkling wine and it's available in either rosé or white. Made by the Champagne method, it's a good cheap alternative to the real thing – though nowadays there are plenty of New World lookalikes to compete with as well.

Wine and religion have always been closely linked. The relics of St-Vincent of Saragossa, patron saint of vignerons, were acquired by Mâcon in the 6th century, no doubt with the idea of giving the region an unfair advantage.

Champagne

Now here's a paradox: to make really good sparkling wine you need wine that you probably wouldn't choose to drink as still wine.

It might sound odd, but it's true. Full-bodied, really ripe still wine doesn't make good sparkling wine. If you want proof, buy a bottle of Coteaux Champenois, the still wine of Champagne. The white is distinctly lean stuff; balanced, yes; elegant, yes; but lean. Put it beside an Australian Chardonnay and it will look distinctly unripe. And yet when that wine is made sparkling it's transformed, and its lightness becomes its greatest virtue. And to get that lightness you need vineyards that are cool, even cold.

The Champagne region is certainly chilly. It's a rather blank, monotonous stretch of open chalk farmland north-east of Paris which, around the towns of Reims, Epernay and Château Thierry, becomes squeezed and squashed into a series of hills and valleys jutting up from the plain. This jumble of slopes is divided into four main areas, the **Montagne de Reims**, **Côte des Blancs**, **Vallée de la Marne** and the **Aube**. And since this far north not all the grapes can be relied upon to ripen equally well every year, and since (for their non-vintage blends at least) what the producers most want is continuity of style from one year to the next, Champagne is almost always a blend of grapes from these various areas.

The more one looks at the wine of Champagne, the more unlikely it seems. These windswept hills are the most northerly and certainly the coldest vineyards in France – and yet they grow red grapes here. Two of the three grapes for Champagne, Pinot Noir and Pinot Meunier, are red. (The third, Chardonnay, is white.) Yet most of the wine is white. And as if the acidity imparted by the cool climate weren't enough, the chalk soil actually emphasizes the acidity in wines grown on it.

There's something else unusual about Champagne, too. If we look at the aims of the person usually credited with 'inventing' Champagne, the Benedictine monk Dom Pérignon of the Abbey of Hautvillers near Epernay, we find that he didn't

WINE AREA OF CHAMPAGNE
- Champagne AC wine area
- Village AC wine
- Main vineyard areas

want to make sparkling wine at all. In fact, he detested the sparkle.

Dom Pérignon began his work in the 1660s. Winemaking was a commercial business for the Abbey, a way of getting an income from its vineyards. But the wine of the region was always unpredictable: the fermentation would die down in the autumn, stopped by the encroaching cold, and then start again in the spring, resulting in a persistent sparkle in the wines. Dom Pérignon saw no future in this: he wanted a serious white wine to compete, at the top of the market, against red Burgundy. So he concentrated on the red grapes of the region because they seemed less likely to produce wines with this tiresome sparkle.

Unfortunately the fashionable world of Paris and London showed itself to be sadly frivolous. It loved the sparkle, and could hardly get enough of it. And, of course, Dom Pérignon knew more about how to achieve the sparkle – through his efforts to avoid it – than anybody else. His work on viticulture, on how to prune and train the vines for best results, how to select the best grapes and get them to the presses before they spoiled, was also invaluable in producing better-quality wine. So yes, it is fair to think of him as the father of Champagne – though not for the reasons he would have liked. And the method of making Champagne, and keeping all that sparkle in the bottle, has undergone various refinements since his time (see box opposite).

Louis Roederer make some of the best, most elegant, complex Champagne around. The wines are given extra depth by Roederer's extensive stock of reserve wines.

The Grapes

All Champagne is made from just three grape varieties.

CHARDONNAY makes lean, acidic wine with a minerally edge in Champagne; only in the very ripest vintages is it remotely attractive to drink as a still wine. But the best examples of 100 per cent Chardonnay Champagne, from the Côte des Blancs, age superbly in bottle.

PINOT NOIR is turned into white wine by the simple expedient of pressing the juice off the skins as soon as the grapes arrive at the winery; the juice is then fermented as white wine. Even when made as red, the Pinot Noir never attains very deep colour this far north; most wines are hardly more than dark rosés. But the grape's characteristic strawberry scent and flavour come through beautifully, and adds weight to the Champagnes of which it is a part.

PINOT MEUNIER is in much demand for less expensive Champagnes as it makes softer-tasting wine that matures faster. It has less prestige than the other two varieties and most houses make less fuss about it – while still using lots of it.

Pinot Noir

Chardonnay

THE WINE STYLES

The mainstay of any house is its **non-vintage wine**. It is also, from the consumer's point of view, the most affordable. The object of each house is to keep a uniform house style, and so each non-vintage wine will be a blend of several vintages, with some wine of each year being kept back to be used in future blends. This irons out not just differences in style between vintages but also differences in quality, although it is always noticeable that when Champagne has had a run of good vintages the general standard of non-vintage wines rises. The reserve wines, being more mature, add soft, ripe, nutty flavours to the wine. Even so, most non-vintage wines improve with another six months or so in bottle after release.

Vintage wines are 'declared' in Champagne when a house feels that the quality of its wine merits it – so not all houses always declare the same years. Everybody will declare the very best years, but in less than perfect years the quality of a house's wines will depend on where its vineyards are or whether it can lay its hands on enough good stuff. A house may also decline to declare a vintage if it thinks it needs to put lots away as reserve wines to beef up its non-vintage wines in the future. Almost all vintage wines are released before they are ready to drink: vintage Champagne improves dramatically in bottle.

De luxe cuvées come complete with high prices and fancy bottles and are (usually) superior wines: only the cream of the crop is used for these cuvées. The trouble is, wines like Dom Pérignon, Krug and Roederer Cristal are drunk far more as status symbols than by people who really appreciate what goes into them.

A few houses release small quantities of old wines that have been recently disgorged: in other words they have stayed on their lees for much longer than usual, and have been disgorged just

'Champagne is the only wine that leaves a woman beautiful after drinking it.'

MADAME DE POMPADOUR, 1721-64

In the cellars of Veuve Clicquot, Reims. On the left of the picture are *pupitres*, the angled racks of bottles that require daily attention from a *remueur*. But the man on the right is taking a break: he's checking the stocks of bottles which are stacked flat to mature on their lees.

BELOW Sediment collecting in the neck of an up-ended Champagne bottle during *remuage*.

MAKING CHAMPAGNE

The essence of the *méthode champenoise* (Champagne method) of making sparkling wine is that a second fermentation of the wine is induced after the wine has been bottled. The carbon dioxide given off during this fermentation can't escape, so it stays dissolved in the wine, ready to froth up as soon as the cork is released.

So: the still wine is bottled. At the time of bottling a solution of sugar, wine and a little yeast, the *liqueur de tirage*, is added, and the bottle is stashed away in a cool, dark cellar while the wine begins its second fermentation. This lasts between ten days and three months. And the wine is then left alone, because aging it on its lees – the dead yeasts from the fermentation – will enable it to develop a wonderfully rich biscuity flavour.

But of course the lees can't stay there forever and decanting is hardly the answer: the bubbles would disappear along with the lees. It was Champagne's most famous widow, *La Veuve Clicquot* – or, to be strictly accurate, her cellarmaster, Antoine Muller – who came up with the idea of what to do next. It's a technique called *remuage*, and it involves placing the bottles in racks (called *pupitres*) in which they can be progressively turned and up-ended, thus coaxing the lees on to the cork. *Remuage*, if done by hand, is a very labour-intensive and skilled affair. Every bottle must be twisted and turned each day, and *remueurs* do it at tremendous speed. But not as fast as machines; which is why almost all Champagne houses now use automatic *remuage*, in which great crates of bottles are mechanically turned, fraction by fraction.

At the end of the process, the bottles are vertical, upside down, and there is a small grey heap of sludge piled on each cork. In order to get it out, the bottles are placed with their necks in a bath of freezing brine; this freezes the wine in the neck of the bottle just enough for the cork to be whipped out, along with its load of lees, and another one inserted. This process is known as *dégorgement* (disgorging). Some wine will also escape with the lees – and so before the final cork is inserted the bottles are topped up. And since most people don't like absolutely dry Champagnes, a little sweetening is added at the same time. Not a lot, however. Brut Champagne still tastes dry, and contains only up to 15g of sugar per litre, and usually quite a bit less. Extra dry, confusingly, is a little sweeter, and sec (which means dry) is sweeter again. But they still taste only a little off-dry. Demi-sec is medium; doux or rich Champagnes are sweet.

The only thing the wine has to do now is age some more: about three years is ideal for non-vintage, and twice as long for vintage.

before sale. These wines can be really wonderful: mature, but with great freshness.

Rosé can be made in one of two ways: either the red skins are left on the juice for as long as it takes to colour it pink, or a little still red wine can be blended in with the white before bottling. Few companies now use the former method: it's more difficult to get a colour that is uniform year to year. Rosés vary in depth of colour, but all should have rounder, richer, more strawberryish fruit than ordinary white Champagne.

Blanc de Blancs is made only from the Chardonnay grape. It can be very light and delicate, but from the south of the region it can be relatively big and fat.

Blanc de Noirs is made only from the two red grapes of the region, Pinot Noir and Pinot Meunier. It has more body and weight than wines containing Chardonnay.

Coteaux Champenois is the still wine of the region. It can be red or white, but none of it is worth its price and it's only worth trying in the ripest years. The white is chalk-dry, though it

ages within a few years to something a little rounder; the red is strawberryish but lean.

THE CHAMPAGNE TRADE

Some of Champagne's best Pinot Noir is concentrated on the Montagne de Reims; Chardonnay is the only grape on the Côte des Blancs, south of Epernay. Both vines flourish in the Vallée de la Marne, and Pinot Meunier grows here, too. The Aube, situated well south of the main vineyards, is warmer and produces richer, broader wines that frequently dominate less expensive blends.

The difference in style between all these regions means that big houses with a big demand for non-vintage wines need grapes from just about everywhere. Some have large vineyard holdings; others do not. And so we come to the structure of the Champagne trade.

On the one hand there are the big négociant houses who market the major brands. They have built the fame and fortune of Champagne, yet none owns enough vineyards for its needs, and most rely heavily on growers for their grapes.

For many, Krug is the pinnacle of Champagne. Its rare rosé is one of the palest of all: it matches, colourwise at least, the palest of smoked salmon.

HOW TO READ A CHAMPAGNE LABEL

Champagne is the only quality French wine that doesn't have to show its AC status on the label, although some companies do. The name Champagne, however, is protected by law and the production of the wine is very tightly controlled. Knowing how to interpret the information on a Champagne label can help you to choose well. The most important piece of information is the name of the producer.

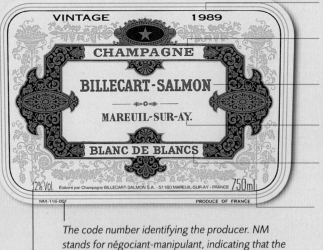

The vintage.
1989 was a good year for this Champagne.

The wine type.

The producer. Billecart-Salmon is one of the few Champagne houses still under family control.

Mareuil-sur-Ay is where the firm of Billecart-Salmon is based.

Blanc de Blancs indicates that the wine is made from white Chardonnay grapes only.

The quantity of wine in the bottle.

The code number identifying the producer. NM stands for négociant-manipulant, indicating that the wine was made in Billecart-Salmon's own cellars.

The alcohol level.

Snow covers Le Mesnil-sur-Oger and its small walled vineyard, Clos du Mesnil, where owners Krug grow Chardonnay grapes for their rare, single-vineyard Blanc de Blancs.

This can be a source of tension: the grape growers want the highest possible price, the houses want to pay as little as possible in order to try to keep within their budgets and maintain stable prices. There are periodic rows, but agreement is always reached because both sides need each other.

There are also many, many growers who make and sell their own wine, usually on quite a small scale, and sometimes only at the cellar door. It can be easier and more lucrative for such small producers to sell a few cases here and a few cases there to visitors from Paris or London than to go to the trouble of seeking agents in each market.

So while there are in theory two sides to the Champagne trade, the merchant houses with their branded wines, and the growers with their grapes, in fact there are a variety of stages in between.

Négociants-Manipulants (NM) are the merchant houses who grow some of their own grapes, buy in the rest, and market branded wines.

Récoltants-Manipulants (RM) are the small growers who make their own wine. Quality varies, but the best are very good. It is supposed not to include growers who take their grapes to the local co-op to be vinified in the communal vats, and then collect an equivalent number of bottles at the end of the process. These are called **Récoltants-Co-opérateurs (RC)**, but strangely few seem to want to put this term on their labels.

Co-opératives Manipulants (CM) are the co-ops of the region; many are very good, and supply wine under a variety of brand names to stores wanting their own label.

There are ten different bottle sizes for Champagne although the ones at the larger end of the scale are rarely made nowadays. Shown below are nine of the sizes: the quarter bottle, half bottle, bottle, magnum (two bottles), jeroboam (four bottles), methuselah (eight bottles), salmanazar (12 bottles), balthazar (16 bottles) and the nebuchadnezzar (20 bottles). The rehoboam (six bottles) is not pictured.

The Food of Champagne

UNUSUALLY FOR A French wine region, Champagne has little tradition of fine cuisine. It has traditional food, of course, but it tends to be of the hard-working, rustic, northern French kind: root vegetables, sausages, pâtés. Nothing, in other words, to match the refinement and glamour of the wine. So the region's chefs (and the Champagne region has an abundance of good restaurants, catering for the many tourists who visit) have more or less invented a cuisine that relies on classic French dishes, made lighter where necessary to suit the style of the wine, and often cooked with Champagne sauces.

Certain combinations of food and Champagne have become classics, but be careful: some, like Champagne and caviar, are actually disgusting together and have been paired off merely because they seem the ultimate in conspicuous consumption. Champagne and oysters are a less good combination than Muscadet and oysters. If you do want to drink Champagne with food, choose a good vintage or weighty non-vintage wine with plenty of bottle age. Rosé is generally a better bet than white. And keep the food quite delicate: scallops, perhaps, or trout.

The Champagne region has its own type of brandy too, Marc de Champagne, which is an excellent finale to a good meal. Marc is the name given both to the cake of skins and pips dug out of the press after the grapes have had their juice squeezed from them, and to the brandy made from it: the skins are fermented and then distilled. Marc de Champagne is quite aromatic but unfortunately it's hard to find outside the region.

Rhône

The Rhône really does deserve the title 'King of the Wine Rivers'. Vines are grown on its banks almost continuously from snow-clad Visp, near the source in the Swiss Alps, right down to the sprawling muddy delta of swamps and marshland on the Mediterranean near Marseille. Even the Loire further north and Germany's Rhine can't match such intense wine activity. And the variety of wines is staggering. The white Visp wines are so pale and feather-like no wine terms are delicate enough to describe them; and the reds and whites of the slopes below Lyon have some of the most intensely exotic flavours ever produced from the grape.

The central stretch of the Rhône Valley, however, the stretch that produces what we think of as Rhône wines, spans some 225km (140 miles) from Lyon down to Avignon. Without doubt all the most memorable wines are made here, yet the differences in style between the reds and whites of the north and the wines of the baking plains around Avignon in the south could not be more marked.

Wines have been made here for millennia: the Gauls knew the value of Côte-Rôtie and the hill of Hermitage, even when the resident Romans were importing wine from elsewhere to drink. The Romans clearly felt at home here: they left behind them a litter of amphitheatres and triumphal arches that punctuate the landscape even today.

The reds of the Rhône are still known as some of France's darkest and most uncompromising wines. In the south as many as nine different red grapes may be blended together, but the predominant variety is the juicy, squashy-edged Grenache, all high alcohol and upfront flavours for quaffing, seldom for keeping.

The whites of the north are rare and remarkable. The Viognier vine produces tiny amounts of brilliant wine at Condrieu and because of the demand for this wonderfully fragrant wine, it's almost as expensive as any in France. Yet it's not for keeping, since its startling fruit is as fleeting

as youth and as easy to miss. In contrast a few miles down the road at Hermitage the Marsanne and Roussanne grapes make whites which often need 20 years to display their daunting breadth of taste. Some can even last as long as 40 years. Further south, among the burly reds, pops up one of the world's most delicious sweet Muscats at Beaumes-de-Venise; while Châteauneuf-du-Pape, whose vineyards are so sunbaked that you can burn your fingers by touching the stones in the noonday heat, somehow manages to produce a few bright, super-fresh aromatic whites.

Carrying grapes up the slopes of Côte-Rôtie, above the town of Ampuis. The steepness of the slopes and the weight of the grape hods – each when full weighs 40kg (90lbs) – make harvesting very hard and labour-intensive work.

It is really only in the last few decades that the top producers of both the northern and southern Rhône have risen to the international prominence that they deserve, and have felt confident enough to stress the value of single-vineyard wines like La Mouline (left).

The Grapes

No fewer than 13 grape varieties are grown in the Rhône: these are the most widely seen.

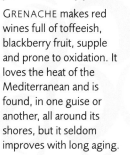

Syrah

Viognier

SYRAH is one of the great red grapes of the world, full of smoky, herby, mineraly, leathery flavours, and able to improve in bottle – indeed often needing to, since it can be tough and tannic in youth – for many years.

GRENACHE makes red wines full of toffeeish, blackberry fruit, supple and prone to oxidation. It loves the heat of the Mediterranean and is found, in one guise or another, all around its shores, but it seldom improves with long aging.

MOURVÈDRE is one of the classiest grapes of the southern Rhône, all herbs and honey, tannin, raisins and plums. It gives structure to Grenache in a blend, and ages well.

CARIGNAN is a gutsy, tannic grape, high in acidity and with plenty of colour, but no finesse. Used in blends it can give backbone; and low-yielding old vines on favoured sites can occasionally give wines of real style.

CINSAUT produces soft, light red – and the more it overproduces the softer and lighter it is. Typically it adds fruit and suppleness to Carignan in blends.

VIOGNIER is the cult white grape of the moment, having suddenly spread from its home in Condrieu and Château-Grillet, where it makes wines of astonishing intensity and apricot fruit, to sites all over southern France and beyond. However, it's a temperamental vine, low-yielding and requiring constant attention.

MARSANNE is the more robust of the twin white varieties of Hermitage. It's also grown in the southern vineyards.

ROUSSANNE is more delicate than Marsanne, and more elegant, with a haunting aroma.

UGNI BLANC is widely planted in the southern vineyards, but has no more character here than elsewhere. A crisp neutrality is the height of its ambition.

MUSCAT is made as a sweet fortified wine in Beaumes-de-Venise, and is always best drunk young.

Northern Rhône

You get your first sight of the northern Rhône vineyards where the motorway sweeps across the river below Lyon at Vienne. If you glance right down the valley, you'll notice a near-vertical cliff of rock, which seems to be cross-stitched with vines. This cliff is home to the terraces of Côte-Rôtie, one of the greatest of the northern Rhône reds.

The Wines

The wines from **Côte-Rôtie** can be heavenly. The Syrah grape, occasionally softened and soothed by the addition of a little white Viognier, is at its most fragrant here, sweet and lilting from a surprisingly early age, the fruit having the chewy ripeness of damsons, the perfume like wild raspberries. The traditional division of the wines into those from the Côte Blonde (earlier-maturing wines with an admixture of Viognier) and Côte Brune (all-Syrah wines, tough and longer-aging) has been somewhat superseded by myriad individual vineyard names: competition between growers to make the most prestigious wines, and charge the highest prices, is rife. Côte-Rôtie, in price terms, is now up there with Classed Growth red Bordeaux and Grand Cru Burgundies, when it seems that only a few years ago (well, a couple of decades, anyway) one could actually afford to buy the stuff. Hey ho.

Condrieu and **Château-Grillet** are two white wine ACs just round the bend in the river below Côte-Rôtie. Both grow the cult Viognier grape, and no other. Viognier is difficult to cultivate, being highly prone to disease, and is unpredictable in yield. However, plantings in Condrieu in the 1990s have soared ahead, turning what looked like a dying appellation into a flourishing one; growers are even experimenting with oak-aging and with making sweet late-picked Viognier. Château-Grillet, at just four hectares (ten acres), is one of the smallest ACs in France, and is in single ownership; its Viognier tends to be more austere than that of Condrieu. But it still has that seductive ripe apricot and mayflower flavour. Below Condrieu nature relents a little and the vineyards flatten out.

St-Joseph is a curious appellation. The locals regard it as light red – the sort of thing you might take on a picnic. Well, it's generally light in comparison to Hermitage or Côte-Rôtie, but the best still need a few years' aging. Quality does vary, though: in the 1970s and 1980s the area under vine expanded dramatically on to the flat riverside, and few of these new vineyards can match the quality of the terraced vineyards at the heart of the AC. Happily the better growers now realize this, but it's still not worth buying St-Joseph from lesser producers. Expect soft, almost sweet fruit packed with spicy blackcurrant flavours.

Jean-Louis Chave's Hermitage is one of the world's great wines, a thick complex expression of the Syrah grape at its best. Condrieu from André Perret shows off fragrant Viognier to stunning effect and is one of the leaders of the current revival in the AC.

Crozes-Hermitage is the largest of the northern Rhône ACs and makes both red and white wine. The white can be very good, appley and nutty, soft but briskly refreshing, while the red is strong, firm Syrah, sometimes rather earthy and peppery, but with a good dollop of raspberry fruit to soften things up.

And then, as the river narrows and forces its path between the towns of Tain and Tournon, the great hill of Hermitage rears up on the left bank, one last burst of rocky splendour before the river valley fans out and flattens to the south.

Hermitage – what a place to live! And yet somebody did – so legend would have us believe. When crusader Gaspard de Stérimbourg returned home from the Holy Land he built a chapel on the hill of Hermitage and lived there for 30 years; the chapel is still a local landmark. And what a view!

Hermitage a century ago produced a red wine as famous as Château Margaux, and a white as sought after as Montrachet. Those were the days when grand, roaring flavours were prized more than delicacy and refinement, and the wines of Hermitage bellowed and thundered their wares. It's only now that we are prepared to listen again.

Marsanne and Roussanne are the white grapes, and good examples of white Hermitage are thick with taste, throwing together a remarkable array of flavours – pears, apples, peaches, toffee, mint, pine resin, licorice – which, after 15 or 20 years, blend into an exotic throat-warming mix of nuts and fruit. Some winemakers are making modern, fruity whites that are lovely at one or two years old by fermenting at cooler temperatures and shunning the use of wood.

Red Hermitage is one of the world's great red wines. When it's young it is so harsh with tannin, tar and dark, leathery power that it pummels your gums and fuddles your senses. But leave it for ten years or more and the brawn is tamed. The thick black, treacly consistency is now the fragrance of wood smoke, of chargrilled meat, of tar. And there's fruit, too: strawberries and raspberries and plums, then blackcurrants, blackberries, seasoned with mint and licorice and pine, soothed with cream. Great Hermitage can do all this. Any Hermitage can suggest at least a part of these pleasures. Nothing else in the Rhône matches Hermitage at its best, but there are two other appellations just south of Tournon.

Cornas is undergoing a renewal at the moment, making ever higher-quality wines in a sort of mini-Hermitage mould: dense, long-lived but with deep plum-skins fruit as well. It's a great deal more reliable than St-Joseph.

St-Péray makes the last sort of wine you would expect from the northern Rhône – sparkling white – and pretty solid, humourless sparkling white it is too. Wagner drank it when he was writing *Parsifal*, which says it all. There's also some foursquare still white.

OPPOSITE **The famous hill of Hermitage with its steeply terraced vineyards dominates this stretch of the Rhône.**

THE MISTRAL

Both the northern and southern vineyards of the Rhône Valley are affected by the notorious Mistral wind which is said to blow for three days at a time. It not only causes physical damage to the vines as it howls down the valley, but also reduces ripening. However, its drying effect can help to combat disease and, just before harvest, concentrates the fruit. It's supposed to drive you mad, but not if you are a grower whose crop has just been saved by its fierce, drying force.

Southern Rhône

You only have to stand by the chapel on the peak of the hill of Hermitage and look about you to understand the difference between the characters of the northern and southern Rhône wines. Below you, dwarfed beneath the precipitous slope, is the town of Tain; to the west and north are the rugged, exhausting cliff faces where terraces of vines produce wines of stark brilliance. Then look to the south. The plains fan out as far as the eye can see. The Rhône seems to lose its force, content to snake its way through the fields and villages as though the hard work has been done and the increasingly torrid sun makes further exertion irksome. So it is with the wines. You don't need to struggle to appreciate the flavours of the southern wines as you sometimes must with a young Hermitage. These are broad, open flavours, rounded, ripened by relentless sun, eased into existence to offer pleasure without pain; thirst-quenching, not thought-provoking.

The lack of definition in their flavours is partly owing to the increasingly fierce conditions in which the grapes grow, since overripe grapes rarely give distinctive flavours, and it is partly the result of the basketful of different grape varieties which are permitted in the region. As many as 13 different varieties are permitted for Côtes du Rhône and Châteauneuf-du-Pape, though Grenache dominates most blends. Although this abundance frequently produces rather fuzzy-edged flavours, modern growers take advantage of the freedom to experiment permitted them under the law.

The southern Rhône can be pretty uneven quality-wise, but good producers are making excellent wines which are well worth seeking out.

The Wines

The majority of southern Rhône wines, from some 40,000 hectares (100,000 acres) in 100 communes, come under the **Côtes du Rhône** appellation. They can be red, white or rosé. The regulations are reasonably tight, demanding 11 degrees minimum alcohol, and limiting the yield of the vines to 50 hectolitres per hectare (hl/ha), though this, like all legal limits on yields, is frequently flaunted in the name of profit. If you want proof, look at the vast range of styles and qualities, from overstretched, dilute and dull to spicy and concentrated.

Côtes du Rhône-Villages wines usually demonstrate a leap of quality that is well worth the extra cost. They come from 16 villages that may append their names to that of the appellation, and the rules are stricter, with yields limited to 42 hl/ha, and a minimum alcohol level of 12.5 degrees for reds. Most of the best vineyards are strung along the foothills of the Dentelles de Montmirail to the east of the river, jagged teeth of bleached rock, where the scrub and pine can hardly gain a foothold. The best Villages wines, often from **Cairanne**, **Valréas**, **Visan**, **Rasteau** and **Beaumes-de-Venise**, are full wines with a slight earthy, peppery edge to their raspberry fruit. They're generally best young; a few will age. The best whites are from **Laudun** in the flatter land nearer the river, while nearby **Chusclan** makes good rosé. The villages of Rasteau and Beaumes-de-Venise also make sweet fortified wines called *vins doux naturels* (see box on p.107); from Grenache in Rasteau and from Muscat in Beaumes-de-Venise.

Châteauneuf-du-Pape takes its name from the papal palace, which was indeed new when it was built for John XXII. It was Clement V who moved the papal court to Avignon in 1305 at the start of the Great Schism and the new palace, situated up in the hills, was intended as a summer

---

BARON LE ROY AND THE APPELLATION SYSTEM

In the 1920s French wine – indeed the wine of all Europe – was in a parlous state. The late 19th century had seen a series of disastrous diseases and pests – powdery mildew, downy mildew and phylloxera – and producers were still licking their wounds. Adulterated and fraudulent wine was widespread, and in France laws were passed to bring these practices to an end by specifying the geographical region from which named wines had to come. Baron le Roy de Boiseaumarié, a producer in Châteauneuf-du-Pape, went further, and devised a set of rules controlling permitted grape varieties, pruning and training methods, and a minimum alcoholic strength for the wines in his region. These rules became the basis for national appellation contrôlée regulations after the Institut National des Appellations d'Origine was set up in 1935. The AC system became the model for other European countries.

residence, away from the stifling heat of the town. The wine comes in red and (more rarely) white; the red has a marvellous dusty softness, redolent of high summer heat in a dusty country lane, and the softness is coated with raspberry fruit and spice. You can drink most of them young, but if you leave the best for a few years you'll catch glimpses of blackcurrant, chocolate, cinnamon and plums, all wrapped in the warm smoothness of the south.

The white is made only in tiny quantities, but can be absurdly good when young, mixing peaches and licorice, herbs, lime and nuts in a surprisingly fresh, mouth-watering wine.

Gigondas, near Vacqueyras to the east of Orange, makes some splendid reds and rosés, rather more rustic and solid than Châteauneuf-du-Pape but not dissimilar in flavour. Most drink well with five years' age, some a little more. Whether they're worth their increasingly ambitious prices is another matter.

Vacqueyras is a sort of mini-Gigondas, going a step further in rusticity though often with good dusty fruit.

Lirac and **Tavel**, to the west of Orange, are rather appetizing: Tavel only makes rosé and it's too expensive, but it does have a good dusty cherry taste even if it's a bit high in alcohol. Lirac rosé is just as good, but lighter and a bit cheaper, while the red can be good beefy stuff. The white is full of fruit when young, but doesn't age.

Clairette de Die is the last wine to mention, although it comes from the isolated Drôme Valley, way over towards the Alps. It is attractive apple-scented sparkling wine made half with the Clairette grape and half with Muscat; **Crémant de Die**, the all-Clairette version, is duller. There's also some still **Coteaux Diois**, but it's hardly ever exported.

The papal insignia of crossed keys is a familiar sight on bottles of Châteauneuf-du-Pape.

The best vineyards in Gigondas are on the higher terraces of the Dentelles de Montmirail where the grapes ripen later.

Alsace

It's hard to imagine this wine region being called Elsass. And yet that's exactly what it was called for much of its history; because Alsace has only relatively recently become part of France. For centuries it was German; then in the 17th century France annexed it. In 1871, after France's resounding defeat in the Franco-Prussian war, it returned to Germany, only to be bounced back to France after World War I, to Germany again in World War II and, then, finally back to France. Not surprisingly, many of the locals think of themselves simply as Alsatian.

One look at the region, however, makes you think of Hansel and Gretel. It's the tiny villages of steeply gabled, half-timbered houses that strain towards their neighbours across narrow streets; it's the shadow of the forested Vosges hills; it's the window boxes of bright geraniums in summer; and if these days it all speaks of peace and plenty there are enough ruined fortresses, even fortified churches, up in the hills to act as a reminder of the days when being a border region between ambitious and quarrelsome neighbours was a recipe for intermittent invasion. (Some villages, Bennwihr or Mittelwihr, for example, are largely concrete and plaster, because some of the worst fighting in World War II raged through their streets.)

The wines, too, bear the marks of this mixed history. Put simply, they are French wines from largely German grape varieties: which means that the wines are drier, higher in alcohol and altogether winier than they would be in the hands of most German winemakers. The German wines to which they bear most resemblance, in fact, are the dry wines from the Pfalz – and the Pfalz vineyards are just over the border, a northerly continuation of the same slopes.

Geography is the key, then, to the wines of Alsace. The Vosges mountains run from north to south, and shelter their eastern slopes from the damp westerly winds, so that this northerly outpost of the vine is the second driest place in France (the driest is around Perpignan in the Midi). There's plenty of sun, too, stretching until well into the autumn, and packing so much ripeness into the grapes that the wines taste rich even when they're bone dry. At their best they have a distinct flavour of terroir; and the soils in Alsace are immensely varied. There are about 20 different major soil types here, including sandstone, schist, granite and volcanic soils; each imparting its own subtlety to the wine.

Nearly all the wines are varietals, and are named after their grape variety; Alsace was doing this long before the New World thought of it. The simplest blends are sold under the name of Edelzwicker, and can be very basic indeed.

CLASSIFICATION

The only appellation is **Alsace** but there are 50 vineyards classified as Grand Cru.

Grand Cru is where you will find the finest reflections of the subtleties of Alsace's terroir. Yields must be slightly lower than for

OPPOSITE **Hunawihr with its 15th-century fortified church – a reminder of Alsace's war-torn past.**

Zind-Humbrecht's wines are excellent examples of their type – this Gewurztraminer is enormously concentrated with exotic fruit, floral, spicy and smoky aromas.

The Grapes

A mixture of French and German varieties given a distinctive local twist.

Gewurztraminer

GEWURZTRAMINER is the most opulent of Alsace's wines with scents of lychees and roses. It's extravagantly spicy, sweet or dry and rich. It can lack acidity.

RIESLING can be sweet or dry here and is excellent with food. It is riper and 'winier' than German examples.

PINOT GRIS (formerly known as Tokay d'Alsace) has an earthy, spicy flavour and is made either sweet or dry.

MUSCAT is planted in tiny quantities. It's nearly always made dry and has a wonderfully crisp aroma.

PINOT BLANC is light, everyday wine, slightly spicy.

SYLVANER is light, everyday wine which is best drunk young. Vieilles Vignes versions can have extra depth.

PINOT NOIR is the only red grape of Alsace and it's generally light in flavour.

WINE AREA OF ALSACE

- ▨ Alsace AC wine area
- ⚜ Main wine villages

WISSEMBOURG

N

Marlenheim
Dahlenheim
Bergbieten
Molsheim
STRASBOURG ■

Mittelbergheim
Andlau
Barr
Nothalten
Dambach-la-Ville
■ SÉLESTAT

St-Hippolyte
Rodern
Bergheim
Ribeauvillé
Hunawihr
Riquewihr
Mittelwihr
Bennwihr
Kientzheim
Sigolsheim
Niedermorschwihr
● COLMAR
Wintzenheim
Wettolsheim
Turckheim
Eguisheim
Gueberschwihr
Pfaffenheim
Rouffach
Soultzmatt
Westhalten
Orschwihr
Bergholz
Guebwiller
CERNAY
Thann
■ MULHOUSE

Bruche
Giessen
Liepurette
Fecht
Thur
Rhine

GERMANY

VOSGES

| 0 km | 10 | 20 |
| 0 miles | 10 | |

Hugel is a famous family name in Alsace. The top wines are the rich Alsace Vendange Tardive and Sélection de Grains Nobles of which Hugel has been a pioneer.

basic Alsace (although arguably they are still too high), and Grand Cru wines should have extra depth and staying power. Basic Alsace wines are usually at their best within a few years of the vintage, but a Grand Cru from a good grower can easily last ten years. Only the four best grape varieties (Riesling, Pinot Gris, Muscat and Gewurztraminer) may be grown for Grand Cru wines.

Vendange Tardive are the sweet wines, encouraged by those long, warm autumns. Vendange Tardive, or late-harvest wines, are off-dry to semi-sweet, but rich and fat and sensuous.

Sélection de Grains Nobles are rare, expensive, and picked berry by berry: they are usually only made when noble rot has attacked the grapes, which doesn't happen every year. The aroma of the grapes is dulled by the noble rot, so even the Gewurztraminer smells less of roses; but instead they gain an unctuousness that makes them ideal with certain foods: *foie gras*, for example.

Crémant d'Alsace is Alsace's own sparkling wine. It's not seen much for export but can be very good, and is usually a blend of several grapes. It can have a touch of musky spice if Pinot Gris has been added to the blend, or some raciness if it contains Riesling. The backbone of the blend is usually Pinot Blanc.

The Food of Alsace

ALSACE IS A gourmet's paradise. The charcuterie here is magnificent, the summit of excitement being fresh *foie gras* or *pâté de foie gras* – created in Strasbourg around 1780. *Foie gras* needs a sweet wine to match its richness. Then there are the various *pâtés en croute*, the smoked Strasbourg sausages, numerous salami-type *saucissons* – and quiche!

Those real men who swear they don't eat quiche have never been to Alsace for a *tarte à l'oignon*, a *tarte flambée* or a proper *quiche lorraine*, and a jug of fresh Pinot Blanc.

The food of Alsace isn't light and the portions are generous. Desserts are based on the fruit of the region – cherries, plums and pears, made into yet more tarts.

Tarte à l'oignon

Loire

The river Loire rises deep in the heart of France and heads north and then west, travelling through the agricultural heart of the country before pouring into the Atlantic, providing a centuries-old highway for both merchandise and culture. No wonder it was a centre of political power. The châteaux here were not built so that their inhabitants could tend vineyards, as in Bordeaux: they were built by an aristocratic ruling élite that imposed its power by force, and often by blood. Yet it was also an educated, sophisticated élite, and the châteaux of the Loire were at the heart of the French Renaissance.

The Loire, by virtue of its length (it is the longest river in France) and its variety of soils and climates (continental in the east, with cold winters and hot summers, and maritime in the west, with mild winters and warm summers), can produce almost any sort of wine one might want. There is the lightest and driest of whites in Muscadet; some of France's most pungent white in Sancerre; some of her longest-living dry white and sweet white in Anjou and Touraine, as well as sparkling wines and fragrant reds.

The Loire region divides roughly into four areas: Muscadet at the river's mouth; Anjou; Touraine; and the Upper Loire. There are no special classifications in any area. The appellation system is so comprehensive that small areas able to make a distinctive style have their own AC.

Muscadet

Muscadet occupies a niche no other wine does. For a start, it is neutral in flavour; for another thing, it is low in acid yet very dry. Acid wines need time in the bottle to harmonize; low-acid wines you can drink as soon as the fermentation is finished. It's also low in alcohol, and all of this makes it the perfect partner for the local oysters and shrimps. The most basic wine is simply called **Muscadet**, and frankly this isn't the one to choose. **Muscadet des Coteaux de la Loire** or **Muscadet Côtes de Grand-Lieu** are a bit better,

One of the Loire's fairytale châteaux – Château du Nozet, near Pouilly. Such architectural gems are part of the heritage of the Loire.

THE SWEET WINES OF THE LOIRE

The Loire – or more specifically Anjou and Touraine – has some of those rare mesoclimates where the autumn fogs coil off the river and drift up through the vineyards as the sun heats the air. The clammy warmth clings to the Chenin grapes and encourages noble rot to attack them, concentrating the sugar so that they give small amounts of intensely sweet juice. Quarts de Chaume and Bonnezeaux in Anjou are two such spots. Both are tiny. Not quite as sweet as Sauternes from Bordeaux, they are very slow to develop and can seem surprisingly dry when young. This is because the Chenin's very high acidity masks the fruit until time softens the wine. At ten to 20 years old they have a wonderful gentle richness, all quince and peaches, but always fresh. Coteaux du Layon and Coteaux de l'Aubance are less intense and can be drunk younger. Moulin Touchais, which has only the simple Anjou AC, is an even more extraordinary sweet wine, all toffeed and rich and lasting for decades. And over in Touraine, Vouvray Moelleux is another contender. It often gets less noble rot than Quarts de Chaume, but in a good year has great intensity and will live for well over a decade.

Meticulous producer Pierre Luneau specializes in Muscadet for the long haul, which is a rarity in a region that concentrates on wine for drinking young.

but best of all is **Muscadet de Sèvre-et-Maine**, which should have more character and style. Always look, too, for the phrase 'sur lie' on the label: it means that the wine has been left in barrel or tank on its lees. These not only keep it fresher until it's bottled, but give it more depth.

Anjou

Anjou's vineyards lie almost entirely to the south of the river. It isn't all vines here by any means, because Anjou's wide, gently undulating fields are used for grain and vegetables as well.

That **Anjou Rosé** is an AC wine is a disgrace – or perhaps it's a disgrace that an AC wine can be allowed to be so bad; I don't know. Either way, it's vaguely sweet, often stale and sulphurous and usually best avoided. **Cabernet d'Anjou** and **Rosé de Loire**, the one a slightly sweet and Cabernet-Franc-based rosé, and the other drier, are better. **Anjou Rouge** can be good: slightly grassy, slightly earthy blackcurranty red that is quite chunky in a warm year. There's also **Anjou-Villages** for red from the best villages. Only Cabernet Franc and Cabernet Sauvignon may be used. **Anjou Blanc** can be excellent: good fresh, minerally Chenin Blanc with a touch of honey.

Savennières, **Savennières la Roche-aux-Moines** and **Savennières Coulée-de-Serrant** are some of the peaks of Anjou. Not physical peaks: instead these dry Chenin whites come from the north bank of the river Layon and are made in a style that is hopelessly unfashionable in a world that demands instant gratification. The wine can be austere, even dull when young; it needs ten years or so to reveal an astonishing dry richness of honey and steel, like sparks struck off granite.

Saumur is known mostly for its Champagne-method sparkling wine. It's made from Chenin, often with some Chardonnay, Sauvignon or even Cabernet Franc added, and the blending does

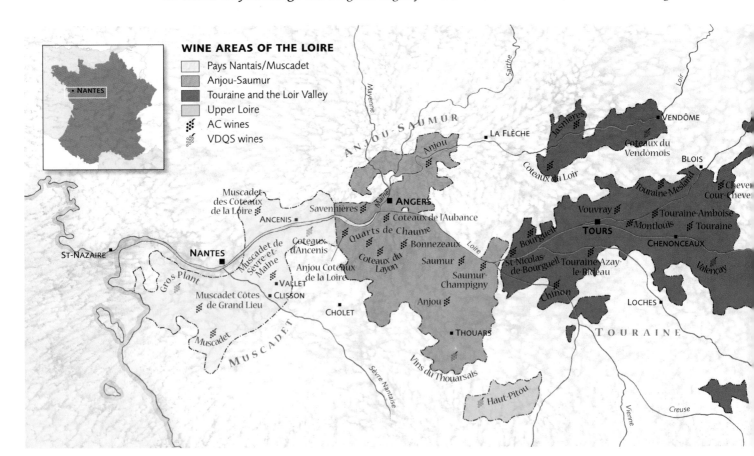

WINE AREAS OF THE LOIRE

- Pays Nantais/Muscadet
- Anjou-Saumur
- Touraine and the Loir Valley
- Upper Loire
- AC wines
- VDQS wines

help to produce rounder fruit. All are best drunk young. **Saumur Blanc** is decent still dry white, as well, and here again the Chenin can be blended. **Saumur Rouge** is attractive, grassy red made from Cabernet Franc; the best red, however, is **Saumur-Champigny**. When the vines are old and the wine well made, it's like drinking essence of blackcurrant and raspberry.

Touraine

Move eastwards and you'll discover meandering rivers, forests full of game, orchards and gardens, and wines with an easy, refreshing quality. High spots include **Bourgueil**, **St-Nicolas-de-Bourgueil** and **Chinon** – all reds from Cabernet Franc. They can have a most unforgettable personality: strangely earthy, dry and sharp-edged, yet with a beautiful, almost searing laser-beam of blackcurrant and wild strawberry. Although delicious young, they can last for years.

The Grapes

The Loire is where the grapes of Bordeaux meet the Pinot Noir of Burgundy.

MUSCADET is one of the most neutral white grapes in the world. Its virtue, when grown in the maritime climate near Nantes, is that it retains freshness and goes well with the local seafood. Its proper name is Melon de Bourgogne, but the Burgundians washed their hands of it long ago.

SAUVIGNON BLANC, although a world traveller, needs a relatively cool climate to express its pungency, its gooseberry-grassy freshness. In too warm a climate it turns flabby; which is why the warmest years in the Loire are good for the reds, but not so good for Sancerre.

CHENIN BLANC needs warmth: unripe Chenin is raw and harsh stuff indeed. Few other places in the world take Chenin Blanc seriously; but then nowhere else does it even begin to reach the heights it does here. The greatest dry and sweet Chenins from the Loire last for decades and mature to a honeyed, minerally richness.

Sauvignon Blanc

CHARDONNAY is very much a bit player here, used for blending into Saumur whites to soften them, though some simple wines may be all Chardonnay. These are light, crisp and attractive.

CABERNET FRANC is the best red grape of the Loire, making finer quality in Bourgueil and Chinon than anywhere outside St-Émilion. The best have rich raspberry fruit; lighter ones are grassy and perfect for summer.

PINOT NOIR is never as great on the Loire as it is in Burgundy; but in warm years there will be some fleeting raspberry or strawberry fruit.

CHINON
APPELLATION CHINON CONTRÔLÉE
1992 Vieilles Vignes
CLOS DE LA DIOTERIE
S.C.E.A CHARLES JOGUET VITICULTEUR, 37220 SAZILLY (FRANCE)
Mis en bouteilles à la propriété
12,5% vol. PRODUCE OF FRANCE ℮ 750 ml

Leading Chinon winemaker Charles Joguet uses very old vines to produce wine with dark red and black fruit and penetrating depth, plus spice, coffee and more with age.

Chenin Blanc

appellation SANCERRE contrôlée

Les Monts Damnés

1997

François COTAT - Propriétaire à CHAVIGNOL - Cher · 750 ml

Didier Dagueneau in Pouilly-Fumé has named his wine after the type of soil – silex – which gives it its particular character. Sancerre from Cotat has a more conventional label but the wine has a concentration of fruit few other growers achieve.

Vouvray, a dozen miles upriver, is one of the most tantalizing of Loire wines. It can be great; really great. The Chenin Blanc grape (Vouvray must be entirely Chenin) needs a warm year to ripen on the tough clay and chalk plateaux which crowd over the village houses huddled below. In such conditions, the wines mature to a fuller-bodied version of Savennières, less minerally but more honeyed, but they can be acerbic in youth. **Vouvray Demi-Sec**, which can be anywhere between just off-dry and medium-sweet, and **Vouvray Moelleux**, which is sweet to very sweet, have tremendous peachy fruit, sometimes smoky, sometimes nutty, with quince and pear often wrapped in honey; and will last 20 years or more. **Sparkling Vouvray**, best drunk young, mops up the rest of the grapes.

Montlouis makes a leaner version of Vouvray, without so much honey; and **Jasnières**, north of Vouvray, makes very austere dry white.

Azay-le-Rideau, **Amboise** and **Mesland** make both white from Chenin and some attractive rosé and red from Cabernet Franc or Gamay.

Touraine is the general appellation for the region: it covers everything from gooseberry-fruited white **Sauvignon de Touraine**, Chenin-based sparklers sold as **Crémant de la Loire**, to light reds and rosés from Cabernet, Gamay or Groslot.

Upper Loire

Sauvignon Blanc takes over here from Chenin as the ubiquitous white grape. The wines with their sharp, grassy, nettly, green character, their gooseberry or asparagus taste, sometimes with a whiff of coffee, have been copied all over the world, most notably in New Zealand. **Sancerre** and its neighbour, **Pouilly-Fumé**, are the most famous, producing pungent whites. **Menetou-Salon** and **Reuilly** are similar in style, though usually a little lighter; **Quincy**, too, is in the same mould, and often the most pungent of the lot.

There are also reds and rosés grown in Sancerre and Menetou-Salon, from the Pinot Noir grape. Red Sancerre can be lovely, rather ethereal red, perfumed and cherryish; the rosé is less often seen but can be good.

The Food of the Loire

THERE IS AN ease and plenty to the food of the Loire. The presence of the wealthy châteaux along its banks meant that new fruits and vegetables were tried out here – and flourished in the mild climate. It's why the Loire came to be known as 'the garden of France'.

Artichokes, peas and lettuce were all brought here as foreign exotica; so were plums, apparently first brought back by returning crusaders. The greengage, or *Reine Claude*, takes its name from François I's queen, herself an enthusiastic gardener; and the horticultural gardens of Angers, closed in 1925, specialized in the development of new types of pear: *comice* and *belle angevine* came from here.

Tarte Tatin

Not surprisingly, fruit features in all sorts of Loire recipes. Prunes are added to fish or meat stews, served with noisettes of pork or poached in wine; fruit tarts and cakes (including *Tarte Tatin*, the famous upside-down apple tart) are also the perfect accompaniment for the sweet wines of the region, with their high acidity.

The river is teeming with fish and these may be served simply in *beurre blanc* sauce, in a *matelote*, or stew, with the local wine, red or white, or if plenty of small fish are to

hand, deep-fried *petite friture*. Sorrel sauce is another favourite partner for the local salmon, pike or *sandre* (pickerel). Near to the ocean you can find every possible form of seafood, still reeking of the brine and iodine of wave-splashed, weed-strewn rocks and absolutely brilliant with Muscadet.

Rillettes are another speciality: pork, goose, rabbit or duck baked and then shredded with a fork, packed into pots with the melted fat and served like pâté, with crusty bread.

Mushrooms also play a great part in the cuisine of the region. The French grow these in the tufa (chalky freestone) caves of Saumur where it is cool and dark. They are delicious either grilled or sautéed in oil and garlic.

And then there is cheese. The sharp, sour *crottin* goat cheeses of the Upper Loire make a surprising, but entirely successful partnership with white Sancerre. Port-Salut, first created by Trappist monks near Le Mans, was sent to Paris in 1873, and apparently sold out within an hour.

Southern France

This is an enormous tract of land, stretching from the Atlantic coast in the west, scraping the peaks of the Pyrenees, swooping along the Mediterranean up to the border with Italy, and then heading north to the border with Switzerland. Phew. How can you generalize about such a vast region? The answer is that you can't. In any case it's several regions, not one, and each has its own culture and its own traditions. The only unifying factor is that those traditions, ever since the vine was first brought here, have involved wine.

Grape vines first arrived in France at Massalia, the Greek city (later called Marseille) founded by Phocaeans in 600 BC. From there they spread northwards up the Rhône Valley and eastwards along the coast and overland towards the Atlantic; by the 3rd century AD they had reached Bordeaux.

As the Roman Empire collapsed, so winemaking and the whole Roman system of export fell into disarray. But wine was always a staple in the south; indeed, in some places it was one of the few crops that would grow, along with olives and figs. Life in the arid hills of Provence or Languedoc was not, in the past, the holiday fantasy it is now; instead it was a region of grinding poverty where wine had to be coaxed from unresponsive soil. No wonder people preferred to plant on the more productive plains. After the arrival of the railway, the flat lands of Languedoc became the supplier of cheap everyday red to Paris and the north; if the wine was too light it was bolstered by an admixture of alcoholic red from North Africa.

Only in more recent years, as the demand for cheap wine fell away, did a problem of surplus develop. The surplus swelled to a lake; the EU decided to act. Vineyards all along the Mediterranean were ripped up; and more ambitious growers began to look towards quality.

But I'm running ahead of myself. Let's start in the South-West, where there never was a glut, and where the steep, damp foothills of the Pyrenees harbour vines that arrived there in the early centuries of winegrowing, and never left.

The South-West

These are some of the most remote vineyards in all France. **Irouléguy**, tucked right up against the Spanish border, makes rustic reds; **Jurançon** and **Béarn** make some ravishing, peachy, dry and sweet white, and some rather undistinguished red, white and rosé respectively; **Madiran** makes spicy reds that can be remarkably attractive. The Tannat grape is the unifying thread running through these reds, generally blended with, oh, some Cabernet, some Fer, some Manseng Noir, a bit of this, a bit of that. The whites can be Gros Manseng, Petit Manseng, Courbu or Camaralet to name but a few. **Gaillac**, whose wines were exported to Britain long before the Médoc was planted, is even more individual, with a grape mix that includes Mauzac, Len de l'El and Ondenc, plus Sauvignon Blanc and Sémillon for the whites; and Duras, Fer, Syrah, both Cabernets and Merlot for robust reds.

Some of France's most southerly vineyards in the Pyrénées Orientales. They are planted high in the hills above Vinca to avoid the worst of the heat.

The Grapes

There are umpteen grape varieties in Southern France: these are the main ones.

Syrah

REDS Cabernet Sauvignon makes characteristically blackcurranty wines, often aged in oak; Merlot is softer, more blackberryish; Malbec makes gutsy, pruny wines in Cahors; Tannat, one of the main red grapes of the South-West, is tough and tannic; Mourvèdre makes gloriously spicy reds; Syrah tastes of herbs and smoke; Carignan gives acidity and structure to a blend; Cinsaut is softer and lighter; Grenache is a vital ingredient in red *vins doux naturels*.

WHITES Sauvignon Blanc is grassy and pungent; Sémillon smooth, round and lemony; Petit and Gros Manseng have lovely peachy fruit; Muscat is grapy and aromatic; Clairette is crisp but otherwise not thrilling; Mauzac has good acidity and an appley flavour; Grenache Blanc produces soft, fat wines; Bourboulenc keeps its acidity well.

Buzet produces good Bordeaux-style red wines from the same mix of grapes, at a lower price. They can age for around five years.

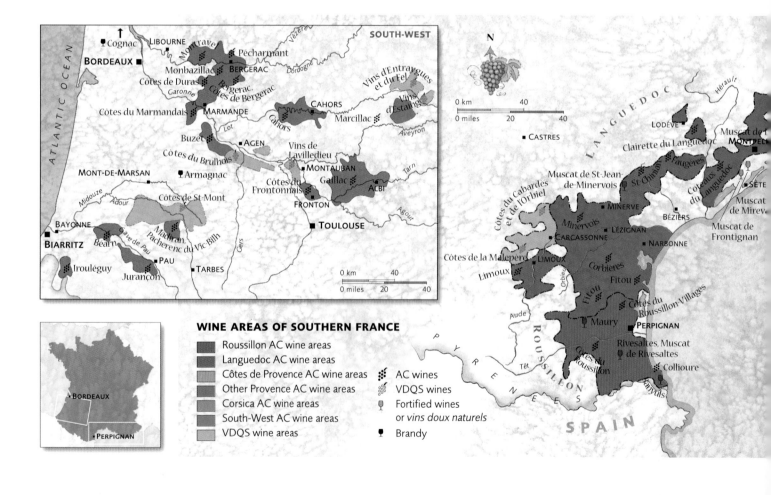

Mas Jullien show what can be done with the traditional grape varieties of the Midi when talented viticulture and winemaking is applied.

But then things change as one approaches Bordeaux. Its influence can be felt from a distance: the proportion of both the Cabernets, Sauvignon Blanc and Sémillon in the wines increases, until by the time one reaches the borders of the Bordeaux region the wines are complete copycats. Look at **Buzet**: the reds here can actually beat basic Bordeaux at its own game. **Cahors** specializes in the Malbec grape, these days a very minor player in Bordeaux, and does it extremely well; like so many of these wines upriver from Bordeaux, it suffered in the Middle Ages from protectionist measures imposed by the merchants of Bordeaux, who disliked the threat to their own light reds posed by wines from more reliable climates. Taxation was heavy, and when it came to shipping wines from the port, priority was given to Bordeaux's own wines.

But to continue. **Côtes du Marmandais** – yes, soft, juicy Bordeaux lookalike reds, with a bit of Fer and Abouriou added to the Bordeaux blend; **Côtes de Duras**: more simple Bordeaux-style reds and whites, often very attractive. And then we come to **Bergerac**, source of some really rather good reds and whites, by now completely in the Bordeaux mould. **Monbazillac** tends to be at its best in those years which are also successful in Sauternes: this is a good source of nobly rotten (in the best years) sweet whites, lighter than Sauternes but often delicious.

Languedoc-Roussillon

This is where the land dries out, where the influence of the Atlantic gives way to that of the Mediterranean, and where the hot south really begins. There are two sides to winemaking here: one follows the pattern of appellation contrôlée, making often good, sometimes very good indeed,

WINE AREAS OF SOUTHERN FRANCE

- Roussillon AC wine areas
- Languedoc AC wine areas
- Côtes de Provence AC wine areas
- Other Provence AC wine areas
- Corsica AC wine areas
- South-West AC wine areas
- VDQS wine areas

- AC wines
- VDQS wines
- Fortified wines or *vins doux naturels*
- Brandy

wines in AC regions like Minervois and Corbières; the other is a less traditional, newer way of thinking, a way of using the vin de pays regulations to produce wines that don't fit any local tradition but which are showing the way forward for much of the south. The two are not incompatible: it would be a shame if every winemaker abandoned AC wines and headed full tilt for vin de pays. But then that's not likely to happen.

Minervois and **Corbières** at their best have a lovely dusty quality to their fruit. Much Corbières is softened these days by the use of carbonic maceration (see p.22), but there are also some serious reds made for aging – which prove that grapes like Carignan, however unfriendly they are when overcropped, can make sensational wine when the vines are old and the yields low. **Fitou**, too, is big, gutsy, dusty red, also based on Carignan, but Syrah and Mourvèdre are making

COGNAC AND ARMAGNAC

Oh, the good life. You've just finished dinner, and the last of the wine is being passed round – a Sauternes, perhaps, with some white peaches. Or is it winter? Perhaps you polished off a pheasant with some Pinot Noir, and now your host suggests a Cognac or an Armagnac. You're not driving, so you think, why not?

Both these brandies come from the South-West but there's a difference between the two which is reflected in the fierier character and greater depth of much Armagnac. It derives partly from the distillation method. Cognac is distilled twice, in pot stills; most Armagnac goes just once through a continuous still. (Some Armagnac, to confuse the issue, is also distilled in pot stills.) The single distillation of Armagnac leaves more congeners (flavour compounds) in the spirit; it is less pure, therefore, but also richer.

Both, however, rely on neutral, acidic base wine. The most common grape is the dreary Ugni Blanc, which reaches its apogee via the still; in Armagnac it is joined by the more aromatic Folle Blanche and others.

Most Cognac and Armagnac is sold quite young: simple Armagnac can be as young as two years, while VO, VSOP or Réserve denotes a spirit of about five years old. Six-year-old Armagnacs can be labelled as XO, Extra, Napoléon or goodness knows what else. (These years are spent mellowing in oak barrels.) Cognac can't be sold before the age of three, when it is called three star or VS; VSOP must be five years old. Again, older Cognacs bear all sorts of impressive names like Napoléon, XO and so on. In addition Cognac produces an aperitif called Pineau des Charentes, which is partially fermented grape juice with young Cognac. It can be deliciously sweet and grapy, but it's after dinner now and too late for an aperitif. So I think I'll have the XO, please.

ABOVE A sample of 25-year-old Cognac being taken from one of the many barrels aging in the warehouses of Courvoisier in Jarnac.

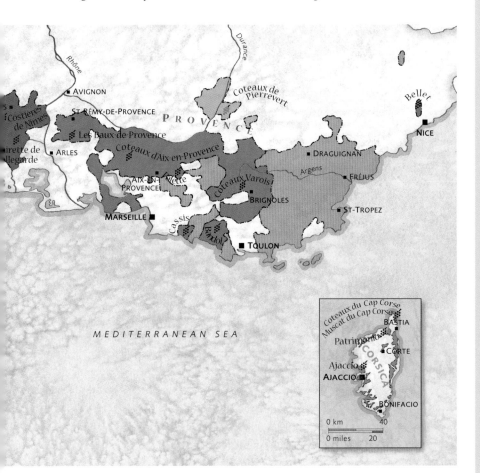

MEDITERRANEAN SEA

0 km 40
0 miles 20

This Cabernet Sauvignon and Syrah blend is one of the finest wines to come out of Provence in the last decade.

increasing inroads as *cépages améliorateurs*, or improving varities: they add fruit and suppleness to the tough-structured Carignan. **Roussillon** is still lagging behind these regions in winemaking terms, and there's considerable Spanish influence here – or rather Catalan, since the locals often consider themselves to be Catalan rather than French.

All these regions make some white, except Fitou; at its best it's crisp and has some character, though frankly it's never going to set the world on fire.

Other AC wines come from **Faugères**, which makes classy, leathery, cherryish reds that involve no Carignan at all, and **St-Chinian**, also a source of good, slightly earthy reds and rosés. And then there is the **Coteaux du Languedoc**, a huge sprawling region of decent whites and increasingly classy reds. There's also some sparkling wine from down here: appley **Blanquette de Limoux**, made from the Mauzac grape, or **Crémant de Limoux**, a more rustic number.

Provence and Corsica

Provence is in some ways the victim of its own success. It's been a tourist destination for so long, and has had such an easy market for its wines, that it hasn't had to try too hard. Think of all those bottles of rosé consumed uncritically in the waterfront cafés: when your customers don't notice that you're charging remarkably high prices for not very thrilling wine, what incentive is there to stop?

But that's only part of the story. There are ambitious producers in Provence (ambitious for quality, that is), particularly in the appellations of **Coteaux d'Aix-en-Provence** and **Les Baux-de-Provence**. The wines of the latter tend to be the more concentrated and generally more complex, but both regions boast some top-class growers. There are some in **Côtes de Provence**, too; it's just that you have to wade through more dross to get to them. Reds in this part of the world focus on Syrah, Mourvèdre, Grenache, Cabernet Sauvignon and Cinsaut, with Carignan gradually being reduced. Grenache is also good for rosés; the small quantities of less than exciting whites rely on Ugni Blanc, Grenache Blanc, Sémillon and Sauvignon. If you want good everyday reds and whites that won't break the bank, **Coteaux Varois** is a good bet.

Provence boasts four tiny individual appellations, as well: **Cassis** (excellent, unusual, expensive), **Bellet** (rather good, also unusual, also expensive), **Palette** (reds and rosés; expensive) and **Bandol** (first-class reds and whites, the reds based on Mourvèdre; and for their quality, not as expensive as all that).

There's wine on **Corsica**, too, and it comes in every possible colour and style. It should be

Stunning scenery used to be the best thing about Coteaux d'Aix-en-Provence. Now there are some good wines too.

VINS DOUX NATURELS

Now, here's a misnomer if ever there was one. These wines are no more 'naturally' sweet than any other fortified wine: they're sweet because the fermentation is stopped by the addition of brandy. They come in both red and white. Muscat is used for the whites: they're made in Rivesaltes, Frontignan, Lunel, Mireval and St-Jean-de-Minervois, as well as in Beaumes-de-Venise in the Rhône Valley. The reds are more difficult to appreciate. They're made from the Grenache grape, come from Maury, Banyuls or Rivesaltes and are sometimes made *rancio*, or maderized, by being exposed to heat or air. This gives them a sour, nutty tang much beloved by aficionados.

The Cazes brothers make outstanding Muscat de Rivesaltes with a spicy orange and rose petal perfume, ripe exotic fruit and a bitter orange finish.

good, characterful stuff and these days it can be. We've been promised a wine revolution in Corsica for some time, and there are good individual producers in ACs like **Patrimonio**, **Ajaccio**, **Coteaux du Cap Corse** and **Muscat du Cap Corse**. Simple **Vin de Corse** is the least promising. But winemaking generally has improved and flavours are fresh and attractive.

Jura and Savoie

The landscape here couldn't be more different to that of Provence. To get there you have to follow the Rhône up towards Switzerland, past the crisp Chardonnays of **Bugey**. Then, in the various tucks and folds of the Alps, from the shores of Lake Geneva down to the Isère Valley near Grenoble, you'll catch glimpses of Savoie. The vines here claw up the slopes; and the wines are light, even ethereal. Most get drunk in the ski resorts. There are reds as well, light ones from Pinot Noir and gutsier ones from Mondeuse.

If the Savoie mountain wines are mostly marked by lightness of touch, the Jura wines are more caveman in style. They mix the Pinot Noir and Chardonnay of Burgundy with red Trousseau or Poulsard; but *vin jaune* is the local speciality. This is a sherry lookalike (though without the finesse of good sherry), also unfortified, matured under flor and made from the Savagnin grape. Searingly dry, almost sourly pungent, it's a fitting full stop for the end of our journey.

The Food of the South

IN THE SOUTH-WEST, the further one goes from Bordeaux towards the Spanish border, the more the food resembles that of the Basque country. Red peppers flavour dish after dish: fish soups, salt cod, *pipérade*, all have to have their share. Very good they are too, sweet and melting. Béarn is the home of *poule au pot*, which Henri IV wished every peasant to eat on Sundays, but not of *sauce béarnaise*, which is a purely Parisian invention.

Head towards Roussillon on the Mediterranean coast and Catalan influence is strong. Peppers are a dominant influence here as well, as are green olives; fish stew is excellent near the coast, as it is all along the Mediterranean. It's a way of using the enormous selection of sometimes dull-textured fish, and flavouring them with garlic, olive oil and herbs (and in Provence, tomato, saffron and hot *rouille* paste to make *bouillabaisse*), all of which are found in abundance here.

Red mullet, rascasse, sardines, anchovies, octopus and shellfish all find their way into the stewpot. Or fish might be grilled over fennel or herbs; anchovies and tuna might go into *salade niçoise*.

The strong, even garish flavours of Provence also include *tapénade* and *anchoiade*, spreads made mainly from olives, anchovies and olive oil, and *aïoli*, the garlic mayonnaise that sometimes seems more garlic than mayonnaise. There is *pistou* as well, the local version of Italian *pesto*. Local reds stand up well to these pungent flavours as do crisp whites.

If you want meat there is lamb, grilled with herbs, and, if you insist, songbirds like larks and thrushes.

Pudding usually consists of fruit or cheese: sheep's milk Banon from Provence, perhaps, with its wrapping of chestnut leaves. Or Roquefort from the Languedoc.

Jura and Savoie are, however, cheese country *par excellence*. Gruyère is eaten as it is, or in fondues, or in sauces with chicken, or in souffles, or melted in onion soup.

Vin de Pays

Ah, country wines. Just the sound of the phrase makes me think I'm sitting in the shade of an olive tree breathing the scents of thyme and rosemary, twisting the cap off a bottle of something cool and fresh that a local vigneron has just decanted. Or perhaps I'm further north, on the banks of the Loire, and there's goat's cheese and fresh bread for lunch, and a bottle of local Sauvignon cooling in the river. Either way, the principle is the same: vins de pays are the wines of the locality; simple wines that nevertheless have the character of their region.

The term was coined in 1968 in an attempt to encourage producers of the completely anonymous and usually dreadful vins de table to upgrade quality, regain a bit of self-respect and increase their earnings. It was placed just above the bottom rung of the quality ladder, vins de table, but beneath VDQS.

For a while it was difficult to see that the introduction of vin de pays was doing much to improve quality, but then a number of factors conspired to bring about a revolution. One factor was the perverse insistence of a Frenchman named Aimé Guibert that fine wine – not just good wine – could be made in a part of southern France that had always been despised as fit only for filling the wine lake. Another was the experience of Australian-trained winemakers in producing decent wine in climates just as hot and unpromising as the Midi. As with all revolutions, the strands leading to it came from many different directions. And they came together in the south; the hot, dispirited, overproducing south.

I should say here that vins de pays are made all over France. There's a great swathe of them along the Loire, with the general title of Vin de Pays du Jardin de la France; like all **regional vins de pays** (there are in all four of these, covering all the vineyards of France) it is subdivided into **departmental vins de pays**, so that a producer near Sancerre can choose to make wine under the name of, say, Vin de Pays de Cher, or under the name of Vin de Pays du Jardin de la France. There are, in all, 39 departmental vins de pays through-

out France. And then there are a further 96 **zonal vins de pays** covering specific regions within departments, making a total of 139 vins de pays.

Sixty of them are in the region of Languedoc-Roussillon. This is the Pays d'Oc, the land of Oc, where the local word for 'yes' was not 'oui' but 'oc'. It has also long been the land of the co-operative cellar. Now, a bad co-op means, effectively, poor wine from a whole area. Improve a co-op and you raise the standard of a whole area. There are various ways of achieving a rapid rise in quality. One is to improve cellar hygiene; another is to install proper temperature control; another is to plant better grape varieties.

All these are things which come naturally to internationally trained winemakers, and it is

Innovation in the south takes different forms: on the one hand companies like Skalli are producing international flavours from vines like Cabernet Sauvignon, while on the other, individual producers like Aimé Guibert are using the best of local traditional varieties to make world-class wines.

OPPOSITE **Lavender thrives in the same hot, dry climate that produces the pungent, herby flavours of the south.**

these winemakers, often Australian-trained, who have brought about the main phase of the vin de pays revolution in the south. They're making varietal wines from Cabernet Sauvignon, Merlot, Syrah, Chardonnay, Sauvignon Blanc, Viognier – all the fashionable international grapes – and selling them as vins de pays, full of upfront juicy fruit and new oak. New World style wines from the south of France, in other words. But they're also making blends from traditional, indigenous varieties given the New World treatment.

What they've achieved is remarkable. The Pays d'Oc is now a byword for inexpensive, tasty, well-made wines. They're not driving out local styles because the innate curiosity of good winemakers means that once they've cleaned up the winery and started producing something they can sell, they'll start looking at what they can play with next. That means exploring terroir and local traditions. And they've shown the AC wines of the south that if they want to justify their higher status they've got to improve their act, too.

But elsewhere in France the vin de pays story is different. Vin de Pays de Bas Rhin is not a big seller, for example; nor is Vin de Pays de Côte d'Or. It's not surprising: hardly any is made. Why? Because the Bas Rhin department covers the northern end of Alsace, where almost everything is AC, sells at a high price, and is good quality. The Côte d'Or department covers the vineyards of Burgundy. They don't need a vin de pays there either. In that respect the vin de pays revolution has been ideal: it has been extremely effective precisely where it was most needed.

Vin de Pays du Jardin de la France covers most of the Loire Valley. Production is large and mainly of Chenin Blanc and Sauvignon Blanc although there is an increasing amount of good Chardonnay too.

MAS DE DAUMAS GASSAC

When Aimé Guibert bought this property, tucked into a tiny valley west of Montpellier in the Languedoc, no vine had ever been planted there. But the soil had caught his attention: pinkish, crumbly, stony soil which struck him as being potentially excellent for growing vines. So that's what he did: never mind that his estate had no appellation contrôlée and wasn't likely to get it; never mind that people thought him eccentric, to say the least. Here, in this remote spot, he created some truly remarkable wine – wine that sells as Vin de Pays de l'Hérault but at Classed Growth prices.

The red is a Bordeaux-style blend of Cabernet Sauvignon, Cabernet Franc and Merlot, thick with tannin and extract, huge and old-fashioned and needing time to mature. The white is equally unusual: it's a blend of Viognier, Chardonnay and other grapes, with an intense floral aroma; unlike the red, it is best young.

Mas de Daumas Gassac's flagship red wine has a wonderfully powerful combination of fruit and tannin, smoke, cedarwood and blackcurrants.

ITALY

Wine pervades every aspect of life in Italy in a way that is found nowhere else in the world. It's as natural a part of a meal as bread or olive oil; and vines are grown all over the peninsula, from the foothills of the Alps in the north right down to Sicily and even beyond, to the tiny island of Pantelleria which almost touches the African shores of Tunisia.

Yet there's a paradox here. It is so basic to life that until recently little notice was taken of it: winemakers grew the grapes, made the wine and sold it to whoever wanted it. They didn't worry too much about the finer points of quality, and neither did the customer. For a country which exported the vine to much of Europe, Italy for many years made a pretty poor fist of her own.

Just think how far back that history goes. It was the Greeks who brought the vine to Italy, and in turn named it Oenotria, the land of wine. But centuries passed and power, economic and political, moved elsewhere. In fact it was only after World War II, and the economic boom that brought prosperity, that Italy's wine industry began to catch up with the rest of Europe. And the wine renaissance that has put her finest wines to the fore worldwide is even more recent, dating from just 30 years ago.

The beautiful Palladian church of San Biagio in Montepulciano dominates the surrounding countryside. Wine is just as everyday a part of life in Italy as fine architecture.

ITALIAN WINE LAWS

The first step in this modern renaissance was the passing of DOC (Denominazione di Origine Controllata) laws in 1963. They came into effect in 1967 and 1968, and were intended to be the equivalent of French appellation contrôlée: they imposed a map and a structure on the chaos that was Italian viticulture. Italian wine had been in the doldrums for years, with low prices, virtually no investment and no reputation. It took the most determined individual growers to build on this, and take Italian wine to its new levels. And how did they do this? Actually, by ignoring the new laws. But before we get into this, let's just run quickly through the basic structure of Italian wine as it existed after 1968.

Vino da tavola was the lowest rung of the ladder, the most basic wine.

Denominazione di Origine Controllata (DOC) wines were the top rung, covering only a few of Italy's wines, but specifying grape varieties and viticultural and winemaking techniques.

Denominazione di Origine Controllata et Garantita (DOCG) was added later. This super-tier was supposed to guarantee the quality, as well as the origin, of the very best wines.

The most adventurous producers, however, wanted their wines to be as prestigious as the best French wines, and so they started to import French grape varieties and French techniques. These meant that their wines could not be sold as DOC; so they sold them as basic vini da tavola instead, gave them snappy brand names, fancy bottles and high prices. They sold like hot cakes and soon had overtaken even the best DOCs in fame. The time had come for a new law.

The new legal structure is far more flexible than the old, and is effectively built around the need to bring Italy's finest wines under the umbrella of the law. A new category, **Indicazione Geografica Tipica (IGT)**, has been inserted between vino da tavola and DOC; in theory it is for wines that are typical of their regions but don't qualify for DOC; in practice it is there for those vini da tavola that don't want the constraints of a DOC. Every so-called super-vino da tavola must opt for an IGT or a DOC.

But there is another twist to the story yet. You remember all those French vines that were being imported, all those French techniques? As the producers experimented and practised with these so they discovered more virtues in their native grape varieties. So now, far from becoming standardized, Italian wine is more varied than ever – and higher quality. Oenotria indeed.

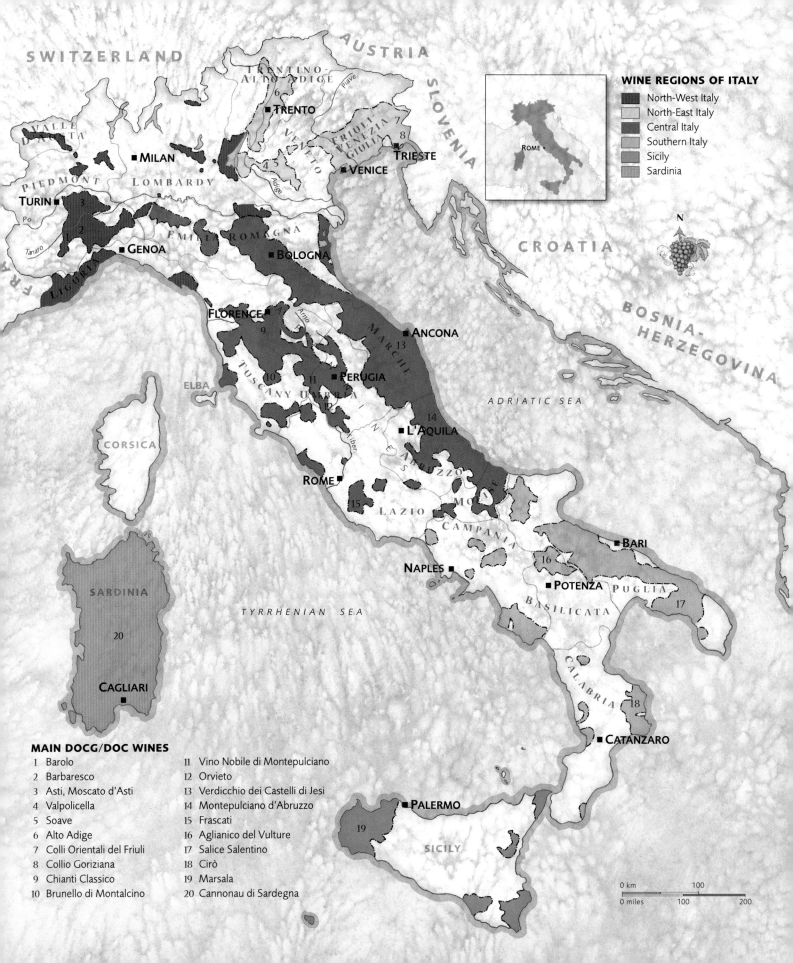

SWITZERLAND

AUSTRIA

TRENTINO-ALTO ADIGE

SLOVENIA

Piave

6 ■ TRENTO

VENETO

FRIULI VENEZIA GIULIA 7

8

■ MILAN

Adige

VALLE D'AOSTA

LOMBARDY

■ TRIESTE

VENICE

PIEDMONT

4 5

TURIN ■

3

EMILIA ROMAGNA

Po

1 2

Tanaro

■ GENOA

■ BOLOGNA

LIGURIA

FRANCE

FLORENCE

ARNO

9

MARCHE

■ ANCONA

ELBA

TUSCANY

UMBRIA

13

10

11

PERUGIA ■

CORSICA

12

L'AQUILA ■

14

ADRIATIC SEA

Tiber

A B R U Z Z O

ROME ■

15

MOLISE

LAZIO

CAMPANIA

■ BARI

NAPLES ■

16

POTENZA ■

PUGLIA

SARDINIA

BASILICATA

17

20

TYRRHENIAN SEA

CALABRIA

18

CAGLIARI ■

■ CATANZARO

PALERMO ■

19

SICILY

WINE REGIONS OF ITALY

- North-West Italy
- North-East Italy
- Central Italy
- Southern Italy
- Sicily
- Sardinia

ROME ●

N

CROATIA

BOSNIA-HERZEGOVINA

MAIN DOCG/DOC WINES

1 Barolo
2 Barbaresco
3 Asti, Moscato d'Asti
4 Valpolicella
5 Soave
6 Alto Adige
7 Colli Orientali del Friuli
8 Collio Goriziana
9 Chianti Classico
10 Brunello di Montalcino
11 Vino Nobile di Montepulciano
12 Orvieto
13 Verdicchio dei Castelli di Jesi
14 Montepulciano d'Abruzzo
15 Frascati
16 Aglianico del Vulture
17 Salice Salentino
18 Cirò
19 Marsala
20 Cannonau di Sardegna

0 km   100
0 miles   100   200

North-West Italy

The north-west of Italy was always described to me in history lessons as the 'serious' part of Italy. Here people worked hard, made money, and occasionally raised armies, which won battles. I was always a little unnerved by these ultra-efficient Lombards and Piedmontese, and harboured a sneaking regard for what was portrayed as the feckless, corrupt but colourful life of the Neapolitans and Sicilians to the south of Rome.

Piedmont

If we just took Piedmont and its most famous red wines, Barolo and Barbaresco, as examples then this grim-faced seriousness could be seen to be typical of the region's whole attitude to life. The Piedmontese are closed, mountain people, suspicious of outsiders. Charming, yes, but suspicious.

The best way to approach Piedmont is from the south. As you climb into the high Apennines above the Mediterranean, the roads become tortuous and pitted with use, the forest-covered mountain slopes only barely disguising the jagged rawness of the rock face as it careers down to the valley floor. But you keep on climbing, and all of a sudden the effort eases, the slopes drop back from the roadside and billowing waves of high vineyard take the place of rock and pine.

From **Diano d'Alba**, where they make succulent, soft Dolcetto, you can see into the heart of Piedmont. To the right are the gentle hills of **Asti**, coated with Muscat vines; ahead, as the road snakes down towards the plain, are the slopes of **Alba** with their Barbera vines and the more distinctive, steeper parcels of land which grow Nebbiolo to make Barbaresco; and way below to the left is a plain interrupted by eruptions of rock shaped like Indian tepees. This is **Barolo**, and the finest Nebbiolo vines clamber up

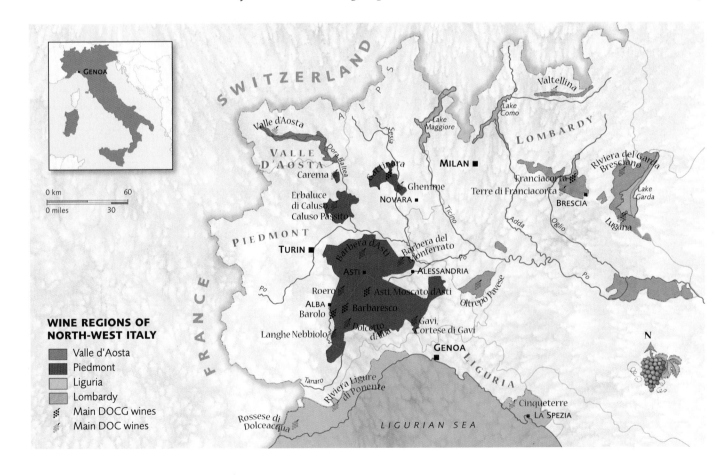

**WINE REGIONS OF
NORTH-WEST ITALY**

- Valle d'Aosta
- Piedmont
- Liguria
- Lombardy
- Main DOCG wines
- Main DOC wines

The Grapes

A region dominated by fine, long-lived reds, with just a few interesting whites.

NEBBIOLO is the star grape of the region. Powerful and long-lived, it makes wines redolent of tar, roses, blackberries, prunes, chocolate, licorice, tobacco and herbs. It reaches its peak in Barolo and Barbaresco.

BARBERA makes reds with high acidity and good tobaccoey, brown-sugary,

cherry and raisin fruit. It is much earlier-maturing than Nebbiolo.

DOLCETTO is lower in acidity (a rarity among Italian red grapes in this respect) and is often best young, when its succulent honeyed cherryish fruit can best be appreciated.

BONARDA is a licoricy variety which is quite mouthfilling and juicy.

MOSCATO(MUSCAT) makes light, low-alcohol semi-sparkling wines of tremendous freshness, bursting with apple and grape flavours.

ARNEIS is Piedmont's most distinguished white grape which makes lovely peachy, appley wines.

CORTESE is the grape that goes into white Gavi. It is attractively fresh but lacks any strong character.

ERBALUCE gives light, acidic whites which are quite attractive, though rare *passito* versions can be really exciting.

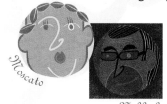

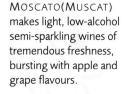

Moscato

Nebbiolo

the sides of these cones of rock topped by villages whose names are as familiar to Barolo lovers as the villages of Burgundy's Côte d'Or or Bordeaux's Médoc are to lovers of Burgundy or Bordeaux.

But Piedmont has for some years now been intent on proving its credentials as a world-class fine wine region, and so the producers make distinctions not only beween villages – Nebbiolo from the villages of Barolo and La Morra are softer, more aromatic, earlier-maturing wines than those of Castiglione Falletto, Monforte d'Alba and Serralunga d'Alba, because of differences in the soil – but also between vineyards. Nowadays the very top Barolos are single-vineyard wines bearing such names as Cannubi or Brunate from Barolo itself, or Rocche in La Morra, or Monprivato in Castiglione Falletto. There is no official classification of Grands Crus or the equivalent, but a *de facto* one is emerging.

The same phenomenon can be seen in **Barbaresco**, though to a lesser extent: Barbaresco has moved less far along the road to international

GAJA

SORÌ TILDÌN
1993

BARBARESCO
DENOMINAZIONE DI ORIGINE CONTROLLATA E GARANTITA
IMBOTTIGLIATO DA – BOTTLED BY GAJA, BARBARESCO, ITALIA, B.F.V. 224/CN
RED WINE, PRODUCT OF ITALY
750 mL 13%Vol   alc 13% by vol

Angelo Gaja, the leading name in Barbaresco, is an adherent of barriques for aging his wines. This use of small barrels is one of the ways in which he makes these traditionally tough wines drinkable younger.

BAROLO OLD AND NEW

Great Barolo used to be a mythical wine – mythical because you knew it existed, yet you hardly ever glimpsed it. No more: these days, winemaking standards have improved enormously. But these days, too, there are two camps in Barolo. Put simply, one camp (we'll call them modern, for want of a better word) favours aging the wine in new French oak barriques after a short fermentation. The result is wines that mature earlier and are more approachable young. The other camp (the traditionalists) stick to the big old Slavonian oak casks that have been used for aging Barolo for generations. Fermentations here are generally longer, and the wines are tougher young and need longer in bottle to come round.

Which is better? There's no easy answer, particularly since there are brilliant growers on both sides. Using French oak barriques certainly gives a more commercial flavour to the wine; and some producers prefer to compromise by using both methods, and blending the wines together.

ABOVE **The town and vineyards of Serralunga d'Alba, well known for its structured style of Barolo.**

MONFORTE   RUSSIA

BAROLO

DENOMINAZIONE DI ORIGINE CONTROLLATA E GARANTITA

BUSSIA SOPRANA

IMBOTTIGLIATO DAL VITICOLTORE NELL'AZIENDA AGRICOLA

PODERI
ALDO CONTERNO

PRODOTTO MONFORTE (Italia)
75cl ℮   B.F.V. 805/Cn   14,5% VOL

Conterno produces Barolo with a tendency towards the traditional. Though accessible when young, the wines need years to show their majesty.

Vines growing on pergolas above the village of Carema in the valley of the Dora Baltea river. The Nebbiolo grape, known locally as Picutener, is grown here.

Two leading producers of wines typical of the region. Barbera is the more assertive grape while Dolcetto, in comparison, is lighter.

are now aiming for wines that can be drunk early and will still age. Barbaresco (a DOCG wine like Barolo) is almost always a little gentler than Barolo. The tannin is still there, though the acidity is rarely so marked, and although the dark, shadowy richness of prunes and raisins steeped in brandy does linger, the fruit can be easier – more damson skins, raspberries and redcurrants, licorice, mint and chocolate, although there is often a slight dusty dryness cooling down the brightness of the flavours. Basic Barbaresco is released at two years old, Riserva at three and Riserva Speciale at four.

Lighter versions of these flavours can be found in **Nebbiolo d'Alba**, **Langhe Nebbiolo** and **Roero**; **Carema** is lighter and relatively refined. Also in northern Piedmont, in the Novara-Vercelli hills, **Gattinara** and **Ghemme**, which both include a small percentage of Bonarda, are softer.

But I mustn't forget Piedmont's other red wines. Barbera covers more of the vineyards than Nebbiolo and DOCs like **Barbera d'Alba**, **Barbera d'Asti** and **Barbera del Monferrato** are excellent, vibrant reds with a whiff of tobacco and resin and strong, rather brown-sugary fruit and a sour-raisins bite. Far more Barbera than Nebbiolo is barrique-aged – the top examples command similar prices to Barolo and Barbaresco.

Dolcetto, too, can be incredibly good. It's an early ripener, so can be planted where Nebbiolo won't work, and while it's moderately tannic it's not that high in acidity, which means that in comparison with Nebbiolo it's practically sweet – hence its name which means 'little sweet one'. There are seven DOCs but the best wines are mostly **Dolcetto d'Alba**; **Dogliani** and **Ovada** are also good. Almost every example you taste seems different, but when it's young it should be bursting with plummy fruit, honey and cream, and even angelica and cinnamon. A few producers make Dolcetto to age, but most is best young.

stardom, though one or two of its growers, notably Angelo Gaja, are already there.

But why are there these two DOCGs for the same grape, Nebbiolo, in the same region? And why, come to that, are there so many other Nebbiolo DOCs? What is it about Nebbiolo?

The answer is that this tough, late-ripening, surly grape gives red wines with flavours of tar and roses, blackberries and prunes, chocolate and licorice, tobacco and pine and herbs. Add to that huge concentration, complexity and longevity. That's Nebbiolo at its best, which effectively means Barolo and Barbaresco. Lesser wines, if they're good and ripe, can have some of the tar and roses fruit; if they're not ripe they just have green tannin and acidity. And the Nebbiolo is late-ripening: it takes its name from the word for fog, *nebbia*, which gives a clue to the weather conditions that prevail when it does eventually ripen. Plant it in the wrong site, with little sun, you'll get lean, astringent wine.

Straight Barolo is released at three years old, Riserva at four years old, Riserva Speciale at five. Light Barolos can be delicious at five years old, but top wines need ten, although some producers

There's also some Cabernet Sauvignon grown in Piedmont, but it's a minority grape here.

Piedmontese whites are a mixed bunch. The Moscato wines, **Asti** (DOCG) and **Moscato d'Asti** (DOCG), are delicious – wonderful, surging fruit blending apples and juicy, crunchy, green grapes. They're low in alcohol, too. The non-DOC versions tend to be less good, however.

Gavi is made from the Cortese grape; the wine is very dry and at its best has a stony, lemony streak of acidity. It's good young, but honestly isn't worth its price. **Erbaluce di Caluso** is similar but creamier, and **Arneis** can be delicious, with a peach and licorice flavour sharpened with apples. There is also some Chardonnay and Sauvignon Blanc grown here, and frequently treated to too much aging in new French oak.

Lombardy

Prosperous Lombardy has the huge industrial city of Milan as its focal point, and the wines tend to come from the furthest-flung corners of the region. In the south is **Oltrepò Pavese** – the name means 'across the Po from Pavia'. There are red, white and sparkling wines here, but not much gets exported except the fizz, which is generally Champagne method and based on the Pinot family (Nero, Grigio and Bianco). The reds, which are often quite decent, come from Barbera, Uva Rara or Bonarda (Croatina) grapes.

Valtellina is in the north, near the Swiss border. Subzones are Inferno, Grumello, Sassella and Valgella. The reds here are based on Nebbiolo, but the wines are seldom more than tough and uninspiring. **Franciacorta** produces Italy's most prestigious sparkling wine; the best of the areas's still wines are varietal Merlot, Cabernet, Pinot Nero or Chardonnay, or Bordeaux blends.

Lugana produces Trebbiano-based whites to the south of Lake Garda. It's one of Italy's better Trebbianos – the wine is full, soft and nutty.

Liguria

Liguria is a crooked finger of coastline and towering mountains. The vineyards are squashed into little patches of terrace where the unrelenting mountain slopes ease off for a few yards. The wines are scarce, to say the least, yet more than 100 grape varieties grow here. **Cinqueterre** is the most famous wine, dry, white and fresh at best. Red **Rossese di Dolceacqua** can be good, curiously heavy but perfumed, and **Ormeasco**, from the Dolcetto grape, can't compare to the Piedmontese versions but can be attractive. The most common whites are made from Pigato and Vermentino, though seldom seem to be well made.

Valle d'Aosta

Valle d'Aosta doesn't have much wine of its own: what vineyards it has are terraced on to the dizzying mountain slopes. Nebbiolo-based **Donnaz** is surprisingly good, and there are some Swiss grapes like Petite Arvine and Petite Rouge which are interesting. But it's the sweet and richly aromatic **Chambave Moscato** which is perhaps the finest wine these steep slopes have to offer.

Fontanafredda's Asti is typical of the style, displaying good intensity and a floral, grapy character.

The Food of the North-West

THE TIME TO visit Piedmont is autumn. That is, if you fancy almost every dish at almost every meal having white truffles shaved over it. Personally I can't get enough of Piedmontese white truffles, whether they're shaved over risotto, or pasta, or *fonduta*, the local version of cheese fondue.

Game, particularly wild boar, hare and venison, also features high on a Piedmontese cook's list of priorities. Roast kid is popular too: all rich, strong flavours that go well with the local red wines. Boiled meats of various kinds may be served together as *bollito misto* and eaten with *bagnet verd*, a sharp sauce that cuts through the richness.

Richness and strong flavours are the key-notes of Piedmontese cooking. *Bagna cauda* is a favourite, a mix of olive oil, anchovy and garlic into which raw vegetables are dipped. It's best with a glass of Barbera.

In the mountain regions there are high-altitude specialities like *bresaola* (wind-dried beef sliced wafer thin) and soups made more substantial by the addition of cheese, like *zuppa valpellinentza*; and Milan is the home of *risotto alla milanese*, cooked with bone marrow and meat stock and coloured and flavoured with saffron. Polenta is everywhere, even chocolate flavoured for pudding – which can be a big disappointment if you're expecting chocolate mousse.

Piedmontese white truffle

North-East Italy

If you want an example of the jumble of different identities and different nationalistic pressures that make up modern Italy, you only have to look at the north-east of the country. Only around the central town of Verona does it seem truly Italian: Alto Adige, a breathtaking mountain region to the north of Verona, is practically Austrian, and the locals are far more likely to greet you with the words 'Grüss Gott' than anything more Italian. Venice has always had an exotic tinge: for centuries its trade links were with Constantinople and the East, and rich silks and rare spices entered Europe through its port. The Friuli region up by Trieste is, in turn, heavily influenced by its Slovenian neighbours.

Inside this patchwork of influences are wildly differing styles of wine. But of all the Italian regions, this was the first to modernize its approach. And here, along with some fascinating indigenous grape varieties, the French and German classics have been grown for well over a century: Pinot Blanc (Bianco), Chardonnay, Riesling, Cabernet Franc, Cabernet Sauvignon, Merlot and Pinot Noir (Nero). But, gratifyingly, they do not swamp wines made from genuine local varieties like Tocai Friulano, Verduzzo, Lagrein and Refosco. Let's start at the top – in altitude terms anyway.

Alto Adige

This, at least, is what Italian-speakers call it. It's the Adige river which runs between dizzy mountain slopes towards the Adriatic. The German-speaking majority call it the Südtirol, and this long fringe of land reaching high into the Alps above Trento only became Italian when it was traded to Italy as the spoils of victory after World War I. Before that it had been part of Austria since 1363, and the majority of the inhabitants would be more than happy for this state of affairs to return.

As it is, it means that the consumer has to cope with wine labels that can list grape variety, village of production and name of DOC in either Italian or German. But it's made simpler by the fact that the wines are almost always sold by grape variety. There is one general DOC for the region, Alto Adige, plus a number of sub-zones, of which **Santa Maddalena** is the best known, made from the red Schiava or Vernatsch grape, which is also the most widely planted grape in the whole region. Alto Adige reds generally have a slightly grassy or smoky quality, depending on their grape variety, with often a hefty lick of acidity and piercing fruit. There's nothing remotely international about them, although some new oak is now being used for aging, which does give them a bit more polish. Reds ripen here because summers are hot in the valleys; Bolzano and Merano can even sometimes boast Italy's highest July and August temperatures. So the whites are often planted way up the hillsides, and have a clean lightness to them that is terribly attractive. Here I'm not so sure about the use of new oak: light Chardonnay aged in new oak tends to lose its individuality. There are also some stunning rich Muscats from here, particularly the rare, tea-rose-scented Rosenmuskateller. It's a shame that this grape is not planted more; but the good news about the Alto Adige is that increasingly producers are making an effort to match grape varieties with the most appropriate sites and there is a lot of excellent wine now being made – much of it varietal – including Pinot Grigio, Pinot Bianco, Chardonnay, Gewürztraminer, Sauvignon Blanc, Pinot Nero, Merlot and Cabernet Sauvignon.

Trentino

Politically paired with Alto Adige, Trentino is more truly Italian and looks south to the Mediterranean. Again, most wines are labelled by grape variety (the grapes are similar to those of Alto Adige), and there is one regional DOC and several smaller ones. **Teroldego Rotaliano** is often seen here, made from the Teroldego grape, and with a delicious light plums and cherries flavour; Schiava-based **Caldaro**, which stretches over the boundary into Alto Adige, is also good stuff, smoky and strawberryish. There's also

OPPOSITE **The view up the Adige Valley from above San Michele all'Adige in Trentino. The best wines come from the slopes rather than the floor of the valley.**

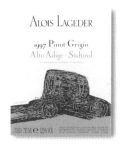

ALOIS LAGEDER
1997 Pinot Grigio
Alto Adige · Südtirol

Südtirol labels like this look both ways, to the region's dominant language, which is German, and to its political reality as a part of Italy.

The Grapes

There is a greater variety of grapes here than in any other Italian region.

Pinot Grigio

SCHIAVA is the main red grape of the Alto Adige. It has low tannin and acidity, but plenty of light strawberry fruit and a flavour of wood smoke.

LAGREIN makes both reds and rosés; the former have a tarry roughness matched by plums and chocolate richness.

CABERNET FRANC and CABERNET SAUVIGNON can both be good, though both tend to earthiness rather than blackcurrant.

TEROLDEGO makes lovely light reds full of cherries and a touch of chocolate.

PINOT NERO (NOIR) is usually rather light but has good plums and cherries fruit.

CHARDONNAY has sharp appley fruit sometimes softened by oak-aging.

PINOT BIANCO (BLANC) is light and creamy in Trentino-Alto Adige, but it can be quite complex in Friuli.

GEWÜRZTRAMINER may well have originated in the Alto Adige village of Tramin. Tends to be light, with fragrant fruity spice.

MÜLLER-THURGAU and SYLVANER can both produce lovely sharp nettles and green grape flavours.

MOSCATO wines can be sensational in Alto Adige: richly perfumed and bursting with flavour.

ROSENMUSKATELLER (MOSCATO ROSA) is increasingly rare, but worth searching out for its scent of tea-roses.

PINOT GRIGIO (GRIS) makes lightly spicy dry wines in Friuli.

TOCAI FRIULANO is a marvellous grape, nutty, smoky and spicy, with a touch of grassiness.

VERDUZZO makes nutty, soft whites with low acidity. When made sweet it is gloriously full of apricots and apples.

PROSECCO is used for soft, creamy sparkling wine in the Veneto.

MALVASIA can be peachy and nutty in Friuli.

RIESLING here is mainly the real Riesling Renano. The best wines have good structure and flowery or peachy fruit.

CORVINA makes the best reds in Valpolicella – all almonds and cherries.

TREBBIANO DI SOAVE is a much more characterful variety than the widely planted Trebbiano Toscana, which provides bulk and little flavour.

GARGANEGA gives good delicate lemony fruit to the better wines of Soave.

Legendary Friuli winemaker Mario Schiopetto is known for his high-quality, intensely concentrated white wines and his success with aromatic grape varieties.

some decent **spumante** made here, from Pinot Bianco and Chardonnay, but overall Trentino is lagging behind Alto Adige in quality terms, and has yet to learn that overproduction doesn't pay in the long run.

Friuli-Venezia-Giulia

Friuli is where the cool-fermented, fruit-fresh styles of Italian white wine began to make their mark as early as the 1970s. These days it is home to some very swanky growers indeed, making wines of immense subtlety and complexity, but also to some overproducing ones who happily coast along on the region's reputation as the source of many of Italy's best whites. Again, the wines are labelled by grape variety, and in addition there are seven DOCs.

Sounds complicated? Just remember that the best wines come from hillside sites, and that means the DOCs of **Collio Goriziano** (known simply as Collio) and **Colli Orientali**. Colli Orientali wines tend to be fuller than the delicate wines of Collio. The other four (**Friuli Latisana**, **Friuli Grave**, **Friuli Aquileia** and **Friuli Isonzo**) are all on the plain. The wines are generally fresh and very attractive, but the hillside sites

GRAPPA

Well, there's grappa and there's grappa. By which I mean that there's brilliantly good and there's also downright horrible – because when you're fermenting and distilling a brandy from the skins and pips dug out of the press after you've made the wine (and that's what grappa is) you can either aim for some fiery anonymous spirit that will keep the cold out and give you a colossal hangover, or you can aim for something with the character and aroma of the original grapes.

The best grappas have the latter. They're often stored by the producer in glass containers rather than wooden barrels before bottling in order to retain all that aroma – and it's the aroma that makes grappa special, not the alcohol. If you really want the best, look for one made from a single grape variety, like Nebbiolo or Brachetto, for a wonderfully delicate flavour.

will always give wines of more individuality and character. Friuli Isonzo in particular has seen a real upsurge in quality, particularly in the past five years or so.

What to look for? Try in particular the indigenous red Refosco, all smoke and acidity, and the nutty, spicy Tocai. And there's Verduzzo di Ramandolo, a fabulous dessert wine tasting of mint, apricot, apple skins and smoke. The region's more famous sweet wine, Picolit, is only sometimes as sweet or as special as its exalted price suggests.

The reason there is this multiplicity of grape varieties is simple: the region has been occupied at various times by Romans, Byzantines, Venetians and Habsburgs, and all brought their favourite vines with them. That adds up to quite a collection. Quality in Friuli would be higher across the board if there was more of a tradition of matching specific vines to specific sites, but on the whole, there isn't. The best growers do it to some extent (and there are a number of excellent producers in the region), but the local tradition is for each grower to offer as full a range as possible. That means a patch each of as many as possible of the following: Cabernet, Merlot, Chardonnay, Refosco, Sauvignon Blanc, Pinot Grigio, Tocai, Verduzzo, Malvasia, Pinot Bianco, Riesling Renano, Gewürztraminer, Ribolla, Picolit, Schiopettino, Pignolo, Tazzelenghe, Riesling Italico, Pinot Noir. Phew.

Veneto

Ah, Venice. In the Middle Ages Venice had no vineyards of its own – no agriculture of any sort, in fact. Instead it built its wealth, and its empire, on trade, and quite a lot of that trade was in wine. The wines in which her traders specialized were the sweet Malvasias and Muscats of the Aegean – Crete, Corfu, Cephalonia and many other places.

The Veneto, however, had been making wine for centuries. Nowadays it's a huge area, stretching from the Adriatic Sea inland to Lake Garda, from the high Dolomite peaks in the north down to the featureless flatlands of the Po Valley. Wine production is enormous and centres on three

wines: white Soave, red Valpolicella and Bardolino. Now, all these can be superb. Careful growers exist in all three appellations who are producing first-class wines of great style and personality, made usually from the original, and best, hilly central sections of the regions. All the appellations have expanded hugely into the surrounding plains, but if you want some idea of why the wines became so famous in the first place, it's these top wines, which will be labelled 'Classico' and come from a leading producer, which are usually the ones to go for.

This is a story of grapes and clones, so I hope you're concentrating.

Soave is a perfect example of how the original DOC laws of 1963 led to the utter debasement of certain Italian wines. The original Classico zone had been delimited in 1927 and consisted of less than 1500 hectares (3750 acres). Under the DOC regulations this was increased by another 5000 hectares (12,500 acres) in 1968. Were these good vineyards? No, they were not; they were on the plain, whereas the original Classico zone vineyards were on hillsides. In addition, replanting in these years was with the Trebbiano

If this looks like a tiring job, it is. These men are picking high-trained Corvina grapes for Valpolicella, in the vineyard of Masi, in Gargagnano.

Single-vineyard Soave like this, from a top producer like Pieropan, will be a revelation to anyone who thinks Soave has to be dull and dilute.

The best Valpolicellas are generally those from single vineyards, like this from Allegrini. They can have considerable character and a pleasing bite.

Toscano variety – an inferior, high-yielding clone of the Trebbiano di Soave, which was mostly there before. Other varieties include Garganega, Chardonnay and Pinot Blanc, but any Soave based on Trebbiano di Toscano will have nil personality. And there'll be too much of it. That's why most Soave is dull, dull, dull. Yet good growers work wonders with Garganega and Trebbiano di Soave to produce delicate, nutty wines with surprising depth. There's also Recioto di Soave, a sweet white wine made from dried grapes (see box opposite).

The story in **Valpolicella** is similar: here overproduction, an over-extension of the vineyard, low prices and the limiting of the proportion of the characterful Corvina grape in the blend have reduced what should be a delicious light red with a bitter cherry flavour to a dilute wine of no interest. The other grapes, Molinara and Rondinella, add acidity and bulk respectively. Yet here again there is some wonderful Valpo-

licella about, usually labelled 'Classico'; there is also some first-class vino da tavola made entirely from Corvina grapes. 'Ripasso' on the label indicates that wine has been refermented on the skins and lees of Amarone wines (see box opposite); this adds an exciting sweet-sour dimension to the wine.

Bardolino, too, has suffered from extra territory being tacked on to the Classico zone, although Bardolino even at its best is light and simple, hardly more than a rosé. The grapes are the same as for Valpolicella, and if you get a good one you get a lovely rush of fresh, simple cherry fruit with just a twist of bitterness at the end. The even paler version is called **Bardolino Chiaretto**. All Bardolino must be drunk young.

The Veneto doesn't consist of just these wines, though often they seem to get all the attention. Soave has two lookalikes in **Bianco di Custoza** and **Gambellara**, both of which can be attractive, providing they're fresh. In fact, the

The Food of the North-East

THIS IS WHERE Austria and Italy overlap. In the Alto Adige, where nobody worries about calories or cholesterol, the food is basically Austrian, and shades into Italy in Trentino. Both regions have a great fondness for meat, preferably smoked, stewed, marinated or packed into sausages.

Polenta

There is excellent freshwater fish from the lakes and rivers, but it's meat – pork, beef, venison or lamb – that gets the popular vote. *Knödel*, little bread-based dumplings, are served with it, as is *sauerkraut*. Fresh Alto Adige reds with plenty of acidity are just the thing to cope with all that rich meat.

Cabbage and potatoes are the main vegetables here – it's not really vegetable-growing country – but there are good apples, pears, cherries and plums, and these can be pressed into service with meat dishes.

Pastries – baked, fried, filled with jam or fruit – are a great favourite at any time. The amazing thing is that after meals like this the locals manage to walk up mountains.

Further east, in Friuli, *gnocchi* take over from *knödel*, and they're made with potato. Polenta (made from maize flour and water) accompanies everything (except *gnocchi*), even being made sweet for desserts, and perhaps stuffed with prunes. There's a sensational variety of fish and shellfish here, too. Oysters, scallops, spider crabs, sardines, tuna, eels,

turbots, scorpion fish and a host of others appear on the fishmonger's slab. A well-chilled Tocai from Friuli's Collio is a good accompaniment. Meat often takes the form of hare or venison stews, served with polenta, or San Daniele ham. This is very sweet, air-cured ham. It's totally delicious and perfect with a glass of creamy, soft Prosecco.

Venice is rice country, the home of risotto and that other local favourite, *risi e bisi*, rice and peas. Rice may be combined with the wealth of seafood from the Adriatic – squid, mussels, mullet, bass and many

others. Soave goes well with most Venetian fish dishes. Meat is often poultry but liver is also especially popular: *fegato alla Veneziana* is calves' liver with onions.

Sweet cakes and biscuits abound, as well: *crema fritta alla Veneziana* is squares of thick custard, deep fried in breadcrumbs; and no *carnevale* would be complete without *fritole alla Veneziana*, deep-fried little offerings of flour, eggs, sugar, nuts and candied peel. Again, Prosecco is delicious with these types of sweets.

Guia, near Valdobiaddene, on the Strada del Vino Prosecco in Veneto. All you need is a pecan tree and you have the basic ingredients for a perfect Bellini.

addition of up to three per cent of Tocai Friulano in Bianco di Custoza can give it extra breadth and richness than basic Soave. **Breganze** has some rather good peppy whites, some deliciously blackcurrant reds and a wine called Acininobili from dynamic producer Maculan which is so creamy and honeyed and sweet it could almost be a dessert Chardonnay. Made from Vespaiolo grapes affected by noble rot, it is one of Italy's most esteemed sweet wines. **Colli Euganei**, in the sheer hills south of Padova, produces an array of wines, still and sparkling, which for the most part are light and unexceptional. Way above the ordinary, however, is the Vignalta estate, whose Cabernet Riserva and Merlot/Cabernet Gemola have become rivals to Italy's best in their categories. In **Conegliano** the Prosecco grape gives gentle but refreshing and scented sparkling wine. This, not Champagne, is the correct fizz to use in Bellini cocktails. Superiore di Cartizze, or simply Cartizze, from a vineyard area of that name, is the most refined. Most of the rest of the region is concerned with producing quaffing wine. The two main regions for this are **Piave** and **Lison-Pramaggiore**. Much of the produce is light, unmemorable Cabernet, Merlot and Pinot Bianco. Raboso is gutsier, and Verduzzo is nutty, low-acid, ultra-soft white. There's Tocai too, sharp yet also nutty, and sometimes ever so slightly spicy.

Masi are a driving force in Valpolicella. This wine is a classic Amarone with a smoothness allied to richness – it's often very dry with a characteristic bitter finish.

RECIOTO AND AMARONE

This is your chance to taste the sort of wine the Ancient Greeks drank. Dried grape wines were once produced all over the Mediterranean, their advantages being that they were lusciously sweet in an age when sweetness was rare, and that they kept much better than other wines. Nowadays such wines survive only patchily, in the *passito* wines and Vin Santo made in parts of Italy, in the straw wines (the grapes are picked and dried on straw) sometimes found in corners of France, Austria and other parts of the Mediterranean.

The Recioto and Amarone wines of Soave and Valpolicella in the Veneto are among these survivors. You make them by picking ripe, healthy grapes and hanging them to dry under the rafters over the winter. They shrivel almost to raisins – and that's when you crush and ferment them. They make just about the thickest, stickiest must imaginable, and they turn into magnificently sweet, rich wine. If you want to know what Recioto della Valpolicella tastes like, imagine a cross between vintage port and a classy northern Rhône Syrah, mixed with raisins, honey and bitter cherries; Recioto di Soave is stuffed with citrus peel and raisiny flavours, all bound together with acidity – because the acidity is concentrated by the drying process, too.

Sometimes the winemaker will take things a stage further and ferment a Recioto della Valpolicella to dryness: what you get then is Amarone, which has the same cherries and raisins and honey of its sweet cousin, but with a pronounced bitter cherry dryness. At its best it's one of the great reds of the world.

Grapes being dried for Recioto di Soave.

Central Italy

Lovers of Tuscany talk of Michelangelo and Botticelli, of the effortless rise and fall of the Tuscan hills and the columns of cypress trees stalking the horizon. In Umbria there is the huge rocky outcrop of Orvieto; in Lazio the vine-clad Alban hills above Rome where the Pope takes refuge from the summer heat. In Marche the beach stretches almost unhindered along the region's entire length, and behind it the hills rise towards the Apennines. Then there is mountainous Abruzzo and flat, gourmandizing Emilia-Romagna. Central Italy is hugely varied. But it is also the home of the modern wine renaissance, which began, appropriately enough, in Tuscany.

Tuscany

The heart of Tuscany's wine regions, indeed the heart of Tuscany, is the hauntingly beautiful hinterland of twisting, dipping hill valleys between Florence and Siena. These are the Chianti hills, and the site of the Classico region of Chianti, although other parts of the Chianti region – Montalbano, Colli Fiorentini, Rufina, Colli Senesi, Colline Pisane, Colli Aretini and just plain Chianti – stretch out much further. To see why quality is so mixed in Chianti and indeed why a wine renaissance in Tuscany was so necessary, we'll have to go back to the Middle Ages.

That was when some of today's leading producers – notably the Frescobaldi and Antinori families – came on to the wine scene. Florence was the banking centre of Europe, and these families were bankers and merchants. It was natural for them to do what the Antinoris did in 1385, and join the Arte dei Vinattieri, the wine sellers' guild. While they owned large tracts of land they didn't farm it all themselves: under a system called *mezzadria* the land would be leased out in return for half the produce; this was how much of Tuscany was farmed right up until the system collapsed in the 1950s and 1960s. When it fell apart, largely because of the flight of labour to the towns, there was nothing to replace it. The land was neglected, and vines and other crops were often all planted together. Italian wine was at its lowest ebb. Into this wasteland, in 1963, came the DOC laws.

In Chianti the DOC did little except codify existing practices. These included the admixture of a large proportion of white Trebbiano and Malvasia grapes. White grapes in red wine? Doesn't sound a good idea, does it? And it wasn't. It was done partly in an attempt to soften the natural

WINE REGIONS OF CENTRAL ITALY

- Emilia-Romagna
- Tuscany
- Umbria
- Lazio
- Abruzzo
- Marche
- Main DOCG wines
- Main DOC wines

0 km 50
0 miles 25 50

N

ROME

PIACENZA
Colli Piacentini
PARMA
Lambrusco
Parma
Po
EMILIA-ROMAGNA
MODENA
BOLOGNA
Sangiovese di Romagna
Trebbiano di Romagna
Canina
PISA
Arno
Chianti Rufina
Albana di Romagna
RIMINI
ADRIATIC SEA
Vernaccia di San Gimignano
FLORENCE
Pomino
Chianti
Chianti Classico
SIENA
AREZZO
Verdicchio dei Castelli di Jesi
ANCONA
Rosso Cònero
Rosso Piceno
Bolgheri
TUSCANY
Vino Nobile di Montepulciano
Brunello di Montalcino
ELBA
Ombrone
PERUGIA
Verdicchio di Matelica
Torgiano Rosso Riserva
MARCHE
Morellino di Scansano
UMBRIA
Orvieto
Sagrantino di Montefalco
Est! Est!! Est!!!
LAZIO
Montepulciano d'Abruzzo
Trebbiano d'Abruzzo
L'AQUILA
Tiber
ROME
Frascati
ABRUZZO

The vineyards of Castello di Volpaia high in the hills of Chianti. The finest wines in this region come from the slopes.

One of the pace-setters in the Chianti Classico zone. This wine is characterized by a clean, elegant and spicily perfumed fruit.

acidity and austerity of Sangiovese (particularly underripe, overcropped Sangiovese) and partly because the white vines were there and needed using up; but it was no way to make serious red wine. The recipe was supposedly based on one evolved by Baron Ricasoli in the mid-19th century; Ricasoli must have turned in his grave to see his work on revitalizing Chianti so distorted. (He had only advocated that white grapes be used in wine meant for drinking young; the DOC laws included them in all Chianti.)

The next few years saw mass planting of vineyards in Tuscany; and yes, to have proper vineyards at last, instead of a mix of wheat and olives and vines, was a step in the right direction. The trouble was that the clones that were used were inferior high-yielding ones that produced poor wine, but plenty of it. It became clear to the best producers that Tuscan wine, under the new DOC dispensation, was going nowhere fast. So they decided to bypass the law.

The result was a whole new breed of top-quality wines, often referred to as super-Tuscans, which adopted French techniques (like aging the wine in small new French oak barriques) and French grape varieties like Cabernet Sauvignon. In 1984 Chianti was promoted to DOCG and the regulations tightened and modernized; three of Tuscany's other top reds, Brunello di Montalcino, Vino Nobile di Montepulciano and Carmignano, are also DOCG. But it took a complete reworking of Italy's wine laws, in the form of the 1992 Goria Law, to establish Tuscany (and indeed the whole of Italy) on a more logical basis. Now Bolgheri has a DOC, and Sassicaia (see box on p.124) has its own DOC within that. All the super-Tuscan vini da tavola are required to slot into either a DOC or an IGT, and both categories have been tailored to fit them.

TUSCAN RED WINES

Let's get back to the hills of Chianti to start our tour proper. The grapes now permitted for Chianti are at least 90 per cent Sangiovese and

This super-Tuscan from Tenuta San Guido has done a great deal to gain credibility for Italy's wines abroad.

Olive oil, the everyday oil of the ancient world which was used in lamps as well as in cooking, has become an expensive status symbol.

Low acidity is a sign of quality and at the top of the range is Extra Virgin olive oil with acidity of less than 1.5 per cent. It requires careful handling of the olives, which are picked slightly unripe for oil purposes: acidity rises as the olives mature. Youth is also important, and olive oil is best consumed while very fresh, preferably within a year of pressing.

Tuscany produces pungent, peppery oils which have the reputation of being the best. And, while it's possible to pay as much as for good wine, price is not an automatic guide to quality.

Canaiolo, and at most ten per cent of other grapes, which in practice often means Cabernet, with perhaps a dash of Syrah or Merlot; Chianti made with 100 per cent Sangiovese is at last legal. Winemaking has improved dramatically, and the wines are rounder and more concentrated – thanks in part to better clones in the vineyard. There's even a programme called Chianti 2000 which aims to replant the old high-yielding clones with better, smaller-berried ones.

The above applies to the better producers, who are concentrated in **Chianti Classico** and **Chianti Rufina**. Basic Chianti without a regional name attached is still a pretty basic wine – no longer sold in straw-covered *fiaschi*, it's true, but remarkably undistinguished.

Bolgheri is now home to some top reds, including Cabernet-based Ornellaia and all-Merlot Masseto, made by Piero Antinori's brother Ludovico. The DOC covers red, white and rosé. South of Bolgheri, in the coastal province of **Maremma**, other new super-Tuscan stars are emerging, mainly around the sheltered Suvereto.

Nearby **Scansano** also has its share as well as **Morellino di Scansano**, a chunky red based on Sangiovese.

In spite of the inroads of Cabernet, Sangiovese is still the main red grape of Tuscany. It's capable of making everything from pitifully underpowered, lean reds to wines that will age for decades and come up tasting powerfully of cherries and prunes and tea. Sangiovese has acidity, and it has power, but it doesn't always have flesh: it only gains that when it's planted in the right place. It needs warmth: it's not found much north of the Arno river for the simple reason that it gets too chilly there. The place where it makes its richest wine is **Montalcino**.

Brunello is simply a synonym for Sangiovese, as are Prugnolo or Sangioveto. So **Brunello di Montalcino** is 100 per cent Sangiovese. It was brought to prominence by Ferrucio Biondi-Santi in 1888, and it's held the limelight ever since: high quality, high price. But it's not a big region: there are only 126 producers here, and the diversity of mesoclimates mean that styles and quality

THE SUPER-TUSCAN REVOLUTION

When you get a situation like the one in Tuscany in the late 1960s – a law that compels you to make wine that will never be taken seriously abroad, while other countries like France are surging ahead with new research and higher quality – it is only the most defiant, individualistic producers who can force change. And they did.

Marchese Piero Antinori of Chianti, his winemaker Giacomo Tachis, and Marchese Nicolo Incisa della Rochetta over at Bolgheri on the coast, took the lead. They experimented with winemaking techniques being used in Bordeaux: better extraction of tannin and flavour from the grapes, the use of small new French oak barriques for aging, and earlier bottling. They also started using

blends of grapes that were not possible under the Chianti DOC regulations. This was the original recipe for Tignanello, Antinori's pace-setting red, released as a vino da tavola with the 1971 vintage. The first vintage, 1968, of Incisa della Rochetta's Sassicaia Cabernet Sauvignon was released at much the same time; this was labelled as vino da tavola because no DOC existed at Bolgheri.

Both these wines sold at high prices. The packaging, the producer's name all spoke of status and quality. And the fashion spread. Soon grapes that were not permitted under the DOC regulations, notably Cabernet Sauvignon, were being planted. Sometimes Cabernet was blended with Sangiovese; sometimes it was

made as a varietal. The number of these non-DOC wines – dubbed super-Tuscans – multiplied. White wines joined the party, too, usually in the form of Chardonnay, which although fashionable wasn't always successful.

Super-Tuscans spread even beyond Tuscany, to Piedmont, even the Veneto. Criticism began to mount: Cabernet Sauvignon and other foreign 'invaders' were taking over Italian wine. But then things took another turn. The close study of winemaking and of their vines by these leading producers brought them to a new appreciation of their native varieties. Nowadays the foreign invaders are part of the Tuscan wine scene, but they're not the whole of it, or even the major part.

vary. So it's not the most reliable of great reds; but at its best it is superb, with great complexity and depth and an almost viscous richness of prunes and licorice, meaty savouriness and bitter black chocolate, all held together by acidity and tannin. It has by law to have at least four years aging in the cellar before release, and producers who want to bottle a younger, lighter wine – a sort of baby brother – can call it **Rosso di Montalcino**. These can be more modern in style and don't need the five to ten years that a Brunello needs in bottle to come round.

Tuscany's other star red, the immodestly named **Vino Nobile di Montepulciano**, also has a 'lesser' DOC, for the same reason; it's called **Rosso di Montepulciano**, and it's the solution for producers afraid of aging their wines too long in wood. Here again Sangiovese rules, though only the best producers attain the elegance or finesse of the best Chianti or Brunello. The best have a ripe cherry-berry fruit matched with a creamy oak softness, a good lick of acidity, plus blackcurrant, cedar and dry sandalwood.

Carmignano never seems to attract the same attention as the others, even though it can be exceedingly good. It's a mix of Sangiovese and Cabernet and has lots of blackcurranty fruit with a characteristically tea-like edge from the Sangiovese. There's also some white and rosé.

TUSCAN WHITE WINES

The whites, leaving aside the super-Tuscans which tend to be made from international varieties like Chardonnay, are mostly variations on a theme of Trebbiano. There's some Vernaccia, particularly from **San Gimignano**, which can blend a peppery edge with a surprisingly nutty fruit and a lick of honey, and there's some Pinot Bianco, blended with Chardonnay and Trebbiano in

Two noble Tuscan reds. Legendary producer Biondi-Santi claims to have created Brunello di Montalcino, and its reputation for longevity and the Falvo brothers of Avignonesi led the revival of Montepulciano as one of Tuscany's best zones.

'We drank Lambrusco from a black bottle which held two litres ... The wine was deep purple and it seethed in the glasses with its own natural gas.'

ERIC NEWBY, *LOVE AND WAR IN THE APENNINES*, HODDER & STOUGHTON

The Grapes

The wines of central Italy are largely based on Sangiovese and Trebbiano.

Sangiovese

Cabernet Sauvignon

SANGIOVESE is the main red grape of central Italy. Its name means 'Blood of Jove' and at its best it's superb – but it must be of a small-berried clone, not the large-berried ones that were planted in the 1970s. Typically it has a delicate bouquet of cherries, both black and red, a flavour of plums, prunes and tea, with noticeable acidity. It has various synonyms, including Prugnolo and Brunello. It is the grape of Chianti, Brunello di Montalcino and Vino Nobile di Montepulciano.

CABERNET SAUVIGNON is now allowed for many DOC and DOCG wines, and seems brilliantly suited to Tuscany. Its flavours here are deep and complex but also fresh and blackcurranty; it blends superbly with Sangiovese.

CANAIOLO is not particularly exciting, adding neither structure nor aroma to the Chianti blend; Cabernet or Merlot is now more popular for filling out the Sangiovese.

MERLOT is being used by some producers to make wines in the mould of serious Pomerol. Elsewhere it's blended successfully with Sangiovese or Cabernet.

MONTEPULCIANO is the main red grape of Abruzzo; it has quite solid plummy, herby fruit.

LAMBRUSCO is used for the wine of the same name and has light, fresh raspberry flavours.

TREBBIANO is the ubiquitous white grape of central Italy. It's seldom exciting, although it can, if handled with care, make good, fresh, nutty whites.

MALVASIA has a good, soft, nutty, smoky quality, but fades quickly.

GRECHETTO is remarkably characterful for a central Italian white grape, with smoky apple and greengage fruit.

VERNACCIA can give crisp fruit with an attractively bitter edge.

VERDICCHIO has a fresh lemony flavour with good acidity and can be quite full. Poor ones taste of glue, although standards are pretty high these days.

VIOGNIER is not widely grown but displays its usual aromatic apricot fruit.

Teruzzi & Puthod, nestling in the rolling hills of San Gimignano, has one of the world's most fashionable and recognizable wine labels.

DOC **Pomino**. At its best Trebbiano is dry and neutral; sometimes it's given some oak-aging, which doesn't really suit it. The trendy Viognier is now being planted in some parts of Tuscany.

There's another wine, too, for which Tuscany is famous, though it is widely made outside the region, and that is Vin Santo. It's a dried grape wine in a similar mould to the Recioto of the Veneto, and the name means 'holy wine': it was traditionally racked off its lees during Holy Week, when atmospheric pressure was reckoned to be most suitable. It can be sweet, semi-sweet or dry, and Trebbiano and Malvasia grapes are used; quality varies but the best are delicious.

Umbria

There's a heady mix of wine styles here, from Orvieto to Torgiano to Sagrantino to some exciting new-wave reds that are popping up so fast it's hard to keep track of them. But the grapes provide a link with Tuscany: there's a thread of Sangiovese running through the reds, and Trebbiano through the whites; Trebbiano isn't usually desperately exciting, but good **Orvieto**, where the Trebbiano is blended with Verdello, Grechetto, Drupeggio and Malvasia, can be full, nutty and smoky, with a touch of honey and some peachy freshness. Can, but usually isn't; it's nearly all made dry, fresh and standardized these days, and

characterful wines are rare. Varietal **Grechetto** wines are more interesting, with full, licoricy, apple and greengage fruit and a touch of smoke.

Sangiovese-based reds include **Torgiano** (where there's also some crisp white) which is round and mellow, though the Riserva is oaky and smooth like creamed coconut, but backed up with masses of almost sweet fruit. Most of the DOC is owned by Lungarotti – a prime mover in the resurrection of much of Umbria.

Rosso di Montefalco is a mix of Sangiovese and Sagrantino; there's also **Sagrantino di Montefalco** which is, well, Sagrantino. Both are splendidly rip-roaring wines, plummy, strawberryish, raisiny and tobaccoey all in turns. Sometimes they're made sweet, and the damson and plum and chocolate richness, balanced by acidity and tannin, can be very exciting.

The new-wave reds are as diverse as they are in Tuscany, but tend to be gutsy and quite solid with good aging potential. Pieve del Vescovo and La Palazzola are two estates to watch out for.

Lazio

There's yet more Trebbiano in Lazio. It's primarily a white wine region, and **Frascati** is its standard-bearer, based on Malvasia and Trebbiano – and, as usual, the less Trebbiano the better the wine. Good Frascati can be delicious, though, with a flavour that veers between apples and nuts, with a distinctive sour-cream nose. It should be drunk as young as possible; even so, too many bottles taste tired and stale.

There's the almost always inferior **Est! Est!! Est!!!**, which hardly ever has the rounded almond and angelica flavour of which it is capable.

There are a few exceptional whites from **Castelli Romani** and **Colli Albani** but there's greater potential for reds as shown by Falesco in **Montefiascone** to the north. There are also some interesting Cabernet and Merlot blends.

Marche

A real transition in quality has occurred here in the last ten years and Marche is now home to some of Italy's best whites. There's some good

BALSAMIC VINEGAR

This is the apotheosis of the Trebbiano grape, the transformation of one of the world's least characterful grapes into something as close to heaven as unfermented juice ever gets. Yet strictly speaking it's not vinegar at all.

Balsamic vinegar is what you get when you boil Trebbiano must and age it in very small barrels for several years, moving it from barrel to barrel in a way reminiscent of the solera system (see box on p.145). Over the years it oxidizes and its flavour deepens; and the different woods used for the barrels – cherrywood, ash, mulberry, chestnut – all add their own character.

The best balsamic vinegar comes from Modena, though it is produced all over Italy. At three or four years old the vinegar is still thin and runny, but with age it thickens and darkens, until a 20-year-old balsamic vinegar is thick as cream and dark as tar. It can even be found over 50 years old. Economics dictate that few of us are likely to have anything that old in our kitchens. But the more you pay, the better the vinegar is likely to be.

white Verdicchio with lovely smoky apples fruit and a touch of honey. There are two DOCs, **Castelli di Jesi** and **Matelica**, of which the former is the most commonly seen.

Of the reds, **Rosso Piceno** and **Rosso Cònero** are the most interesting: they're both Sangiovese plus Montepulciano, though Rosso Cònero is mostly Montepulciano, Rosso Piceno mostly Sangiovese. They're good strong reds, more or less biting according to how much Sangiovese is in the blend, and more or less plummy, raisiny and herby according to how much Montepulciano there is.

Emilia-Romagna

Emilia-Romagna is mixed as far as quality is concerned; quantity is its strongest suit. A lot of the white vines are Trebbiano, and make **Trebbiano di Romagna**; a lot of the red ones are **Lambrusco**, and make the high-acidity, sharply refreshing, raw raspberry-flavoured wine of the same name. Worth seeking out is good, dry **Lambrusco di Sorbara**. One or two other grapes can be used and there is even white Lambrusco.

Other wines here include varietal Barbera and Bonarda, which are often made slightly frothing and can be attractive young; **Colli Piacentini** is home to some good dark, grapy wines from these varieties. Red **Gutturnio**, also Barbera- and Bonarda-based, can mix licorice with good acidity and raspberry freshness. And then there's **Albana di Romagna**, pleasant but hardly distinguished white. In the **Sangiovese di Romagna** DOC hillside pockets planted to low-yielding old vines provide wines of real class.

Abruzzo

Head down to Abruzzo and the same grapes – Trebbiano and Montepulciano – are responsible for whites and reds respectively. The first is usually adequate, sometimes nutty; the second, of which there is an increasing number of good examples, can be full of strong plummy fruit matched by chewiness and acidity. Don't confuse it with Vino Nobile di Montepulciano: in Abruzzo it's a grape, the other is a town in Tuscany.

Falesco's Montiano is among the top Merlots made in Italy and shows the potential of reds in Montefiascone in Lazio.

This stylish wine from Umani Ronchi, a well-known producer on the Adriatic coast, shows how Verdicchio is blossoming into central Italy's most promising white variety.

The Food of Central Italy

TUSCAN FOOD tends to be prepared simply: meat, including the superb beef of the native Chianina cattle from the Val di Chiana, is grilled in the form of *bistecca alla fiorentina* and served with white Tuscan beans (*fagioli*). A glass of Sangiovese-based wine is the perfect accompaniment. Game, especially wild boar and hare, is also popular. Hare may be turned into sauce and eaten with pasta as *pappardella alla lepre*.

Olive oil is the universal dressing: *pappa di pomodoro* is a delicious mush of stale bread with fresh tomatoes, basil and lashings of olive oil. Bread is used too in *ribollita*, a hearty vegetable soup made with the addition of white beans, olive oil and chunks of *pane toscano*, traditionally served reheated.

Tuscany is also home to some of the country's finest pecorino cheese.

Umbrian food again is simple, though they're fond of truffles, especially the black variety, *tartufo nero*.

In Rome, meat may be just roasted with rosemary, especially if it's milk-fed lamb, *abbacchio*, or kid, *capretto*. But there are hefty stews as well, of oxtail or beef featuring wine, tomatoes and garlic. Artichokes are a Roman speciality: those served *alla romana* are flavoured with mint, parsley and garlic.

Emilia-Romagna, by contrast, has some of the richest cooking in all Italy. No pig is safe here: every part of its anatomy can be turned into sausages and salamis. Parma ham comes from here, as does parmesan cheese, and the best balsamic vinegar in Italy.

Southern Italy

This is the Mezzogiorno, a scorchingly hot, blindingly bright land where the grapes used to shrivel on the vine in the midday heat and the best thing you could say about the wine was that it was wet.

No longer. This is the source of some of Italy's most exciting new wines, like the reds of the Salento Peninsula. They're found only patchily – this is still a stupefyingly poor region, where for generations people have been fleeing the land in search of a better life – but when the wines are good they're very, very good.

Molise

Molise, which isn't that far south, is not in the lead when it comes to creating splendid new wines. The main grapes here are Trebbiano and Montepulciano, and **Biferno** is the main DOC. But some of Molise's few good wines have remained outside the DOC.

The Grapes

The grape varieties of southern Italy were often brought over by the Greeks.

NERO D'AVOLA can give wines of great richness and complexity.

MONTEPULCIANO has lots of sturdy plummy fruit.

FRAPPATO gives fruity Sicilian reds with a taste of berries.

AGLIANICO has good chocolate and licorice fruit.

NEGROMARA has spicy, herby flavours.

MALVASIA NERA has an attractive chocolaty taste.

PRIMITIVO produces rather rustic, foursquare red in the main.

CATARRATTO gives quite spicy, full wine.

INZOLIA has good aroma and best examples have a nuttiness.

GRECO DI TUFO has light almondy fruit.

GRILLO is a relatively neutral white grape.

FIANO DI AVELLINO has a honey and pear-skins flavour.

Villa Matilde leads the way in the revived DOC of Falerno del Massico. Its label harks back to the days of the famed Roman wine Falernian. Again, on an ancient theme, the Aglianico grape was brought to Italy by the Ancient Greeks.

Campania

This beautiful region round the Bay of Naples, and beneath Mount Vesuvius with its crumbly volcanic soil, was the home of Falernian, the most famous wine of the ancient world (see p.12). There's now a newish DOC, **Falerno del Massico**, which is supposed to be a revival of its glories. There are now some very good Aglianico-based reds from **Taurasi** and elsewhere – Aglianico has a wonderful chocolate and licorice richness with high acidity to match.

Lacryma Christi del Vesuvio is less interesting. The white **Fiano di Avellino** is better, with a honey and pear-skins taste, and white **Greco di Tufo** has a good almondy taste, and these two whites are worth seeking out if only because they're made from the sort of ancient grape varieties in which southern Italy abounds.

Basilicata

The most interesting grape here is the red Aglianico, which the Greeks brought to Italy with them and which can be found dotted all over the south. In Basilicata the main spot for it is Mount Vulture; **Aglianico del Vulture** can achieve an amazing chocolate richness, the bittersweet bite of almonds and the perfume of green peppercorns, with a stark southern dustiness and a streak of acidity.

Calabria

More vines of Greek origin can be found in Calabria: Gaglioppo, for example, which produces sturdy reds at **Cirò**. Aglianico and Cabernet are also becoming more important. **Greco di Bianco**, a dessert wine made from partly dried grapes, has strong personality and sweet orange-peel fruit.

Puglia

Puglia has long had massive production of grapes. Some are table grapes, but a great deal of wine pours out of here as well, and most of it isn't much good. The vermouth industry in the north of Italy looks to Puglia for its base wine, and by the time it's been doctored with herbs and other flavourings it presumably doesn't matter too much what it tasted like in the first place. But Puglia does have a remarkable centre of quality in the Salento Peninsula, where the Negromaro grape, plus some Malvasia Nera (both are black, as the names suggest) make reds of an intense bitter chocolate and herbs flavour. Of the eight DOCs of the region the ones we mostly see are **Brindisi**, **Copertino** and **Salice Salentino**.

There's also some Primitivo in Puglia; this is the same grape as California's Zinfandel, and as more New World winemakers trickle into the south (we're already seeing the first fruits of their work) we are beginning to see Primitivos that are worthy of the grape.

We're also starting to see blends of southern Italian grapes with international varieties like Chardonnay and Sauvignon Blanc and this, too, could be a way forward. Chardonnay and Sauvignon on their own often lack acidity and aroma, even if the vineyards are planted at high altitude, but they can be attractive in a blend.

Sardinia

Wines in every conceivable style, from the sherryish **Vernaccia di Oristano**, to light, dry **Vernaccia** made in a more standard mould, are produced in Sardinia. Dry, white **Vermentino di Sardegna** is fashionable and can be wonderfully aromatic, full and stylish. Reds from Cannonau can be good, particularly when made sweet and plummy. Other premium reds are based on Cabernet and Carignan, known here as Carignano.

Sicily

Sicily is the home of Marsala and, from even smaller islands nearby, Moscato di Pantelleria and Malvasia delle Lipari, all of them usually sweet and sticky. **Marsala** has a distinctive smoky, acidic tang and veers between nuttily dry and syrupy sweet; **Moscato di Pantelleria** is a dark, gooey Muscat from a tiny island within a giant's spit of Africa, and **Malvasia delle Lipari** is a lovely raisins, brown sugar and peaches sweet wine from islands just north-west of Messina. But there is also good table wine from Sicily

itself: deep plums and chocolate reds, and substantial but fresh whites from white grapes like Catarratto, Inzolia and Grillo, and reds like Nero d'Avola and Frappato. Cabernet Sauvignon and Chardonnay – whether used varietally or in blends – are found in some of the best producers' wines. The key to better flavour and freshness in Sicily is improved winemaking – usually this amounts to nothing more elaborate than cool fermentation and perhaps, for the whites, some skin contact before fermentation. The result can be a transformation of what was pretty ordinary into something remarkably attractive. Sicily can no longer be dismissed in terms of wine production. Its early pioneers for quality are now being joined by a mounting wave of others.

Vines planted in the black volcanic soil on the southern slopes of Mount Etna, near Nicolosi, Sicily. This soil is exceptionally good for vine growing.

SPAIN

Spain to me conjures up pictures of a harsh, sunbaked land where boys tend goats beside dusty villages, where fountains play in shady courtyards and where the starkness of life breeds extremes of temperament: on the one hand a strong sense of honour, on the other a sense that *mañana* is quite soon enough for anything.

As always, there's some truth in the stereotype. Spain is a land of extremes, and the extremes of weather and topography – mountains, a high central plateau covering most of the country, lush greenery along the northern coasts while the southern coasts almost touch Africa, and an unforgiving climate that veers sharply from icy cold to roasting hot – are reflected in the extremes of its history. Think of the Moors, bringing their sophisticated culture of mathematics and medicine and an easy tolerance of wine (technically it was forbidden by Islam, but many of the caliphs grew grapes and drank wine); think then of the Reconquest and the rigidity of thinking that was imposed on Spain. Yet it's also the land of Cervantes, of picaresque comedy and of the lunch that starts at three in the afternoon and goes on until who knows when.

We can carry the extremes through into wine. Spain has more land under vine than any other, yet the yields are so low that it only ranks third in production terms. It's the sun again, drying the vineyards and sucking the juice from the grapes. Spain claims to have some 600 varieties of vine, yet only about 20 of those are important, and the ones that pop up again and again are Tempranillo, Garnacha, Cariñena, Airén and Macabeo.

Nevertheless, the last few years have seen a sea change in Spanish wine. It always used to be that long aging in wood was admired in Spain. Now a new generation of winemakers has practically been supporting the steel industry on its own, judging from the quantity of shiny stainless steel vats that cram winery after winery. Cold fermentation and early bottling are in; long wood-aging is out, except for the top traditional wines. A word that was seldom applied to Spanish wine in any approving sense – *joven*, meaning young – is now found on bottle after bottle. There has been a remarkable growth in seriously fine wine in the last decade or so – areas such as Ribera del Duero and Priorato are producing top-class wines that are making their mark internationally.

At the more basic level, it's true that there's a certain sameness about many of these wines. The grape varieties don't vary much, and the aim is a youthful fruitiness. They are not wines for long contemplation, but the point is that they're inexpensive, and they're very attractive.

CLASSIFICATION

The structure of Spanish wine is basically the same as that of other EU countries.

Vino de Mesa is the simplest table wine.

Vino Comarcal is a category of regional wines that applies to certain good-quality wines that happen not to be from a DO area.

Vino de la Tierra are country wines, the equivalent of French vin de pays.

Denominación de Origen (DO) is the equivalent of French appellation contrôlée. There are over 40 of them.

Denominación de Origen Calificada (DOC) is more or less the equivalent of Italy's DOCG, and applies to leading DOs with a proven history of quality. There is only one so far: Rioja.

The town of Jerez at the heart of the sherry industry has inspired artists throughout the ages. It's no suprise it's home to one of the world's most famous and traditional wines.

FRANCE

BAY OF BISCAY

N

SANTANDER

OVIEDO

GALICIA

CORDILLERA

CANTÁBRICA

SANTIAGO DE
COMPOSTELA

Miño

PAÍS
VASCO

PAMPLONA

VITORIA

NAVARRA

LOGROÑO

CATALONIA

2
3
5 6

CASTILLA Y LEÓN

RIOJA

Duero

Ebro

ZARAGOZA

BARCELONA

4

7

10

8 9

16 17

ARAGÓN

ATLANTIC
OCEAN

18

19

19
23
22
21
24

25

26

27

20

MEDITERRANEAN
SEA

PORTUGAL

SIERRA
DE GREDOS

MADRID
MADRID

37 38

38 39

CASTILLA-LA-MANCHA

36

28

VALENCIA

VALENCIA

EXTREMADURA

Guadiana

35

Júcar

29 28

MÉRIDA

34 27

32 31 29

30

33

SIERRA MORENA

Guadalquivir

SIERRA
NEVADA

MURCIA

33

40

SEVILLE

43

ANDALUCÍA

41

42

CÁDIZ

41

WINE REGIONS OF SPAIN

North-West Spain
North-East Spain
Central Spain
Southern Spain
Islands

CANARY ISLANDS

45 50 51
49 52
46 47 48

BALEARIC ISLANDS

PALMA DE
MALLORCA

44

0 km   200
0 miles   100   200

0 km   100
0 miles   50

MAIN DOC/DO WINES

1 Rias Baixas	12 Chacolí de Guetaria	23 Conca de Barberá	34 Almansa	43 Condado de Huelva
2 Ribeiro	13 Rioja DOC	24 Penedés	35 Valdepeñas	44 Binissalem
3 Ribeira Sacra	14 Navarra	25 Pla de Bages	36 La Mancha	45 La Palma
4 Monterrei	15 Campo de Borja	26 Alella	37 Méntrida	46 El Hierro
5 Valdeorras	16 Calatayud	27 Ampurdán-Costa Brava	38 Vinos de Madrid	47 Ycoden-Daute-Isora
6 Bierzo	17 Cariñena	28 Valencia	39 Mondéjar	48 Abona
7 Cigales	18 Somontano	29 Utiel-Requena	40 Montilla-Moriles	49 Valle de la Orotava
8 Toro	19 Costers del Segre	30 Alicante	41 Málaga	50 Valle de Güímar
9 Rueda	20 Terra Alta	31 Yecla	42 Jerez-Xérès-Sherry y	51 Tacoronte-Acentejo
10 Ribera del Duero	21 Tarragona	32 Jumilla	Manzanilla de Sanlúcar	52 Lanzarote
11 Chacolí de Vizcaya	22 Priorato	33 Bullas	de Barrameda	

North-West Spain

This section of Spain gives us both its top whites and some of its most prestigious reds – and by coincidence both come from regions that have only recently made much impact abroad.

Ribera del Duero

Spaniards knew about Ribera del Duero, of course: it's where Spain's absolutely top red, **Vega Sicilia** (see opposite), comes from, but until other bodegas started setting up there it was pretty irrelevant to most of us because we couldn't get the wines, and if we could get them we couldn't afford them.

Well, Vega Sicilia has been there since the last century, presiding over vineyards on the banks of the Duero and surrounded by sugar beet. Why didn't other people plant vines there sooner? I don't know. It wasn't until the 1980s that other wine producers moved in and made this into a proper wine region, instead of a one-producer fiefdom.

Pesquera wines – richly coloured, firm, fragrant, plummy and tobaccoey – are helping to broaden Ribera del Duero's reputation in international markets.

The Grapes

Grapes here are at the two extremes: either weighty reds or crisp whites.

TEMPRANILLO rules the reds of Ribera del Duero and Toro, producing gutsy, intensely flavoured wines full of plums and brown sugar that take well to oak-aging, and will live well in bottle as well.

VERDEJO is the main white grape of Rueda, where it makes soft, nutty whites.

VIURA is a minority grape in Rueda, where its acidity makes it useful for blending with Verdejo.

SAUVIGNON BLANC is found in Rueda, where it is often made as a varietal.

ALBARIÑO, the main grape of the Rias Baixas, gives acidic, aromatic wines with a discernible flavour of apricots.

TREIXADURA gives crisp, aromatic wine in Galicia.

Vega Sicilia has long set the pace in Ribera del Duero. Top wine Unico is full-bodied, firm and powerful with intense complexity and elegance.

The river Duero is a pretty important wine river. Not only does Rueda straddle its banks further downstream, but when it crosses the Portuguese border and becomes the Douro it is the artery linking the great port wine vineyards with the port from where they are shipped. It's in a league with the Rhône and the Rhine in terms of quality wine production. It alss helps to maintain a more uniform balance in temperature.

The altitude of the vineyards up here in Ribera del Duero is about 700-800 metres (2300-2600ft) above sea level, and because it's well inland summers are hot, if short, and temperatures fall sharply at night even in summer. That all makes for acidity in the grapes, but the main red grape, Tinto Fino, a local version of Tempranillo, produces wines with terrific colour and depth to balance that acidity, and with a flavour that's a turbulent whirlpool of chocolate and moist brown sugar and sweet-sour overripe plums. The wines need aging in bottle after release if they're to be tasted at their best, and there are some stunners around. They're not cheap but they're not mega-expensive either, especially compared with the sky-high price of Vega Sicilia.

There's a bit of white made, from the Albillo grape, but it doesn't have the DO, and some rosado (rosé) as well, mostly from Garnacha, which is also non-DO.

Rueda

Heading downstream, we move swiftly from rich, long-lived reds to fresh whites – and what's more, fresh characterful whites. Rueda always used to produce fortified wines a bit like coarse, cheap sherry, and still does, for those locals who like that sort of thing. The reputation of Rueda was retrieved in the 1970s when Rioja producer Marqués de Riscal moved in. The company rescued the Verdejo grape variety from possible terminal decline and then successfully introduced Sauvignon Blanc. These newer creations are the wines the rest of us go for, pungent whites based on the nutty Verdejo and sharpened up with the

VEGA SICILIA

How do you make the most expensive wine in Spain? It's simple when you know how. First, you pick one of the most inhospitable spots you can find. It's not too isolated, though, because there are other vineyards around you, and Madrid is only 130km (80 miles) away, so at least you can sell your wines. You plant the vineyards with Tinto Fino, white Albillo, and the red varieties of Bordeaux: Cabernet Sauvignon, Merlot and Malbec. (You planted these in 1864.)

Over the next few years your neighbours get fed up with battling the late frosts and the low yields (you yourself get around 20 hl/ha, which is very low indeed) and rip up their vines: sheep and other crops take over.

When you make your wine you age it in a mixture of new wood and old, large vats and small, and you age it for perhaps eight years in all before bottling it. You then store the bottled wine for about another decade, and your customers will cellar it for a further decade.

The main wine you call Unico. You don't make it every year; only when the vintage is good enough. Lesser wines go into Valbuena, which is bottled younger, after two to three years, and sold after five.

So you see, it's simple. Providing you have endless dedication and endless attention to detail, you too can make the most expensive wine in Spain. And each bottle, opened after several decades, will be a complex mix of leather and coffee and chocolate and tobacco.

Now there are other wineries in Ribera del Duero, indeed Vega Sicilia has bought a neighbouring winery and makes a less expensive red, Alión, there. It was Alejandro Fernández who spotted the potential of the region more recently, and started making Pesquera, a red which quickly rose to international stardom. The 1980s saw a considerable expansion – although none of the newcomers so far rivals Vega Sicilia.

The vineyards of Vega Sicilia are subject to harsh climatic conditions – they bake in summer, freeze in winter and the temperature plummets with every sunset.

more acidic Viura. The Sauvignon Blanc here is very much in the same mould: grassy, flavourful and well structured.

Other Regions in Castilla y León

Next door and just to the west there's the splendidly named region of **Toro**, which just happens to produce reds which can only be described as beefy. Again, it's Tempranillo, or a local version of it called Tinto de Toro, that's responsible, and the wines are terrifically powerful and solid, again with that flavour of brown sugar and plums.

To the north there's the not very inspiring region of **Cigales**, which makes some okay rosado from Tempranillo and Garnacha, although little is exported. So let's head west to Galicia.

Galicia

If one needed yet another example of how national boundaries have a limited effect on wine styles, one would only have to look at the whites from here. To the south, over the Portuguese border, it rains a lot, the wine is called Vinho Verde

and is aromatic and acidic. In Spain a few miles to the north it rains a lot, the wines are made from the same grapes (Albariño in the main, with a bit of Treixadura, Loureira and others) and they're aromatic and acidic. They're perhaps a bit fuller than the Portuguese versions, perhaps even a bit heavier, but the idea is the same.

There are five DO regions of which Rias Baixas, Ribeiro and Valdeorras are the most exciting, in that order. **Rias Baixas**, named after its flooded coastal valleys, or *rias*, concentrates on the characterful, aromatic Albariño grape, making creamy-rich, fruity wines with a glorious fragrance. The very best examples can be compared to the wines of Condrieu from France's Rhône Valley. **Ribeiro** grows more Treixadura and Torrontés, both aromatic and crisp though less exotic than Albariño. Lightweight reds and rosés are also made here. **Valdeorras** makes some fairly aromatic white from Godello (an indigenous variety almost extinct just 20 years ago) which has a highly distinctive appley character and intriguing aging possibilities. The Mencía grape is used for lively young, unoaked reds.

An example of the sort of aromatic, modern white in which Spain now specializes, from Terras Gauda, a winery at the forefront of the Rías Baixas region.

The Food of Northern and Central Spain

IN INLAND SPAIN the cooking is based on hardship: it's designed to use up whatever is left over, plus as much or as little as can be afforded from the market. So dishes are elastic, shrinking back to the bare essentials in times of shortage, and expanding munificently when food is plentiful. *Migas*, or crumbs, for example, consists of fried breadcrumbs with green peppers and garlic plus, if the purse allows, sausages, olives, vegetables and whatever else comes to hand. Meat is stewed slowly with beans and vegetables; odds and ends of the pig are made into a hundred different sorts of sausage,

as well as the prized Serrano ham of the mountain areas. You'll be offered slices of *jamon* (ham) and *chorizo* sausage in bars, too, not to mention prawns and slices of cheese. Even the simplest Spanish bar will have several kinds of *tapas*, or bar snacks, on offer.

On the coast fish and shellfish take over: crab is baked with garlic, onion, parsley, tomato, breadcrumbs and cheese, and there are umpteen ways of using fish of every size and style, from

mixtures of tiny fried fish to garlicky stews. In Valencia you'll find *paella*, made here without the additions of chicken and rabbit often found in other parts of the country.

Most meat, bean and vegetable dishes are best washed down with traditional styles of white or strong local reds which can stand up to pungent flavours.

Finally, for the sweet-toothed only, there's *turrón*, Alicante's nut-and-honey nougat, on sale in every confectioner's shop.

North-East Spain

For wine lovers, this has long been the most famous part of Spain, apart from the sherry country, because it is home to Rioja. But these days, it has even more to offer.

Rioja

It's difficult to go anywhere in north-east Spain and not sense the shadow of Rioja. Its influence is everywhere, simply because it is Spain's best-known region for table wine. And Rioja itself was influenced not so very long ago by Bordeaux.

It happened because Spain became affected by phylloxera considerably later than France. So when France was suffering wine shortages, what did the merchants do? Hopped over the Pyrenees, of course, and did some serious shopping. As a result the late 19th century was a period of great prosperity in Rioja – you can see from the elaborate bodega buildings (bodega is the Spanish term for a cellar and is often applied to a wine company as a whole) that this was a time of boom – and it was then, too, that Rioja imported the idea of aging wines in small oak barriques as in Bordeaux. But whereas Bordelais winemakers always used French oak, the Riojanos preferred American.

Bad times followed: phylloxera reached Rioja in 1901, by which time Bordeaux was recovering. The decline of Rioja's wine industry was helped by the Civil War, and it wasn't really until the 1970s that the region got back on its feet.

So let's look a little more closely at what exactly makes up the Rioja region. It spreads some 130km (80 miles) along the river Ebro's banks in a high mountain valley, and gets its name from the little Rio Oja which joins the main flow of the Ebro at Haro – one of the region's main towns. The Rioja DOC divides into three sub-regions: Rioja Alta, Rioja Alavesa and Rioja Baja. Each gives very different characteristics to the wines, and most Riojas are a blend of wines from two or more of these regions.

Rioja Alta is right at the north-western end of the valley, where the mountains crowd in on the town of Haro and the River Ebro relaxes a little after its battle through the Cantabrian gorges. Haro is a lovely, quiet, rather idiosyncratic town, with no real centre but substantial outskirts and bodega buildings of wild eccentricity dating from a super-confident late 19th century. In general the Alta vineyards produce wines which have a strong, firm style; the reds age well.

Rioja Alavesa swoops down from the foothills of the Cordillera Cantábrica to the Ebro's north bank. As in the Rioja Alta, the climate comes under the joint influence of mountains and ocean, giving warm, wet springs, short hot summers and mild autumns. The Alavesa wines are the softest, most lightly coloured and most perfumed of Riojas and the reds are seldom seen unblended, though they are delicious young and yet age surprisingly well.

Vineyards on the banks of the river Ebro near Haro. The river here is the border between Rioja Alta and Rioja Alavesa.

Cosecheros Alaveses is an up-and-coming co-op producing impressive Rioja under the Artadi label. Excellent fruit and modern, clean vinification are key.

Display boards for Rioja bodegas are a common sight in many towns in this part of Spain.

OPPOSITE **Fonzaleche, west of Haro in the Rioja Alta, is typical of the many villages which nestle in the hills of this region.**

Rioja Baja, which starts at the gate of Logroño and continues right to Rioja's eastern boundary, is lower, flatter and hotter. Within reach of Mediterranean sunshine, the wines are rougher, heavier and higher in alcohol – around 13 degrees as against 10-11 degrees elsewhere in Rioja. Although much in demand for adding colour and brawn to lighter wines, they don't on their own have much complexity.

There are many more single-estate wines than there used to be, which is good, but the majority of Rioja is made by the merchant houses or the co-operatives, and the key to the style of Rioja is not so much in the vinification, which is pretty standard, as in the aging. It's those Bordeaux-style barrels in which the wine spends long years that give it its mellow smoothness. New oak is not the essence of this style, though a proportion of new American oak will give extra vanilla flavours to the wine; most bodegas like a mix of new and old, and some of the barrels may be very old indeed. It's this long aging that gives the reds their warm vanilla softness, and gradually lightens the Tempranillo strawberry fruit.

Only a few white Riojas are aged in wood

Spanish wineries, like this one belonging to Raïmat in Costers del Segre, Catalonia (see p.138), are now as high-tech as any in the world and gleam with stainless steel.

these days, although those that are can gain a marvellously complex waxy richness from it. The fashion is for cool-fermented young, crisp whites, and most bodegas go down this road.

There are four different levels of aging for reds:

Sin Crianza wines have less than a year's aging in wood, or none at all. The words Sin Crianza do not appear on the label, unlike those of the other categories.

Crianza wines have a minimum of 12 months in wood and further time in bottle. They may not be sold before their third year. Whites have at least six months' aging in barrel before bottling.

Reserva wines are supposed to have been better from the start, not just be old Crianza wines that didn't find a buyer. They have at least 36 months' aging in cask and bottle, of which at least 12 months must have been in cask. They can't be sold before their fifth year. Whites have a minimum of six months in cask, and 24 months' aging in total.

Gran Reserva wines have at least 24 months in cask and 36 months in bottle, or vice versa. They cannot be sold before their sixth year. Whites have six months in cask and 48 months' aging in total.

Navarra

Rioja's nearest neighbour, Navarra, has long had to play second fiddle. But the DO's rapid development since 1985 has produced a modern, dynamic, winemaking environment which has been dubbed as Spain's answer to the New World. There are lots of good fresh reds and whites to be had. Many foreign grape varieties have been planted, leading to a spate of juicy reds from Cabernet Sauvignon and Merlot, as well as Tempranillo. In addition, there is an increasingly impressive array of barrel-fermented Chardonnays. The recovery of the local Moscatel de Grano Menudo grape (Muscat Blanc à Petits Grains) and renewed interest in young Garnacha reds are the latest developments in a buzzing region.

The Grapes
Varieties with great potential
— when they're made well.

TEMPRANILLO is by far the most important grape here in quality terms, and it dominates the best red Riojas, giving lovely gentle strawberry and raspberry fruit. In hot years, however, this early-ripening variety yields deep, dark spicy wine which will require years of aging. Although it can be fairly tannic, Tempranillo has low acidity, so often needs to be blended with more acidic varieties. In Catalonia it turns up under its local name, Ull de Llebre.

GARNACHA TINTA (GRENACHE NOIR) produces strong, rather coarse, peppery wine in hot Rioja Baja, but in the best spots can give stunning raspberry and pepper flavours.

GRACIANO is a minority grape in Rioja, but gives strong, fragrant blackberryish wine with dark colour and good ability to age. But its yields are low and farmers prefer the easier pickings of Tempranillo.

CARIÑENA (CARIGNAN) goes by the name of Mazuelo in Rioja: much of it gives just tannin and rough-and-tumble fruit.

CABERNET SAUVIGNON can be added to Rioja, and is often found unblended in Penedés where it gives piercing blackcurrant fruit rounded out with new oak.

Tempranillo

Garnacha Tinta

VIURA (MACABEO) is the main white grape in Rioja, and is spot-on for the modern razor-sharp, grapefruit-tart whites.

MALVASIA used to be Rioja's great white grape, but is now only rarely grown. It gives fat, nutty, musky wine, honeyed and fragrant, but it isn't suitable for the ultra-modern whites: it's quite weighty and it oxidizes quickly.

GARNACHA BLANCA is grown in Rioja to some extent, but makes rather heavy, alcoholic wine which fades quickly.

PARELLADA is fresh when vinified cool, but will win no personality of the year awards. At best it's peppery and has some aroma.

XAREL-LO makes heavy, earthy, alcoholic wine used for sparkling wine in Catalonia.

CHARDONNAY is grown in Penedés and made both as a varietal, often aged in new oak for a fat, tropical style, and for blending into Cava, generally to the benefit of the blend.

Alvaro Palacios moved to Priorato in the late 1980s. His obsession was to make world-class wines from very old vines in a unique location. He uses 70-year-old vines to produce L'Ermita, a dark, hugely concentrated wine with plummy aromas and complex flavours.

País Vasco

Let's nip up and take a quick look at the Basque coastline. There are two DOs here, **Chacolí de Guetaria** and **Chacolí de Vizcaya** (if you happen to speak Basque you'll know them as Getariako Txakolina and Bizkaiako Txacolina respectively). You'll be lucky to see them exported, but if you find yourself in San Sebastian look out for them. They're fresh, simple young whites, and they go down a treat with the local seafood.

Aragón

Campo de Borja is lightening its style from the hefty reds it used to concentrate on. Cariñena and Garnacha, neither of them suited to great complexity, are the grapes.

Cariñena, in spite of its name, grows mostly Garnacha and makes perfectly pleasant soft reds, and some okay whites and rosados. **Calatayud** has yet to make much of a mark for its young reds; but **Somontano**, stuck out near the Pyrenees, is an exciting spot. Some stylish whites and reds are emerging from here, made from both Spanish and international grape varieties.

Catalonia

Ampurdán-Costa Brava is trying less hard, but with all those tourists to flog its rosado to, it doesn't have to. **Alella** makes some rather nice dry and off-dry whites, and **Conca de Barberá** is producing young, fruity reds and whites under the influence of flying winemakers. **Tarragona** is looking more hopeful than it was, with some quite tasty reds appearing, **Priorato** has undergone enormous changes in just a decade. Having acquired a reputation for rich, thick, slightly rustic reds, it is now producing (thanks to a group of enterprising young winemakers back in the 1980s who started to plant some French grape varieties to give added complexity and aging ability to the wines) some very serious and long-lived reds indeed. These new wines are now the most expensive and potentially the best in Spain. **Terra Alta** isn't in the same league, but produces some reasonable reds. And near Lerida there's the DO of **Costers del Segre**, producing very attractive reds and whites from various combinations of Tempranillo, Garnacha, Cabernet Sauvignon, Pinot Noir, Merlot, Chardonnay and Macabeo.

Penedés

In the 1980s this was the most innovative region in Spain – it had installed stainless steel and temperature control in the cellars before most places, thanks to the influence of Torres, the company that still leads the region. It also planted international grape varieties like Chardonnay and Cabernet Sauvignon, Sauvignon Blanc and Pinot Noir and Merlot before other regions, and Torres in particular went in for experimental vineyards in a big way, trying out all sorts of different vines.

Now I suppose it's going through a period of consolidation. Few of those experimental varieties ever found their way into the wines, which still rely on the international favourites plus typically Spanish varieties like Parellada, Tempranillo and Garnacha. But the wines are actually better than ever: the more extreme examples of overoaking have been toned down.

The range of wines is as great as ever, helped by the three main parts of Penedés, each of which has a different climate and favours a different style of wine.

Bajo Penedés, along the coast, is pretty sauna-like in summer and is best at producing sweet wines, or else quite beefy and full-bodied reds.

Medio Penedés, the traditional quality area, centres on Vilafranca del Penedés, about 200 metres (650ft) above sea level. It's still fairly hot but the vineyards are mostly planted with white grapes, especially Xarel-lo and Macabeo, because Spain's **Cava** sparkling wine industry is based here, at San Sadurní de Noya (see box below). The reds are better balanced than in the Bajo and there are grapes like Cabernet Sauvignon, Merlot and Pinot Noir alongside the traditional Ull de Llebre (the local name for Tempranillo), Monastrell (ditto for Mourvèdre) and Garnacha Tinta.

Penedés Superior is the highland section, very mountainous and wild, ranging up to 800 metres (2600ft). Here the grapes may not ripen until as late as November, but if they are French varieties like Chenin Blanc or Chardonnay, they will have a startling intensity of fruit unlike any others in Spain. The Parellada is the main native grape, and a variety of imports like Chardonnay, Gewürztraminer, Riesling, Muscat d'Alsace and Chenin Blanc also produce racy, perfumed wines of high quality.

Miguel Torres makes good wines with local grapes in Penedés and is also renowned for his plantings of French varieties. Fransola combines Sauvignon Blanc with some local Parellada.

CAVA

Cava, the Spanish name for Champagne-method fizz, can legally be made in many parts of Spain, although in fact most wines come from Penedés. It has improved hugely in recent years – at least, to foreign tastes. The Spanish used to revel in its slightly rooty, earthy flavours; now they are getting used to greater freshness and fruit. Although the wines are made by the Champagne method, hand riddling of bottles as shown on the right is a rarity: the Cava cellars have equipment that is uniformly high-tech. The grapes used, principally Parellada, Xarel-lo and Macabeo, are not the world's best by a long way, and a dash of Chardonnay can perk up a blend no end. The best-value, fruitiest Cavas are generally the youngest, with no more than the minimum nine months' aging.

RIGHT **Performing the *remuage* on bottles of Cava in the cellars of Raventos i Blanc, San Sadurní de Noya.**

Central Spain

It's the flatness that first strikes you, and the monotony: the bleak, scorched-brown landscape with its crosshatching of stubby vines, its huddled clumps of stunted olives, and its dusty sweeps of grain stretching away like an artist's exercise in perspective. Then it's the heat: searingly insistent in this high, waterless plain. You can see why Don Quixote went barmy out in these wide open spaces – scudding white clouds in the burning sky, disturbingly flat prairie, and then the shimmering mirage of a windmill – or is it a giant? – on the far horizon.

The Wine Regions

La Mancha is at the heart of this region but vines abound in the provinces of Murcia and Valencia as well, and are even found on the Mediterranean coast at Alicante. But La Mancha is the biggest of them all – it's the biggest demarcated wine region in Europe – and so inevitably it sets the tone.

And how things have changed. It's the availability of stainless-steel vats and temperature-controlled fermentation that's done it, encouraged by changing tastes abroad and made possible by EU money. New, relaxed DO regulations adopted in 1995 allow for much-needed irrigation of vineyards; potentially creating an area which could compete with Australia's Riverland, Murray River and Riverina. Reds and whites which were cheap, coarse and usually oxidized are now cheap, fruity and fresh. They're never going to be great wines – the growing conditions see to that – but they're a great source of everyday drinking. The whites are nearly all made from Airén, the reds from Tempranillo. There's a bit of Chardonnay and Cabernet Sauvignon being grown, too,

The traditional round white windmills above Consuegra overlook the plain of La Mancha below.

Bush-trained Cencibel (Tempranillo) vines growing on a remote estate in Valdepeñas – note the sparse planting.

The Grapes

Tempranillo and Garnacha dominate the reds; Airén the whites.

TEMPRANILLO, here known as Cencibel, is central Spain's great red hope. It gives much less delicate wine than it does in Rioja; here, further south, it ripens enthusiastically to make rich, deep, plum-skin and pepper wine in Valdepeñas and, picked earlier, juicy light reds in La Mancha.

GARNACHA TINTA is planted pretty widely, giving soft, toffeeish wines that age quickly.

BOBAL makes big, tannic reds that keep their acidity even in searing heat; it's used for grape concentrate as well as for wine.

MONASTRELL is the same as southern France's Mourvèdre, a heat-loving grape that ripens late. It's the mainstay of Jumilla, Valencia, Yecla, Alicante and Almansa, and it has great potential for quality, if made properly. It makes big, alcoholic red wine with strong flavours of game and plums.

AIRÉN is by far the most planted white variety in La Mancha and Valdepeñas, which makes it the most widely planted variety in the world. These days it is mostly young and fresh, fairly neutral but vaguely fruity.

Monastrell is the basis of the red wines of Jumilla, and earlier picking and better balance is resulting in more modern styles that nevertheless retain the character of the region.

and plantings of red grapes are being increased at the expense of white, so there'll be lots more juicy Tempranillo coming on stream.

To the north-west of La Mancha is **Méntrida**, where Garnacha is grown for some pretty hefty reds, and to the south-east is **Almansa**, where Garnacha and Monastrell do the same sort of thing; it's hard to see what either region has done to deserve the status of DO. **Valdepeñas**, tucked into the southern end of La Mancha, is much better news: the grapes are Airén and Tempranillo again (the latter is called Cencibel in these parts), and the wines to look for are the oak-aged red Reservas and Gran Reservas, which taste of coconut cream, toffee and plums and cost remarkably little. And to the north, **Vinos de Madrid** is producing some decent young stuff, again mainly from Tempranillo and Garnacha, but it's mostly drunk in the bars of the capital.

Yecla and **Bullas** are both fairly undistinguished, though Yecla is also making some rather better modern styles; **Jumilla** is responding to foreign investment and turning out some attractive everyday reds. Avoid the traditional beefy styles, however: they're a form of bottled headache.

Alicante and **Utiel-Requena** also go in for this sort of thick, heavy red, although the latter also has a nice line in rosados from the Bobal grape; **Valencia** is making some reasonable, inexpensive reds, but apart from the odd good brand has yet really to make its mark. The sweet Moscatels can be perfectly pleasant, but don't have a lot of finesse.

In all of these regions there has been a growth in outside investment and expertise; an invasion of new equipment and a focus on new techniques that are gradually transforming quality. And it's not just in the wineries; viticulturalist Richard Smart's (see box on p.245) work on pruning and training techniques, for example, is paying dividends in the vineyards.

"But now, by the remembrance of her you love best, pray thee, tell me, is not this your right Ciudad Real wine?" "Thou hast a rare palate," answered the Squire of the Wood, "it is the very same, and of a good age too."

DON QUIXOTE DE LA MANCHA, CERVANTES, 1547-1616

Southern Spain

If you want the Spain of your dreams, this is it. This is where you'll find whitewashed villages perched on clifftops that overlook undulating fields of biscuit-pale corn; Gothic churches that were once medieval mosques; cool, creeper-hung courtyards with magenta bougainvillea tumbling from balconies, and the mournful semitones of flamenco drifting from darkened bars. And this, where the soil turns blindingly white with chalk, is where you'll find one of the world's most unlikely wines: sherry.

But if sherry is the finest wine of the south, it has many imitators. This (to go back a few hundred years) was where sack came from; it was a generic term that encompassed all the thick, sweet wines of southern Spain and the islands, and it had two great advantages. One was that same sweetness: sugar, remember, was expensive, and people have always craved sweet flavours. The other was that the sweetness of sack helped to preserve it on the sea journey from Cádiz to London, Bristol or wherever.

More recently the success of sherry meant that other, similar wines from nearby – Montilla, Málaga and Condado de Huelva – were not able to compete on quality, and were increasingly seen as second best. On the whole that's a reasonable judgement, although there is now some superb Montilla to be had and it's remarkably cheap too. If you think top sherry is underpriced, they're almost giving this stuff away.

The Wines

The reason Jerez and its neighbouring towns make better wine than elsewhere down here is twofold: chalk and flor (see p.144). **Montilla-Moriles** has some very chalky soil at its heart, and this is where its best wines are grown, but most of it is sandy. The climate is harsh and extreme, too, without the moderating sea breezes of the sherry country. Pedro Ximénez is the main grape, and there's some Airén, known locally as Lairén, and some Moscatel. The styles of wine are the same as those of Jerez: fino, amontillado and oloroso, but they can't be called by those names outside Spain as the names legally belong to sherry; ironic, since amontillado actually means 'in the style of Montilla'. Pale dry, medium-dry, pale cream and cream are the designations used; pale dry matures under flor, but there's never as much flor as in Jerez, because it's so much drier here. Montillas rarely need fortification, since the very hot ripening season produces grapes of at least 16 degrees potential alcohol. The wines are generally softer and less assertive than sherry although the top dry amontillado, oloroso and rich Pedro Ximénez are really worth seeking out.

Málaga can be interesting, with a smoky, raisiny taste, but since the area's best producer, Scholtz Hermanos, closed its doors in 1996, the matter is increasingly academic. The wines range from sweet to dry, and the sweet ones are best. Pedro Ximénez and Moscatel are the main grapes.

Condado de Huelva is the least famous of these wines, although its history is as long as any. It comes in a dry, flor-aged version, an older, somewhat *rancio* style (oxidized – deliberately so – to give a pungent tang to the flavour), and an unfortified young wine. The grapes are Zalema, which don't have much flavour, and Palomino.

There's also some wine made in the **Canaries**, and on **Mallorca**, which serves mainly to quench the thirst of the tourists.

OPPOSITE **Harvesting Palamino grapes. Winemakers these days know how to match the soil to the style of sherry they want.**

Rich Pedro Ximénez styles from Montilla-Moriles can be very good indeed. Don't be misled by the date on this label – 1927 here refers to the solera, not the vintage.

The Osborne bull is a traditional sight on Spanish hilltops. Osborne is the biggest drinks company in Spain and these wooden silhouettes, far larger than life size, dot the bare hills.

Sherry

Sherry is one of those wines, along with port and 'claret' (see p.51), that has been partly shaped by British and Irish merchants. Like the companies in those other regions, the names of many of the great sherry houses – Harvey, Croft, Osborne, Sandeman and others – are the names of traders who saw an opportunity and headed south.

As so often, it was the proximity of a busy port, in this case Cádiz, that encouraged the growth of the wine trade. And the wine was special because the last outcrop of chalk soil in Europe occurs just north of Cádiz, in the sherry triangle composed of the three towns of **Jerez de la Frontera**, **Puerto de Santa María** and **Sanlúcar de Barrameda**. In spite of the blistering heat, the white chalk vineyards give Palomino grapes with light, delicate juice which ages under flor (see box below) to provide one of the most memorable tastes in the world.

The finest vineyards are on chalk soil called *albariza*, and they constitute almost all the vineyard land here. Chalk's ability to produce light-bodied wine is the key, along with its capacity for water retention – vitally important in an area which gets 295 days of sun a year, but only 560mm (22 inches) of rain, hardly any of which falls in summer. Both *barro*, a brownish clay

which yields fairly hefty wine, and *arena*, or sand, are allowed for vine growing, but are less and less used.

The winemaking is pretty much the same as for white wine; the young wines are fermented dry and then fortified with brandy. What makes sherry sherry is the aging process in solera (see opposite) and under flor. It is those two factors by which sherry is categorized.

SHERRY STYLES

Fino is light, dry sherry, aged under flor, with a pale colour and a biting dryness, almost a baker's yeast sourness. Some commercial ones are sweetened as the shippers think consumers can't take the real thing. Well, if they can't they should drink something else, because to my mind to soften fino is to lose the dry pungency which is its essence.

Manzanilla is a type of fino, but even lighter; it comes from Sanlúcar de Barrameda, where the damp sea air encourages the growth of a particularly thick layer of flor, so the wines have even more of that austere yeastiness. Like Jerez fino or Puerto fino they should be drunk as soon as possible after bottling, never decanted and always chilled. You should also always finish the bottle in one go – buy half bottles, if you like. A fino

Ripe Palomino grapes on vines growing in almost pure chalk soil. There are different varieties of Palomino – Palomino Fino is the typical Jerez one.

Barbadillo is the largest sherry company in the town of Sanlúcar de Barrameda. Manzanilla styles are salty and dry.

FLOR

For years flor was a mystery, a benevolent presence on the new wine, and one that was anxiously awaited every spring after the vintage. Now it is much better understood, and more predictable. It's a yeast – in fact it's the same yeast that is used in Jerez to ferment the must. When all the sugar in the juice is used up and turned to alcohol, instead of dying, which is what most yeasts do, it changes its nature and continues to live and grow on the surface of the wine, forming a thick white coating. It has a curious texture, not unpleasant, and usually described as creamy or porridgy; and while it lives it feeds on the wine, changing its biochemical make-up and its flavour. Instead of the dull, flat flavour of Palomino, fino matured under flor has a pungent, appley, nutty, yeasty sourness.

But flor is quite a touchy creature, and won't live on wine that is too strong or weak in alcohol. So sherry has to be fortified to above 14.5 degrees but not more than 16 degrees for the flor to flourish; if you want to make oloroso, which is not aged under flor, you simply fortify it to a level that flor won't like. Hey presto, no flor.

Flor also prefers the cooler, damper conditions of Sanlúcar de Barrameda and Puerto de Santa María, both of which are on the coast, to those of Jerez, which is further inland, and grows more thickly in the first two. This accounts for the subtle differences in flavour between Puerto fino and Jerez fino and manzanilla.

THE SOLERA SYSTEM

This is a system of fractional blending which keeps the flor alive – and flor is crucial to the style of finos and amontillados. Left to itself the layer of flor would feed off the wine until there was nothing left for it to feed on; it would then die. But in order to have the maximum effect on the wine it has to be kept alive, and to do this you need to add fresh new wine at intervals.

Imagine, then, a row of barrels. The oldest wine is at the far end, and at intervals you withdraw wine from here for bottling. You top up with wine from the next oldest barrel, and in turn top that up with wine from the next oldest, and so on, topping up the youngest barrel with wine from the most recent vintage. That, in essence, is a solera system, except that every stage may contain many hundreds or thousands of butts. Strictly speaking only the final stage is called the solera: all the others are criaderas, or nurseries. A solera system for a fino may contain three or four criaderas and the solera; some for very old and rare olorosos contain many more criaderas before the wine finally reaches the solera, but quantities for these wines may be very small.

At work in Osborne's La Palma bodega in Puerto de Santa.

OPPOSITE **The cooler seaside conditions in Sanlúcar de Barrameda help produce the characteristically pungent and salty manzanilla.**

left open, even in the refrigerator, is a fino spoiled.

Manzanilla pasada is an older manzanilla that has been left to age in barrel past the usual four- to five-year span and has gained some delicious nuttiness.

Palo cortado is another oddity, a fino which changes personality as it ages in barrel, and combines the zesty tang of a fino with rich demerara sugar nuttiness, while remaining bone dry. It's a wonderful style, both delicate and rich.

Amontillado sherry, in its authentic form, is always dry. Commercial blends intended for export markets are sweetened, but you wouldn't catch a Jerezano touching that sort of thing. Amontillado – proper amontillado – is fino which has stayed in barrel until the layer of flor has died, and the wine has oxidized and matured to a nutty, dried-fruit richness, while still remaining dry.

The Grapes

Sherry is effectively a one-grape wine, although others are permitted.

PALOMINO is the sherry grape *par excellence*. Practically all sherry is made from it, with the addition of Pedro Ximénez for sweetening now being relatively rare. Most sweetened sherries are made so by the addition of some Palomino that has been dried in the sun and then pressed and fermented. Palomino produces rather neutral wine with low acidity which, when made as table wine, is usually the epitome of dullness. It is fortification, the solera system and the growth of flor that makes Palomino special.

PEDRO XIMÉNEZ is more common in Málaga and Montilla-Moriles than it is in Jerez. When made into table wine it is generally heavy and flabby, but when dried in the sun and fortified it makes rich, dark, grapy sherry.

MOSCATEL is a minority grape in sherry, and is grown in sandy soil and used for sweetening.

You'd expect a sherry called Matusalem to be pretty opulent, and so this is. It's immensely concentrated and rich and best sipped in small quantities.

Oloroso is a different kettle of fish. These wines start out bigger and sturdier and are fortified to a higher level (generally to 18 to 20 per cent alcohol) to prevent any growth of flor. They are aged in solera, just like finos, but without the flor they darken and the flavour deepens to a raisiny, brown sugar, nuts and coffee flavour, like fruitcake and toast; they are immensely complex wines, with some of the most attention-grabbing tastes to be found in a bottle. And again, in their natural state, they're completely dry. Here, though, even the finest wines may be sweetened a little before sale; they may not taste even off-dry, but without any sweetening at all they can be just too austere. Commercial versions will be labelled 'cream' and are unlikely to have been made from top-quality base wines. Pale cream sherries are basically sweetened inexpensive fino. Top-class sweet olorosos, labelled 'oloroso dulce', are another matter, and are wonderful dessert wines.

There's another kind of sweet sherry made as well: **Pedro Ximénez**. The grapes are left to dry in the sun on *esparto* mats and then pressed and fermented. The wine is thick and black and sticky as treacle, tastes of grapes and is increasingly popular as a dessert wine. It is one of the very few wines that is delicious served with vanilla ice-cream.

Sherries are sweetened with a dash of Pedro Ximénez if they're very good; with sun-dried Palomino if they're not so good.

The Food of the South

IN THE SOUTH it can be difficult to know when the *tapas* end and the meal begins. You'll be offered *tapas* all over Spain, but this is where they come into their own: not just *jamon* or squares of *tortilla* (potato omelette), but dishes of shellfish, anchovies, *chorizo*, kidneys in a sauce made with sherry, green olives, grilled peppers, Manchego cheese, slices of dried tuna and a hundred others, depending on the whim or skill of the cook.

There's also *gazpacho*: not just the familiar, refreshing cold soup of tomato and chopped peppers, but also a white version made with almonds.

After that comes fish: there is meat in the south, but fish is far more common, and excellent. A speciality of Sanlúcar and Cádiz is fried fish, caught that morning. Or you might be served elvers cooked in olive oil with chillies.

Afterwards there's more Manchego cheese, served with *membrillo*, or quince jelly, or the egg-yolk-based tarts and puddings found all over Spain – they're a way of using up the leftovers, when the egg whites have been used for fining the wine.

Dry sherry of all sorts goes superbly with *tapas*; sweet sherries are best kept for dessert, or for drinking after your meal. In Jerez and the rest of the sherry region you're likely to be offered table wine from elsewhere in Spain with your meal proper: Rioja, perhaps, or Ribera del Duero.

A typical *tapas* bar with meats hanging from the ceiling and a wealth of dishes on offer. *Tapas* means tops or lids and derives from a time when bartenders used to cover glasses of wine with a small plate to protect against flies. They would place free appetizers on these.

PORTUGAL

Traditional ceramics, often to be found in railway stations like the above piece from Pinhão, celebrate the local wine and scenery.

Portugal is the last undiscovered wine country of Western Europe.

Yes, I mean it. There are port and Vinho Verde, two diametrically opposed wine styles, next door to each other in the north. Dão and Bairrada occupy the hills a little further south, and further south again are Estremadura, Ribatejo and Alentejo, all pouring out vast quantities of wine. Offshore, nearer Africa than Europe, is Madeira, making fortified wine.

And yet it's only in the last few years, as EU funds have poured in, that we've begun to see what Portugal might mean in wine terms.

Portugal's long history of isolation from the rest of Europe is responsible for this. It's a country that has always preferred to turn its back on the great land mass to the east, and instead look west and south, over the sea. Portuguese mariners rounded the Cape of Good Hope in the 15th century; the great late 15th- and early 16th-century age of discovery under Manuel I, the Fortunate, saw Portuguese trading posts established in the East Indies, eastern Asia, South Africa and Brazil; Vasco da Gama discovered the sea route to India and Portugal vied with Venice for control of the valuable pepper trade. It's a small country, but it operated on a global scale.

But then times changed. Brazil became independent in 1822; phylloxera destroyed the vineyards at the end of the 19th century, and for most of the 20th century Portugal looked inwards. The Salazar dictatorship was followed in 1974 by revolution, and only in 1986, with membership of the EU, did Portugal really start to look around again at the outside world.

1986 was, by coincidence, the 300th anniversary of the Treaty of Windsor, which established Portugal and England as allies. It's thanks to that alliance (helped along by the 1703 Methuen Treaty which gave favourable terms of trade to Portuguese wines imported into Britain), that Britain developed its taste for port wine: when

The Food of Portugal

TO EAT WELL IN Portugal you must eat simply. Eschew the Frenchified restaurants with their international cuisine: it won't be as good as you can get at home, and you'll be missing everything that makes Portuguese food special.

Instead head for the places that serve *bacalhão* – dried, salted cod that can be prepared in, they say, 365 different ways. It has a strong flavour that takes some getting used to, but can become addictive.

In the north it may be preceded by *caldo verde*, cabbage soup, perhaps with some slices of *chouriço* sausage at the bottom: to my mind this is not one of the greatest triumphs of the Portuguese kitchen, but in the north you're given it twice a day.

Meat – lamb, kid, chicken – is simply grilled or roasted; in the centre of the country suckling pig is a speciality, and it is unbelievably tender and succulent.

Fresh fish, as opposed to *bacalhão*, is available freshly caught and grilled all round the coast: sardines, turbot, squid, prawns and lobster are all favourites, and the quality is superb.

Accompaniments are simple: just boiled potatoes and green salad to let the freshness of the fish sing out. Vinho Verde

Tinto (red) is delicious with both *bacalhão* and oily types of fresh fish such as sardines. Decent local reds are the best thing to go with meat dishes.

Further south, aromatic, spicy flavours dominate, and meat and shellfish may be cooked together: pork and clams, stewed slowly and flavoured with coriander, is a traditional dish of the Alentejo.

Pudding may be *pudim flam*, the local version of *crème caramel*, or one of any number of sticky puddings based on egg yolks. Rice pudding, *arroz doce*, is another option.

There's always cheese too. Serra cheese ripens to a marvellous runniness and is eaten with *marmelada*, or quince jelly, but there are many others, local and nameless, like the sheep's cheese I once brought home: it had such an authentic reek of the sheepfold that nobody would touch it.

If you want to eat your cheese with bread, there's a wide and delicious choice including *pão de milho* (corn bread) which is beautifully fragrant.

Britain was at war with France, as it so often was then, Portuguese wine was the obvious alternative.

Port was in fact one of the earliest wines to be demarcated by law: the Marquis of Pombal, intensely disliked by the British merchants because he cracked down on abuses in the port trade, mapped the boundaries of the port wine region in 1756.

There are vineyards, however, almost everywhere in Portugal; only the highest parts of the mountains grow no vines, and they are given over to scrub and patrolled by eagles. Everywhere else a vine will be found somewhere, even if only in a back garden, alternating with the leggy cabbages and scratching hens that between them provide the basic diet of many rural areas.

Ask the owners of such vines what variety they are and they're unlikely to know. Even where vines have been corralled into vineyards there may well be different sorts growing together, and nobody knows or cares what they are. Sorting out Portugal's vineyards is a massive task, and it's only just beginning. Discovering the potential of varieties that have hitherto been buried in anonymous blends is just as big; and thanks to a handful of ambitious winemakers, we're starting to see the fruits of it.

CLASSIFICATION

Portugal's wines are divided into four tiers of quality.

Vinho de Mesa is the simplest everyday table wine.

Vinho Regional is regional wine, the equivalent of French vin de pays.

Indicação de Proveniência Regulamentada (IPR) wines are the equivalent of French VDQS, and are in theory eligible for promotion to DOC status. The category is also known as **Vinho de Qualidade Produzido em Região Determinada (VQPRD)**.

Denominação de Origem Controlada (DOC) is the equivalent of French appellation contrôlée. It replaced the earlier category of Região Demarcada in 1990.

WINE REGIONS OF PORTUGAL

- DOC wines
- IPR regions/VQPRD wines

DOC WINES

1. Vinho Verde
2. Porto/Douro
3. Dão
4. Bairrada
5. Bucelas
6. Colares
7. Carcavelos
8. Setúbal
9. Portalegre
10. Borba
11. Redondo
12. Reguengos
13. Vidigueira
14. Lagos
15. Portimão
16. Lagoa
17. Tavira
18. Madeira

Table Wines

One never thinks of Portugal as being wet – and yet there it is, right next to the Atlantic, with the clouds and the wind coming in from the west, drenching the land so that everything grows lush and green. Only when one gets right down in the south does the seaboard dry out. Most of the table wine regions start a little way inland, although there are exceptions, and the Vinho Verde region runs right up to nudge the Atlantic.

Vinho Verde is the big DOC table wine region of northern Portugal. The Douro, though, is increasingly important as a source of first-class reds and whites – it may even turn out to be Portugal's finest table wine region in the future (for further information, see p.153). Heading south, Dão and Bairrada stretch across the country south of the Douro, but then there are nothing but IPR zones, some of them producing very good stuff, until the Alentejo's clutch of DOCs (Portalegre,

Borba, Redondo, Reguengos and Vidigueira). There are some smaller, historically important DOCs west of Lisbon (Colares and some fortified ones, see p.151) and the IPR zones within Estremadura and the Ribatejo. The Algarve's DOCs, right down on the south coast – Lagos, Portimão, Lagoa and Tavira – are producing much lesser-quality wine than many of the IPRs, which seems pretty daft. Politics, as ever, seems to have played a part in getting them their DOCs.

The overall picture, in fact, is one of go-ahead winemaking in the IPRs and stick-in-the-mud winemaking all too often in the DOCs. But that's not an infallible rule, thank goodness. And some of Portugal's best wines are simply Vinhos Regional. It's the producers who are all-important.

Vinho Verde

I love Vinho Verde. I love sitting in the sort of tiny restaurant in which Portugal specializes, perhaps in some remote town, perhaps overlooking the sea, eating *bacalhão* and drinking red Vinho Verde. Red Vinho Verde? Yes, certainly. About half the Vinho Verde produced is red – acidic, slightly fizzy, with astringent cherry fruit that cuts through the strong flavours and oiliness of the fish (everything is dressed with olive oil here) like nothing else. It's one of the world's great simple meals.

It's not that easy to buy red Vinho Verde abroad, however. The white version is much more accessible. And yes, white not green. The green of the name refers to its youth, because it's always drunk young. The grapes – Alvarinho, Loureiro, Trajadura, Avesso, Padernã and others – make light, acidic, aromatic wine which unfortunately is often sweetened for export. If you want the real thing, look for a single-estate wine rather than a brand.

Dão and Bairrada

Dão and Bairrada are undergoing something of a renaissance and a number of small, quality-driven estates are emerging. Many producers are putting

---

Esporão, in Alentejo, employ Portuguese-domiciled Australian David Baverstock, one of the most influential of contemporary Portuguese winemakers. Trincadeira, a grape variety of the south, is increasingly made as a varietal.

The Grapes

This is where Portugal's treasury of unique grapes is beginning to show its worth.

BAGA is the red grape of Bairrada, and it's found in Dão and the Ribatejo, too. It makes deep-coloured, tannic wines with high acidity and lots of herby, strawberryish, plummy fruit. Increasingly, winemaking is aimed at bringing out the fruit and bottling earlier rather than beating it into submission in old oak casks.

ARAGONEZ, known as Tinta Roriz in northern and central Portugal, is the local name for Tempranillo. It's widely grown in the Alentejo and makes well-structured, strawberry-flavoured reds.

CASTELÃO FRANCÊS is found pretty well all over southern Portugal, sometimes under the names of Periquita or Santarém. It's a grape with very good potential, making juicy, generally rich, beefy reds.

ALVARINHO is the same as the Spanish Albariño, and makes similarly light, acidic, apricot-scented wine in Vinho Verde.

TOURIGA NACIONAL, the main port grape, is increasingly used in the Dão region, giving deep-coloured, tannic and concentrated wine.

LOUREIRO is an aromatic white grape grown for Vinho Verde. It has an attractive scent of peach.

TRAJADURA is normally blended with other Vinho Verde grapes; it adds body to the blend.

ROUPEIRO makes light white in the south, best drunk young.

FERNÃO PIRES is planted all over Portugal for white wine and can have quite an attractive grapy aroma.

ARINTO (alias Padernã in Vinho Verde) has high acidity and can even age rather well. It's common in the Ribatejo.

a huge amount of effort into producing modern, fruity styles that are a world away from the tired old oak of yesteryear. Dão, hidden high in the hills, makes reds (increasingly based on Touriga Nacional) that taste of strawberries and plums baked with herbs; Bairrada, coming from a scrubby, placid lowland area, and based on Baga, is fruity but tannic, with peppery, plum and blackcurrant flavours. The whites of both areas, especially those based on Encruzado, Maria Gomes (Fernão Pires) or Bical, are good. When they're from a modern producer they can be fresh and herby and unusual.

Alentejo

The Alentejo is the source of both good juicy, inexpensive reds and whites from the local co-ops and some exceedingly good wines from private estates. The latter are much more expensive, but they really are worth it. The reds have the typical cherry-and-chocolate fruit of local Aragonez, Castelão Francês and Moreto grapes aged in Portuguese oak, but with depth and complexity as well, a combination of power and finesse. The top whites are also unusual, and can combine local varieties like Roupeiro with a touch of Chardonnay.

Don't bother too much about whether a wine has a DOC, an IPR or is simply Vinho Regional Alentejo: it's the dedication of the producer that counts, and while most of the DOC wines are good value and cheap and cheerful, some of the most thrilling are from IPRs.

Other Regions

The same holds true of the west of the country, except that we actually don't see that many DOC table wines from here. **Colares** is grown in clifftop sand dunes overlooking the Atlantic, and its main claim to fame is that phylloxera never reached here, since the louse couldn't live in the sand. The red is fantastically tannic, and there's a bit of white, from the Malvasia grape.

But it's the IPR regions round here, and all the way up the coast, that are leading the way. Look for the regions of **Estremadura**, **Ribatejo** and **Terras do Sado**. The latter is the source of some excellent blends of local and international varieties (often made by Australian winemakers) as well as being home to sweet fortified white Moscatel de Setúbal (see p.157). There are some great wines from all of these, at all price levels. The inexpensive whites are not quite as good as the inexpensive reds but the reds have more of that lovely cherry-and-chocolate fruit.

Harvesting grapes for Vinho Verde in the Minho. Vines are traditionally trained high above the ground on trellises to avoid damp and to enable cabbages and other crops to be grown below.

Port and Douro

The astonishing thing about port is not that it's so good, but that it exists at all. It is a product of trade as much as of nature, and the first merchants to trudge unwillingly on muleback up the hot, desolate Douro Valley, staying at inns that were so infested with fleas that they preferred to sleep on the tables rather than on the beds, to buy raw, rustic wine from growers who didn't even speak French, never mind English, were not at all happy with their purchases. They would have preferred to have been staying in civilized comfort in Bordeaux, buying claret.

But this was the late 17th century, and Britain's regular quarrels with France meant that French wines were either taxed at punitive levels or prohibited altogether. An alternative source of supply had to be found.

The Methuen Treaty of 1703 decreed that the main substitute would be Portuguese wine. The merchants must have been dismayed. What was there, after all? The thin, acidic wines of the coastal regions? Hardly John Bull's sort of thing. The wines from further inland were just the opposite: black, tannic wines of no subtlety or finesse. They would have to be brought downriver and treated to make sure they didn't deteriorate on the journey to Britain. The best treatment would probably be a hefty dose of brandy.

Thus was born one of the great wines of the world. Those early ports were simply red table wines fermented out to dryness, and then given a slug of alcohol. British drinkers, accustomed to something slightly more refined, were not impressed. It was not until brandy began to be

Quinta do Crasto, positioned above the Douro river between the towns of Regua and Pinhão, is the new sensation of the Douro. Wine previously sold as bulk is now fashioned into delicious ports and red table wines.

added during the fermentation, to kill the yeasts and leave residual sweetness in the wine, that port began to take the form we know now.

The Douro vineyards stretch along the banks of the river and its tributaries almost as far as the Spanish border. They are mostly on terraces, supported by painstakingly constructed drystone walls, and so narrow that they cannot be worked mechanically. Newer plantings are on broader terraces built with a bulldozer, or are unterraced, in rows running up and down the slopes. All are on crumbly schist soil: any granite outcrops in a vineyard may not be planted. In the 1980s money poured into the region in the form of loans from the World Bank, and subsidized vineyards, all of excellent quality, sprang up all over. Not all these are being used for port – the port market simply wouldn't be able to cope with all the extra wine. Instead it is going into what the Douro is discovering is a nice little earner – table wine.

DOURO TABLE WINES

Many of the most famous port companies still prefer to focus on fortified wines, leaving the table wine field wide open to innovative companies able to exploit the quantities of high-quality grapes available. Some employ Australian winemaking expertise, but it is noticeable that all insist on maintaining the character of the local grapes, and often use the most traditional winemaking methods, updated where necessary. Styles vary between light and juicy and made for drinking young, to big, tannic wines full of smoke and spice and plums that will age well in bottle. These are some of the best red table wines in Portugal.

MAKING PORT

Let's get back to port, however, and the process by which it is made. Once picked, the grapes are brought to the farm, or quinta. Traditionally they were then piled into wide granite troughs called *lagares*. Then, as soon as the men returned from the vineyards, they washed their feet and jumped into the *lagar* to spend the rest of the night treading the grapes.

The Grapes

There are 80 or so varieties grown in the Douro. Here are the five best.

TOURIGA NACIONAL is one of Portugal's best red grapes, if not the best. It has elegance and structure as well as concentration, and a flavour of ripe plums, spice and violets.

TOURIGA FRANCESA is a perfumed variety, less concentrated than Touriga Nacional, but with good rich fruit.

TINTA BARROCA adds good colour and tannin to the port blend.

TINTA RORIZ is the same as Spain's Tempranillo, and contributes strawberry fruit and good structure and longevity to the blend.

TINTA CÃO has finesse and longevity.

Two top Douro table wines that show the enormous potential of this region. Both use local grape varieties: Barca Velha is mainly Tinta Roriz while Quinta do Crasto is made from a blend of Tinta Roriz, Touriga Nacional, Touriga Francesa and Tinta Barroca.

Some quintas still use this method, and reserve it for their finest vintage wines. The human foot exerts just the right pressure on the grapes: enough to extract colour and tannin, but not enough to break the bitter pips. The cheaper alternative is autovinification, done in huge vats like coffee percolators, that are also designed to extract maximum colour and tannin during the short fermentation. Because whichever method is used, once the alcohol level reaches about six degrees the wine is run off the skins and fortified with brandy. In the spring it is brought down (by lorry, these days) to Vila Nova de Gaia, the town that faces Oporto across the mouth of

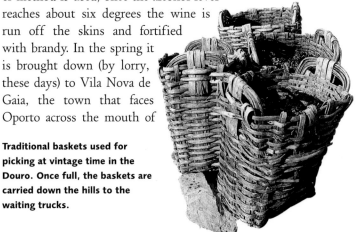

Traditional baskets used for picking at vintage time in the Douro. Once full, the baskets are carried down the hills to the waiting trucks.

The grapes for finest vintage port are still trodden in *lagares* in the traditional way.

Taylor's vintage ports are always among the longest-lived, acquiring great finesse and superb flavour after 20 years or more. Ferreira is well known for its excellent tawny ports. This example is creamy, nutty and consistently fine.

the Douro, there to age in the merchants' lodges, or warehouses. (Some port is also aged up in the Douro Valley these days; it used to be considered too hot, but air conditioning and insulation can do wonders.) How they are aged, and when they are bottled, varies according to their style.

PORT STYLES

There are many different styles of port; choosing can be a complicated business.

Vintage ports are the product of a single year, bottled about two years after the vintage, when they are still tough, fiery, uncompromisingly savage, rich and heady, and will need ten to 15 years in bottle to soften into something sweet, perfumed, with the most delicious blend of blackberry, blackcurrant, cherry and damson fruits, a tobacco or herby spice and a peppery heart. Many ports are now accessible younger, however, due to changes in the vinification methods. Vintage ports are only 'declared' in the best years, which usually means three or four years in ten.

Single-quinta or **off-vintage ports** are the alternative, in the next best years. These too are the products of a single year, and are made and aged in exactly the same way as traditional vintage ports. (The difference is that traditional vintage ports are not single-estate wines – Taylors, for example, bases its vintage port on Quinta de Vargellas, but releases Vargellas as a single-quinta port in the next best years.) They are based on

single estates of high quality and are released when the year isn't quite good enough for a vintage declaration. They mature in bottle, but are usually released when almost mature, at eight or ten years old. They're less intense than vintage wines, but have the same characteristics.

Crusted ports are a blend of several years, bottled young and maturing in bottle; and throwing a 'crust' or deposit as they age. They are good quality, and need decanting before being drunk.

Late Bottled Vintage, or **LBV**, is wine from a single year, but is not in the same bracket as vintage port or single-quinta because it is bottled after four to six years in cask, when it is ready to drink. The best LBVs are the unfiltered ones that need decanting; these have lots of character, which is more than can be said for the others, most of which are merely sweet and on the light side.

Vintage Character wines are similar, but are not from a single vintage and have none of the character of vintage port.

Tawny ports are aged entirely in cask and should be drunk immediately they are released. They are soft, subtle-flavoured ports, with a sweetness akin to brown sugar and raisins, though younger ones can be plummy, too. The best have an age designation – ten, 20, 30 or over 40 years – and are of excellent quality. Younger, cheaper tawnies are blended from lesser-quality wines.

Ruby ports are inexpensive, and bottled young while the wine is still strong and fiery, with a simple grape-skin sweetness.

Colheita ports are a style favoured by the Portuguese houses, and they can be very good too. Basically they are tawny ports from a single year, aged in cask and then sold when ready to drink.

White ports are more common than they once were although they're not seen, or indeed drunk, that often outside Portugal. They are much fresher and lighter than they used to be, but are still often best drunk with tonic water and plenty of ice.

CORK

Corks have been used to seal bottles since the early 17th century, although the ancient world also knew about cork and used it to seal amphorae. As a bottle stopper it has many advantages: it's elastic, so if it's squeezed into a bottle neck it will expand outwards to fit it snugly; it's impervious to most liquids, and providing it's kept damp and not allowed to shrink, it's airtight. It comes from the bark of the cork oak, *Quercus suber*, which likes mild, relatively damp conditions, and thrives in Portugal. It also grows in Catalonia, North Africa, Italy and southern France, but most of the world's wine corks come from Portugal.

You can easily spot a cork oak. Its bark is stripped every nine years, and so there'll be a line roughly where the branches start, below which the bark is thinner. If it's been stripped recently the exposed wood will be a rich red colour, right down to the ground. Sometimes you see cork oaks interspersed with other trees in mixed woodland – the cork oaks can be perched on the most inaccessible slopes and outcrops, and yet there's that bright reddish-brown trunk, indicating that someone has braved the rocks and scree to harvest the bark. In the Alentejo, cork oaks dot the land as far as the eye can see. They provide shelter from the sun for the herds of black bulls, intended for the bull ring, that graze these plains.

The bark, once removed, is left outside to dry before being cut. You can tell the quality of a wine cork by its length and by the number of imperfections on its surface: the longer and smoother the better is the rule. A really good wine cork will have hardly a mark on it.

The biggest problem with cork is not visible to the eye. When a wine is said to be 'corked', it has a strong musty, drainy smell that can come from a chemical compound called Trichloranisole, or TCA, and this can come from corks that have been treated with chlorine as part of the production process. Unfortunately you don't know a cork is tainted until you taste the wine.

Even the best cork won't last for ever. Wines may be recorked every 20 or 25 years (if you're really grand the cellarmaster of the property that made the wine might come to you to do it); agglomerate corks, made of cork trimmings stuck together, are used for everyday wines and are not suitable for long aging.

FAR LEFT **Cork trees growing outside Arronches, near the city of Portalegre.**
LEFT **A close up of a piece of cork oak.**

Madeira and Other Fortified Wines

When the first Portuguese explorers got to Porto Santos, an island that sits in the Atlantic within spitting distance (almost) of Madeira, all they could see of the latter was a turbulent pile of dark clouds. The seamen decided that these were 'vapours rising from the mouth of Hell'; who can blame them for heading back to the Algarve?

If they'd peered beyond the clouds they'd have seen sheer and jagged rock, thick with forest. When the Portuguese did begin to settle it, their leader, Zarco 'the blue-eyed', burnt the forest to make way for houses and agriculture; the blaze lasted for seven years and left behind it a thick layer of wood ash. This, combined with the volcanic soil, gives wines with high acidity – crucial for longevity.

Madeira, by virtue of its position 645km (400 miles) off the coast of Morocco, became a useful stopping-off point for merchant ships. They picked up casks of local wine on their way, and soon discovered that this wine tasted even better after it had been through the Tropics, pitching and rolling in the hold of a ship. When, as late as the 1900s, it became too expensive to induce this special cooked, smoky flavour by sending the wine halfway round the world and back, the producers devised an alternative, and nowadays the wines are cooked at home.

MAKING MADEIRA

There are various ways of producing Madeira, however, and they depend on the quality of the base wine. The cheapest wines are heated in estufas, which are large tanks with heating coils inside; the wines spend at least three months at a temperature of 40-50°C (104-122°F).

Better wines go into 600-litre (132-gallon) wooden casks and are stored in heated rooms for longer, perhaps six months. It's an altogether gentler way of treating the wine.

The very best wines have no artificial heating at all. Instead they rest in 600-litre casks under the eaves of the lodges, or warehouses, for at least two to three years – and remember that Madeira is subtropical, so it's quite warm enough here to impart the typically smoky-sour flavour of great Madeira. They are then moved but kept in cask for a further 20 or so years. These are the wines that go into the rare vintage Madeiras.

CLASSIFICATION

Madeiras are classified by quality and by grape variety. **Three-year-old** Madeira is called Selected, Finest or Choice. The next rung up is **five-year-old**, known as Reserve or Old. Old Reserve or Very Old Madeira will have been aged for a minimum of **ten years**; wines aged

The Grapes

The first four grapes are the noble varieties of Madeira; Moscatel is grown on the mainland.

SERCIAL makes the driest Madeira, with a light gold colour, steely acidity and savoury 'attack'. It is the most shocking of Madeira flavours, and needs a good ten years to be remotely ready to drink.

VERDELHO gives the softest of the four types of Madeira. But soft is a relative term here, since the wine is still pungent and smoky, although with a fair amount of medium-sweet fruitiness.

BUAL, or Boal, gives rich brown wine with the ever-present Madeira acidity.

MALMSEY is probably the Greek Malvasia grape, which was the first planted in Madeira some 500 years ago. This dark brown wine is startlingly sweet, yet its almost caramel richness is intertwined with a smoky perfume and a refreshing nip of acidity which is unexpected in such a luscious wine.

MOSCATEL, the basis of Setúbal, has the typical grapy aroma and flavour of all the Muscat family. When made sweet it takes on a spicy, raisiny note.

An ornamental Madeira barrel end. The barrels used are always made of old wood because the flavour of wood is not desirable in the finished product.

Most of the vineyards in Madeira are near the coast – further inland, the terrain is too mountainous. These new plantings are in the north of the island near Santana.

HENRIQUES&HENRIQUES

MADEIRA
MALMSEY
10

Under EU law, you can now rely on a wine called Malmsey being at least 85 per cent made from the grape of this name.

for **15 years** are known as Extra Reserve. At the top of the quality ladder are the **Vintage** wines. These are not sold until a minimum of 22 years after the vintage. During this time they will have spent 20 years in cask and a further two in bottle. They seem to live forever.

Now, grape varieties. There are four main 'noble' varieties on Madeira: Sercial, Verdelho, Bual and Malmsey, of which Sercial makes the driest wine and Malmsey the sweetest. Until Portugal joined the EU and became subject to the EU rule that says that if a grape variety is named on the label it must constitute at least 85 per cent of the blend, a Madeira could bear the name of a grape while in fact containing very little of that grape. The workhorse grape was Tinta Negra Mole, which could be made sweet or dry and bore as little resemblance to Sercial, Verdelho or the rest as crab sticks do to fresh crab. Well, not any more. If a Madeira says Sercial or whatever on the label, at least 85 per cent of it, these days, will be Sercial. Wines based on Tinta Negra Mole just call themselves pale dry, dark rich and so on.

OTHER FORTIFIED WINES

There are a couple of fortified wines from mainland Portugal which also deserve a mention: Setúbal and Carcavelhos. **Setúbal**, from the Setúbal Peninsula south of Lisbon, is based on Moscatel, and the fermentation is stopped by the addition of brandy, just like port. The Moscatel grape skins are then left to macerate in the wine, which gives it its strong Muscat aroma; it is then aged in oak until it is deep and raisiny.

Carcavelhos is more like tawny port: it's fermented dry and then fortified, and aged in cask. It has a good nutty flavour and is rather attractive, but there's hardly any made now, and only one vineyard left.

GERMANY

German wine walks a tightrope. First there's the tightrope of quantity versus quality with, on the one hand, the lure of the mass market and the ease of shipping huge quantities of overstretched wine at low prices. On the other hand there is the quality option, with all the care, risks and restriction of yields that that implies. Due to the extremely cool climate, all German wine has to choose between quantity and quality.

But the tightrope metaphor can be extended, too, to the taste of fine German wine. It's the taut balance of sweetness and acidity that gives the best wines a high-tensile strength; these wines are not high in alcohol, and can seem fragile, but that taut balance enables them to live for years.

Rivers are vital to German wine. They map the vineyards simply because when the weather is as cold as it is here a large body of water can moderate the climate sufficiently for grapes to ripen. The best vineyards are often on slopes overlooking the rivers which greatly increases the amount of sunlight that reaches the vines. If you are determined to grow vines on the very margins of where they can ripen, you have to employ every trick available to beat the climate.

You even turn the soil to your advantage. Have you ever tried to walk up a steep slope of decomposed slate, and felt it slipping from under your feet, the smooth shards slithering away as you try to stand on them? Some of the most northerly German vineyards are on just such slopes – and if it's difficult to walk there, just imagine trying to plant vines. Yet slate retains the heat, and when there's not much heat to be had, every bit you can retain means another fraction of ripeness.

This problem – that to produce fine wine in Germany involves a great deal more effort, time and expense than it does in, say, Bordeaux's Médoc region – has been at the heart of Germany's vinous troubles in recent decades. Because while it is immensely difficult to make good wine in Germany, making poor wine is a doddle. And if customers (particularly customers abroad) are prepared to buy poor wine in large quantities, it's hard to blame producers for supplying it.

How do you make poor wine in Germany? First of all you uproot your Riesling vines. In most regions of Germany, Riesling is the finest grape: if you want that wonderful taut balance, Riesling is what you grow. But much German research in recent decades has been devoted to producing vine crosses that will yield riper grapes under almost any conditions. They don't taste like Riesling, but goodness, do they give quantities of grapes. So you'll plant Müller-Thurgau (actually bred by a Swiss in the last century), or Kerner, or Bacchus, or Optima or Ortega or any of a couple of dozen others. You won't choose the steepest vineyards, either; you'll find land elsewhere where it's practically flat and where you can work your vineyards with tractors. Costs are lower, yields are higher, and never mind what it tastes like.

The trouble is that the flood of these cheap wines to overseas markets has pretty well destroyed Germany's reputation as a producer of fine wine. The fine wines are still being produced, and they're better now than they were ten or 20 years ago; but it's harder and harder to sell them outside Germany. And yes, the good producers recognize the problem, and for some years now have been finding ways of addressing it.

One way has been to reduce the sweetness of the better wines. Sugary, insipid flavours

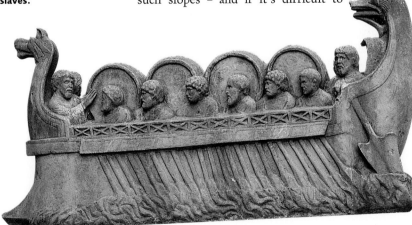

Trier, in the heart of the Mosel, was the northern capital of the Roman Empire and a centre of winemaking. This copy of a Roman carving found near Neumagen shows a Mosel wine ship complete with barrels and galley slaves.

POLAND

BERLIN ■

Elbe

■ LEIPZIG

S A C H S E N

Unstrut

S A A L E - U N S T R U T

DRESDEN ■

Saale

CZECH
REPUBLIC

■ COLOGNE

BONN ■

Rhine

A H R

M I T T E L R H E I N

Ahr

KOBLENZ •

M O S E L - S A A R - R U W E R

Mosel

BAD
KREUZNACH •

• TRIER

N A H E

Nahe

R H E I N G A U

WIESBADEN •

FRANKFURT

• MAINZ

R H E I N H E S S E N

WORMS •

P F A L Z

F R A N K E N

Main

WÜRZBURG

HESSISCHE
BERGSTRASSE

HEIDELBERG •

W Ü R T T E M B E R G

KARLSRUHE •

B A D E N

BADEN-
BADEN •

STUTTGART

Neckar

Danube

Rhine

F R A N C E

A L S A C E

FREIBURG •

■ MUNICH

A U S T R I A

KONSTANZ •

S W I T Z E R L A N D

N

0 km   50   100
0 miles   50

BERLIN •

QUALITY WINE REGIONS OF GERMANY

- Ahr
- Mittelrhein
- Mosel-Saar-Ruwer
- Rheingau
- Nahe
- Rheinhessen
- Pfalz
- Hessische Bergstrasse
- Franken
- Württemberg
- Baden
- Saale-Unstrut
- Sachsen

OPPOSITE **The town of Bernkastel on the Mosel is overlooked by its world-famous Doctor vineyard. It's an ideal site with slopes facing south and south-west, heat and light reflection from the river and wind protection from the wooded Docterberg hill behind.**

Egon Müller-Scharzhof wines are the most famous and expensive of German Rieslings. This Trockenbeerenauslese is one of the world's most intense and concentrated wines.

are the hallmarks of cheap German wines, goes the reasoning; therefore we must distinguish our fine wines from the others by emphasizing the acidity and the body, not the sweetness. In the Rheingau there is an association of top growers (Charta) dedicated to producing dry or half-dry wines; many of the new-wave wines of the Pfalz are also dry. There are also moves afoot in almost all regions to classify the finest vineyards, and even map the finest parts of such vineyards. Such moves may well find their way into law but at the moment they are still informal. This brings us neatly to a look at how German wine is currently classified.

CLASSIFICATION

There are two sides to look at in the German classification system: how the vineyards are categorized and how the wine is categorized. We'll do the vineyards first.

There are 13 wine regions, or **Anbaugebiete**, in Germany: Ahr, Mittelrhein, Mosel-Saar-Ruwer, Rheingau, Nahe, Rheinhessen, Franken, Hessische Bergstrasse, Rheinpfalz, Württemberg, Baden, Sachsen and Saale-Unstrut.

Each of these 13 regions is divided into **Bereiche**, very broad groupings of villages. A great deal of wine is sold under Bereich names, and it is seldom exciting.

Grosslagen are groupings of vineyards with supposedly similar characteristics within a Bereich. The worst are as poor as Bereich wines, but some small Grosslagen produce nice stuff.

Einzellagen are single vineyards. The wines of an Einzellage should nearly always be better than that of a Grosslage, but unfortunately it is pretty well impossible to tell which is which from the label.

Einzellage wines, you see, generally bear the name of their village followed by the name of the vineyard. Piesporter Goldtröpfchen, for example, means the Goldtröpfchen vineyard in the village of Piesport. So far, so simple. But Piesporter Michelsberg, which sounds as though it should be the Michelsberg vineyard in the village of

---

RIPENESS LEVELS

Now, I don't want to get too technical, so I'll just say that in Germany the ripeness of the grapes is measured in degrees Oechsle: they're a way of measuring sugar content, based on specific gravity. The ripeness categories of Kabinett, Spätlese, Auslese and so on all have lower and upper levels of Oechsle degrees laid down by law, and these can vary according to the region and the grape variety: Baden, being warmer, demands higher Oechsle degrees in nearly all categories. All serious growers, if they have a wine which could just scrape into, say, Spätlese, because its Oechsle reading is just high enough, will always demote it to Kabinett and opt for a top Kabinett rather than a lean Spätlese.

The problem is that the sugar content of the grapes is only a general indication of their ripeness. Other factors, such as the vineyard cultivation policy, vine age, vineyard site and the state of the grapes (clean, with noble rot or grey rot), are more decisive for wine quality than sugar content.

The man who gave his name to the system was the Pforzheim physicist Ferdinand Oechsle. During the 1830s he spent a great deal refining the work of another scientist, J-J Reuss, who from his base in Württemberg had been the first person in Germany to develop the method of weighing grape must. A similar scale, devised at Klosterneuburg, is also used in Austria.

Piesport, is in fact a Grosslage, and wine sold under its name is likely to be of no distinction whatever.

Now the wines. The legal classification here is by ripeness of grapes, measured by sugar levels, or Oechsle degrees (see box left).

Deutscher Tafelwein is the lowest level, and is generally very low indeed. Exceptions can be found in the Pfalz and Baden, where some growers make fine oak-aged wines outside the rules and sell them (expensively) as Deutscher Tafelwein.

Landwein is the supposed equivalent of French vin de pays, but is seldom used.

Qualitätswein bestimmter Anbaugebiete (QbA) is wine from one of the 13 demarcated regions and can have sugar added to the juice to increase alcohol.

Qualitätswein mit Prädikat (QmP) is where fine wine usually begins. These wines are higher quality, and are divided into six sub-categories:

Kabinett is wine made from ripe grapes (without any special selection, unlike Spätlese and Auslese) and is usually low in alcohol and medium-dry.

Spätlese is late-picked wine, usually dry to medium.

Auslese is made from selected overripe bunches of grapes. The wine is rich and concentrated, and can be anything from dry to really quite sweet.

Beerenauslese is made from selected overripe berries, often affected by noble rot. These wines are rare, concentrated and sweet.

Trockenbeerenauslese (TBA) is made from individually selected berries that have been shrivelled by noble rot. These wines are intensely concentrated and very sweet.

Eiswein is made from grapes frozen on the vine and picked at temperatures of -8°C (18°F) or below. They are intensely sweet and long-lived (see box on p. 165).

Trocken wines are dry, **halbtrocken** wines are half-dry; these terms will sometimes appear on the label.

HOW TO READ GERMAN WINE LABELS

I've picked three labels to show you how to find your way through the complicated nomenclature of German wines. One is reasonably ornate, with the Gothic lettering that's actually not found much these days on German labels; one is a model of clarity and one is of a high-quality Tafelwein.

First, Dr Loosen's Erdener Prälat. The more old-fashioned style label actually disguises the fact that this wine comes from one of the most modern wine producers of the Mosel. Erden is the village from which the wine comes, Prälat is the name of the vineyard. It's a single-vineyard wine in other words and that single vineyard, the Prälat, is arguably the greatest site of the Middle Mosel. 1997 is the vintage and Riesling Auslese tells us both the grape variety and the QmP category. Dr Loosen is the producer, and Bernkastel/Mosel is his address. Erzeugerabfüllung Weingut Oekonomierat Dr Loosen means 'bottled at the winery'. Alcohol levels are low so the wine will contain a lot of unfermented sugar and be sweet. 750 ml is the volume of the bottle. Mosel-Saar-Ruwer is the region.

J-J Prüm's label couldn't be easier to read. The main section of the label has the producer's name, the vintage, the name of the vineyard (the Sonnenuhr vineyard in the village of Wehlen in the Mosel) and the QmP category, in this case Spätlese. Move to the side of the label and you get the rest of the legally required information: the address where it was bottled, in this case at the estate; the black eagle which is the logo of the VDP (Verband Deutscher Prädikats-und-Qualitätsweingüter), an association of top estates and always the sign of a good producer, the alcohol level (low), the bottle volume, the grape name, the wine region and the quality category.

Karl Heinz Johner, down in the Pfalz, likes to do things his own way. He specializes in making fine wines that don't quite fit the official mould, so he sells them as Tafelwein, or table wine. So, reading from the top is the vintage, the grape variety (Weisser Burgunder, or Pinot Blanc), the table wine region (Oberrhein; table wine regions are different from quality wine regions); the fact that it was bottled by the grower, and his address; the alcohol level; the official quality level and the bottle volume.

Mosel-Saar-Ruwer

OPPOSITE The Goldtröpfchen vineyard just to the west of Piesport produces excellent Rieslings with the intense blackcurrant and peach aromas typical of Mosel-Saar-Ruwer.

For sheer, heart-stopping beauty you can't beat the Mosel Valley: the river is so tranquil as it twists and loops between Luxembourg and Koblenz, the 130-odd villages dotted along both banks are so picture-book pretty, and the vines tumble down the towering slopes that rear almost vertically above the river. It's a surprise to see anything growing on such precipitous slopes, such loose slate scree, let alone this carpet of vines unwinding along the hillside. Although the vines grow on both sides of the river, in all the best areas the river has carved an amphitheatre facing south as it has twisted and turned to find a way through the rock, and because the Mosel is so far north, it is really only on these slopes that the grapes fully ripen.

The Romans, who always had a good eye for a vineyard, knew this: wine from the Mosel supplied the great city of Trier, just downstream from the confluence of the Mosel and the Saar;

The Grapes

The invasion of the Mosel by Müller-Thurgau has done nothing for the region's reputation.

RIESLING is one of the great grapes of the world, and perhaps the finest white grape of all. On the Mosel-Saar-Ruwer it produces wine that is almost water-pale in colour yet with a piercing intensity that enables it to live for years.

MÜLLER-THURGAU, invented only a century ago as a Riesling lookalike which ripened earlier and gave more juice, has spread like wildfire through Germany, supplanting Riesling in many areas. In the Mosel it produces slightly raisiny fruit and a rather sharp flowering-currant nip to its usual pot-pourri perfume.

ELBLING is still grown in the Upper Mosel, near the Luxembourg border, mostly for use in Sekt. It produces clean, fresh wine with little character or finesse.

Riesling

if you want to get an idea of the importance of Trier to the government of the Roman Empire, just take a look at the massive Porta Nigra (the Black Gate) still standing in the city today: as blunt statements of power go, it certainly is hard to beat.

The Romans, though, mostly grew Elbling, and Riesling is the great grape of the Mosel today. It's not the only grape, however: there are, unfortunately, vineyards planted on flatter land, land with poor exposure to the sun, richer land – sites suited to many crops other than vines – which are planted with lesser grape varieties, and which sadly help to devalue the name of the Mosel. I've said it before but, as always in wine, you should trust the name of the producer above all.

The best wines are all Riesling. It produces some of the world's most thrilling flavours here, all apples and smoky slate and lean, steely acidity that after a few years is suffused by honey; these are light wines, but their fragility is deceptive. They live for years. Even a simple QbA will need two or three years, and a Kabinett can improve for at least five, and will live for ten. Spätlesen need seven or eight years, and will live for 12, 14 or more.

Most wines are made traditionally, which means medium-dry to medium-sweet. They're seldom very sweet – there's not a lot of Beerenauslese made here, and a Mosel Auslese is honeyed rather than richly sweet. If the wines are fermented out dry then it's usually better if they are of Spätlese level or higher: Mosel Kabinett can tend to taste a bit on the bony side if it's trocken.

Vines are grown along the whole length of the Mosel, from the German border right up to Koblenz, but the finest part is the Middle Mosel, where the river winds back and forth, seeking a route through the slate cliffs. The differences between individual vineyards and growers are often greater than the differences between villages, so let's take a tour of the Middle Mosel then, heading north from Trittenheim to Zell.

Sundials, like this one in Zeltingen in the Middle Mosel, feature in quite a few German vineyards.

Middle Mosel

Trittenheim's finest vineyard is the Apotheke (pharmacy) site; Altärchen is also good and steep. The wines are sleek, crisp but relatively light examples that need a good vintage to have much weight.

Piesport is an even more famous name, and one that has been shockingly devalued by the dross sold under the Grosslage name of Piesporter Michelsberg. Piesporter Goldtröpfchen will be a very different kettle of fish: ripe, slightly spicy, with lovely balance and very long living. The wine can be drunk after two years but will be better with up to ten. The village itself lies in a horseshoe-shaped bend, where the river swings right round and leaves a south-facing amphitheatre; the vineyards facing it on the flatter land of the opposite bank are simply not in the same league; they're where much of the poor Grosslage wine comes from. Yields here

will be much higher, and the vines may not even be Riesling: the wine will be softer, grapy, simple and dull.

At **Brauneberg** there's a sight that is familiar along the Mosel: the town on one bank, the vineyards facing it across the river. It makes perfect sense: why build houses on top-quality vineyard land? Especially when it makes wine of the robust, peachy style of Juffer or Juffer Sonnenuhr. Both have an ideal, precipitous, southeast exposure. Sonnenuhr means sundial: it's one of many German vineyards where a sundial is set into the vineyards for the convenience of the townspeople on the far bank. The wines are more elegant than those from Piesport but with power and structure.

Bernkastel – or, to give it its full name, Bernkastel-Kues – has had its name devalued just as much as that of Piesport. Bernkasteler Kurfürstlay or Bernkasteler Badstube are Grosslage wines; Bereich Bernkastel is a Bereich name. Bernkasteler Doctor, on the other hand, is one of the finest vineyards on earth: a steep patch of slate high above the town that can give wine of infinite complexity, all smoke and spice, honey and steel, delicacy and strength. The top wines show their potential only after eight to ten years.

Graach is in the same league of quality, though its Domprobst or Himmelreich sites are less famous; **Wehlen,** also just as good, has Sonnenuhr which produces powerful, firm wines. There's another Sonnenuhr at **Zeltingen.** At **Ürzig** the wines are suddenly spicy, and its top vineyard, Würzgarten, means spice garden. The wines are the ultimate in elegance and charm. In **Erden** the superb Prälat vineyard is the best and produces the most opulent and exotic of all Mosel-Saar-Ruwer wines. The steep terraced slopes have a perfect southern exposure and the vineyard enjoys the warmest mesoclimate in the region. The site immediately to the east, the Treppchen, is next best, giving wines with a similarly exotic fruit, almond and mineral character, with almost as much intensity as the Prälat.

KOBLENZ

Winningen

ZELL/MOSEL

Mosel

Rhine

COCHEM

Zell

WITTLICH

Ürzig   Erden   TRABEN-TRARBACH

Zeltingen

Wehlen   Graach

Piesport   Bernkastel-Kues

Brauneberg

Trittenheim

LUX.

TRIER   Lieslbach

KONZ   Kasel

Ruwer

Wiltingen

Ayl   SAAR-   RUWER

Ockfen

Saarburg   Serrig

OBERMOSEL

MOSELTOR

Saar

Nahe

BERNKASTEL

BEREICHE WINE AREAS OF MOSEL-SAAR-RUWER

- Moseltor
- Obermosel
- Saar-Ruwer
- Bernkastel
- Zell/Mosel
- Main wine villages

KOBLENZ

0 km   20
0 miles   10   20

N

Saar

The Upper Mosel, nearer the German border, has fewer famous villages; but it is here that the tiny river Saar joins the Mosel. The spring comes late to the Saar, and autumn often sinks into a dank, early winter before the Riesling has had time to ripen. In those years the wines tend to provide the base wine for **Sekt** (see box on p.170), German sparkling wine. But when the sun continues long into October, then the wines can achieve a scarcely credible mixture of sharpness and fruit and perfume, combined with a slaty, steely character from the soil. And the hard winters mean that **Eiswein** (see box opposite), a rarity in most regions, can be made almost every year here.

A surprising number of vineyards are in single ownership here; this is a rarity in Germany, where the vineyards have been divided and subdivided over generations. Schloss Saarstein is one such, at **Serrig;** other vineyards here are Vogelsang and Herrenberg. (It's worth remembering that any vineyard with a name ending in 'berg' is likely to be steep; and steepness, as already mentioned, is an aid to quality in Germany.) **Ockfen** has its great Bockstein vineyard and **Ayl** has Kupp, making extraordinarily honeyed and steely wines. **Wiltingen's** best site is Scharzhofberg; Wiltinger Scharzberg, by contrast, is a Grosslage wine.

Ruwer

The Ruwer, flowing into the Mosel downstream from Trier, makes only tiny quantities of wine from a meagre 280 hectares (690 acres) of vineyards. Like the Saar, it needs a good warm year to make the sort of honeyed, intense wines of which it is capable. It's so much colder here than in the main part of the Mosel because the Ruwer flows more or less north, and has very few sites with really good southerly exposure to the sun. But the Riesling grape dominates, and at least the region hasn't been devalued by a flood of cheap wine. And its two best estates, Maximin Grunhäus and Karthäuserhof, are truly world class.

Maximin Grünhaus in the Ruwer Valley is one of Germany's greatest estates. Carl von Schubert vinifies separately the wines of his three vineyards under sole ownership (Abtsberg, Brudersberg and Herrenberg), making chiefly dry and off-dry wines of subtlety and distinction.

EISWEIN

It is winter – December, or even January. It could even be Christmas Eve or New Year's Day. Your Riesling vines, high on their hill in Serrig, or Bernkastel, or the Ruwer, are bare of leaves, but some grapes remain. You have left them there deliberately, protected as best you can from the birds, and now, as night falls, you are listening anxiously to the local weather forecast. The announcer says the magic words: ' a low of -8°C'. You're on the telephone within a matter of minutes. Be ready, you tell your pickers: we may start before dawn. You set the alarm for the early hours, and stumble in the dark to read the temperature outside -7°C: that's fine. It will be colder in the vineyards, with the wind sweeping through the vines. You summon your pickers: they're awake, and waiting.

By the time the sun comes up over the hills the vines are stripped and the grapes are in the press. Their water content, frozen solid, stays behind with the skins, and the juice runs thick and sluggish into the tiny vat prepared for it. It will take the rest of the winter to ferment, and even then will have intense sweetness to match the intensity of acidity. It will also have a characteristic tang of snow in the aroma, and it will age for decades, unless it all gets drunk young.

But in the meantime, the hard, cold work is over for another year, there is gluhwein and sausages for breakfast, and the pickers are definitely in party mood.

Dr Richter's Mülheimer Helenenkloster vineyard is rare in Germany for producing a magical Eiswein virtually every year. Exotic fruit flavours yet bracing acidity are features of both this and Karthäuserhof.

The Rhine

The Rhine shapes a vast proportion of German winegrowing culture. It runs through Lake Constance, draining the southern Baden vineyards and forms the northern border of Switzerland. At Basel it finally deserts Switzerland and flows north through a wide, fertile basin, with Baden's main vineyards crowding the eastern bank. Then it's up past the Pfalz and Rheinhessen to the west and northern Baden and Hessische Bergstrasse to the right, until Mannheim, where the river Neckar, along whose banks Württemberg's vineyards flourish, joins the main flow.

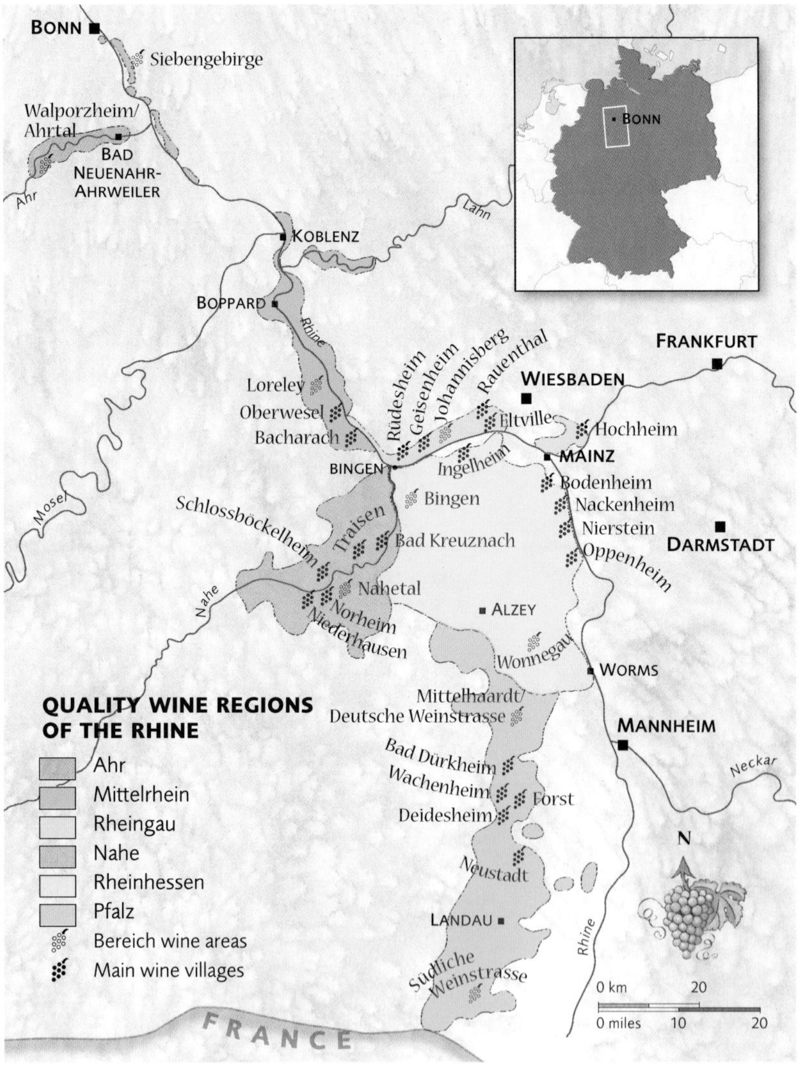

At Mainz the river Main pours its waters into the Rhine, nearly 80km (50 miles) west of its own Franconian vineyards, then the Rhine meets the mass of the Taunus Mountains and sweeps west, providing the perfect south-facing slope of the Rheingau. Finally, at Bingen where the Nahe joins the flood, it forces a gap through the hills and sets off north past the Mittelrhein to Koblenz, where the Mosel joins. And as the river surges up to Bonn, even the tiny Ahr trickles its offering into the mighty Rhine.

The Rheingau

If the Rhine didn't take a left turn where it does we would be deprived of some of the world's greatest white wine vineyards. It's because the river, heading gently north past the lazy hills of the Rheinhessen, suddenly hits a wall of slate and has nowhere else to go. Only about 50km (30 miles) later does it find a way through; and those 50km of steepish slate provide the ideal site for wines with a taste of grapes and honey, cut by the cold steely flavour of minerals and rounded by a smoky warmth. The German dessert wine tradition has its roots here: it's a prime area for nobly rotten wines. Auslesen are relatively easy to make in this warm climate, and Beerenauslesen and Trockenbeerenauslesen can also be found. Nearly all the vineyards are planted with Riesling, though Spätburgunder (Pinot Noir) is on the increase. And while the best of the wines are sensationally good, some of the most famous have been resting on their laurels, so choose with care.

The Rheingau, more than almost any other German wine region, is a land of great estates. In the past the Church and the nobility pretty well divided it up between them: Kloster Eberbach, now seen as the cultural wine centre of the region, was founded by the Cistercians in 1135, and a few years earlier the Benedictines had founded what later became known as Schloss Johannisberg; the schloss still crouches on the slopes above Geisenheim. Geisenheim itself is the site of an important viticultural research institute that has contributed a number of new

QUALITY WINE REGIONS OF THE RHINE

- Ahr
- Mittelrhein
- Rheingau
- Nahe
- Rheinhessen
- Pfalz
- Bereich wine areas
- Main wine villages

This small chapel, set in a perfect spot for contemplation, is between the Schonhell and Würzgarten vineyards, north of Hallgarten.

A leading light of Charta, Georg Breuer produces modern wines with modern labels from various sites in Rüdesheim.

vine crossings to German viticulture; thankfully these have taken little hold in their native region.

Hochheim, the first major village of the Rheingau, is separated from the main part by the town of Wiesbaden; the slopes are gentler here and the wines are full-bodied, deep and with a certain earthiness. Indeed, the Rieslings from the top Domdechaney, Kirchenstück and Hölle sites are the most powerful wines in the region. The old British term for Rhine wine, 'hock', was an abbreviation of Hockamore, a clumsy British attempt to pronounce Hochheim. Queen Victoria, who adored all things German, allowed a vineyard to be named after her, the Königin Victoria Berg, after she stopped there for a picnic.

Walluf has some good Spätburgunder, and **Rauenthal** produces spicy wines which often show their best at Auslese level, particularly from the Baiken vineyard. **Eltville's** vineyards are less famous individually, but it is the home of the local branch of the State Wine Domain; and if you go up a little valley you come to **Kiedrich,** where the wines are always best in the warmest vintages, and where the best site is Gräfenberg.

Erbach springs a surprise: its Marcobrunn vineyard, one of the best in Germany, is so low it's practically in the river yet it is a perfect suntrap, giving deep, sultry wines with full flavours and good structure. Exceptional vintages may last for 20 years or more. **Hattenheim** has some suntraps too, in the form of Nussbrunnen, Wisselbrunnen and Mannberg. Higher up is the Steinberg vineyard, and above that is the great grey pile of Kloster Eberbach. It's hard to find an exciting Steinberger these days but when good, they're sleek and racy. **Hallgarten** makes big, slow-developing wines; those of **Oestrich** are rich and honeyed, particularly when from the Lenchen or Doosberg sites. These are classic Rheingau wines, with crisp acidity and a hint of earthiness. At **Winkel** princely estates dominate the view, although they are not necessarily leaders in quality terms. Hasensprung is the best vineyard, giving wines of delicacy and perfume.

The Grapes

Riesling is the quality wine of the north, but makes room further south for others.

RIESLING is the grape that dominates the Rhine regions in quality terms, though in quantity it often lags behind Müller-Thurgau and others. In the Rheingau it gives wines of supreme elegance and longevity, reaching Beerenauslese level or higher; in the Pfalz it is richer yet drier, in the best parts of the Nahe it is fierier. The best vineyards in the Rhinehessen give well-structured Rieslings with a smoky tang; in Baden they are fuller-bodied, dry and honeyed.

MÜLLER-THURGAU is important in terms of quantity, but not quality. It gives ripe, pot-pourri-scented wines that are at their best in the Pfalz or Baden, and are usually blended.

GRAUBURGUNDER, alias Ruländer, alias Pinot Gris, is a grape of the southern Rhine, where it flourishes in Baden and the Pfalz. When made dry it has honeyed, earthy, spicy fruit, full and broad; when sweet it has a rich, honeyed, almost mushroom-rich flavour, but less aroma.

Riesling

Pinot Gris

WEISSBURGUNDER produces dry, well-structured wines, sometimes given some oak-aging in Baden and the Pfalz. Oak makes it more substantial; without it Weissburgunder is fresh and winey.

SILVANER is a speciality of the Rhinehessen, where it makes light, softish wines with a slight earthy tang.

TRAMINER, alias Gewürztraminer, is found in Baden and the Pfalz; as in Alsace, it needs acidity to keep its blowsy spiciness in check.

SPÄTBURGUNDER, or Pinot Noir, produces some very good wines indeed in the Rheingau, Pfalz and Baden, but it needs a dedicated grower and a market that has turned away from the German taste for sweet, jammy reds which developed in the 1960s and 1970s. Dry versions will probably be labelled as Spätlese or Auslese trocken.

Spätburgunder

Bodenheim is one of the Rheinhessen's oldest wine villages. As this sign says, it was first established in 754.

Geisenheim, where the viticultural institute has its home, nevertheless sticks to Riesling for its local vineyards; look for perfumed wines from the Rothenberg site. At **Rüdesheim** the mountains rise higher than ever, giving polished, rich wines from Berg Schlossberg and Berg Rottland.

And then the river turns. **Assmannshausen** faces away from the main part of the Rheingau and grows Spätburgunder. A trend for deeper-coloured, dry reds in recent years has greatly improved quality. At **Lorch** there's Riesling again, and it's pretty good, even if it doesn't have the fire of the best of the Rheingau.

Nahe

The Nahe touches the Rheingau and Rheinhessen and reaches out towards the Mosel, and there is no doubt that the best wines have something of all three regions. They have a bit of the floweriness of the Rheinhessen, and a little of the light tongue-tingling fresh acidity of the Mosel, but above all they have the grape and honey fruit of the Rheingau, and a little of the slate and smoke, too. This makes the top wines some of the loveliest in Germany, because the perfume of the fruit is more open, more orchard-scented than in the Rheingau, yet the acidity and slate are always there to keep the flowers and perfumes in place and add a mineral sheen to the fruit. However, this only applies to the central vineyards of Traisen, Norheim, Niederhausen, Schlossböckelheim and Monzingen, whose wines can also add a fiery spice to the mix. Elsewhere much merely adequate, soft wine is made, usually sold under Bereich or Grosslage names.

So let's take a closer look at the top villages. **Schlossböckelheim's** top sites are the Kupfergrube, which was a copper mine until early this century, and Felsenberg, which is centuries older. **Niederhausen** boasts the great Hermannshöhle though Steinberg, Hermannsberg and Klamm are pretty nearly as good. **Norheim** has Dellchen, Kirschheck and Kafels, though none of these is as famous as Traiser Bastei, the most remarkable vineyard of **Traisen**. It sits, insignificantly small, right at the foot of a towering red porphyry cliff, the Rotenfels. It's so small that the road and the railway probably take up more room than the vines, but it produces intensely fiery wines. The bigger Rotenfels is practically as good. **Bad Kreuznach** (a spa town, as you might expect) numbers Steinweg, Krötenpfuhl, Brückes and Kahlenberg among its top sites.

Rheinhessen

This is Germany's largest single wine region, and it's a curious blend of world fame and complete anonymity. Although it has 165 wine villages, scarcely half a dozen have any sort of fame, and even the most renowned, Nierstein, is famous largely because of the abuse of its reputation.

Nierstein is on a thin strip of angled valley bank sloping down to the Rhine. It has some wonderful sites which produce delectable Riesling, soft, intense and fragrant, with sweet grapes and spring flowers mingling deliciously. It also has one rather poor vineyard on less good slopes, called **Gutes Domtal.** This name has caught on, so much so that it has become the name of a Grosslage, while poor old Nierstein has had to give its name to the Bereich covering all the vineyards in the east of Hesse. Altogether the name of Nierstein is attached to a third of all the wines of the Rheinhessen, almost all of them unmemorable, while the true growers of Nierstein struggle to differentiate their products from the mass-produced plonk.

The vast majority of wine from the rest of the Rheinhessen is mopped up by **Liebfraumilch**. Since most villages grow light, flowery Müller-Thurgau or soft, fat Silvaner or new crossings, they are ideally suited to such cheap bulk blends.

The other villages that are worth seeking out are mostly on the Rheinterrasse (or Rhine front), the western side of the Rheinhessen. **Oppenheim** makes good Silvaner with a slightly earthy local style, and Nierstein on form is as scented and as fragrant as any wine in Germany. Wine from **Bodenheim** is a slightly lesser version in the same mould but **Nackenheim** is the source for some of the greatest Rieslings being made in

Germany today. Wines from Weingut Gunderloch are particularly impressive. Then in the north, looking across the Johannisberg in the Rheingau, is **Ingelheim**, which makes some tasty red, and at the junction of the Nahe and Rhine stands **Bingen**, with one superb hill which produces steely, coal-smoky Rieslings touched with honey.

Pfalz

The Pfalz, which used to be called the Rheinpfalz, is a region of astonishing richness and fertility; and there is something of this, too, in the wines. They're rich, luscious, even exotic, with mangoes and apricots and lychees all emerging with age. They also have enough body to them to be successful as dry wines. Not all are made dry, by any means; but particularly in the south, where some of Germany's most adventurous winemakers are experimenting with new techniques, dryness is common, and wines may even be oak-aged. At the opposite end of the scale is the large amount of bulk wine produced here for Liebfraumilch, which is of no more distinction than bulk wine from anywhere else in Germany.

The traditional fine wine area of the Pfalz is the north, just above **Neustadt**. The best sites are

The Hipping vineyard, just north of Nierstein village, ranks alongside Pettenthal, Brudersberg, Oelberg and Orbel, as one of the best vineyards on the entire Rhine.

Rainer Lingenfelder is a leading exponent of this grape – in his hands a simple Scheurebe becomes superb and really shows what this variety is capable of.

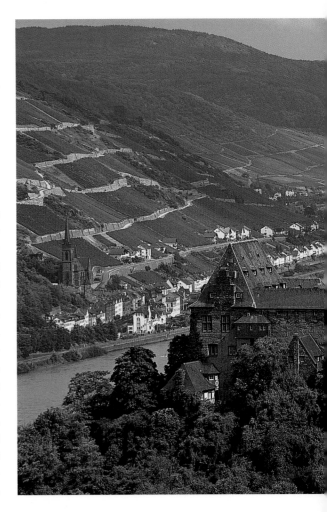

Since leaving the regional co-operative to go solo in 1987, Bernard Huber has shot to fame winning a whole series of blind tastings with his powerful Spätburgunder, his barrel-fermented Chardonnay and his rich, dry Gewürztraminer.

SEKT

In German-speaking countries the sparkling wine is known as Sekt – but beware, in Germany, of anything labelled 'Sekt' as opposed to 'Deutscher Sekt'. The former will be imported from anywhere with cheap wine to sell and merely fizzed in Germany, whereas the latter is German through and through. Riesling is the best grape, and if the wine is Riesling it will say so on the label; the Pinot family (Weissburgunder, Ruländer alias Grauburgunder, and Spätburgunder) also make successful wines.

Germany is also fond of red Sekt, and this can be surprisingly sweet; so check the label for the word 'trocken' if you don't want a mouthful of fizzy jam.

steeper than they are further south. In **Kallstadt** a warm climate combined with the excellent Saumagen site result in some of Germany's richest dry Rieslings. **Bad Dürkheim** is not only a spa town but hosts an annual wine festival; **Wachenheim** has more elegance to its wine and makes superb-quality Rieslings from its Goldbächel and Gerümpel vineyards.

Forst wines are riper, more honeyed: wines from the Jesuitengarten are especially concentrated, but most Forst wines need warm years to produce their fullest flavours. **Deidesheim** also makes great wine, though they won't be found under the Grosslage name of Deidesheim Hofstück – yet another example of the legal abuse of the greatest names of German wine. Look instead for wines from the top sites of Grainhübel, Hohenmorgen, Kalkofen and Leinhöhle.

In the south, villages to look for include **Leinsweiler, Siebeldingen, Birkweiler** and **Burrweiler**. As in the north, but perhaps even more so, there is Traminer, Weissburgunder, Scheurebe, Grauburgunder and Spätburgunder, few of which ripen very successfully further north. Scheurebe excels itself in the Pfalz, and gives wines with spice and fire.

Baden

This is the warmest of all German wine regions; the vineyards sit along the east bank of the Rhine, on the foothills of the Black Forest, looking across to Alsace; there are also some vineyards north of Baden-Baden, and there are some pleasant summer resort wines made along the north banks of the Bodensee (Lake Constance).

This is also a region where Riesling, except for a few spots, plays second fiddle to the Pinot family. Pinot Gris (known variously as Ruländer or Grauburgunder), Weissburgunder and Spätburgunder all ripen well here, with the white grapes giving honeyed dry wines and the red Spätburgunder producing good fruit and structure, although the flavours can sometimes be a little jammy; the German taste for sweetish reds is changing, but it hasn't yet vanished. Gewürztraminer makes almost blowsily rich wine here,

and even the Müller-Thurgau and the notoriously neutral Gutedel take on a sunny southern flavour. The Riesling's main home in Baden is at **Durbach**, where they call it Klingelberger.

Hessische Bergstrasse

Bensheim in this tiny side valley vineyard region east of Worms is the hottest town in Germany. Arriving there you notice first the fruit trees and the balmy Mediterranean warmth rather than the vines, which isn't that surprising: there aren't many of them. The Riesling is the main grape, and most of the wines are made at co-operatives.

Mittelrhein

If you want fairytale castles, near vertical sheets of vineyard rising out of tumbling river water, with picturesque gabled villages snuggling into the foot of the rockface, and the distant strains of the Lorelei maidens humming away in the depths of your imagination, then this is the place for you (along with several million other like-minded tourists). This stretch of the Rhine between Bingen and Koblenz is intensely beautiful. The wines are impressively strong-tasting, racy and slaty with good rough fruit and a sting of acidity. They are nearly all Riesling and the best are generally from **Boppard, Bacharach** and **Oberwesel.**

Ahr

Most of the wine here is pale, cherry-tasting red, usually from the Spätburgunder grape, although there are some growers producing serious Burgundian-style Spätburgunder aged in oak barrels.

The impressive Burg Stahleck looks across the Rhine to the town and vineyards of Lorch at the eastern extremity of the Rheingau.

The Food of Germany

IN THE LAST COUPLE of decades there has been something of a revolution in German cuisine. The country now boasts more Michelin-starred restaurants than any other, apart from France.

Germans are primarily meat-eaters but they do serve freshwater fish like pike, trout and carp, and in the north there are herrings.

Meat can take the form of wild boar, venison, or other types of game. Hare and wild duck are common. Beef features too, but the animal that is most beloved of the German kitchen is the pig. Sausages and hams of all kinds find their way into many different dishes, often matched with fruit – cranberries, perhaps, or apples. The sweet and sour, smoky and piquant flavours of traditional German food are complemented perfectly with off-dry grapy white wines.

In the north, you can find hearty dumplings, often flavoured with ham or cheese. Cabbage is a popular accompaniment. Green cabbage is pickled as *sauerkraut*; the red variety is often cooked with apple as *apfelrotkohl*.

In the south, freshwater fish – pike or trout – is cooked in Riesling and fresh herbs abound in soups and sauces. But the pig is never forgotten for long: a favourite dish is *Himmel und Erde,* or Heaven and Earth: blood sausage, fried onion, apple sauce and mashed potatoes, all mixed together.

You should also look out for specialities like white asparagus between April and June and wild mushrooms in the summer and autumn.

Bread is a another distinctive feature of German cuisine. Rich-tasting black rye bread, known as *pumpernickel* is a national favourite as is the salted *brezel*.

And the Germans love their *kaffee und kuchen* (coffee and cakes). Black Forest gateau is an example of a famous product sadly debased.

Black Forest gateau

Other German Regions

The Rhine and Mosel are the best-known sources of German wine abroad, but there are other parts of Germany that also produce wine. Most of them have considerable local renown, and often thirsty local markets that drink the lot.

Franken

Franken wines are unusual in Germany: they are dry and not that aromatic, and the finest come from the Silvaner grape. In this, Franken seems a long way from the Rhine and Mosel.

In fact Franken, or Franconia, is a good 80km (50 miles) away from the Rheingau, and it hugs the river Main as it crosses the country in a great wobbly W before joining the Rhine at Mainz. Its centre is Würzburg, where the 12th-century Marienberg castle and the baroque Residenz, with its Tiepolo ceiling, are among the glories of Germany; but there are few concentrated stretches of vineyard land and forest, rock and pasture occupy much of the landscape. Apart from the traditionally German south-facing river valley slopes, there are vineyards scattered in small pockets haphazardly across the region, wherever there is a particularly warm cranny or the risk of frost is low. Frost is a terrible problem here; harsh winters are commonplace and the summer is short, and it can cause wildly fluctuating yields.

The main grape is the Müller-Thurgau, which can produce reasonable quality here, and there are umpteen others, including Scheurebe, Bacchus, Rieslaner (a cross of Riesling and Silvaner), Kerner and Riesling. But Silvaner is Franken's star grape. It gives wine with something honeyed and earthy, with a vegetal overtone which is more tomatoes than cabbage. It needs the best sites, and then produces wine which ages well: the Stein vineyard at Würzburg is a top site by any standards, and Riesling grows here as well. Randersacker's Pfülben vineyard, the Lump vineyard at Escherndorf and the Julius-Echter-Berg vineyard at Iphöfen are almost equally splendid.

Württemberg

The river Neckar and its numerous tiny tributaries run a tortured, convoluted course as they head north to join the Rhine at Mannheim. This provides a thousand small, steep, south-facing slopes to capture the summer and autumn sun. But many of these south-facing folds in the river bank can only squeeze in a few hectares of vines, and most of the wine gets drunk locally. More than half the wine is red and the best comes from Limberger grapes. A local favourite is pallid, vaguely red wine from the Trollinger grape tasting of coal smoke and strawberries. Isolated steep sites on the Neckar produce fine Riesling.

Sachsen and Saale-Unstrut

The climate in these two regions of the former Democratic Republic is continental, with cold winters and the danger of late frosts but warm summers. The wines are fermented out to dryness and can have good body. The best wines are from Grauburgunder, Riesling and Traminer.

Franconians were bottling their wines in these dumpy little flasks (*Bocksbeutels*) long before Mateus Rosé from Portugal was a gleam in its inventor's eye.

The Grapes

No one variety dominates, though each region has its favourites.

SILVANER reaches its greatest heights in Germany in Franken, producing soft, earthy dry wines that age well, but are untypical of German wines in that they are not aromatic. In a sheltered site the grapes reach good levels of ripeness but even so wines of above Auslese level are rare.

RIESLING is a minority grape in all these regions, and seldom hits the heights of excitement that it does in, say, the Mosel. But the wines are appley and peachy and have good acidity.

MÜLLER-THURGAU produces more solid, structured wine in Franken than elsewhere.

KERNER is one of the better modern vine crossings. Bred in 1969, it has a leafy, appley aroma, slightly coarse but attractive. It's a minority grape in Württemberg and Franken.

LIMBERGER is at its best in Württemberg where it produces respectable red.

TROLLINGER is known as Schiava or Vernatsch in northern Italy, where it probably originated. In Württemberg it is made rather pale and sweet.

Juliusspital's dry Silvaner from top vineyard Würzburger Stein in Franken is an excellent example of the style – full-bodied, with ripe apple and citrus, and a fresh aftertaste.

AUSTRIA

It's impossible to travel for long in the wine regions of Austria without thinking of empire. The Austro-Hungarian Empire, that is: that great mixture of cultures that straddled central and Eastern Europe, and shaped both Austria's world view and its wine.

Austrian wine veers more towards the spicy flavours of Hungary and Slovenia than the floweriness of German wines. The grape varieties demonstrate a shift to the east, as well: there is Riesling here, and Müller-Thurgau, Gewürztraminer, Sylvaner, Ruländer (alias Pinot Gris), Weissburgunder (Pinot Blanc) and Scheurebe; but there is also Furmint, Grüner Veltliner and St-Laurent, grapes that spread eastwards beyond Austria's modern boundaries; and Rotgipfler, Zierfandler, Blauer Wildbacher and Zweigelt to balance international imports like Cabernet Sauvignon, Chardonnay and Sauvignon Blanc. The grape varieties grown in Burgenland are the same as those of Hungary; just down the road, those of Styria are also found in Slovenia, and the vines of the Weinviertel are the same as those of the Czech Republic and Slovakia.

There is another factor which affects the development of Austrian wine, and that is the habit of all Austrians to spend their free evenings sitting in country inns, or *Buschenschenken*, eating *schnitzel* and drinking local wine. It has to be local because the rules state that a *Buschenschenke* can only sell what is made on the premises (that goes for the food as well as the wine). Each inn naturally wants to have a full range of wine styles to offer its customers, and so has to grow as many vine varieties as it can squeeze in; this tends to mitigate against the sort of site selection that is common in top wine regions worldwide. Nevertheless, the best Austrian growers are developing the sort of national and international reputations that allow them to go beyond a purely local clientele, and the best wines of Austria are, without a doubt, absolutely world class.

It has been, in fact, a remarkable recovery. In 1985 Austrian wine seemed to have suffered a

WINE REGIONS OF EASTERN AUSTRIA
- Lower Austria (Niederösterreich)
- Vienna (Wien)
- Burgenland
- Styria (Steiermark)
- Wine areas

mortal blow: a scandal erupted when some producers were discovered to have been adding diethylene glycol to their wines to make them taste sweeter and fatter; the additive was not harmful, but it wasn't legal either.

A new wine law followed in double-quick time, and public taste changed overnight: suddenly people wanted dry wines and a new, dynamic generation of Austrian winemakers set about creating entire new wine styles.

The wine country is divided into four zones: Lower Austria or Niederösterreich, which is by far the biggest and covers the northern section; Burgenland, which curves around the Hungarian border and is strongly marked by Hungarian influences; Styria, a big sprawling area in the south which makes lean, acidic wines, and Wien, or Vienna itself.

The Grapes

A huge array of grapes, reflecting Austria's position at the heart of Europe.

GRÜNER VELTLINER is the workhorse white grape of most regions, producing light, peppery wine. It is usually best drunk young, though top examples can age and be very powerful.

Riesling

WELSCHRIESLING makes clean, fresh wine which can be surprisingly good as a dessert wine.

RIESLING is the true Riesling, producing superb, racy, steely wines in the Wachau, Kremstal and Kamptal.

GEWÜRZTRAMINER here usually has decent acidity and structure to balance its intense flavours of roses and lychees.

FURMINT is seldom grown, even in Rust, where it makes superb Ausbruch. A pity: it has a tantalizing smoky, spicy aroma.

CHARDONNAY is increasingly widely grown, and sometimes aged in new oak for international-style, buttery whites.

MÜLLER-THURGAU is widely grown and aromatic, though seldom exciting. It's known as Riesling-Sylvaner in Austria.

SAUVIGNON BLANC is very good at its best, grassy and pungent, with good acidity. Lesser versions have more acidity, less aroma.

RULÄNDER is found most in Styria and Burgenland; in the latter it produces some splendid sweet wines, full of earth and spice.

WEISSBURGUNDER, alias Pinot Blanc, is found almost everywhere, and makes some excellent, well-structured wines with a leafy, nutty taste.

MUSCAT OTTONEL is the dominant member of the Muscat family in Austria. Relatively light in flavour, it nevertheless produces beautifully elegant, sweet late-harvest wines.

BLAUBURGUNDER, or Pinot Noir, can produce some well-structured wines in Austria.

BLAUFRÄNKISCH makes attractive raspberryish wine, often these days aged in oak.

CABERNET SAUVIGNON is ever more fashionable; the best are aged in oak and have plenty of body.

Chardonnay is a relatively new arrival in Austrian vineyards and, from a good producer, it can be remarkably complex. This Chardonnay comes from the top estate in Langenlois in Kamptal, Austria's most productive wine town.

Alois Kracher is known as Austria's greatest sweet winemaker. This full-bodied powerful example is all dried apricot, raisins and spice.

Wien

Yes, there are vineyards within the city boundaries. But those in the suburbs are prettier, and you can while away the evenings in a *Heurige* (a sort of *Buschenschenke* or local wine inn, typically serving the young wine of the year, itself called *Heurige*). Not all Viennese wine is made to be drunk young, however, and there are some serious growers here. Grüner Veltliner, making light, slightly peppery white wine, is the most common grape, but there's Riesling and members of the Pinot family as well.

Lower Austria

This is subdivided into seven regions. The **Weinviertel** is the biggest, but also produces the least distinguished wine: it's mostly everyday stuff from high-yielding vines, some of which goes to make Sekt. The exceptions are some rather good reds from **Mailberg** in the north.

Kamptal and **Kremstal** used to be one region, called Kamptal-Donauland. Standards are very high, and it is home to some of Austria's finest producers. Grüner Veltliner seems to do very well here, giving concentrated wines that are several notches above the average stuff sold by the half-litre mug; Riesling also takes on some polish and finesse.

In the **Wachau**, where the vineyards rise on steep terraces above the Donau (Danube), the dry Riesling is the best in Austria, racy and long-lived. The producers are so proud of their region that they've established style categories that are unique to the Wachau, and that demand higher standards than the national wine law: Steinfeder are the lightest, most delicate wines, Federspiel wines are more substantial, with a higher alcohol level, and Smaragd are bigger still, fermented dry and with an alcohol level of over 12, and up to 15, degrees.

Donauland, or Danube Land, is the region immediately to the west of Vienna. White wine dominates, and vine varieties are the usual Austrian selection; at the centre of the region is **Klosterneuburg**, both a monastery which owns large tracts of vineyards and a viticultural institute. The specifically Austrian measurement of must weights, Klosterneuburger Mostwaage (KMW), was developed here; the principle is similar to that of Germany's degrees Oechsle.

Carnuntum's warm, dry climate produces well-structured wines from a variety of grapes; its best wines are red. On the whole, however, its a rather diverse region without much individuality. **Thermenregion** is even warmer: hot spas abound here, and the wine speciality, semi-sweet wine of great spiciness and considerable longevity, made from Rotgipfler and Zierfandler (known here as Spätrot), went out of fashion after 1985. There are red vines planted here, too.

Burgenland

Of the four sub-regions here, **Neusiedlersee** and **Neusiedlersee-Hügelland** are the most remarkable. They lie either side of a broad shallow lake, the Neusiedlersee; a paradise for water birds, holiday-makers and noble rot. On the west side of the lake the area where noble rot affects the grapes is relatively narrow, and the land rises in hills, whereas on the eastern side it stays flat and interspersed with mini-lakes for mile after mile. There's a huge amount of noble rot on the eastern side, year after year; the wines here are intensely sweet and rich, with tremendous balance and structure. There are also some substantial reds, and good dry whites made. The village of **Rust**, on the edge of the lake near the Hungarian border, has its own sweet wine speciality: Ausbruch is made from noble rot, and comes between Beerenauslese and Trockenbeerenauslese in terms of sweetness and intensity.

Mittelburgenland makes stylish, well-structured red wines from Blaufränkisch, and blends of other grapes (Zweigelt, Cabernet Sauvignon, St-Laurent) with Blaufränkisch. **Südburgenland** is a bit of a backwater, making attractive reds from Blaufränkisch and whites from Welschriesling.

Styria

The lean, acidic white wines of Styria are tailor-made for the modern Austrian palate. The region is divided into **Südsteiermark, Süd-Oststeier-**

mark and **Weststeiermark**; the speciality of the last is an austere rosé called Schilcher, made from Blauer Wildbacher grapes. Nothing that dissolves your tooth enamel so effectively should cost so much. The other regions of Styria are a better bet: Sauvignon Blanc, Chardonnay, Traminer, Welschriesling, Pinot Blanc, Gelber Muskateller and others flourish, although when they're very young (and they usually are) differences between grape varieties tend to be masked by piercing acidity.

CLASSIFICATION

The classification of Austrian wine is similar to that of German wine but with just enough differences to confuse you. There is **Tafelwein** (the most basic), **Landwein** (rarely seen) and **Qualitätswein**, of which **Kabinett** (which must be dry) is a sub-category. **Prädikatswein** includes **Spätlese, Auslese, Eiswein, Beerenauslese, Ausbruch, Trockenbeerenauslese** and another Burgenland speciality, **Strohwein**, which is made from grapes dried on straw to concentrate their sweetness.

Vineyards rise on steep slopes above Dürnstein in the Wachau. Richard the Lionheart was imprisoned in the castle here but probably didn't get much of a chance to enjoy the view.

The Polz brothers are consistent producers of top-quality dry whites in Hochgrassnitzberg in Styria. Styrian wines make a virtue of their leanness and dryness.

SWITZERLAND

It won't come as much of a surprise to learn that Switzerland has the highest vineyards in Europe – at Visperterminen in the Valais grapes grow at 1128 metres (3700ft) – or that it has some of the most beautiful – in the Vaud, where the vineyards tumble down to the edge of Lake Geneva, or in the Valais where the vines cling to the mountain slopes high above the valley of the fledgling river Rhône. Yet these vineyards are not as chilly as one might think. They get plenty of sun, and the abundance of lakes raises the temperature a notch or two – most of the country's vines grow on slopes overlooking lakes or rivers.

Most are in French-speaking Switzerland, though all 24 Swiss cantons, French-, German- and Italian-speaking, grow some wine. Chasselas is the most widely planted variety, and it really does produce some interesting wine here – which is more than it does in most places. The thing about Chasselas is that it reflects the character of

the soil it's grown on – it's like Riesling in that respect. So Chasselas from different regions really does taste different. Yes, the differences are subtle, but they're there.

This emphasis on terroir marks out Swiss wines from the styles currently fashionable in many countries. They don't have upfront fruit to attract the novice; they can have quite strong flavours, but they're always subtle. And some of the grape varieties found here – like Petite Arvine, or Amigne, or Humagne Blanc – are found almost nowhere else. Müller-Thurgau was a Swiss invention, so of course it's widely planted in German-speaking Switzerland; other varieties include Gamay, Pinot Noir, Merlot in the Italian-speaking cantons, and even Syrah, which ripens surprisingly well in certain spots.

Most of the vineyards are in the French-speaking cantons, and **Valais** has the lion's share. Around 40 per cent of the Swiss crop comes from

WINE REGIONS OF SWITZERLAND

- Valais
- Vaud
- Geneva
- Neuchâtel
- Fribourg
- Bern
- Jura
- Eastern Switzerland
- Ticino

The mountains are never far away from the vineyards in Switzerland. Here, at Sion in the Valais region, there is plenty of sun however; the south-south-east-facing slopes bask in a rain shadow which makes irrigation obligatory most years.

mould. The Italian-speaking cantons concentrate on Merlot, which varies from light to really rather serious and structured. **Ticino** is the major producer in Italian-speaking Switzerland: look for the words Merlot del Ticino on the label. The best bear a VITI seal, a quality guarantee.

CLASSIFICATION

In the Valais, appellation contrôlée d'origine implies a wine made to stricter standards than mere appellation contrôlée; in Geneva, in addition, there are Grands and Premier Crus which are precisely delimited. Generally speaking in Switzerland, wines can come from a canton, a region within a canton, or from an area larger than a canton.

Petite Arvine is one the finest grapes of the Valais but is not planted elsewhere in Switzerland. This example has a characteristic salty tang.

here. Vineyards crowd the mountain slopes, seeking out the driest nooks and crannies in the less well-favoured spots, broadening where the land allows. And wouldn't it be disappointing to explore this region, which is hardly known outside Switzerland, and find that it grew the same grape varieties as everyone else? Well, you're safe from disappointment on that score. Yes, it's true that these mountain terraces produce Chasselas (alias Fendant here), and Pinot Noir and Gamay, which can be blended together to make Dôle, and which generally seems to be less than the sum of its parts, but there are also intense, elegant, unusual dessert wines made from late-picked Amigne, Petite Arvine, Marsanne and others. There's even Vin des Glaciers, made from Rèze grapes and aged high up in the mountains; it's deliberately maderized and aged in solera, like sherry, but it's extremely rare, so you'll be lucky to find any.

The **Vaud** is also Chasselas country, though there's some Pinot Gris and Chardonnay as well, and some Gamay. Chasselas likewise dominates **Geneva** and **Neuchâtel** (where they also make a pale rosé oeil de perdrix from Pinot Noir).

The German-speaking cantons, when they're not growing Müller-Thurgau (which they call Riesling-Sylvaner), grow Blauburgunder for reds. These are generally in the light, off-dry German

The Grapes

Three cultures mean three different traditions; but Switzerland has unique vines of its own, too.

Merlot

CHASSELAS (also known as Fendant in Valais) is Switzerland's main grape. It makes light white which has the knack of reflecting its terroir.

RIESLING-SYLVANER (MÜLLER-THURGAU) was bred by a Herr Müller of the canton of Thurgau, although he was working at Geisenheim in Germany at the time. It produces characteristically flowery, aromatic wines here.

SYLVANER is important in the Valais, where it makes quite well-structured wine.

PINOT NOIR makes generally light wines here, sometimes hardly more

than rosé, but some good examples in a Côte de Beaune style have been made in recent years.

GAMAY is light in Switzerland but never as good as it is in Beaujolais. A lot is blended with Pinot Noir.

MERLOT is the main grape of the Italian-speaking cantons. Some are weighty and oak-aged; most are quite light.

PETITE ARVINE is elegant and ages well but is not widely planted.

AMIGNE, a speciality of the Valais, makes intense spicy wine. It can be dry or late-picked and sweet.

ENGLAND AND WALES

Winemaking in England goes back a very long time, and for a very long time, as far as we can tell, it was pretty successful. It was probably the Romans who brought the vine to England, and by the 11th century, according to the Domesday Book, there were at least 38 vineyards. Vines and wines flourished for the next century – the success of English vineyards during the Middle Ages was partly due to the prevailing climate of northern Europe which, on average, was at least 1°C (33°F) warmer than now – but in 1152 Henry II married Eleanor of Aquitaine, and the English love affair with the red wines of Bordeaux began.

English vineyards survived this, especially since most were attached to monasteries with a constant need for sacramental wine, but they did not survive the Dissolution of the Monasteries in 1536; this was the death knell of English wine. A few private vineyards survived into the 18th century, notably one at Painshill in Cobham, Surrey, but apparently only the owner thought the wines were worth drinking.

That's how things stayed until 1952, when Hambledon Vineyard in Hampshire was established. It seemed like a false dawn: when the English Vineyards Association (EVA) was formed in 1967 there were barely a dozen members, and rather fewer acres of vines. But the universal surge of interest in wine during the 1970s provided a spur, and the 1980s and 1990s have seen increasing professionalism and increasing quality.

That is, when the weather allows. Sun (not enough) and rain (too much) are the usual British moans, and where the vine is concerned, they're justified. Measuring the temperature needed to ripen grapes by the degree days system (see box on p.192), 1000 degree days is generally reckoned to be the bare minimum. Even in relatively warm southern England the average is only 762, and in the frequently blustery conditions any warm air collecting between the vines is quickly blown away; in the west, the rain-bearing westerlies, and in the east those icy blasts straight from Siberia can crucially lower the temperature in a vineyard.

Late frosts and rot are the main problem, and the grapes are often not ripe enough to pick until late October, or even November. So it's not surprising that vineyards congregate in the southern counties of England and Wales (it's still called English wine even if it's from Wales) although there are vineyards in all but six English counties, and the most northerly are in Durham. Site selection and canopy management play an important part in the battle against the climate.

Early ripening grape varieties are essential. Müller-Thurgau, Seyval Blanc and Reichensteiner

The Grapes

The ability to ripen well in a cool, damp climate is crucial.

MÜLLER-THURGAU in England tends to lose its muskiness and become elderflower-fresh.

SEYVAL BLANC is often blended, but from a talented producer is pungent when young, aging to a mature, almost Burgundian complexity.

REICHENSTEINER is best made slightly sweet, when it has a good smoky quince taste.

BACCHUS gives strong, rather obvious flavours of elderflower and gooseberry.

MADELEINE ANGEVINE gives apple and elderflower fruit.

CHARDONNAY is used especially for sparkling wine as it produces very suitable acidic base wine.

PINOT NOIR is used mostly for sparkling wine, when it gives good light strawberry flavours.

Surrey-based Denbies is the giant among English vineyards, producing a range of wines. Recent venture Chapel Down specializes in commercial quantities of good, inexpensive sparkling wine from bought-in grapes.

are the main grapes, with the hybrid Seyval Blanc being frowned on by the EU for Quality Wine but often making the best, most complex wine of the lot. There's a bit of Chardonnay, too, and various German crosses. Some wines are made off-dry, though dry styles are increasingly successful, and there's even a bit of oak-aging being used. The typical flavour is a sort of hedgerow freshness, a touch of elderflower, a touch of grapefruit. The best, from the leading producers, age rather well.

Winemaking methods are much the same as in any other northern region – chaptalization is the rule, as it is all over northern Europe and, as in Germany, sweet unfermented grape juice is sometimes added to the fermented wine. However, there is a general tendency to drier wines with more character in England.

Sparkling wine production is a promising area. The best English sites should provide ideal grapes for base wines. The chalk soils, which are naturally well drained, encourage ripe flavours and the climate provides correspondingly high acidity.

An official classification system has not yet been introduced but an EVA seal on a label is generally a quality pointer.

The traditional Kent countryside, complete with oasthouses, is given a rather European feel by the vines growing in vineyards at Lamberhurst.

THE WINE TRADE

Lacking any vineyards to speak of of its own, England has always imported wine from outside. For 300 years, from 1152 onwards, Bordeaux owed allegiance to the English crown, and the love of claret that was planted in England has never died.

It has, however, been unrequited for long periods. In the 18th century Britain and France were intermittently at war, and French wines were subject to prohibitive taxation, or were banned altogether (which did not prevent Sir Robert Walpole, Britain's prime minister, from smuggling in claret and Burgundy, via Holland, bribing the customs officers with brandy if necessary).

In these years port was the Englishman's preferred wine. Spanish wine was much drunk, and mostly consisted of Canary, Málaga and other sweet wines, the successors to the sack of Tudor England. Italian wine was also available, but was considered not to travel well. The Methuen Treaty of 1703 between England and Portugal established preferential terms for trade for Portuguese wines and the port of King's Lynn in Norfolk even became known for the lighter style of port shipped through it.

King's Lynn, in 1700, was the second biggest wine port in England; the biggest was London. But Bristol also played a vital part: Bristol Milk Sherry is one of the first examples of wine merchants blending and treating wines to suit the taste of their customers.

In Scotland, the port of Leith, serving Edinburgh, was the centre of the wine trade. The Scots and the French have generally had a warmer relationship than the English and French, and the Scots shipped claret in vast quantities. Indeed, in 1616 legislation was passed to restrict the amount of wine that Highland chieftains could use in their households. Important chiefs were to be limited to four tuns (16 hogsheads, or about ten litres per day) for the household's annual supply.

A 19th-century painting of a wine-tasting.

EASTERN EUROPE

Harvest time in the vineyards at Suhindol, in Bulgaria's Northern Region.

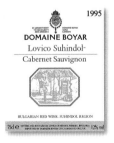

The first Bulgarian Cabernet Sauvignon to make an impact abroad. This creamy, curranty, throat-soothing style of Cabernet is now synonymous with Bulgaria.

The last few decades have not been easy on Eastern Europe. The rule of the Ottoman Empire (which included Romania and Bulgaria) wasn't exactly conducive to winemaking, although vine growing continued, as the Ottomans had a fondness for table grapes; and there was only a relatively short interregnum between the end of the Ottoman Empire and the beginning of the Communist one.

But the history of winemaking in these parts goes back long before the Ottomans erupted from Central Asia. The first known pips from grapes ever to have been cultivated by man have been found in what is now Georgia; they have been dated to 7000-5000 BC.

Ironically, the Soviet scientists who dated the pips themselves lived under a regime which promoted quantity over quality: anyone who visited the ex-Soviet Union will recall the erratic nature of the wine. And you remember when Bulgarian Cabernet Sauvignon first started appearing here, and how good it was? Well, you couldn't get anything like that inside the country. Eastern Bloc wine was mostly dreadful, collectivized and mistreated, and when the Iron Curtain collapsed and we all peered into the depths of an unknown landscape, what did we see? Acres and acres of vines, frequently planted in the wrong place (hillside vineyards being more difficult to work); wonderful potential for unusual flavours, but a sad lack of investment. Indeed, a lack of everything: bottles, corks, winemaking equipment were all in short supply.

The obvious answer, to a Western world replete with winemakers, equipment and investment, was to send some of it eastwards. Flying winemakers duly arrived in the hills of Hungary, the former Czechoslovakia and elsewhere and started scouting around for likely spots for making wine that would appeal to consumers in the West. Now, a few years further down the line, it's possible to have a clearer picture of what's been achieved, what has been salvaged, and what is still possible.

Bulgaria

Bulgaria is the exception to the 'no investment' rule, since back in the 1960s it started planting better varieties like Cabernet Sauvignon and Merlot, and was aided in its efforts to improve quality by the University of California at Davis; the two sides were brought together by Pepsico, which was keen to sell its cola in Bulgaria and wanted to receive in return something it could sell (not tractor parts, in other words).

But then came President Gorbachev's campaign to reduce alcohol consumption in the ex-Soviet Union. He forced a lot of Bulgarian vineyards to be uprooted; discouraged growers turned to other crops, and the disintegration of the Soviet Bloc and the threat or promise of land privatization didn't help. It is much to the credit of the producers that they are still turning out juicy

young reds and greatly improved whites. The main attraction being the easy drinking renderings of the classic red grape varieties. Local red varieties, plummy Mavrud, meaty Gamza and the deep though less common Melnik, can be good too. Richer, fuller reds come from the mountainous south and south-west, whites and lighter reds are mainly from the north and east (the freshest whites coming from the Black Sea coast). We should see accelerating change and improvements now that privatization is effectively complete.

Hungary

This is where there really should be some sensational flavours: indigenous varieties include Furmint, Hárslevelü, Ezerjó and Mezesfehér. Hungary shares some varieties with other countries of central and Eastern Europe: Olasz Rizling (the Welschriesling of Austria), Zöldveltelini (Austria's

WINE REGIONS OF EASTERN EUROPE

- Czech Republic
- Slovakia
- Hungary
- Romania
- Moldova
- Ukraine
- Russian Federation
- Slovenia
- Croatia
- Bosnia-Herzegovina
- Fed. Rep. of Yugoslavia
- Bulgaria

Using local grape varieties, flying winemakers and consultants from Australia, New Zealand and elsewhere are helping to bring much-needed improvement to Hungary.

The Grapes

There's an enormous range of grapes here, but not all will ever appear on a label.

CHARDONNAY is widely grown. Quality can be fair from Bulgaria, but beware of over-oaking. Flying winemaker Hungarian Chardonnay is a good buy.

FETEASCĂ comes in two kinds: Albă and Regală. Both make spicy, perfumed whites which can, however, lack acidity.

FURMINT is a terrific grape, with marvellous smoky greengage fruit. It ages well, too. It's the main grape in Tokaj, and is also made into dry wines.

GEWÜRZTRAMINER is found all over Eastern Europe, and is typically spicy in style.

GRÜNER VELTLINER is found in the Czech Republic and Slovakia, and gives light, leafy whites that can be too high in acidity for comfort.

HÁRSLEVELÜ is the second most important grape in Tokaj, after Furmint, and gives weighty, peachy wines.

IRSAY OLIVER is found in the north of the region and gives Muscatty, perfumed wines.

RKATSITELI is well suited to the cold and has good levels of acidity and sugar.

RHINE RIESLING is usually well balanced but never as exciting as in Germany.

SAUVIGNON BLANC needs cool sites to be properly pungent.

TĂMÎIOASĂ ROMÂNEASCĂ makes wonderfully incense-perfumed nobly rotten whites in Romania.

WELSCHRIESLING, alias Olasz Rizling or Laski Rizling, can be good and fresh.

CABERNET SAUVIGNON produces its best quality and richest flavours in Bulgaria and Moldova.

GAMZA is found in Bulgaria and makes soft, early-drinking reds.

KADARKA makes Hungarian reds which could be better (richer, more tannic) than they usually are.

KÉKFRANKOS is also known as Frankovka or Blaufränkisch and has some potential for quality. It can be vegetal if not properly ripe.

MAVRUD gives sturdy reds in Bulgaria.

MERLOT makes decent softish reds in Bulgaria.

PINOT NOIR is widely grown, but is generally jammy at best.

SAPERAVI makes good rich, spicy red in Moldova.

Cabernet Sauvignon

TOKAJI

This used to be known in the West as Tokay, but the Hungarian spelling is now more common: Tokaj is the region, Tokaji the wine. Western investment (from France and Spain) has changed the flavour of the wine, too: it's now far fresher than it ever was in the Communist past, and far more able to show the flavours of noble rot, and the smoky flavours of the Furmint grape. There's a debate going on in Hungary as to whether the old oxidized style should be allowed to die or not: I say yes – in general. But if one or two dinosaurs want to continue in the old way – let them, for the sake of comparision.

The grape varieties used for Tokaji are Furmint, Hárslevelü and Muscat Lunel. Botrytized grapes (called *aszú*) are added to dry base wine, and the numbers of *puttonyos* added indicate the sweetness of the final wine (a *puttonyo* is simply the local measure): three *puttonyos* will be quite sweet, five *puttonyos* very sweet. You might just see some Essencia: this is so sweet it can barely ferment and is usually employed to beef up lesser wines.

Prices of Tokaji have risen with investment, but so has the range of wines available.

Tasting wine in the cellars of Tokaj Kereskedöhóz (formerly the Tokaji Wine Trust).

Grüner Veltliner), Leányka (Romania's Feteascǎ), Cirfandli (Austria's Zierfandler), Kékfrankos (Austria's Blaufränkisch), Rkatsiteli and Zweigelt. It also has vines from further west: Chardonnay, Sauvignon Blanc, Riesling, Tramin (Gewürztraminer), Muscat, Cabernet Sauvignon, Cabernet Franc, Merlot and others.

And indeed Hungary is beginning to show what it can do. Flying winemakers are producing some good stuff, and the region of Tokaj (see box left), best known for its sweet wines, is producing some excellent (and excellent-value) dry Furmint, showing just how good this grape can be.

Romania

There's great potential here, but so far we haven't seen much sign of modernization. Prices are low, and there are some wonderful wines to be had, but unreliability and lack of consistency are big problems. Styles to look out for include the botrytized wines of **Cotnari**, on the slopes of the Carpathians, made from the Tǎmîioasǎ Româneascǎ grape, botrytized Chardonnays from **Murfatlar** on the Black Sea Coast, and perfumed dry whites from the Feteascǎ grape. There are also some rather jammy Pinot Noirs.

Czech Republic and Slovakia

The vineyards here are in a southern strip along the Austrian and Hungarian borders, and most of them are in Slovakia. They even include a chunk of the Tokaj vineyard, which in the bad old days had been pretty well ignored: Czechoslovakia had happily swapped the right to the appellation for the right to export beer to Hungary. Bizarre.

Wine styles resemble those of Austria, though on a less intense scale, probably because they haven't really got their winemaking sorted out yet. But the potential is there, particularly with many protected south-west- and south-east-facing slopes in Slovakia, along with grape varieties such as Riesling, Traminer, Pinot Blanc, Pinot Gris, Sauvignon, Welschriesling, Müller-Thurgau and Irsay Oliver. There are some reds, from Cabernet Sauvignon, Frankovka (Blaufränkisch) and others.

Western Balkans

The main producer here is **Slovenia**, which makes some quite high-quality stuff, but at prices which do not make it attractive in export markets. The best come from private producers, who are surprisingly well equipped with stainless steelery, particularly if they happen to be near the border with Austria or Italy. The reason is that under Communism these borders were a great deal more permeable than most, and it was possible for private producers (who were always allowed to own a few hectares of land) to sell their wine in the West and translate the proceeds into new equipment.

Styles tend to echo those found the other side of every border (all Slovenia's vineyards are round the edges of the country). Those that are an extension of Italy's Collio vineyards share the same grape varieties and flavours; those that border Styria have the same lean, clean fruit; the rest are near the Croatian border and produce some surprisingly good Welschriesling. The stuff that for years has been imported to Britain (generally as Olasz Rizling, a synonym) clearly doesn't come from the best vats.

Inland **Croatia** produces mainly bulk whites; the best-quality vineyards are on the Dalmatian coast, turning out gutsy, mouthfilling Postup, Peljesac and Faros reds. There are also wines produced in the other lands of former Yugoslavia, **Serbia**, **Bosnia-Herzegovina**, **Montenegro**, **Kosovo** and **Macedonia**, but they are seldom seen abroad.

CIS States

These countries of the ex-Soviet Union produce a pretty mixed bag of wines. As a rule of thumb the further east you go the less familiar the wines become. When you get to **Georgia** you start finding tannic whites fermented on their skins.

The countries of most interest abroad are **Moldova**, which can make good solid Cabernet Sauvignon as well as white from Rkatsiteli, and the **Crimea**. Here it's warm enough for some hefty sweet and fortified wines with the Massandra winery producing some superb examples.

Primorski, near the Italian border in southern Slovenia, is in part an extension of Italy's Collio region. Varieties such as Merlot abound here.

An old plaster relief on a house at Hogilag in the Tirnave area of Transylvania, a cool-climate region where Romanian families have made wine for generations.

EASTERN MEDITERRANEAN

This, the centre of the classical world, is where wine as we know it began. Over 2000 years ago wines were being shipped from country to country, and individual growths prized above the common run of the mill wines, just as they are today – it's just that now the focus of wine has moved westwards (and southwards too, to the southern hemisphere).

Greece

Now, here's an irony: we know more about the wine of Ancient Greece than that of any other country of the ancient world, and the wine of Greece was prized in every civilized nation. Greek colonists carried the vine to Sicily and mainland Italy, to southern France and the shores of the Black Sea. Yet nowadays Greece is outpaced by almost every European country in wine quality, modernization, investment and so on.

Ask most non-Greeks to name five Greek wines and they won't get much further than Retsina.

Greece's long period as part of the Ottoman Empire is largely to blame for this. Wine was by no means forbidden to Christian Greeks, but there was no incentive to develop a modern, export-oriented wine industry. And for much of this century tourists have provided an easy market; so the surprise is not that Greek wine has been left behind. Rather, the surprise is that it is now showing such promising signs of catching up.

Reds are mostly spicy with a rich plummy centre: good ones include Náoussa (from Xynomavro grapes), Côtes de Meliton and Neméa (from Agiorgitiko grapes), but look out too for wines from individual estates. Good whites include sweet Muscats from the island of **Samos** and from **Pátras** on the northern coast of the Peloponnese Peninsula, but again, look out for

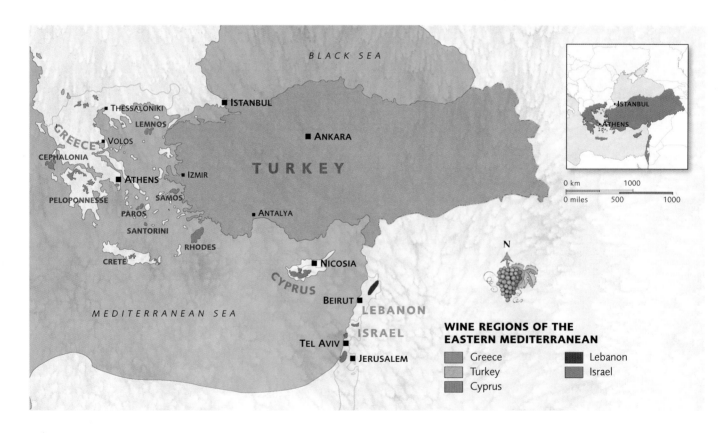

WINE REGIONS OF THE EASTERN MEDITERRANEAN

- Greece
- Turkey
- Cyprus
- Lebanon
- Israel

Vineyards planted on slopes below the rock pinnacles of the Meteora, in Thessaly, central Greece.

light, dry single-estate wines blended from such varieties as Moscophilero, Rhoditis and other indigenous varieties: these are Greece's secret weapon and so far, happily, Greek producers seem keen to do research into their native grapes rather than rely on Cabernet and Chardonnay. Both these and other international varieties like Cinsaut, Merlot, Grenache and Syrah, are grown, but they are not Greece's only answer.

Retsina can be deliciously oily and piny, especially if young and fresh. It is made by adding small pieces of resin to the must before fermentation, and the quality both of the resin and of the base wine are crucial to the quality of the final wine. Savatiano is the main grape, sometimes blended with Rhoditis.

Cyprus

This is another country with a splendid past and a not-so-splendid present. Again there was Ottoman domination; after that Cyprus shipped a lot of wine to the famously unfussy ex-Soviet Union, and exported grape concentrate to other countries, including Britain, to be turned into cheap, locally made fortified wines. It also makes sherry-style fortifieds of its own. **Commandaria** is a relic of Cyprus's winemaking past and it could be wonderful. It's a strong, sweet, dark wine, usually fortified and redolent of raisins and

Domain Mercouri is one Greek company which is convinced of the need for new winery equipment, new grape varieties and new wine styles to help boost its country's international reputation.

The Grapes

Greece has a wealth of native grapes; otherwise it's mostly French varieties.

AGIORGITIKO is a red grape native to the Peloponnese, where it has good fruit but needs to be planted at high altitude to retain acidity. When it does, it ages well.

CABERNET SAUVIGNON is found in Greece, Lebanon and Israel, and produces characteristically blackcurranty wine.

CINSAUT grows in the Lebanon and is generally blended.

CARIGNAN is also grown for blending in the Lebanon.

MAVRO, meaning black, is the main grape of Cyprus and covers three-quarters of the vineyards; it is used for everything from sherry-style fortifieds to red table wines. At best it has a slightly vegetal blackcurrant flavour, and with a few years' aging this vegetal character becomes more pronounced.

XYNOMAVRO is a black grape widely grown in northern Greece for its good acidity and abliity to age.

CHARDONNAY is grown in relatively small quantities in Israel and Greece and in even smaller quantities elsewhere.

MOSCOPHILERO makes strongly perfumed whites and rosés (it has pink skin) in Greece.

SAVATIANO is widely used for Retsina, and is relatively neutral with low acidity.

RHODITIS is a late-ripening, pink-skinned grape grown in Greece and favoured for its good acidity.

XYNISTERI is the most common white grape in Cyprus. If picked before full ripeness it can (or could) produce earthy wines with good acidity and aroma.

MUSCAT is usually the superior Muscat Blanc à Petits Grains in Greece although there is also some Muscat of Alexandria. Many of the Greek islands, especially Rhodes, Lemnos and Samos, produce excellent sweet Muscats.

ASSYRTIKO is a fine-quality white with good acidity, widely grown in Greece.

ROBOLA is a pungent citrus-flavoured white grape with good acidity, grown especially in Cephalonia in Greece. It's the same grape as the Robolla of north-eastern Italy.

Stained glass depicting events from the Old Testament (Book of Numbers, Chapter 13) in which Israelite spies carry a huge bunch of grapes from the Promised Land (from Château Vilmart, Marne, France).

nuts. Red Mavro and white Xynisteri grapes are partially dried and then fermented: the fermentation stops naturally before all the sugar has been converted to alcohol, though its strength may be increased by the addition of spirit afterwards. Cyprus table wines have for long been utterly dreadful; better ones are promised, year after year. Well, I'm still waiting.

Turkey

There are masses of grapes grown in Turkey – absolutely masses – but they nearly all get eaten as table grapes or turned into raisins. Less than three per cent end up as wine, and, if I'm to be honest, I have to say that the wine that is made isn't actually very good. It has potential, it's true, but there doesn't seem to be a cat's chance in hell of that potential being realized. The reds are solid and earthy – they probably have to be pretty solid

to survive the wineries – and whites, which survive less well, are generally oxidized. And yet one can sense at their heart that there was once a good wine in there trying to get out.

Lebanon

Lebanon, to all intents and purposes, means Chateau Musar (see box below left). Both Chateau Musar and Lebanon's other main producer, Chateau Kefraya, have vineyards located on east-facing slopes of Mount Barouk overlooking the Bekaa Valley.

There are other estates in the Lebanon but they're not in the same league yet. Although, with excellent reds like Musar's and Kefraya's, it is hoped that a more stable future will provide a stimulus for ever better wines from a land which is, after all, one of the world's oldest sites of wine production.

CHATEAU MUSAR, LEBANON

This long-aging red, tasting of chocolate and musky plums with hints of spice and smoke, must surely be one of the world's most remarkable wines. It's made by one of the world's most remarkable winemakers, too: when Serge Hochar took over the family winery he spent years searching for somewhere else – somewhere calmer and safer – to make wine, before deciding that he would brave Lebanon's civil war. His vineyards are in the Bekaa Valley, and sometimes the front line ran between the vineyards and the winery, which made getting the grapes in even more fraught than usual, and sometimes the winery and his house were shelled. But in spite of all this 1976 and 1984 were the only vintages when he was unable to make any wine.

The red wine is a blend of Cabernet Sauvignon, Syrah and Cinsaut. It takes about 12 to 15 years to mature and develop superb perfume and flavour and can last for another 15. There is also a white wine but it is less often seen and is made from the indigenous Obaideh and Meroué.

Israel

Most, but not all, Israeli wines are kosher, although kosher wines can be and are made elsewhere. Modern versions of kosher wines, made in thoroughly high-tech wineries, are more in tune with modern tastes than they used to be. All stages of kosher wine production come under the control of a rabbi, and wines must be made by practising Jews. Vineyards within the biblical area must be left fallow every seventh year (the risk this poses to the wellbeing of the vines is often got around by selling the vineyard to an obliging gentile for the year), and only kosher materials may be used in wine production. Non-practising Jews working in the winery may not handle must or wine. The strictest rabbis insist on wine being pasteurized, which does little for its flavour. Israel's leading quality wine producer is the **Golan Heights Winery**, see box opposite.

GOLAN HEIGHTS, ISRAEL

This is both the name of a winery and the name of a wine region: the first is the most go-ahead winery in Israel, which set new standards of freshness and flavour back in the 1980s when it started applying modern winemaking techniques to kosher wine; the second is Israel's finest wine region, growing red and white grapes at high altitudes. The bad news is that the Golan Heights may one day be given to Syria as part of a peace agreement, and Syria has not expressed any sympathy with winemaking; the even worse news is that at the time of writing peace looks further away than ever.

As well as kosher wines, good barrel-fermented Chardonnay and sparkling wines are also being produced. The grape varieties are the international ones of Cabernet Sauvignon, Chardonnay and Sauvignon Blanc; the Yarden range is the best, followed by the Golan range.

ABOVE **A vineyard above the Sea of Galilee, Israel. Under kosher law this has to be left fallow every seventh year.**

The Bekaa Valley, near Kefraya, in the Lebanon.

There's a paradox here: the peace that the region so desperately needs is likely to mean the end of Israel's finest wines.

UNITED STATES AND CANADA

It seems hard to believe now that the first European vines to be planted in the United States died. And, come to that, the second ones, and the third ones. Attempts to produce drinkable wine to ease the lot of the early colonists failed miserably.

Before they got as far as trying out European vines, those first settlers in Virginia and Carolina had found the land thick with native American species of vine. Think how they must have rejoiced. Here at least was a gift of nature: wine, in the new colonies, would be plentiful and good.

At least, they thought that until they tried it. It turned out to be not at all attractive to European palates: it had a pungent mayblossom scent and flavour, heavy, with no subtlety; if they'd known what nail varnish smells like, they'd have recognized that aroma, too. So they imported European cuttings. And, thanks to phylloxera, the cuttings died.

At first by chance, and then deliberately, they started breeding hybrids of the native and the European species. These were better: they lived, and the settlers could actually drink the wine. It was these vines that were the basis of the early American wine 'industry': grapes like Concord, Delaware, Isabella, Catawba and Norton.

Yet over on the West Coast things were taking a different path. There the Spanish settlers were having no trouble in cultivating European varieties: their favourite was an undistinguished red vine called Mission. After the states of the south-west joined the other states of America, plantings increased and other varieties were found to thrive: the foundations of California's winegrowing supremacy were in place.

In 1919 it was nearly wrecked. With the advent of Prohibition, which lasted until 1933, grape concentrate became the focus of the growers. Vineyards proliferated, but any interest in or taste for fine wine among the public was destroyed. With Repeal the industry took refuge in producing highly alcoholic sweet wines of no particular quality, from the easily irrigated Central Valley. These, in any case, were the cocktail years; spirits, not wine, were fashionable.

The 1960s changed all that. In the new cosmopolitan climate wine emerged as a sophisticated social drink, ideal for entertaining. The necessary market finally existed and California grasped its chance with both hands. The number of wineries grew. California was the leader of the New World.

It wasn't long before the Old World began to take note of what California was doing, and copy it. Varietal labelling, for one thing. It was merchant Frank Schoonmaker who first came up with this idea in the 1940s: it wasn't unprecedented in Europe – Alsace had been doing it for years – but in California, where the inaccurate use of such generic terms as 'Chablis', 'Burgundy' and 'Sauternes' was rife, it was revolutionary.

The use of technology, too, came naturally to California winemakers when it was still anathema to many Europeans. With vineyard mechanization, scientific selection of good clones, night picking, scrupulously clean wineries and temperature-controlled fermentation the winemakers of California produced good, fruity, enjoyably fresh wines in places that would previously have been considered far too hot to make anything other than the cheapest plonk: and yet this wine was both tasty and cheap. At this point the Old World should have scented trouble. A new kind of wine drinker was finding a new kind of wine.

But California learnt from Europe, too. In particular it took note of the vanilla richness of red Bordeaux and the buttery, nutty flavour of white

Banner advertising a wine auction in St Helena, Napa County. Wine auctions such as this are an important part of the Californian social calendar.

WINE REGIONS OF THE UNITED
STATES AND CANADA

US AVA and other wine areas
Canada VQA and other wine areas

Opus One, Oakville, Napa County, is a joint venture between Californian pioneer Robert Mondavi and the late Baron Philippe de Rothschild of Mouton-Rothschild, Bordeaux. The architectural brilliance of many Californian wineries echoes the prosperity of the region.

Burgundy; it looked at the numbers of new oak barriques in the cellars, and put two and two together. At much the same time that Europe was making its first tentative moves towards new technology, the United States was putting wines into new oak barriques. Both sides took a while to get their new toys right: new oak is easily overdone, can dominate the flavour of a wine to the exclusion of fruit, and doesn't sit well with all grape varieties. A lot of 1980s California wines were hugely over-oaked, and it took a move towards 'food wines' – wines you could drink with food, instead of with great effort – to tone things down a little. Current trends are very much towards red wines, with health concerns

pushing up demand. Merlot is benefiting here: Cabernet Sauvignon is no longer the red wine of automatic first choice for every Californian drinker and winegrower. Merlot has the advantage of being soft and supple – buttery and toffeeish, even – at a young age, but has enough structure to make it a serious competitor to Cabernet Sauvignon in the fine wine stakes, too.

VITICULTURAL AREAS

Wine production, however, is not confined to California. Wineries – some big, some small 'boutique'-sized – exist in most states as well as in Canada, with some concentrating on hybrid vines, and some on fruit wines from fruits other than grapes. There is a nationwide system of **American Viticultural Areas (AVAs)** in the United States – which are supposed to have some geographical identity, but which impose no European-type restrictions on grape varieties or wine styles. If an AVA is stated on a wine label, the wine must be 85 per cent from that AVA, and if a grape is stated, the wine must be 75 per cent from that grape. Individual vineyards within a recognized AVA may also be named, with the proviso that the wine must be 95 per cent sourced from that vineyard. If a wine bears a vintage date on the label it must be 95 per cent from that vintage.

In the northern states, like those of New England, Ohio and Michigan, cold winters are the problem and hybrids and even native American vines are often the grower's ally, though vinifera varieties are slowly increasing. Vinifera vines are found in Maryland, Virginia, North Carolina and Georgia, but high summer humidity is the problem here, leading to rot. Virginia, however, has had success with Cabernet Sauvignon as well as Rhône varieties such as Viognier and Syrah. New Mexico, Arizona and Colorado also grow vinifera vines in spite of hot summers and cold winters. Texas, surprisingly, is showing more promise than any of them, with Chenin Blanc, Sauvignon Blanc, Chardonnay, Cabernet Sauvignon and others all having potential. Canada is very cold indeed and its speciality is Icewine.

PHYLLOXERA

This tiny aphid was the reason why those early European vine cuttings planted on the East Coast invariably died. Native American vine species were immune to it, and passed that immunity to hybrids. California, in those early days, was free of phylloxera, which was why European vines would grow there.

These naturally resistant native vines provided the cure for Europe's devastated vineyards at the end of the 19th century. Virtually all the world's wine vines are now grafted on to American rootstock, with different strains of rootstock being selected to suit different conditions. Not all, however, have the same degree of immunity to phylloxera. The widespread planting of Californian vineyards on a rootstock known as AXR1 has proved something of a disaster: it's just not immune enough, and is susceptible to the so-called Biotype B strain of phylloxera. So in recent years vast tracts of Californian vineyard have been uprooted. But California's growers are having the best chance they've ever had to consider precisely which varieties to plant in which sites. The long-term effects on quality should be excellent.

California

Most people never refer to American wine. For them, if it comes from the United States it must come from California. And they're not far wrong: over 90 per cent of US wine comes from here. And California, to millions of people around the world, means something else, too: sunshine.

But the secret of California – the factor that allows it to make fine wine, not just juicy everyday jug wine – is just the opposite of unlimited, all-day sunshine. Some of California's finest vineyards are downright chilly. And they are moulded by two major geographical features: the Pacific Ocean, and the Coastal Range of mountains.

Cold water flowing down from Alaska makes the warm air above the sea condense into fog. The high coastal mountains mostly keep this away from inland areas – but now and again there's a break or a dip in the mountains. When that happens the fog pours through, cooling the temperature and mitigating the effects of the burning sun – because California is far south, on a similar latitude to Spain and North Africa. You can even stand on San Francisco's Golden Gate Bridge around noon and watch the fog approach: first it's a sea mist on the horizon, and then the fog slides underneath you into the bay and on inland.

So all California's fine wine areas – with a few exceptions where high altitude does the cooling job equally well – are situated where a break in the Coastal Range or a river valley heading seawards creates a funnel for this cold air blanket. Where there's no gap for the cool air to penetrate, the valleys behind the mountains boil. It is climate that shapes the different styles of California wine more than any other single factor (except, of course, for grape variety).

With the enormous variety of climates that this gives, you might expect a similarly large range of grapes. But no: California's success has been built on just a handful of international favourites. Cabernet Sauvignon, Chardonnay, Merlot, Zinfandel (okay, that's not so international) and Sauvignon Blanc are the favourites,

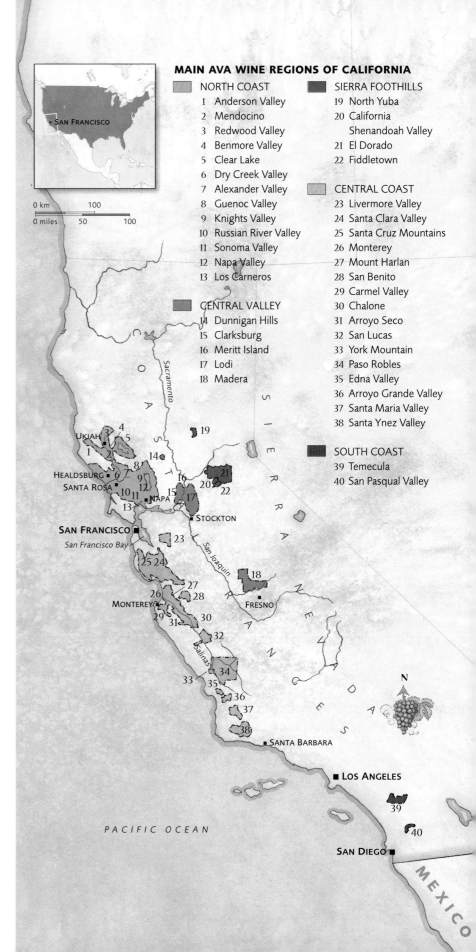

MAIN AVA WINE REGIONS OF CALIFORNIA

NORTH COAST
1 Anderson Valley
2 Mendocino
3 Redwood Valley
4 Benmore Valley
5 Clear Lake
6 Dry Creek Valley
7 Alexander Valley
8 Guenoc Valley
9 Knights Valley
10 Russian River Valley
11 Sonoma Valley
12 Napa Valley
13 Los Carneros

CENTRAL VALLEY
14 Dunnigan Hills
15 Clarksburg
16 Meritt Island
17 Lodi
18 Madera

SIERRA FOOTHILLS
19 North Yuba
20 California
     Shenandoah Valley
21 El Dorado
22 Fiddletown

CENTRAL COAST
23 Livermore Valley
24 Santa Clara Valley
25 Santa Cruz Mountains
26 Monterey
27 Mount Harlan
28 San Benito
29 Carmel Valley
30 Chalone
31 Arroyo Seco
32 San Lucas
33 York Mountain
34 Paso Robles
35 Edna Valley
36 Arroyo Grande Valley
37 Santa Maria Valley
38 Santa Ynez Valley

SOUTH COAST
39 Temecula
40 San Pasqual Valley

with Pinot Noir every red winemaker's holy grail. There's some Gewürztraminer and some Riesling, though as yet the latter isn't taken as seriously as it is in Australia. Only recently have Rhône varieties like Syrah, Grenache, Mourvèdre and others been planted with an eye to fine wine-making; and the grapes planted by the early Italian settlers, notably Barbera and Sangiovese, have only now started to be appreciated properly.

California's growers used the opportunity presented by phylloxera B (see box on p.190) to try new varieties. But, like everyone else, they have to make a living, and they can best do so by producing what people want to drink. And what people want to drink, in the main, is still Chardonnay, Zinfandel, Merlot and Cabernet, even if they're planted in sites where other varieties might do better.

Blends are another area of renewed interest, especially ones inspired by Bordeaux and the Rhône. The most innovative winemakers know that a blend of grapes is often more than the sum of its parts: Cabernet can benefit hugely from a bit of softening Merlot, for example. But varietal labelling is such an easy way to sell wine. You don't have to explain anything; your customers know what to expect, and all you have to do is supply it. There's been a huge growth in 'Meritage' wines – Bordeaux blends, both red and white – but the term Meritage had to be coined,

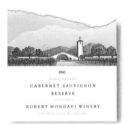

Robert Mondavi is a Californian institution, spreading the gospel of Californian wine from his Napa home base. His Cabernet Sauvignon Reserve shows enormous power and depth.

DEGREE DAYS

In California a classification also exists for climates, intended purely as a guideline to help growers assess which grape varieties will be best suited to their areas. The system, known as 'degree days', is based on averaging out the recorded daily temperatures over the course of the growing season (April to October), then taking an average of the annual totals over a number of years. This produces five regions (roughly, the coolest to the hottest, from I to V), but the sytem has not been applied as rigorously as its originators, the University of California, had envisaged. And quite right, too, since its rather broad brush approach takes little account of individual microclimates.

and publicized, to establish this as an accepted style. Make up your own blend and you might find it trickier to sell – unless you're already so famous and have such a name for quality and imagination that anything you make will have them queuing in the street. And yes, there are California winemakers like this.

Where else is there room for innovation? Paradoxically, in those very areas that Europe has always thought of as being its own: in terroir, in accepting that the wine is made in the vineyard, not the winery, in relegating the role of the winemaker to that of an enabler rather than a creator.

And actually, that's happening too. In parts of Napa, in Carneros, in all sorts of nooks and crannies all over the state, individual winemakers are becoming aware that one patch of land makes distinctly different wine from another patch next to it. Of course, you won't get them to agree on where the boundaries are (they don't agree in

Springtime mustard flowering between rows of dormant vines, seen here in Rutherford, Napa County, is a common sight all over northern California.

Europe, either), but this is how an awareness of terroir develops: in fits and starts, in patches here and there. There are even winemakers in California to whom you can mention the word 'terroir' without their making the sign against the evil eye; it wasn't so many years ago that nearly all California winemakers were quite certain that the only function of soil was to hold the vine upright. Single-vineyard wines are appearing from everywhere these days.

UNIVERSITY OF CALIFORNIA, DAVIS

The University of California at Davis is the centre of American viticultural and winemaking research and where most of its winemakers are trained. It has been a centre for research and teaching since 1880; grapes couldn't be grown at Berkeley, which was where the original University was sited, and so vineyards were established in the warmer climate of Davis. It has since conducted

The Grapes
A combination of top international varieties, plus some quirkier ones.

CABERNET SAUVIGNON is the great red grape of the Napa Valley. Think big, concentrated fruit; think lots of oak, think ripeness and tannic structure. But California Cabernet comes in all possible styles, from simpler wines to the leaner wines of cooler regions.

PINOT NOIR is getting better and better, thanks to the discovery of a handful of seemingly ideal spots by a few Pinot fanatics. Carneros is one such, Mount Harlan, Santa Barbara and Russian River are others. And in the very coolest spots, like the Anderson Valley, it makes excellent Champagne-method sparkling wine.

Zinfandel

ZINFANDEL is a wonderful, bright-faced, easy-going grape which will make almost anything: port-style sweet wines, blockbuster reds or fresh fruity ones, even the sweetish rosé known absurdly as 'blush' and usually called White Zinfandel. The best reds are sturdy and marked by peppery blackberry and raspberry fruit.

MERLOT is used a lot to blend with Cabernet but is wildly popular on its own for rich, soft, plum and cherry fruity red.

PETITE SIRAH, originally France's Durif, makes good, tough, rather raisiny red.

ITALIAN VARIETIES like Sangiovese and Barbera are also making strides and often blended with other red grapes for exciting flavours.

RHÔNE VARIETIES are also on the increase, especially Syrah, Grenache, Mourvèdre, and whites like Viognier, Roussanne and Marsanne.

CHARDONNAY thrives in all but the hottest parts of the state. The best are far more subtle and complex than they used to be; less ambitious wines have an intense blend of fruit flavours: mango, peach, fig, melon.

SAUVIGNON BLANC is at its best in the cooler areas, where it has a chance to produce the grassy, gooseberry flavours that are its *raison d'être*. Those labelled Fumé Blanc may be oaked, or mixed with Semillon for extra fatness.

RIESLING is known here as Johannisberg Riesling or White Riesling, but both mean the same thing – the true Riesling of Germany. The dry wine made in California is seldom very exciting, but late-harvest botrytized versions can be sensational, honeyed and intense, with high acidity.

Chardonnay

Based in the cool Anderson Valley, Lazy Creek has developed a cult following among those who know California wines. This Gewürztraminer has rich, spicy flavours. Sadly, however, plantings of the variety are on the decline.

research into the matching of vine varieties to particular soils and climates, cellar technology and all aspects of grape growing and winemaking. Its alumni have included Albert J Winkler who developed the system of heat summation and degree days for classifying climates according to the number of days per year warm enough to ripen grapes; Harold P Olmo, who developed many new vines crossings, and writer and enologist Maynard Amerine.

It's famous for its rigorously scientific approach to problems; however, it doesn't always get things right. Its advice to California's growers to plant their vines on AXR1 rootstock, which has proved insufficiently resistant to phylloxera, has meant that most of California's vineyards have had to be replanted.

North Coast

The Californian contrast of climates, the great arbiter of style throughout the state, can be clearly seen on California's North Coast. In **Mendocino's** interior **Redwood Valley** the Coastal Range is hardly broken, the cooling fog can't find a way in, and it is warm; in places very warm, so big Cabernets and briary Zinfandels are common.

The northern reaches of the **Russian River Valley** are pretty hot, too; Rhône varieties like Syrah and Grenache can do well here.

Mendocino has a range of AVAs, from the catch-all Mendocino to more specific ones like Anderson Valley, and these by and large separate out different climates: **Anderson Valley** is extremely cool. One of the major Champagne houses, Louis Roederer, makes sparkling wine here. They selected this spot because the weather was just about as grim as it is in Champagne. Still wines from cool-climate-loving grapes like Gewürztraminer and Riesling are good here, too. Neighbouring Lake County, with the AVAs of **Clear Lake** and **Guenoc Valley**, seems to be able to make everything from Sauvignon Blanc to rich Petite Sirah and Zinfandel, depending on the altitude of the vineyards.

One of the great discoveries of recent years – or rather rediscovery – has been old-established vineyards, often of Zinfandel, planted by winegrowers of the last century. They were so deeply unfashionable for many years that it's a miracle they've survived, but now they're being given all the help they need to produce small crops of concentrated wine.

SPARKLING WINES

The first sparkling wines made in California were, perhaps not surprisingly, called Champagne. Cheaper sparkling wines from the state are still labelled Champagne (much to the fury of the Champenois who believe, rightly, that Champagne can only come from the Champagne region of France: it is not a generic term). Such wines are usually made by the *cuve close* or transfer process, which weakens the association still further.

However, there is a breed of top-quality wines made by the Champagne method. Some of these are made by Californian companies, but in recent years companies from Champagne itself, as well as from Spain, have been buying land in the cooler parts of California, building wineries and making sparkling wines on the pattern of their produce at home. The results have been startlingly successful. Some mimic the flavour of Champagne remarkably accurately; a few even seem to make rather better wine in California than they do at home.

Californians use high-tech methods to produce their sparkling wines. No hand *remuage* for them – giropalettes are much more cost effective.

Napa

I f there's one wine that sums up California, it's Napa Cabernet. Rich, deep, tannic when young, but if given time, bursting with black cherry, mint and cedar, they've been dubbed the Pauillacs of the west.

And yet Napa is a remarkably diverse area. It's only some 32km (20 miles) long, and in places less than 1.5km (one mile) wide, and is said to have more different sorts of soil than the whole of France, although it's probably natives of Napa rather than natives of France who say that. It looks a bit like Provence – there are the same scrub-covered hills, the same car-laden roads (although they drive more slowly here), the same prosperous chic. If you build a winery here it's almost obligatory to hire an innovative architect and produce something even more stunning than your neighbours; as a result Napa is a treasury of all that is best in contemporary architecture. Old wineries (which means, basically, pre-Prohibition) are lovingly preserved and used as visitor centres, even if the hard work is done at a space-age installation next door.

The Napa ideal is to have a glamorous winery building surrounded by its own vineyards, Bordeaux-style – and there's a direct parallel here with the Médoc. In the boom years of the 1980s the Médoc was turned into a building site as château after château competed for the smartest new *chai*, the most state-of-the-art installation. Well, Napa is doing that all the time. It is not a coincidence: both the Médoc and Napa focus on Cabernet Sauvignon, and the first Napa growers to make their mark internationally with the grape took as their model the First Growths of the Médoc. A leading figure – indeed the leading figure – here is Robert Mondavi. He has set the pace for Napa, and for all California, ever since he set up his own winery in 1966. His mission was to travel the world, and then apply what he had learnt to his wines in California.

The coolest part of Napa, the southern end, shares with the coolest part of Sonoma the AVA of Carneros. The further north you go the warmer it gets, until at the northern end Zinfandel

flourishes, and big, strapping Cabernets. There are white wines made everywhere, too: since post-phylloxera replanting, Chardonnay, however, tends to be concentrated south of the town of St Helena.

In Napa Valley proper the biggest surprise, to anyone reared on European vineyards, is that nearly all the vines are planted on the valley floor. It's absolutely flat here and the rows of vines jostle for space against the valley walls – and yet they don't climb up them. Well, they do sometimes. More and more, in fact. One of the most exciting developments of the last few years

As well as stunning buildings, some wineries, like Clos Pegase in Calistoga, also boast fine sculptures. Others even house their own art collections.

Two examples of the style of Cabernet that has made Napa famous throughout the world.

Autumn colours in vineyards along the Silverado Trail, south of Calistoga, in the hills of the Napa Valley.

Stag's Leap Cellars were the winners of the famous 1976 Paris tasting (see opposite). The Hess Collection is a showcase not only for wine but also for art which is housed in a gallery at the winery.

has been the emergence of magnificent reds and whites from vineyards high up in the hills; but at first there was no need for this. Rutherford and Oakville were quite capable of making the reputation of the valley on their own.

Rutherford and **Oakville** are next-door neighbours, AVAs with well-drained alluvial soil which (if you believe that terroir affects the taste of wine; skip this bit if you don't) just happens to make Cabernet Sauvignon of startling depth and complexity. The original Napa Cabernets, the ones that made the name of the valley, came from here. No, nobody can actually say precisely why, nor can anyone agree on where the alluvial soil begins and ends. Appellation boundaries in France, too, are mostly the result of political compromise.

There's more great Cabernet – and Merlot, too – in **Stag's Leap District**. These wines have juicier, more supple fruit than those of Rutherford and Oakville, but the best are long-lived. **Howell Mountain** and **Mount Veeder** – both, as their names suggest, are hillside AVAs – also focus on Cabernet, with some good Zinfandel, Cabernet and Chardonnay in Mount Veeder.

But not all wineries in Napa, or indeed anywhere in California, restrict themselves to grapes grown in their home vineyards. Wineries right up near Calistoga may own vines in Carneros, or buy grapes there, and make cool-climate Carneros reds and whites. Or they may blend some into other grapes for the sake of balance. Many wineries, even boutique wineries, produce several single-vineyard wines, plus several wines drawn from a wider area, with a more general AVA. It's the equivalent of, say, a Burgundy grower with his range of single-vineyard wines, village wines and basic Burgundies. It's all part of the business of offering a range of qualities.

These days with California recovering from phylloxera B, the vineyards even look different. In Napa some 8095 hectares (20,000 acres) were replanted; in Sonoma 6070 hectares (15,000 acres). New clones were introduced, a greater variety of rootstocks and closer vine spacing. Improved trellising systems, too, give better air circulation around leaves and fruit. As a result, yields per vine are much lower than they were, and vines are healthier: better for the wines, better for the vines.

THE JUDGEMENT OF PARIS

It was back in 1976 that California won its spurs, vis-à-vis French wine. Wine merchant Steven Spurrier organized a blind tasting of the best of red Bordeaux versus the best of California Cabernet, and the best of white Burgundy versus the best of California Chardonnay. The bottles were all mixed up and unmarked so that the judges (themselves a mixture: top Parisian restaurateurs, top growers from Bordeaux and Burgundy and the senior inspector of INAO, the Institut National des Appellations d'Origine) had no idea which was which.

The results were startling: in both red and white sections a California wine came top. Among the Cabernets, Stag's Leap 1973 beat Mouton-Rothschild 1970; among the Chardonnays, Chateau Montelena beat a Meursault-Charmes.

Afterwards, some commentators were keen to point out that French wines take longer to evolve than California ones, and that the more upfront fruit of California wines gives them an advantage in blind tastings. All this is true: but it was nevertheless a major triumph for the Napa Valley.

Sonoma

Sonoma County is one of California's most diffuse areas, with AVAs layered one on another. It has mountain vineyards producing fragrant, long-lived reds and whites, dense and expensive; but on the whole Sonoma's wines are softer and juicier, more easily approachable than Napa wines, and they are often cheaper. But it doesn't have the concentrated valley floor carpet of wines which distinguishes Napa. Furthermore, Napa fame was built on long-established wineries, some of which had been there before Prohibition, whereas the majority of Sonoma's finest wineries are relative newcomers. Until the 1970s Sonoma wine was generally sold for blending; not now. So perhaps it's even more remarkable that some old vineyards, planted as long ago as the turn of the century, are still producing. Century-old vines give only small crops, but the quality can be terrific.

Sonoma Valley itself runs up through a mixture of farmland, commuter towns and vineyards to Santa Rosa. From here, north to Cloverdale, lies the most concentrated group of Sonoma AVAs.

Alexander Valley is a confusing sort of place to understand, simply because it seems to do everything pretty well; at the same time it's difficult to point to any style that is outstanding here. It's the biggest of Sonoma County's AVAs and has the most vines, the majority of which are planted on the valley floor. There's Chardonnay and Sauvignon Blanc, Cabernet Sauvignon, Zinfandel, Merlot, Sangiovese, Barbera and Rhône varieties. Common sense might say that you can't have a region that produces good versions of all of these; yet that's precisely what Alexander Valley does. **Knights Valley**, to the south-east, makes good Cabernet and Sauvignon Blanc.

The **Russian River**, which runs through Alexander Valley, also has an AVA of its own, where the river swings west at Healdsburg and heads for the sea. It's far cooler here, and sparkling wines from Chardonnay and Pinot Noir do particularly well. Pinot Noir, in fact, is the new Russian River star. Gewürztraminer, too, is good, and there's also top Chardonnay, complex and long-lived. **Sonoma-Green Valley** is a cool-climate sub-AVA of Russian River; **Chalk Hill** is another sub-AVA, giving good Chardonnay and Sauvignon Blanc.

Dry Creek Valley, just north-west of Russian River, has plenty of Italian names among its producers, since it was Italians who planted the first vineyards here. There's sensational Sauvignon

An historic California winery, revitalized by the arrival of influential winemaker Zelma Long in 1979 and the purchase by current owner Moët-Hennessy in 1981.

Bucher presses and rotary fermenters at Gallo Sonoma's Frei Ranch winery in Dry Creek Valley. A high level of investment has obviously been ploughed into this high-tech operation.

ZINFANDEL

Zinfandel is California's very own grape, the nearest thing the state has to an indigenous vine, and it can be anything Californians (or anyone else) want it to be: white (which means pink, or 'blush'); light, juicy red, or strapping, sturdy red that will age for several years. (The last style shows the grape at its best, with rich, fairly simple, berried fruit.)

Yet no vine is really indigenous to California. Zinfandel had to have come from somewhere; the question was where. It clearly wasn't French. It was originally said to have been brought from Hungary by winemaking pioneer Agoston Haraszthy in the early 1860s; the trouble with this theory was that the variety was already being grown on the East Coast before Haraszthy brought his mixed bag of cuttings from Europe. It was only DNA 'fingerprinting' in the 1990s that established the truth: Zinfandel is the same as Primitivo, a red grape found in southern Italy. Ironically, Primitivo might well have remained pretty obscure if it hadn't been for the Zinfandel connection; now it bathes in reflected glory.

ABOVE A delivery of Zinfandel grapes arriving at a winery. Unfortunately, this variety can ripen unevenly which means that you sometimes end up with unripe green berries on the same bunch as those that have reached full maturity. And the grapes can quickly turn into raisins if not picked promptly.

Two Zinfandel specialists. Ravenswood wines are big and powerful though still well balanced. Rafanelli's classic California Zinfandel is from old-vine, non-irrigated, hillside grapes.

Blanc, which is head and shoulders above Chardonnay, and wonderful Zinfandel, which seems to do better than Cabernet. Not surprisingly, it's the northern reaches of the AVA, where the cool fog can't reach, that make the best Zinfandel; the best whites tend to come from further south.

Sonoma Valley is the heart of the region. It runs parallel to Napa Valley, yet the mountains in between are so wild and the roads between the two valleys so few that you could be in a different world. If Napa is California's Bordeaux, all grand architecture and smartness, Sonoma is more like Burgundy: it's far more relaxed about itself. It's more genuinely rural, too, although it has its share of chi-chi hotels. It's popular with tourists but the weekend traffic doesn't seem to jam the roads quite the same way as it does in Napa.

In the south where long-lived Cabernets and dense Zinfandels are produced from high hillside vineyards, it's cool; the further north you go the weaker the Pacific fogs become and the more the temperature rises. So Sonoma's wines range from concentrated reds to elegant whites from Chardonnay, Gewürztraminer and others. There's a sub-AVA called **Sonoma Mountain**, which makes fine Cabernet Sauvignon from hillside vineyards. The move to the hillsides is producing reds which are longer-lived and slower to develop.

This statue of St Francis oversees production of some 100,000 cases of wine at the St Francis winery in Kenwood in Sonoma Valley.

Carneros

Carneros doesn't seem like a world-famous vineyard area at all. The landscape is gently undulating; picture hills like this and in your imagination you automatically dot them with sheep. Well, Carneros means sheep, and there were indeed pastures here until some canny grape growers realized that the climatic conditions mirrored Burgundy. There was a rush to buy up land.

This was actually Carneros's rebirth, rather than its beginning as a wine region. There had been vineyards here before phylloxera struck in the late 19th century; but at that time the cold had been a curse that stopped grapes ripening. Now that growers started planting Pinot Noir and Chardonnay, it became a gift.

It's not just cold that is the secret here, but the fogs that roll in from the sea, and frequent winds: all these factors help to slow maturity and lengthen the ripening period. These fogs are crucial: they roll in early from San Pablo Bay, and in summertime burn off late. The sunshine would be hot if it got an uninterrupted go at the vines: Carneros is on the same latitude as northern Italy, so it's no feeble northern sun we're talking about. But the fog ensures that it is nicely filtered. Rainfall is low and the clay soil is relatively unfertile; no wonder Pinot Noir likes it so much.

Pinot from here has a lightness of touch, a scented quality that is not the same as that of Burgundy but that is nevertheless a true expression of the grape. Chardonnay grown in these conditions is more elegant than any other in Napa or Sonoma (the Carneros region straddles the southern ends of both Napa and Sonoma Valleys), and quietly builds its character over the years into a marvellously refined wine. Merlot is looking promising, too, and Sauvignon Blanc is beautifully fresh and grassy. There's potential for other cool-climate white grapes too. Wineries from all over the North Coast buy Carneros grapes, either doing separate Carneros bottlings or using the grapes to add elegance to blends.

Sparkling wines are also successful here; a blend of Chardonnay and Pinot Noir is common and more than one Champagne house has set up a winery in Carneros.

Carneros Creek has played a key role in establishing the Carneros region as an important area for Pinot Noir; Saintsbury's Pinot Noirs are brilliant examples of the perfume and fruit quality of the region.

The Food of California

CALIFORNIAN CUISINE is a wonderful pot-pourri of cuisines from all over the world; strong, fresh flavours married to the traditions of many countries. You don't have to go far to find restaurants catering to every taste, from Mexican and Italian to Chinese, Japanese and Thai.

Food fashions change so fast on the West Coast that no one, cook or consumer, can surely keep up with them. There's fusion food – the explosion of flavours that is California, plus the herbs and spices of the Far East – and there's CalItal (California meets Italy). There's CalMed (California meets Provence) and I'm sure that by the time this book appears there'll be at least three more.

But there are some enduring characteristics. Bold, intense, exciting flavours are paramount, and usually several of them served all at once (coriander plus olive oil plus grilled peppers plus garlic plus goat's cheese, plus plus plus).

Oaky Chardonnay is good at coping with these strong, mixed flavours. With CalItal food, California Barbera ought to be perfect; just as California Rhône Ranger wines should be the natural match of CalMed; in fact, any good, weighty, spicy California red will go well.

As well as easy access to ingredients from all over the world, there's a wealth of top-quality local produce. There's seafood from the Pacific including crab and salmon. Clams, mussels and oysters are also farmed. Organically produced meats are increasingly abundant as are fruit and vegetables. The state grows its own apples, dates, kiwi fruit, peaches, melons and oranges. Needless to say, fresh fruit salad is a favourite dessert. Salads, too, can be wonderfully extravagant affairs, sometimes a complete meal in themselves. And there's also an ever increasing number of small, specialist producers, catering for every whim of the gourmet market.

Central Coast

While Napa and Sonoma and the vineyards north of San Francisco Bay are California's most famous, they're not the whole story. Some of the best Zinfandels in California come from Santa Cruz, while splendid Pinot Noirs come from Santa Barbara County and the San Benito Mountains, all way south, in a large area called Central Coast. It's an area of such diversity that generalizations are impossible.

Santa Cruz Mountains is the first AVA you come to, south of San Francisco Bay. It's more famous for its wineries than for its vineyards – lots of them buy in or grow grapes elsewhere – but what vines there are grow at every possible altitude and with every possible exposure. It's relatively cool, but can still ripen Zinfandel, Cabernet and Rhône varieties like Syrah, Roussanne and Marsanne. Pinot Noir also does well here. **Santa Clara** doesn't have many vineyards either, but does grow some Chardonnay; **Livermore** grows good Semillon and Sauvignon, but spreads its bets over a wider range of grapes, most of which are unremarkable.

Jim Clendenen of pace-setting Au Bon Climat draws inspiration from both Burgundy and Piedmont; Randall Grahm of Bonny Doon is a fan of Rhône, Italian and Spanish grape varieties. Le Cigar Volant is his homage to Châteauneuf-du-Pape.

OPPOSITE The barrel room at Firestone Vineyard in the Santa Ynez Valley. The large wooden fermentation vats (right) will be made from old oak whereas the smaller barrels for aging the wine will be new oak. This imparts more flavour to the maturing wine.

RHÔNE RANGERS

These growers, and their innovative wine styles, are a welcome change from the otherwise little varied Californian diet of Cabernet and Chardonnay. They're so called because they've adopted the grapes of France's Rhône Valley – principally Mourvèdre, Grenache, Syrah, Viognier, Roussanne and Marsanne – and grown them for both varietals (especially in the case of Viognier) and blends, sometimes with other Rhône varieties, sometimes with Cabernet or Barbera or anything else that takes their fancy. Quality is generally very good, and prices are not low, though certainly not as high as the prices of top Chardonnays and Cabernets. Joseph Phelps, Bonny Doon and Qupé are among the leading names. Often there was no need to import vine cuttings – always a bureaucratic and slow task – because old vineyards of Grenache and Mourvèdre already existed, having been planted for fortified wines by earlier generations of winemakers. The use of grapes from such low-yielding old vines can give extra depth to the wines.

San Benito County would be entirely unremarkable in wine terms were it not for Pinot Noir grown on limestone in the **Mount Harlan AVA**. This is bigger, richer, wilder wine than the Pinot from Carneros; it's more Burgundian than Carneros Pinot, without the delicacy of the Côte d'Or, but with an intensity and unpredictability that puts it into the top league. Calera is the name to look for. There is concentrated Viognier and Chardonnay here as well.

The **Salinas Valley** in **Monterey County** can be a bit on the cool side for grapes. In the past, wines could be too green and vegetal to be much good. That didn't stop people planting here, though now the vineyards are concentrated in the south, where it's warmer. One of the exceptions is an AVA called **Chalone**, which makes remarkable Pinot Noir and Chardonnay from high-altitude, unirrigated vineyards.

If you follow the Salinas Valley southwards you come to **Paso Robles**, where it's anything but cool. The sea fog can't find its way in to chill these vineyards, but the vines planted high on the hills nevertheless get pretty chilly at night. The result is startlingly good reds, from Cabernet, Zinfandel and Rhône varieties. Nearby **Edna Valley**, on the other hand, is distinctly cool by Californian standards, and makes lean, nutty, Burgundian Chardonnay. **Arroyo Grande**, even cooler, is proving highly suitable for sparkling wine. And **Santa Barbara County**? There's stunning, supple Pinot Noir and Chardonnay from both its AVAs, **Santa Maria Valley** and **Santa Ynez Valley**. The former is cool, maybe almost too cool for comfort; the latter has some hot spots that can ripen even Syrah. Santa Maria, in fact, is now producing some Pinot Noir which is giving Russian River and Carneros a run for their money. Elsewhere **Arroyo Seco** makes good Chardonnay and Riesling, and the **Santa Maria Highlands** have a reputation for Cabernet and Merlot.

Central Valley

The Central Valley is home to huge wineries like the Franzia winery, pictured above, at Ripon, near Modesto.

Quady produce good port-style wines in Madera. Elysium is a rich dessert wine with very ripe black fruits.

This vast area, distinguished by the size of its wineries, is unrelentingly hot. The world's biggest winery – E & J Gallo – pumps out huge quantities of very passable wine every year here, and the first impression of the region is of a flat, irrigated desert. Small, wine-oriented towns where you might find, say, a good restaurant? Forget it. Wineries with innovative modern architecture that will welcome you and offer you a glass of wine in a shaded garden with hummingbirds darting between flowers? Some hope. Nobody goes to the Central Valley unless they have a good reason. And tourism is no reason at all.

Nevertheless, this is where California shows what it can do under difficult conditions. We're not talking fine wine here, we're talking technology. This is the sort of wine – well-made, fruity and cheap – that set off the wine revolution worldwide, because once people had discovered that cheap wine could taste nice there was absolutely no reason for them to go on buying the stuff that tasted horrible.

The Central Valley is divided into the **Sacramento Valley** and the **San Joaquin Valley**, and the former does actually have some parts, like **Lodi**, that are slightly cooler and can produce better quality. The San Joaquin Valley produces huge quantities of fruit, vegetables and grapes – but, perhaps not surprisingly, there are some good-quality fortifieds at **Madera**.

Other Regions in California

There are one or two spots in central California producing interesting wine. The **Sierra Foothills** is Gold Rush country and makes good strapping Zinfandels from rugged, high-altitude vineyards that can be the spiciest, strongest-tasting and most memorable in California. The high vineyards of **Temecula** near Los Angeles give some interesting whites.

Oregon

In 1966, when David Lett planted Pinot Noir at Eyrie Vineyards in Oregon's Willamette Valley, there were virtually no wineries producing vinifera wines in the Pacific Northwest states of Oregon, Washington and Idaho. These days it's a different picture.

Oregon has had a bumpy ride – too much hype, too soon – but now it's settling into its stride. And some pundits are saying that one day it will produce the best wine in the United States. Not the most – it could never compete with California on quantity – but the best. And more specifically, the best Pinot Noir.

Although Oregon began making wine as long ago as the 1820s, Prohibition effectively wiped out those efforts and it wasn't until the 1960s that a revival began. It started when some of the wine pioneers of California realized that for one thing, they didn't really like California and what they really wanted was to get away by themselves somewhere. Oregon, with its laid-back, rural atmosphere, became a focal point. And, by coincidence, its cool growing season and plentiful rain seemed just the thing to make vine growing difficult. And Pinot Noir produces the best wine where it has to work hardest.

And it certainly has to work hard here. Summers are so uneven that picking can start as early as September, or as late as November; the Pacific Ocean keeps frost away and keeps winters mild, but it also brings rain which falls west of the Cascade Mountains; which is where the vineyards are.

Not that there are the great tracts of vineyards that one sees in California. They are dotted here and there in Oregon, clustered into a few favoured areas, sweeping down hillsides where low winery buildings sit in the shadow of forest. This is a community of smallholders, feeling their way in a marginal climate with one of the world's most temperamental grapes.

The first winery was started in the relatively warm **Umpqua Valley** 290km (180 miles) south of Portland, but the early growers centred their efforts on the **Willamette Valley** south-west of Portland. In 1979, a 1975 Eyrie Pinot Noir came second to a 1959 Chambolle-Musigny in a blind-tasting competition in Paris, and beat a

David Lett's Eyrie Vineyards' Pinot Noir is medium-bodied with fine lightly spicy, herbal cherry fruit. Not bad for someone who started off making wine in a poultry-plucking shed.

Picking Pinot Noir, the grape that is making Oregon's reputation, in the vineyards of the Sokol Blosser winery in the Willamette Valley.

The Grapes

Pinot Noir is Oregon's main weapon – but it has a couple of others, too.

PINOT NOIR is Oregon's strongest suit – and it's pretty clever for an emerging wine region to have picked on the grape that all the world wants to grow, but few can grow successfully. The best Oregon examples have good depth, concentration and complexity, and there are lighter, jammier versions as well.

PINOT GRIS does well in Oregon – and it's just as well that the region has a second string to its bow. The local style is dry, quite light but with a characterful touch of spice.

RIESLING does fairly well here, making light, peachy wines, but it doesn't receive the attention of Oregon's main grapes.

CHARDONNAY is widely grown but doesn't seem to produce wines of great interest. Most are light and crisp; the best are elegant with some oak. New clones from Dijon in France are helping Oregon producers craft Chardonnays that may rival the best of California.

GEWÜRZTRAMINER is a minority grape but rather successful, with a crisp, spicy character.

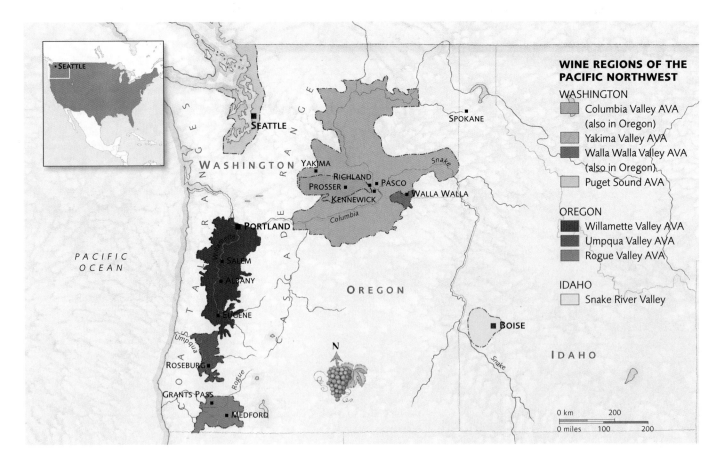

Domaine Drouhin, the Burgundy wine company, bought 40 hectares (100 acres) of land in Oregon in 1987. Laurène, made from estate-grown grapes, is among the finest Pinot Noirs to have come out of Oregon to date.

1961 Chambertin. In a replay in 1985 ten Oregon 1983 Pinot Noirs were set against seven 1983 Burgundies, and took the first three places. Such tastings are never conclusive, but top Burgundy producer Robert Drouhin found them convincing enough to invest in land and a brand new winery in the Dundee Hills, close to Eyrie Vineyards. This move was what really convinced the doubters of Oregon's potential: if a leading Burgundian is prepared to stake money on Oregon Pinot Noir then it must be good. Ironically, Drouhin's Oregon Pinots have been so good that many blind tasters have mistaken them for Côte d'Or Burgundies. Other outside investment has followed, notably from California.

David Lett also introduced Pinot Gris to Oregon and this has proved quite a success, making early-maturing whites that are excellent with seafood. The first clones of Chardonnay planted in the Willamette Valley produced lean and acidic wines that lacked body and balance. New Chardonnay clones imported from Dijon, France, are being planted and the resulting wines have shown dramatic improvements in texture and spice. Gewürztraminer has great promise in the Willamette Valley but unfortunately few producers choose to grow it due to low prices and sluggish sales. There's also a smattering of citrus-flavoured Riesling and gentle Pinot Blanc.

The **Rogue Valley** AVA has a much warmer climate and many fine Cabernet Sauvignon and Merlot wines are beginning to be made. Other developing areas include the **Applegate Valley** and **Illinois Valley**. None of these, however, are suited to producing large yields, and so Oregon's future can only be as a producer of high quality. And California's top Pinot Noirs have become so good in recent years that Oregon is going to have to work pretty hard to keep its reputation as Pinot Noir heaven.

WINE REGIONS OF THE PACIFIC NORTHWEST

WASHINGTON
- Columbia Valley AVA (also in Oregon)
- Yakima Valley AVA
- Walla Walla Valley AVA (also in Oregon)
- Puget Sound AVA

OREGON
- Willamette Valley AVA
- Umpqua Valley AVA
- Rogue Valley AVA

IDAHO
- Snake River Valley

Washington

There is one vital difference between wine in Oregon and wine in Washington State – and it's called the Cascade Mountains.

These mountains, running north to south through the state, ensure that the clouds drop their rain on the western part of the state, which has a climate much like that of Oregon, and can, in its very few vineyards, make similar styles. On the eastern side of the Cascades the story is different. Bakingly hot summers and freezing winters may not seem the ideal conditions for wine, but provided you can irrigate, and provided you can keep the cold at bay during the winter (usually by planting on a south- or south-west-facing slope, so that the cold air drains away) the climate can be beaten. It has been beaten to such good effect in fact that Washington State is now the second biggest wine producer after California – albeit rather a long way after California.

Washington State's wine industry was built originally on the American hybrid grape Concord, and more recently, when vinifera grapes were planted in the 1970s, on the ability to produce large amounts of fresh, agreeable wine at a low price, with more marked acidity and fruit than the bulk wines of California. They're a monument to irrigation: the vines are planted in a wild, dry moonscape of semi-desert, with only 15-20cm (6-8 inches) of rain each year, yet with industrial-scale irrigation they can produce yields three times as high as those of Oregon. And the days are long here: in June Washington State averages 17.4 hours of daylight per 24 hours against California's 15.8. All this makes for a rare combination of very ripe grapes rich in sugar, balanced by high acidity from the cold nights.

These conditions could have created a fruit bowl turning out massive quantities of jug wine at ultra-low prices. Luckily Washington State growers decided that high-quality affordable wine was where the future lay. And they've been proved right: they produce beautifully fragrant Riesling and Gewürztraminer, ripe, soft Chardonnay, excitingly grassy Sauvignon and honey-rich but tangy Semillon. Reds, too, are good. The Cabernets are full of an almost Australian blackcurrant and mint fruit, but are dark and tannic enough for long aging, and the Merlot is softer but equally impressive. In fact, it is Merlot that has made a reputation for Washington State red wines. Leonetti Cellar Merlot has become an icon of the Washington wine industry and its popularity has fostered large increases in the amount of Merlot planted in the state.

The vineyards are concentrated in **Columbia Valley** which contains the smaller but important Yakima Valley and Walla Walla Valley. **Yakima Valley** is cool, relative to the rest of Columbia Valley, but still makes Cabernet, Merlot and even Sangiovese, plus Chardonnay and Sauvignon. The **Walla Walla Valley** crosses the border of Washington State into northern Oregon. Many new vineyards have been planted here and the grapes from these produce big, tannic red wine.

Puget Sound is a more recent AVA, made up

Riesling grapes arriving at the Columbia Crest winery in Paterson. They'll need plenty more to maintain their annual production of 750,000 cases.

One of Washington State's finest wineries producing excellent Cabernet Sauvignon and Merlot and currently experimenting with Sangiovese sourced from the Walla Walla Valley.

The Grapes

A paradoxical combination of rich reds and cool-climate whites.

CABERNET SAUVIGNON from Washington has concentrated blackcurrant fruit and ripe, upfront flavours.

MERLOT has soft, blackcurrant and damson fruit in Washington State, and can age quite well.

LEMBERGER, the Austrian Blaufränkisch grape, makes good juicy everyday young red.

RIESLING has taken to the cold nights of Washington State and Idaho and produces well-balanced, polished wines which reach good levels of ripeness and may be made sweet.

CHARDONNAY is usually soft and barrel-fermented in Washington; Idaho examples may be rich and oaked, or leaner if not.

SAUVIGNON BLANC from Washington State is proving attractively pungent, with good grassy, gooseberry flavours.

SEMILLON does well in Washington State, with good citrus fruit flavours.

Cabernet Sauvignon

Chateau Ste Michelle is a pioneering winery with an enormous range of wines including Sauvignon Blanc, Chardonnay, Riesling, Merlot and Cabernet Sauvignon. Barrel-fermented Chardonnay with layers of new oak is the trademark wine for Woodward Canyon, based in the Walla Walla Valley.

of a handful of growers struggling to ripen vinifera grapes in vineyards located west of the Cascade Mountains. Rainfall at vintage time presents a sizeable obstacle.

And the mountains? Well, there's one mountain in particular, Mount Rainier, that all Washington State growers hope will continue in its present state of stability. An eruption there could wipe out the entire industry.

Idaho

Idaho has a climate as marginal as they come. The trouble is that days here are hot and nights cold – much like Washington State, only more so. The ripening season is shorter, the winters colder, and vines that survive the winters tend to produce wines of startling high acidity, high sugar and lower flavour. Riesling does well under these circumstances, and Chardonnay can succeed, but Cabernet often needs a longer growing period. The way to soften the acidity and bring down the alcohol level in the whites can be to increase the yields, thus going against accepted wisdom in every other region in the world.

The Food of the Pacific Northwest

BLESSED WITH a long coastline and fertile valleys and grasslands, the Pacific Northwest has no shortage of high-quality ingredients.

Seafood is at the heart of the cuisine: clams, crab, lobster, oysters and mussels plus a wide variety of locally caught fish including salmon, tuna, flounder, halibut, cod, red snapper and sole. Pinot Gris is light and dry with enough flavour to go well with most of these.

Fruits and berries are plentiful in the forests – marionberries, blueberries, huckleberries and cranberries. The forests are also home to wild mushrooms – oyster, morel, porcini, shiitake and chanterelle.

Rich grassland feeds a thriving dairy industry. Look out for Oregon's delicious Tillamook cheddar and traditional orange style cheeses from the Rogue and Umpqua Valleys.

Oregon is also nut country. It's the only state with its own nut – the filbert or hazelnut.

As evidence for Yakima Valley's claim to be a premium wine region continues to emerge, new vineyards, like this one at Sunnyside, are springing up.

East Coast

Remember those early wines made by the first settlers in North America, and how unappealing their flavour was generally considered? Well, the grapes responsible can still be found in New York State.

They even make some wine, though they go into grape jelly as well, and they are by no means the whole story of winemaking here. New York State grows native American *Vitis labrusca* vines; hybrids (a hybrid is the product of interbreeding between *Vitis vinifera* and *Vitis labrusca* parents and not to be confused with a vine cross which is the result of interbreeding two vines of the same species) and European *Vitis vinifera* vines. That's enough range of flavours for anybody. Especially given that some hybrids, notably Seyval Blanc and Cayuga, can make attractive wines as well. They are more resistant to the harsh, extreme climate of New York State, and have less of the so-called 'foxy' flavour of labrusca grapes. Why the strange, sweet perfume of labrusca grapes should be called foxy I have no idea; it doesn't in the least resemble the smell of any foxes I've ever got near. But it is pungent and not massively attractive in wines, although in grape jelly it is unexpectedly appealing.

A large industry developed here in the late 19th century, growing grapes both for wine and for grape juice, with Concord as the main grape. Fast forward to the 1950s, when Charles Fournier, the winemaker at Gold Seal Vineyards in the Finger Lakes, got in touch with Dr Konstantin Frank, a Ukrainian-born grape grower, to start work on planting vinifera varieties here. The problem of phylloxera, which had put paid to the early settlers' vinifera cuttings, had been solved: new vinifera vines would be grafted on to American rootstocks, as is the case almost everywhere else in the world. The remaining problem was more intractable. It's the cold winters that are liable to kill off vinifera vines these days.

The best answer proved to be site selection. There are large bodies of water in New York State, and the vineyards congregate near them: Lake Erie, the Finger Lakes, Hudson River and

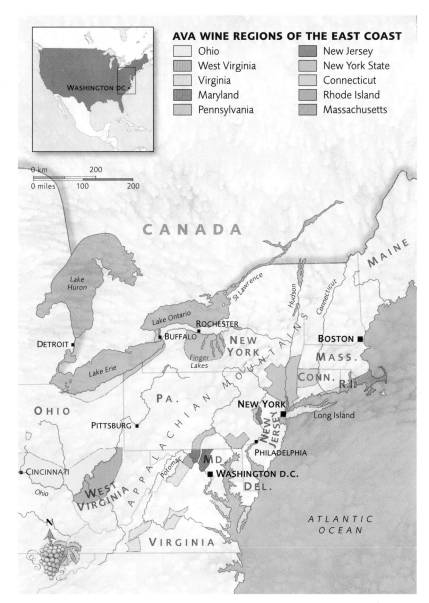

AVA WINE REGIONS OF THE EAST COAST

- Ohio
- West Virginia
- Virginia
- Maryland
- Pennsylvania
- New Jersey
- New York State
- Connecticut
- Rhode Island
- Massachusetts

Long Island are the main areas. Most have some spots warm enough for vinifera varieties, particularly if in autumn the vineyard soil is heaped up around the vine trunk above the graft to protect it from frost.

Another boost to vinifera production was given by the Farm Winery Act of 1976, which permitted farmgate sales of wine. Suddenly it became feasible for small producers to make good wine.

OPPOSITE Vineyards on the west side of Lake Keuka in the cool growing region of the Finger Lakes in New York State.

Lake Erie has the smallest percentage of vinifera vines. About 90 per cent of the grapes grown in the region are Concord and they are sold mainly as table grapes and for grape juice. A few determined souls are trying to make vinifera vines work.

The **Finger Lakes** are long, narrow, deep lakes carved out by Ice Age glaciers; hills rise steeply from their edges, which allows cold air to run from the vineyards, and the lakes moderate the climate sufficiently to allow some vinifera vines to be grown. Back in the last century they were the centre of New York State's wine industry. There's some interesting Chardonnay, Riesling and Gewürztraminer here. Pinot Noir is planted, too, though generally doesn't reach any great heights of quality although a few growers are having success with it. Recent bottlings of sparkling wine have been good. Most wines should be drunk within two or three years.

Hudson River, north of New York City, has some Pinot Noir as well, and some Cabernet Franc, though rather more Chardonnay and Riesling; it was the original New York State wine area, but got involved in modern vinifera winemaking relatively late.

Long Island is where the real action is. This is New York State's newest area, and was first planted as recently as 1973, on what had been potato farmland. The temperate climate proved ideal for vines, and many more vineyards have followed. Long Island is divided into two AVAs, **The Hamptons** and **North Fork**. There's a longer growing season here, which means that even red vinifera varieties can ripen. The weather can cause havoc, however, and several good vintages have been ruined by hurricanes, something few other premium winegrowing regions have to face. Cabernet Sauvignon does better here than Pinot Noir, which finds it too warm. Best of all are Merlot and Cabernet Franc, which really seem to like the maritime conditions and produce excellent subtle flavours and beautiful structure. Chardonnays are crisp, softened a little with oak, and Sauvignon Blanc is brilliantly sharp and grassy – in fact this is the best area in New York State for Sauvignon. There's also some Riesling, Gewürztraminer and Pinot Blanc.

Elsewhere on the East Coast **Pennsylvania**, **Virginia** and **Maryland** are the main wine states. The growers tend to hedge their bets and grow both hybrids and vinifera vines. Virginia with its Cabernet Sauvignon, Merlot, Syrah, Sauvignon Blanc, Riesling, Chardonnay and Viognier looks the best bet for quality.

The Grapes

Cool-climate styles reign, and the length of the ripening season is crucial.

Chardonnay

CHARDONNAY is the main vinifera vine here, making light but ripe wines made buttery by some oak-aging.

RIESLING is mostly light, with attractive appley, peachy fruit.

GEWÜRZTRAMINER makes crisp wines with good acidity and a touch of ripe spice.

PINOT BLANC ripens well and gives balanced, quite creamy wines.

SAUVIGNON BLANC ripens best on Long Island, producing wines with crisp, gooseberry fruit.

CABERNET SAUVIGNON can be a bit green in cool years, but in warm summers makes well-structured reds.

MERLOT shows good promise, making quite rich, blackberryish wines.

CABERNET FRANC produces well-balanced, fruity wine on Long Island.

PINOT NOIR is light and slightly jammy; perhaps the least successful of the reds.

Two influential East Coast figures – Dr Konstantin Frank made the first commercial wine from vinifera varieties in the Finger Lakes in 1959 and Alex Hargrave was one of the Long Island pioneers in the early 1970s.

Canada

If I were to say just one word about Canada's wine industry it would be 'wow'. I've seldom seen such improvement in such a short time. The first commercial vinifera vines were planted in the mid-1970s at Inniskillen: before that Canada had relied on labrusca grapes made sweet and sticky and usually labelled as 'port' or 'sherry'. Canada had had Prohibition, too: it started in 1916 and lasted until 1927, though wine was never included. And the development of a discerning domestic market was not helped (and continues not to be helped) by the government monopoly of all alcoholic drink sales: provincial liquor boards control the distribution and sale of all wines, spirits and beers. Only Alberta and British Columbia have private wine merchants working alongside the liquor boards.

Nevertheless, wine producers in Canada have aimed firmly at quality in the last 20 years, and the results are remarkable. They're never going to produce enough to set the world alight; but in quality terms they're worth noticing. Already there is a characteristic pristine, fresh fruit style that is fast becoming a Canadian trademark. Icewine in particular is a speciality (see box opposite).

The regulatory system, the **Vintners' Quality Alliance (VQA)**, has provided a series of standards that govern most facets of Canadian winemaking. It lays down minimum must weights for wines which bear its seal: they must only be made from locally grown grapes, unlike non-VQA wines from Ontario, which can contain up to 75 per cent grapes or must from outside Canada. In terms of quantity the industry has shrunk since 1988: that was the year a Free Trade Agreement was signed with the United States, and it was accompanied by a vine-pull scheme in Canada. British Columbia, already a relatively small region, lost over half its vines; Ontario lost a third.

Mission Hill shows what Canada is capable of. It exploded on to the world wine stage in 1994 winning the best of show award for its 1992 Grand Reserve Chardonnay at the International Wine and Spirit Competition in London.

The Grapes

A fairly small selection of major grape varieties, but with a few suprises.

RIESLING is one of Canada's success stories, reaching good levels of ripeness balanced by high acidity. It doesn't have the taut raciness of good German versions, but they are getting some elegance into the wines, and some appley, honeyed fruit.

CHARDONNAY is light and well balanced, with some elegance and increasing complexity.

PINOT GRIS has become more important since the vine-pull scheme of 1988, and makes good, gently spicy whites.

PINOT BLANC is used as a basic blending grape and for sparkling wines, but on its own can make creamy, fruity whites, sometimes aged in oak.

GEWÜRZTRAMINER is grown as a minority grape in British Columbia. It's mostly light and crisp.

PINOT NOIR looks very promising in the Niagara Peninsula, where the weather is similar to that of Burgundy.

CABERNET SAUVIGNON won't ripen everywhere, but can produce fairly light reds with attractive blackcurrant fruit.

MERLOT could end up being Canada's best red, with good rich, plummy wines.

Riesling

The Wine Regions

Most of Canada's vineyards are in **Ontario**, though **British Columbia** grows vines in the **Okanagan Valley** and some smaller regions like **Fraser Valley, Similkameen Valley** and **Vancouver Island**. There's a lot of German influence in British Columbia, so it's not surprising to find German vines like Riesling, Gewürztraminer and Ehrenfelser rubbing shoulders with Pinot Blanc and Chardonnay. All these are cool-climate vines: it's the deep Okanagan Lake that moderates the extremes of climate sufficiently to allow vinifera varieties to be grown at all. Styles of wine tend to be Germanic, too.

In Ontario there's more water, in the form of Lake Ontario and Lake Erie, and they have the same effect. In spite of this there are still a lot of hybrids grown in the **Niagara Peninsula**, the main wine area; vinifera vines, however, have good potential, and Chardonnay and Pinot Noir from here have balance and structure reminiscent of Burgundy. Riesling gets beautifully ripe.

ICEWINE

This is Canada's speciality, and it's a perfect example of how to turn a difficult climate to good effect. Canada's winter can usually be relied upon to freeze grapes on the vine, year after year, and there's now more Icewine made here than anywhere else in the world. Even so, quantities are still tiny, and the wines can't help but be expensive: yields are minute. Riesling and the hybrid Vidal are the usual grapes, with Riesling giving more elegant, longer-lived wines, Vidal lower acidity and broader fruit. They don't yet have the stylishness of German examples, but then the Canadians have been making them for a rather shorter period.

LEFT **The chilly task of harvesting grapes for Icewine.**

A big, sweet, unctuous Icewine mixing ripe nectarines, apricots and a touch of tea, with crisp acidity on the finish.

SOUTH AMERICA

OPPOSITE **The vineyards in South America are some of the most dramatic in the world. Here, in Chile's Aconcagua Valley, northwest of Santiago, it's almost entirely planted to Cabernet Sauvignon and Merlot.**

Driving northwards on the highway out of São Paolo in Brazil – just a little way outside the city, where the suburbs are already giving way to eucalyptus forest and cattle pasture – you cross the Tropic of Capricorn. There's a sign by the side of the road telling you so, and it's a magical moment for anyone from a cool northerly climate – the phrase 'the Tropics' conjures up a vision of everything that is not European.

South American wine both is and is not European. The grape varieties are European, and were brought over by successive waves of settlers. The influences that have shaped wine here, and the idiom in which wine is made, are largely European, since the native peoples neither cultivated the vine nor made wine. Yet to make wine within the Tropics, as some South American countries do, isn't remotely European. And it was originally the enormous distance between South America and the mother continent that made the settlers plant vines here – in spite, very often, of orders to the contrary from Spain.

There's something of a paradox here, since on the one hand vine cuttings were being sent out to Cortez in the 1520s, and in New Spain, as Mexico was then called, planting vines was a condition of land grants. On the other hand, Spain still expected to be able to export wine to its New Spanish colonists, and from the late 16th century the Spanish government was demanding that New Spain buy more wine from Andalusia, and even uproot its own vines.

Such is the lot of colonists. Such measures did restrict viticulture in Mexico, but simply meant that the colonists bought their wine from Peru instead. Well, they knew what the alternative meant. Imagine what Spanish wine must have tasted like after it had been halfway across the world in the hold of a sailing ship. 'Undrinkable' would be putting it mildly.

It is sometimes said that the influence of the Church was crucial to the spread of wine in South America – well, it was up to a point. But a lot of the early vines were planted by secular settlers who were not there to convert the natives; they merely wanted to have something fit to drink. Where the Spaniards conquered, there they planted vines: Mexico and Peru were followed by Chile and Argentina. The Portuguese colonized the vast expanses of Brazil, and while Brazil does make wine it's hard to find a Brazilian who'll admit to drinking it. They prefer imported wine from Chile (considered chic) or Spain (considered even more chic), even though neither country sends them its best wines.

In Chile the domestic market for wine is fairly large; and a prosperous, well-travelled consumer market meant a demand for the sort of wines made in France. Consequently these are the most European in style of all South American wines; in Argentina, where an influx of Italian immigrants provided a ready market for cheap domestic wines, the producers have been slower to remake themselves in an export mould. But now that Argentina is becoming an export force to be reckoned with, it's possible to see that the country does have enormous potential for quality.

Peru, in spite of its early dominance of the market, has been left behind. But that could change: vines are grown for wine as well as for the local (lethal) Pisco brandy. And even though the vineyards are well within the Tropics there are plenty of mountains to provide cool high-altitude slopes.

Mountains, and in particular the Andes, are the key to viticulture in much of South America. They run like vertebrae all down the West Coast, and ensure that Argentina's vineyards are very dry indeed. But they have another function, too, as a source of irrigation from melted snow. This water, running from the snowfields at the top of the peaks, has over the millennia carved cross-valleys into both sides of the mountains, and the rivers that run down into both Chile and Argentina are the greatest single factor in sustaining a wine industry.

Argentina is well known for its top-quality beef and the gauchos who herd the cattle. As well as producing large quantities of beef, Argentina is also the world's fifth largest wine producer.

Chile

The Bordeaux of the southern hemisphere: well, that's not such a silly description for Chile. It's true that Bordeaux would be glad of such an even climate and would be glad, too, of the lack of phylloxera and downy mildew. It's true, too, that Chile's best red is its Cabernet Sauvignon, and that it also grows Merlot and Sauvignon Blanc as well as that non-Bordelais variety, Chardonnay. French influence in Chile is stronger than probably anywhere else (vinously speaking) in South America.

The first colonists, however, were Spanish. They brought the vine here sometime in the mid-16th century, and the varieties they favoured were the Pais, a rather dreary black grape that still haunts the wine industry today, Muscatel and others. These settlers had no thought of export: they merely wanted something drinkable on their tables. Wine fashions accordingly took a long while to change, and it was not until the richer members of Chilean society started to travel to Europe in the 19th century (where they were notable for their wealth) that they began to take note of what was being drunk elsewhere.

Such observation bore fruit: cuttings were imported to Chile from Europe before those same European vineyards were all but destroyed by phylloxera at the end of the 19th century. Meanwhile the Chilean wine industry flourished. It's not entirely clear why it should have remained phylloxera-free, and the combined boundaries of Andes and desert are usually cited. Clearly these must form a far more effective barrier than mere seawater: Australia and New Zealand, equally remote, both have phylloxera. It's worth noting that Chile also employs very strict plant quarantine regulations.

As a result Chile has never had to graft its vines. Irrigation is easy and cheap: melted snow from the Andes fills the rivers during the growing season, and runs through the many east-west valleys that cut through the main range. There is also a coastal range of mountains, less dramatic than the Andes, but still high enough to ensure that little rain falls on their eastern slopes.

The plain in question is the long Central Valley, the strip of land running north and south of Santiago for about 1000km (600 miles) in all, and between the two ranges of mountains. On the face of it, it provides a pretty simple situation for the vine grower: the vineyards in the north must be warmer, those in the south cooler. Well, that's true to some extent, but it's not the whole story.

The climatic picture changes not just as you go from north to south, but also as you go from west to east, even though the country is so narrow. On the western side you have the cooling influence of the Humboldt Current, sweeping up the coast and sending cold air inland. Then there's the Coastal Range, forcing the rain clouds to dump their cargo on its western slopes and ensuring that its eastern slopes are warm and dry. On the other side of the Central Valley the western slopes of the Andes have much greater temperature variation between night and day – and

The Grapes

Chile grows the main international varieties, but lacks a speciality.

CABERNET SAUVIGNON is Chile's most famous red, juicy, blackcurranty and often with extra richness from new oak. It's nearly always released when ready to drink and needs no further aging; Reserve and other older wines can have good depth.

MERLOT is another star wine, with beautiful scented black cherry fruit, sometimes softened by oak. Some wines labelled Merlot are from the Carmenère, a 19th-century Bordeaux variety.

PINOT NOIR from cooler regions can have good strawberry flavours and attractive aroma.

SYRAH is being planted in small quantities and should have potential in a climate that's good for beefy reds.

CHARDONNAY is the leader of the whites, and the best balance rich, tropical fruit flavours with good acidity. Cool regions like Casablanca give the best acidity.

SAUVIGNON BLANC is increasingly pungent and aromatic now that the lesser Sauvignonasse is increasingly consigned to cheaper blends. Again, Casablanca and other cool regions give the greatest aroma.

Cabernet Sauvignon

Chardonnay

CHENIN BLANC can do well in cool spots, giving crisp appley fruit.

GEWÜRZTRAMINER isn't as richly spice-laden as Alsace examples, but there are good crisp wines emerging from cooler sites.

A very young vineyard being given its first taste of drip irrigation. It's a system which delivers a specific amount of water to each plant.

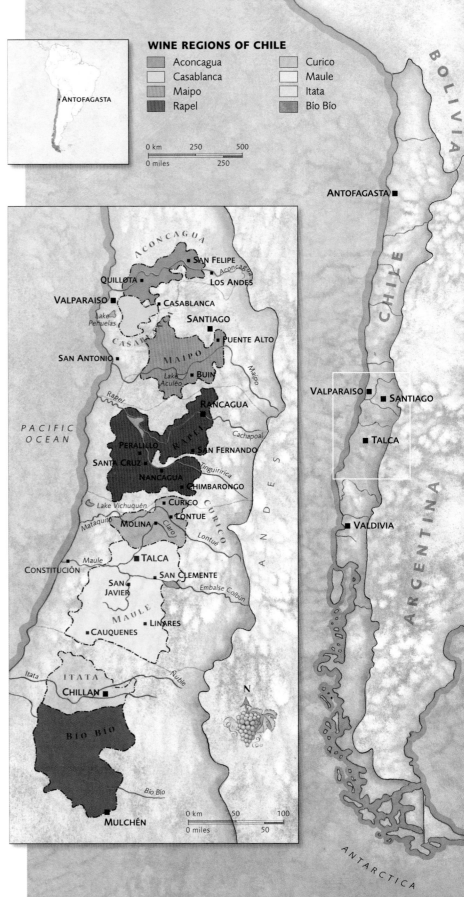

WINE REGIONS OF CHILE

Aconcagua
Casablanca
Maipo
Rapel

Curico
Maule
Itata
Bío Bío

cold nights mean good acidity in the wines. And where the Coastal Range dips and allows more cold air through into the Central Valley there are potentially good cool-climate sites. So it's a complicated picture, and only now are growers really beginning to find the ideal spots for each grape variety. It's a process that will take a long time – after all, it took Bordeaux a good few centuries.

In Chile it's only just beginning, in spite of the country's long history of winemaking, because of the problems the country faced until democracy and economic stability returned in the 1980s. Only then did the country really become determined to make its mark on wine markets abroad. Its progress since has been remarkably fast by anybody's standards. New to Chile in the last year are the release of a number of super-premium wines with price tags to match – most notable are the Errázuriz/Mondavi joint venture Seña and the Montes winery's Alpha M. It's an indication of where Chile considers itself these days. And who knows, eventually it might even become easier to buy decent wine within Chile itself. At the moment the majority of the good stuff goes abroad, and Chileans are reduced to drinking cheap and basic wine based on Pais or

INTERNATIONAL VISITORS

The Spanish Conquistadores, arriving in the 16th century and bringing the vine with them, were the founding fathers of Chilean wine. Other settlers followed, but it was not until the 19th century that the industry began to take on its modern face. In 1830 a Frenchman, Claudio Gay, suggested to the Chilean government that it might not be a bad idea to have a government-backed nursery for the study of all manner of plant specimens. Vines would be among them; and happily the government agreed. The nursery was called the Quinta Normal; and the vines were vinifera cuttings from Europe.

More cuttings arrived in the 1850s, brought by one Silvestre Ochagavía Echazarreta, who also brought over a French winemaker to deal with them. Vine growing became fashionable: to have a vineyard or two, and a French winemaker in the cellar, was the last word in chic in late 19th-century Santiago.

Today foreigners are still arriving, armed with cuttings (which now have to go into quarantine) and new ideas about what to plant where and how to make vines. These days they're known as investors rather than settlers, and they may come from Bordeaux, Spain, California or even Australia. Flying winemakers dart in and out, too, making a vintage in the southern hemisphere during a slack period in Europe; and the more Chile's reputation rises, the more they will come.

ABOVE **Merlot may originally have come from elsewhere, but now it's very much part of the scenery. These young cuttings will soon be ready for planting out in the vineyards.**

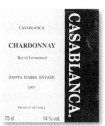

Winemaker Ignacio Recabarren's barrel-fermented Chardonnay from Viña Casablanca is one of Chile's top wines.

other distinctly unthrilling grapes or (irony of ironies) buying imported wine.

CLASSIFICATION
A new appellation system, which came into being in 1995, demarcated five main regions. There are three main wine regions: **Aconcagua** (incorporating the cool sub-region of Casablanca), the **Central Valley** (with sub-regions Maipo, Rapel, Curicó and Maule) and the **Southern Region** (including Itata and Bío Bío). Further north there are the regions of **Atacama** and **Coquimbo**, where table grapes and Pisco brandy are the main products.

There is a 75 per cent rule which governs vintage, exact origin and grape varieties. Under this law, a wine can contain up to 25 per cent of other grape varieties, vintages and wine from other areas. The use of terms such as Reserva, Gran Reserva and Reserva Especial can only be used for wines which state a place of origin. There's no rule yet, however, stating when a wine can be called Reserva.

Aconcagua
Aconcagua is hot and dry and mainly given over to table grapes. It contains one major winery, Errázuriz Estates, who do, however, manage to produce some of Chile's premium reds.

By contrast, Aconcagua's sub-region, **Casablanca**, is anything but hot. It's on the coast, where it catches all the cool air – sometimes too much in fact. Frost is a real problem here. But it's certainly hitting the headlines and making a name for itself as an excellent spot for white wines – much of Chile's best Chardonnay and Sauvignon Blanc comes from here.

Central Valley
Maipo, just south of Santiago, is the heart of the Chilean wine industry, because it was here that the 19th-century rich liked to live and grow vines. Many of the older-established companies still have their headquarters here, and a great deal of Cabernet Sauvignon, Semillon and Sauvignon Blanc is grown. The city of Santiago is expanding,

however, and pressure from the suburbs threatens some of these vineyards. Good reds, especially Cabernet, also come from **Rapel**. Rapel used to sell most of its grapes to wineries in Maipo but now there are increasing numbers of small boutique wineries who are putting the region on the map. **Maule** and **Curicó** are cooler and there are large plantings of Pais still here, though Cabernet Sauvignon, Merlot, Sauvignon Blanc and Semillon are grown for export. Both Chardonnay and Sauvignon Blanc from Curicó are particularly good.

Southern Region

Pais dominates these vineyards, although it's cool enough to offer potential for better grapes. The west is pretty swampy, but there could be good sites elsewhere. **Bío Bío** and the **Valle de Itata** are certainly on the up, with plantings of international varieties – Merlot, Cabernet Sauvignon and Chardonnay – producing some promising flavours. It's cooler and damper here than further north, but with appropriate training and trellising systems the grapes reach good levels of ripeness.

NEW DEVELOPMENTS

Chilean wine, then, is evolving all the time. The big changes of recent years have been better vine identification (in the past a lot of what passed for Sauvignon Blanc was the inferior and less pungent Sauvignonasse); the installation of modern winemaking equipment, in the form of stainless-steel vats with temperature control; and the discarding of the traditional old wooden barrels made of *rauli* wood. New oak barriques have come in instead, and (as is always the case when they're a new toy) have sometimes been used to excess. Chile has made its mark abroad with juicy, blackcurrant and vanilla reds, buttery Chardonnays and increasingly tangy Sauvignons, all sold at good-value prices; the challenge now is to keep the irrigation under control (it's too easy a way of letting grape yields rise, which in turn dilutes flavour), and get greater concentration into the wines. To this end, drip irrigation is increasingly being used. It's more expensive than basic channelled irrigation or flood irrigation but it ensures the vines a controlled supply of water and thus helps control yields.

Merlot Cuvée Alexandre offers sweet damson proof that this grape has the potential to be Chile's trump card. However, Chile's fame was built on Cabernet Sauvignon, of which Don Maximiano Estate Reserva Cabernet Sauvignon from Errázuriz is a top example.

The Food of Chile and Argentina

CHILEAN FOOD is a fusion of European dishes and ingredients, brought here over the centuries ever since the Conquistadores set the tone by importing grape vines, with the rich variety of food that already existed here. The beef that features so strongly in European-style Chilean cuisine was an import from Europe; *empanadas*, the beef pasties popular throughout South America, can also be found in Spain.

But Chile also has an enormously long coastline,

and the seafood is of excellent quality. It may be cooked *à la française*, in recipes brought by the French chefs that were as much a 19th-century status symbol as French winemakers, or it may be more Spanish style: the fish stews found everywhere mix whatever fish and molluscs are to hand with a thickening of breadcrumbs. Ripe, oaky Chardonnay is just the thing to cope with these strong flavours.

You should only visit Argentina if you like beef, because the diet seems to

consist of beef, beef and more beef. The quality is superb, and the simplest dishes are of grilled steak; but if you fancy something more complicated, it can be stewed a multitude of different ways, notably with peaches, corn and pumpkin in *carbonada*, a typical stew from the north-west. Argentina's speciality red grape, Malbec, is the perfect accompaniment.

Chicken is also popular and crab lovers are in heaven, with the Centolla crab, or King crab, from Tierra del Fuego.

Dried and smoked shellfish on display in a market in Angelmo, Chile.

Argentina

It wasn't so very long ago that Argentinian wine was considered a bit of a joke in Europe: all right if you were desperate for a novelty, but not the sort of thing you'd actually want to drink. And yet Argentina has been making wine since the 16th century: why have we only now started drinking it?

For most of its history, Argentinian wine just hasn't been very nice. Nor did the producers ever think that we'd want to drink it: there was an enormous and thirsty population at home, eagerly swilling down some 90 litres (20 gallons) a head each year. Arguably they needed whatever consolation wine could bring: the country was suffering inflation of around 1000 per cent per annum in the early 1980s, and had had decades of political and economic uncertainty.

But let's go a bit further back. The early Spanish settlers planted vines, but they, too, planted them with a view to what would grow most easily ('easily' being a relative term in the semi-desert conditions of the wine areas). They also planted what they happened to have with them – which usually meant Criolla, a version of which grows in Chile as Pais. What they did get right, however, were the irrigation systems they established on the eastern slopes of the Andes to catch the melting snow as it ran off: their systems are the basis of the irrigation systems still in use today.

Rather more variety came into the vineyards with a second wave of immigration after independence in the 1820s. Spaniards, French and especially Italians poured in, all bringing a taste of home with them in the form of vine cuttings. Tempranillo, Sangiovese, Nebbiolo, Dolcetto, Barbera, Lambrusco and (with the benefit of

WINE REGIONS OF ARGENTINA

- ☐ Salta
- ■ Tucumán
- ☐ Catamarca
- ☐ La Rioja
- ☐ San Juan
- ■ Mendoza
- ☐ La Pampa
- ☐ Río Negro

Trapiche is the quality arm of Mendoza-based Peñaflor, Argentina's biggest wine producer. Peñaflor might not yet be as familiar a name as some other giant-sized wine producers but nevertheless it is one of the largest companies in the world.

hindsight, most importantly) Malbec arrived at this time. None of them made great wine; none of them needed to. Quantity was the great thing; and irrigation provided it.

More recently a period of economic stability has meant that investment has become not only a possibility but a sensible measure for any ambitious producer; and a dramatic fall in consumption at home has made such producers look abroad for their markets, which in turn has made investment essential. Argentina is just at the beginning of a process that will, if all goes well, turn it into not only a modern wine-producing country, but potentially the best in South America. It's already the biggest, producing five times the amount that Chile does.

What Argentina has (and what Chile lacks) is a couple of special grapes. One is Malbec, a red grape from South-West France that has never achieved great renown on its home turf, although Cahors is its finest expression. It's also a minority grape in Bordeaux. But in Argentina, where it often has the best, less fertile hillside sites, it produces greater depth of flavour, more damsons and violets, spice and blackcurrants, than ever it does in France.

Argentina's white weapon is Torrontés. It's grown in Galicia in Spain, but Galicia puts more emphasis on its fashionable Albariño, leaving the Torrontés field clear for Argentina. In Argentina it's grown at high altitudes, and it has good acidity (not a quality prized much on the domestic market), lovely spicy, Muscatty aroma and most unexpected delicacy.

CLASSIFICATION

On the classification side, there is no centrally administered appellation system as yet although three Mendoza regions, **Maipú**, **Luján de Cuyo**, and **San Rafael**, all have denominacións de origen, as does **La Rioja**. Argentina is also beginning to think carefully about what grape varieties should be planted and where they should be planted. At the moment, however, your best bet when buying wine is to be guided by the producer's name.

CLIMATE

The Andes both create and solve Argentina's defining grape-growing problem: that of water. In the first place they create a massive rain shadow, so that the land on their eastern side is virtual desert; but in the second place melting snow pours off them, making irrigation easy. Water is held in reservoirs and distributed by one of three ways: by flood irrigation, which is not quite as uncontrolled as it sounds; by the directing of water along the furrows between the vine rows; and by drip irrigation, which is still quite a recent innovation here.

When water does descend from the skies in the summer, it is usually in the form of hailstones – and these are hailstones as big as golf balls, guaranteed to wreck both car bodywork and vines. The only answer is to seed the hail-bearing clouds with rockets, but this is both expensive and unpredictable in its results.

Water from the snow-covered Andes feeds the channels irrigating these vineyards in Mendoza.

OPPOSITE **Vineyards in the high-altitude Tupungato Valley in Mendoza. Some of Argentina's best fruit comes from this area.**

Mendoza

This is by far the main region, nestling against the eastern foothills of the Andes. Two-thirds of the country's vineyards are here. Malbec is the main grape – though there's less Malbec than there used to be, since the massive uprooting of vineyards in the economically troubled 1970s and 1980s. Barbera and Tempranillo grow here, too. Most are on their own roots, as is the case everywhere in Argentina; phylloxera exists here, but doesn't seem to do enormous damage, perhaps because there's a fair bit of sand in the soil. It's also possible that flood irrigation plays a part in keeping phylloxera at bay, the continual dampness of the ground helping to keep the pest inactive. Anyway, grafting has simply never been a possibility, given the state of the economy until recently. A grafted vine can cost up to four times as much as an ungrafted one.

Luján de Cuyo and **Maipú** both have appellations, the former making

elegant whites from Chardonnay, Sauvignon and Riesling in high-altitude vineyards, the latter producing beefy Cabernets and Malbecs. There is also some Tempranillo and Sangiovese, though these generally get blended, and are of little significance for quality.

The cool, high **Tupungato Valley**, where the soil is poor, is also a region to watch, especially for crisp whites from Sauvignon Blanc. Some of the country's best grapes come from Tupungato's Valle de Uco. New plantings in **Agrelo** are also promising for aromatic whites. **San Rafael** makes rich Cabernets as well as Malbec and Chenin Blanc.

Other Regions

North of Mendoza, the regions of **San Juan, La Rioja, Catamarca** and **Salta** are all hotter – yet it is from Salta that the best Torrontés has so far come. High-altitude vineyards are the answer: at 1800 metres (6000ft) these are some of the highest in the world. A number of wineries from the Mendoza area have planted experimental vineyards here, with an emphasis on both Torrontés and Cabernet Sauvignon.

Right down in the south, **Rio Negro** and **Neuquén** might prove to have similarly great potential. It's cooler here and an important area for fruit production, especially apples, but Torrontés, Semillon, Chardonnay and Sauvignon Blanc could be of more interest in the years to come. A longer growing season and chalky soils have encouraged a number of experimental plantings. The area also has the potential to produce good sparkling wine in due course. All that's needed now to help things on their way is a little investment.

The Grapes
Malbec and Torrontés are the grapes to watch.

MALBEC is Argentina's finest red, achieving great depth of spicy, plummy fruit. A great deal was uprooted in the 1970s and 1980s, though that trend has now been reversed.

CABERNET SAUVIGNON is seldom so exciting, and can lack richness. The best are often blended with Merlot.

TORRONTÉS is so far Argentina's best white, grown at high altitude for delicate aromas and flavours. Torrontés Riojano is the main sub-variety.

CHARDONNAY has taken a while to establish itself but latest vintages show considerable elegance and suitability for lighter oak treatment.

Dr Nicolas Catena is probably Argentina's most progressive wine producer. His Malbec has rich scents of blackberry and licorice with the structure for long aging.

Norton's Torrontés displays plenty of characteristics of the style. It's aromatic with scents of roses, lavender and grapy overtones. On the palate, it's fresh, crisp and full of lime and lavender.

Other South American Countries

There must be many, many sites in South America that are capable of making good wine. Altitude is key in most countries; so is the development of a genuine wine culture. A genuine domestic wine culture, that is: one that doesn't automatically think that imported wine is better. (At the moment it generally is – at least, it's better than the domestic wine offered to the domestic market.) But in South America everything imported is smart: cars, clothes, everything.

And yet it's not just the key wine producers like Chile and Argentina that are making the better stuff. Uruguay has good Tannat – another French grape often performing better here than it does – or is usually given a chance to do – back in France. And what about the Petite Sirah of Mexico? In France it's called Durif, and is dismissed with a shrug.

Brazil, Peru, Paraguay, Ecuador, Bolivia, Venezuela and Colombia also produce wine to a greater or lesser extent. In large parts of the continent, however, the climate is simply not suited to wine-drinking, it's just too hot and humid. True, something along the lines of really fresh Frascati would be delicious in these circumstances but this is simply not the sort of wine produced in these countries. The locals therefore turn to spirits which they drink before, during and after meals. But let's take a whirlwind tour of the rest of the continent and see what's what.

Mexico

Believe it or not, Mexico comes fourth in the Latin American league table of wine production, after Argentina, Brazil and Chile. A lot of its vineyards produce table grapes or dried grapes, and a lot produce base wine for brandy. Table wine is pretty mixed in quality, but there are some real stars, notably Petite Sirah from **Baja California** in the north. The best-quality wine comes from up here, from heavily irrigated vineyards; further south it is necessary to plant at high altitudes to escape the searing heat. As it is, reds tend to be jammily soft. Other grapes include Cabernet Sauvignon, Merlot, Nebbiolo, Zinfandel, Grenache and Carignan; there are white grapes as well, but they're not actually terribly good.

Brazil

Rain and humidity are the main problems here; indeed labrusca varieties outnumber vinifera varieties seven to one because of the subtropical climate. However, foreign investment from companies like Moët & Chandon is bringing considerable change to the country and the quality of some labels hints at huge potential.

By going up into the hills of **Rio Grande do Sul**, the state where most of the vineyards are concentrated, it's possible to escape the worst of the heat, but there's no escaping the rain, nor the problems of ripening and rot that it brings. **Serra Gaucha** is the main region – as the name suggests, it's high up in the hills; vines are also grown in the **Frontera** region, near the border with Uruguay. A whole raft of varieties are cultivated: Chardonnay, Gewürztraminer, Welschriesling, Semillon, both Cabernets and Merlot, plus Italian varieties like Barbera, Trebbiano, Bonarda and Moscato, planted by the Italian immigrants who established the Serra Gaucha vineyards.

Uruguay

The traditional wine here is unusual: a dark sweet rosé made from Tannat and Muscat Hamburg, sometimes made even more unusual by the hybrid Isabella. The Tannat was originally planted by Basques, who all in all seem to have had a crucial role in South American wine: it was families of Basque descent who owned most of the Chilean industry until recently. And it is the Tannat, bottled on its own, which is making Uruguay's reputation abroad. There are also some plantings of Petit Manseng, the high-quality grape of Jurançon in South-West France.

Winemaking on the whole is still pretty old-fashioned, even though vinifera varieties are now starting to replace hybrids in the vineyards.

Mexican winery L A Cetto has established its reputation with dark, full-flavoured varietal red wines from Petite Sirah, Cabernet Sauvignon and Nebbiolo. In Brazil, labrusca and hybrid varieties still outnumber classic vinifera varieties although some producers have a go.

There are various wine regions, with most of the vineyards being planted on the hills west of Montevideo.

Peru

What Peruvians really like to drink is **Pisco**, a pretty potent local brandy; and accordingly, most of the vineyards produce base wine for distillation. Even the vineyards by the coast are pretty hot and tropical, and it's common to get two crops a year due to warm temperatures and lack of winter dormancy – well, you don't produce very good wine that way, just lots of it. There are some table wines made from varieties like Moscatel, Torontel, Sauvignon, Cabernet Sauvignon, Grenache, Malbec and Barbera.

Ecuador

The best wines come from the cooler spots, where vintages are restricted to one per year; the vineyards near the coast produce three crops a year, which even beats Peru.

Bolivia

To be honest there aren't many vineyards here, and most of them grow Muscat of Alexandria for distillation into the local brandy. The vineyards, which are mainly in Bolivia's southern region of **Tarija**, are at high altitudes, but are nevertheless pretty hot.

Venezuela

Two harvests a year are the rule here in the tropical conditions. Grape concentrate seems to be the base of most of the wines produced, and hybrids dominate.

Colombia

The production of modern table wines is in its infancy here: wine-based aperitifs, brandy and sweet fortifieds are the usual fate of the vines, few of which are vinifera.

Paraguay

There are a few vineyards in Villa Rica, but the subtropical climate is not conducive to quality.

Cuba

Before leaving this continent, let's head briefly to Cuba. Thanks to a joint venture with an Italian producer, we're just beginning to see a few wines being exported. Some land in the **Pinar del Río** region on the east of the island has been planted with Chardonnay, Pinot Grigio, Tempranillo and Cabernet Sauvignon, although until the vines are in full production it seems that grape must is also being imported from Italy.

A wine harvest festival in Bolivia. The grapes hanging here will be made into table wine and the local aromatic brandy known as Singani.

AUSTRALIA

Australia Felix. That was what it used to be called, and that's how it's marked on early maps made after Captain James Cook first made landfall on that unknown coast in 1770. Happy Australia. What a paradox.

It's a paradox because there is indeed something happy, something sunny and easy-going about the Australian wines we know today: their upfront fruit, their clear flavours, their drinkability. Yet all the while the first experiments in winemaking in the new continent were going ahead, Australia was proving a place of horror for the convicts who had landed in Botany Bay on 26 January 1788. The calm domesticity that caused cuttings of vines brought from the Cape of Good Hope to Botany Bay to be planted in the governor's garden was not the only story.

Those cuttings produced their first fruit in January 1791. Commercial viticulture became a reality after about 1820, and in the meantime the colonies had spread: Parramatta (now a suburb of Sydney) was founded in 1788; Hobart and Launceston on Van Diemen's Land (now Tasmania) and Newcastle in 1804; Port Macquarie further up the coast in 1821; the Swan River Colony in Western Australia in 1829, Melbourne in 1835 and Adelaide in 1836. The convicts provided the labour needed to make the young settlements self-supporting, even profitable; and by the time the final convict ship arrived in Western Australia in 1868, Australian agriculture was flourishing.

Wine flourished with it: at the 1873 Vienna Exhibition a 'Hermitage' wine from Bendigo in Central Victoria was judged best of its type by an international jury. When it became clear that the wine wasn't French, the French jurors resigned in protest, saying the wine was so good that it had to be French. Then in 1882 the Australians attended the Great Bordeaux Exhibition, and Victoria carried off the trophy for the most successful exhibitor from 'the rest of the world'.

But by this time phylloxera had arrived in Australia: it was first discovered in 1877 in Geelong. But it didn't, and hasn't, spread throughout the continent: South Australia is phylloxera-free, and so is much of New South Wales.

Those early table wine successes were something of a false dawn. Local demand was for sweet, often fortified wine, and so as a wine industry became established that was more and more what it produced. The centres of the industry switched to hotter areas like South Australia's Riverland.

The increasing amount of land being planted to vineyard and the growth of its wine industry have prompted Australia to redefine its premium wine areas. The Lachlan Valley in New South Wales (right) is an area to watch.

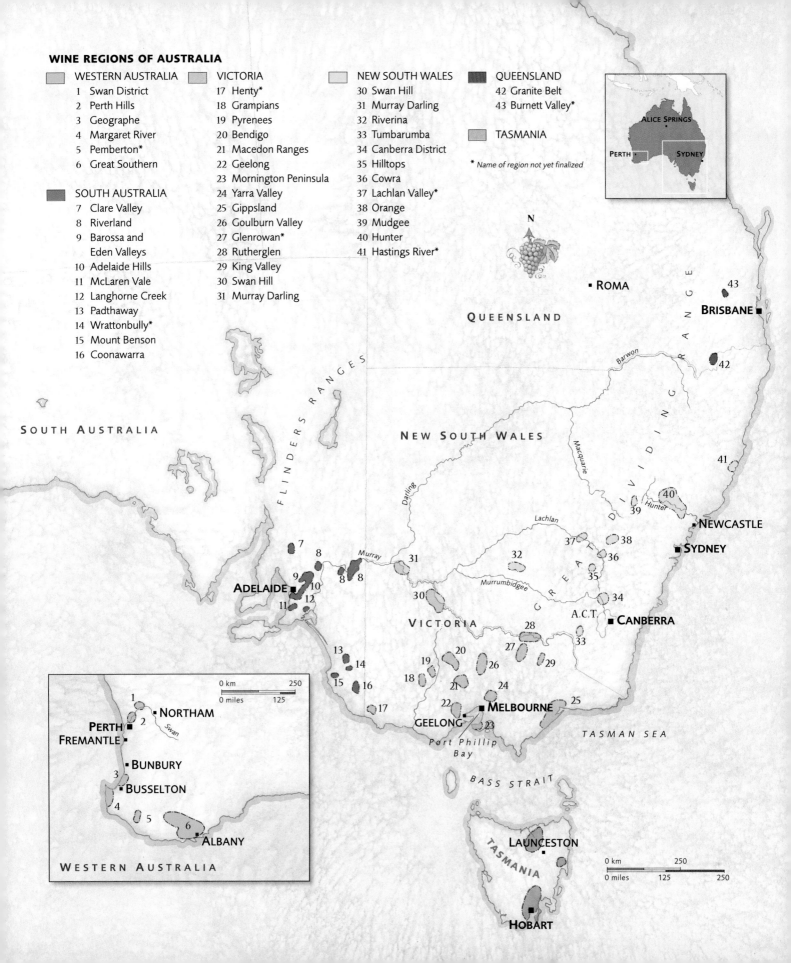

WINE REGIONS OF AUSTRALIA

WESTERN AUSTRALIA
1 Swan District
2 Perth Hills
3 Geographe
4 Margaret River
5 Pemberton*
6 Great Southern

SOUTH AUSTRALIA
7 Clare Valley
8 Riverland
9 Barossa and
    Eden Valleys
10 Adelaide Hills
11 McLaren Vale
12 Langhorne Creek
13 Padthaway
14 Wrattonbully*
15 Mount Benson
16 Coonawarra

VICTORIA
17 Henty*
18 Grampians
19 Pyrenees
20 Bendigo
21 Macedon Ranges
22 Geelong
23 Mornington Peninsula
24 Yarra Valley
25 Gippsland
26 Goulburn Valley
27 Glenrowan*
28 Rutherglen
29 King Valley
30 Swan Hill
31 Murray Darling

NEW SOUTH WALES
30 Swan Hill
31 Murray Darling
32 Riverina
33 Tumbarumba
34 Canberra District
35 Hilltops
36 Cowra
37 Lachlan Valley*
38 Orange
39 Mudgee
40 Hunter
41 Hastings River*

QUEENSLAND
42 Granite Belt
43 Burnett Valley*

TASMANIA

* Name of region not yet finalized

N

ROMA

BRISBANE

QUEENSLAND

43

42

SOUTH AUSTRALIA

FLINDERS RANGES

NEW SOUTH WALES

Barwon

GREAT DIVIDING RANGE

41

NEWCASTLE

SYDNEY

Macquarie

Darling

Lachlan

40

39

Hunter

7

8

9

10

12

11

ADELAIDE

Murray

8 8

31

Murrumbidgee

32

37 38

36

35

34

A.C.T.

CANBERRA

30

13

14

15

16

18

19

17

20

21

26

27

28

29

33

VICTORIA

24

22

23

GEELONG

MELBOURNE

Port Phillip Bay

25

TASMAN SEA

BASS STRAIT

LAUNCESTON

TASMANIA

0 km   250
0 miles   125   250

HOBART

ALICE SPRINGS

PERTH

SYDNEY

WESTERN AUSTRALIA inset

1

NORTHAM

PERTH

FREMANTLE

Swan

2

BUNBURY

BUSSELTON

3

4

5

6

ALBANY

WESTERN AUSTRALIA

0 km   250
0 miles   125

The wines that Australia exported to Britain (and Britain between 1927 and 1939, because of trading advantages given to Commonwealth countries, imported more Australian wine than French) were either fortified, or so heavily alcoholic that it made little difference. Reds were so sturdy that they were sometimes prescribed as tonics.

THE MODERN WINE INDUSTRY

Yet not all Australian wines, even in the early days, were rough and alcoholic. Winemakers in regions such as the Barossa Valley had always produced extraordinarily fine and long-lived reds and whites, and it was wines of this kind that were the forerunners of today's old vine Shirazes. They were overtaken by fashion, which turned to lighter wines in the wake of cold-fermentation techniques introduced in the 1950s. In the 1960s and 1970s they looked increasingly like the wines of the past. But when the first glimmerings of interest in the old vines of the Barossa appeared in the late 1980s, it was to the makers and growers of these earlier wines that a new generation began to listen.

Modern Australian wine really dates from the 1950s, when cold fermentation began to produce lighter wines. Twenty years later the advent of wine casks, typically 4.5 litres (1 gallon) of everyday wine in a box to keep in the refrigerator, proved conclusively that Australia had a remarkable knack of producing inexpensive wine that tasted better than inexpensive wine from almost anywhere else. Chardonnay and Cabernet were planted, and rapidly set about dominating the wine scene. In the early 1980s the first new-style Australian wines were shipped to Britain. It seems curious in retrospect that they didn't catch on immediately; but once they did there was no stopping them.

They made their impact simply because they were tastier than anything else available at the same price. Vivid fruit flavours were (and are) to the fore; appellation counted for very little.

Certainly, the appellation situation has changed, as regional differences have become apparent: the Hunter Valley has one character,

OPPOSITE **Henschke's Hill of Grace vineyard in the Eden Valley produces superb red wine from Shiraz vines which are over 100 years old.**

LEFT **Nowadays these 100-year-old Shiraz vines may not give many grapes, but the flavour of the wine will be intense and concentrated.**

the Barossa another, the Eden and Clare Valleys have their own personalities, and Coonawarra is different again. But the basis of inexpensive Australian wine (and quite a lot of more expensive stuff, too) is the blend.

Grapes can be grown anywhere and be blended with grapes from anywhere else. Every Australian winemaker is imbued with that philosophy, and it is reflected in wines that take some of their grapes from New South Wales, some from South Australia, some from Victoria; interstate blending, with wine being trucked great distances, is an everyday fact.

The reason is that Australian winemakers don't have much time for the concept of terroir, that essentially European idea that a wine is shaped by the combination of soil, climate and exposure to the sun that it obtains in each individual vineyard. Instead they have viewed climate as the major influence on wine style, and Australian wines reflect, and are intended to reflect, the flavour of the grape, not the terroir.

The move towards lighter, more elegant wines has led to a search for higher altitudes at which to plant: cool-climate viticulture is the current vogue. Cool climates are difficult to find elsewhere, except for Tasmania, where it can be almost too cool: nearly all Australian viticulture is concentrated in the south-eastern corner of the country where the weather is warm to warmer, and dry. (New South Wales is the exception to

Grange is regarded as Australia's greatest red wine. Recently Penfolds have launched a 'white Grange' amid considerable publicity.

the dry rule: here it can be too wet for comfort, at the wrong times of the year.)

That being said, certain spots have emerged which have shaken, just a little, this firm belief that terroir doesn't matter. The main one is Coonawarra, in South Australia, where the difference in soil is perfectly obvious to the eye. Now, I'm not saying that Coonawarra is converting Australian winemakers to the importance of terroir, because it's doing nothing of the sort. But it has shown that just occasionally, in certain circumstances, soil can make a difference. Yet Aussie winemakers can be as pragmatic about blending grapes together as they are about blending different regions. Shiraz may be blended with Cabernet, or Semillon with Chardonnay. It's the flavour that counts above all.

The interregional and interstate blends come, of course, from the big wineries, the wine corporations that dominate Australian drinking. The biggest of them, Southcorp, including all of its subsidiaries, controls over a third of the domestic market. Small new wineries do pop up, however, to testify to the everlasting wish of winemakers to do their own thing.

Some Australian and Australian-trained winemakers, not content with doing their own thing in Australia, take their skills all over the world. These flying winemakers, well grounded in the skills needed to make tasty wine in uncomfortably hot climates, have proved themselves better equipped than anyone to turn around the fortunes of underperforming wineries in Eastern Europe or the less favoured parts of southern France. It has all helped (if help were needed) to spread the taste for Aussie-style wine further and further abroad. Australia Felix indeed.

CLASSIFICATION

An appellation system has come into being as part of an agreement with the EU, to which Australia wants to ship more and more wine. Australia is also phasing out the use of European wine names like 'Champagne', 'Burgundy' and the rest. Some of the following categories are also in force; others are following.

Produce of Australia is the most general geographical indication.

South-Eastern Australia is already a familiar sight on labels. The region actually covers the vast majority of Australian wine regions.

State of Origin is the next most specific category. **Zones** are smaller than a state. Mount Lofty Ranges in South Australia, for example, includes the smaller **regions** of Adelaide Hills and Clare Valley. **Sub-regions** are smaller again. The region of Adelaide Hills incorporates the sub-regions of Lenswood and Piccadilly Valley.

WATER, WATER EVERYWHERE

Water is essential for every vineyard in the world. In most European wine regions it's forbidden, so winemakers must rely on rain coming at the right time and in the right quantity; but New World viticulture relies on irrigation. It's perfectly possible to plant a vineyard in a virtual desert, provided that you can get enough water to your vines, and a common sight in Australia is a vivid green patch of vines, all watered by drip irrigation, in the midst of a landscape baked biscuit-brown. In the hot, heavily irrigated bulk wine regions the vines are given a great deal of water; in fine wine areas irrigation is restricted or is not used at all.

Irrigation might be anathema to a European, but in a hot climate it can be crucial to wine quality. In drought conditions, the vine may shed leaves, which reduces its ability to ripen the grapes; in extreme heat photosynthesis stops, which also prevents the grapes ripening. Irrigation is therefore of great benefit.

ABOVE **Pretty well every Australian winery has its own dam, or reservoir and water pump like the one above in the vineyards of Montrose in Mudgee, New South Wales.**

New South Wales

This was where European settlement began; and when the first fleet dropped anchor in Sydney Harbour, then called Port Jackson, vine cuttings came with it. But the first vineyards are now buried under the tarmac of suburban Sydney, and New South Wales's wine industry really only got going when the Hunter Valley was planted in the 1820s.

The Wine Regions

It's a strange place to plant vines, the **Hunter Valley**. It's warm and it's wet, with drought in the winter when you want to fill the dams, and storms in the summer that can go on into the harvest. If vines didn't already exist here nobody, these days, would plant them.

But back in the 1820s it seemed better than the alternatives. The coastal area is far too humid and subtropical, and inland, the other side of the Great Dividing Range, it's even hotter and hopelessly dry. (Irrigation wasn't so easy then.) So the Hunter it was.

Why plant vines at all in such a rough-and-ready new settlement, you might ask. Entertaining was hardly a priority, after all. But wine was seen as an aid to health, far better for the new settlement than rum or whatever home-distilled spirits they might otherwise stun themselves with.

These days the Hunter is no longer Australia's foremost wine region, and the emphasis has moved to more vine-friendly climates elsewhere. But it continues because in spite of everything it makes some stunningly good wines. Not everything is good, because not all vines will succeed here: Pinot Noir, Riesling and Sauvignon Blanc are among the failures (though if you plant higher up, on the slopes of the Brokenback Range, the climate can be cooler). The successes are Cabernet Sauvignon; Shiraz, traditionally distinguished by its sweaty saddle character, though this is found less often than it used to be; Chardonnay, rich, fat and peachy (the first varietal Chardonnay was made by Tyrrell's in 1971); and, above all, Semillon.

I say 'above all', but in fact the traditional style of Hunter Semillon, which is unoaked, is made by only a handful of companies, and then in pretty small quantities. It's a unique wine style and one of Australia's great inventions, but commercial it's not. These wines taste light and lemony, even dull, when they're very young; but after ten years in bottle they've transformed themselves into wines so rich and toasty, so honeyed and complex, that you'd swear they'd been aged in oak from Heaven. When they have been aged in oak, by contrast, they're very good, and the best age quite well; but they never hit quite such heights. But they can be drunk younger, and that makes them easier to sell. Verdelho can do well here, too, but it's not yet much grown, and Merlot has potential.

The Hunter Valley, now known simply as Hunter, divides into two, the Upper Hunter and Lower Hunter. Nearly all the vineyards are

The bottling and packaging line of De Bortoli, producers of sublime botrytis Semillon in Riverina. This photograph gives an idea of the technology that has helped transform the area.

The Grapes

The warm climate here doesn't suit every grape, but can produce some unique styles.

Semillon

One of the Hunter's best Semillons. Winery founder Len Evans has long led Aussie wine from the front.

SEMILLON is the great grape of the Hunter, reaching its highest quality in the unoaked examples. But oaked ones are excellent too, full of toasty fruit. It's grown in Riverina for soft, light everyday whites, and in smaller quantities for top-quality botrytized wine.

CHARDONNAY is fat and rich, full of lush, creamy, tropical fruit in the Hunter and Cowra, and leaner and nuttier in Orange.

SAUVIGNON BLANC isn't much grown, but can be pungent in cool Orange.

VERDELHO is found only occasionally, but has good ripe lime fruit.

TREBBIANO is one of Riverina's main grapes, churning out lots of clean everyday white.

MUSCAT GORDO BLANCO, alias Muscat of Alexandria, produces oceans of fruity, perfumed wine.

SHIRAZ is widely grown: leathery in the Hunter, rather solid in Mudgee and light and fruity in Riverina.

CABERNET SAUVIGNON does best in Mudgee, where it's rather earthy, and the Hunter, where it can be rich and chunky.

MERLOT can be good in the Hunter, with rich, ripe fruit.

OPPOSITE **The Roxburgh vineyards of the Rosemount Estate in the Upper Hunter Valley produce complex, weighty Chardonnay.**

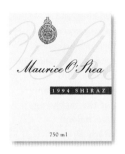

This O'Shea Shiraz from McWilliams is made from the fruit of the original vines used by legendary winemaker Maurice O'Shea to produce his famous reds of the 1920s, 1930s and 1940s from his Mount Pleasant winery in the Hunter Valley.

in the Lower Hunter, and many of the vineyards planted in the enthusiasm of the 1960s and 1970s in the Upper Hunter have been uprooted: the soil is too rich, and the wines lack the concentration of the Lower Hunter wines. The best vineyards in the Lower Hunter are on outcrops of volcanic basalt soil where the slopes give good red wines; but overall in the Hunter the bias is towards whites.

Cowra is a very promising and go-ahead district. It has a much more congenial climate: more reliable, with lots of sun and hardly any rain. Add irrigation and you have a source of rich, lush, creamy Chardonnay – archetypal Aussie Chardonnay, in fact. There's also spicy, cool-tasting Shiraz to be had.

Mudgee (the name is Aboriginal for Nest in the Hills) is red country, where the hot climate (it's well inland) and lower rainfall than the damp Hunter produces solid Shiraz and Cabernet. You don't see that many wines with 'Mudgee' on the label because a lot is blended with wines from other regions, notably the Hunter; in spite of that the region introduced its own appellation system long before the rest of the country did. A big planting boom in recent years will boost its profile.

Canberra District has about 20 wineries, just outside the Australian Capital Territory, because you can't buy land freehold within it. Cool, high altitude (800 metres/2600ft) may sound good but can pose problems with flowering, lack of ripeness and frost damage. Early offerings had a distinct tinge of the home winemaker, but some smart Riesling, Chardonnay and sparkling wine can be found today. There's quite a lot of major new planting going on here too.

If you want cool-climate viticulture in New South Wales, then **Orange** is the place. Spring frosts can be a problem here, but it's cool enough, too, for tangy Sauvignon Blanc. Chardonnay goes nutty here rather than fat, and reds are rather elegant.

Riverina is New South Wales's grape basket. Picture in your mind bakingly hot plains watered by the Murrumbidgee river system (the alternative name for the region is the hopelessly unglamorous Murrumbidgee Irrigation Area); think of large quantities of irrigation and generously yielding vines. These are the sort of vineyards that fuel Australia's wine casks; and it's these vines (plus some pretty high-tech stuff in the wineries) that have proved for the last 30 years or more that Australia is terribly good at producing good, clean flavours cheaply.

And yet there are some seriously good wines made here as well. The large family-owned firm of De Bortoli makes an astonishing botrytis Semillon, Noble One, year after year, which can rival all but the very best Sauternes from Bordeaux. They also produce a fine dry botrytis Semillon to complement it.

New areas are emerging all the time: the wine map of Australia is in a state of permanent transition these days. The latest areas to make their mark in New South Wales include Tumbarumba, Hilltops and the Lachlan Valley and in the next few years I dare say there'll be plenty of others.

Tumbarumba is a very cool, high-altitude region with fine Chardonnay, Sauvignon Blanc and Pinot Noir – much of which goes into the production of sparkling wine. **Hilltops** is to the north of Canberra District. The growing season here is relatively long and production is of full-flavoured Chardonnay, Shiraz and Cabernet Sauvignon. The **Lachlan Valley** is so new that it's too early to tell exactly what they're going to specialize in.

HOW TO READ AUSTRALIAN WINE LABELS

One might think that the New World, and Australia in particular, would have dispensed with the complications that have arisen in Europe, and which find their way on to wine labels. Well, they have; but they've also done a fair job of inventing a few others of their own.

Australian winemakers have a great fondness for identifying their wines by bin numbers which stems from the traditional method of storing unlabelled bottles. These were kept in cellars which were divided into numbered sections, known as bins, each holding a stack of maturing wine. New or experimental wines were known in the winery by their bin number but it became fashionable in the 1940s and 1950s for wines to keep this number even when established. It's just as well that the label on this Penfolds Cabernet Sauvignon Bin 707 goes on to list the grape varieties, because Penfolds have so many different bin numbers that it would be impossible to remember which was which. Bin 707 is entirely Cabernet Sauvignon and is blended from three different areas. The blurb underneath is merely telling you it's a good wine. The name and address of the producer is written around the crest; the catch-all region is South Australia.

Henschke's Hill of Grace 1994 is simpler: this is single-vineyard Shiraz – the understated label could hardly be clearer Note the high alcohol – it's 14 per cent. Ripe grapes with high sugar levels produce this extremely sturdy alcohol level.

Yarra Yering's Dry Red No 1 is the most enigmatic of the three labels. The winemaker has always chosen to call his wines by these anonymous names: Dry Red No 1 is a blend of both Cabernet Sauvignon and Cabernet Franc with Merlot, Malbec and Petit Verdot – a Bordeaux blend, in other words. Dry Red No 2 is Shiraz-based. Aficionados know that these are some of the best and most distinctive wines in Australia.

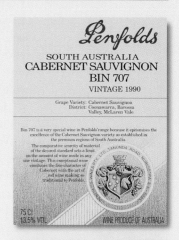

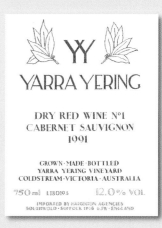

Victoria

If you want boom and bust, followed – touch wood – by boom again, this is the place to look. Around half of all the wine in Australia came from Victoria in the mid- to late 19th century; and then – nothing. Or hardly anything worth talking about. Phylloxera destroyed most of the vineyards, and it took until the 1960s before the industry revived.

Vines were first planted here in 1834, and two of the earliest regions to be established, Geelong and the Yarra Valley, were planted by Swiss immigrants. Ironically, in view of the talent of modern Aussie winemakers for coaxing flavour out of hot, dry regions, it was the Swiss talent for cool-climate viticulture that proved most useful here.

Then in 1851 gold was discovered. As soon as the secret was out, would-be gold diggers started arriving from all over the world. Where gold prospectors flocked to try their luck, vineyards were planted: Avoca, Bendigo, Great Western (now known as Grampians) and Ballarat all date from this time.

But gold fever died and a lot of the vineyards found themselves without buyers for their wine. The arrival of phylloxera in 1875 was an even greater blow. It hit Bendigo and Geelong so hard that the government ordered uprooting of all vines. By the end of the century the only vineyards left in Victoria were in the north-eastern corner, with just a handful of vines still in Great Western, Goulburn Valley and Riverland.

It was Geelong that again led the way to revival in the 1960s but it was only in the 1980s that planting all over the state really gathered pace. Now there are vineyards all over, and Victoria makes every conceivable style of wine, from cool-climate sparkling wines in the far south to sweet fortified Muscats – one of Australia's unique styles – in the North-East.

RESERVE PINOT NOIR

Coldstream Hills is in one of the loveliest corners of the Yarra Valley. Perhaps inspired by this location, the Pinot Noir is one of Australia's best: sappy and smoky with fragrant cherry fruit.

Brown Brothers has planted its Whitlands vineyard 765 metres (2500ft) up in the Great Dividing Range of North-East Victoria to ensure a cool climate for its premium grapes. It's so high here you need to take a jumper – it's appreciably colder than the valley floor.

The Grapes

Victoria has the ability to be all things to all wine lovers.

SHIRAZ can be dense and peppery in the Central Victoria regions of Goulburn Valley, Bendigo and Pyrenees or softer and jammier from the Riverland.

CABERNET SAUVIGNON likewise comes in different styles; the best mint-and-eucalyptus wines come from Central Victoria.

PINOT NOIR is elegant and perfumed, with considerable depth, from the Yarra Valley and other cool-climate regions; in the very coolest it is grown for sparkling wine.

CHARDONNAY flows out of the Riverland, in every style from light and inexpensive to rich, broad and oaky and still quite inexpensive. Finer examples come from cool regions like the Yarra Valley. It is also widely grown for sparkling wine.

RHINE RIESLING can be excellent, lean and long-lived, in high-altitude vineyards; it needs cool climates.

BROWN MUSCAT, alias Muscat Blanc à Petits Grains, makes rich dark fortifieds in North-East Victoria.

MUSCADELLE, often known as Tokay, is the other grape that makes North-East Victoria's luscious fortifieds.

MARSANNE does well in the Goulburn Valley, making intense peach and quince whites.

The Wine Regions

The **Yarra Valley** is Victoria's foremost table wine region. It's an enchanting spot of steep-sided hills and close-growing gum trees, with a little river meandering along the valley bottom. There are no vines down by the river – it's too flat, too boggy. High up on the hills it's too cold. But in between, where the climate is warmer than that of Burgundy, but cooler than that of Bordeaux, the conditions seem tailor-made for ripe, softly structured, perfumed Pinot Noir and elegant, long-lived Chardonnay but also, if you pick your spot properly, dense Shiraz and Cabernet. It's also humid enough for fine nobly rotten wines.

Most of Victoria's vineyards are pretty scattered, with the Yarra being more densely planted than most. The regions between the coast and the Great Dividing Range tend to be cool: **Geelong** gives intensely flavoured reds and whites. Pinot Noir is exciting, but Chardonnay, Riesling, Sauvignon Blanc and Shiraz also impress. The

MORNINGTON PENINSULA

RESERVE CHARDONNAY
1997

PRODUCED AND BOTTLED BY
STONIER'S WINERY, MERRICKS, VICTORIA 3916   750ml
PRODUCT OF AUSTRALIA   14.0% VOL

Commercially, Stonier's is the most important winery on the fashionable Mornington Peninsula. This Reserve Chardonnay has peachy, honeyed fruit with spicy oak characters and considerable finesse.

SPARKLING WINES

For good sparkling wine you need acidity; that means you want a cool climate for growing the grapes. You don't need weighty wines; in fact lighter base wines make better sparkling wines. So anywhere that's almost too cool to ripen grapes can have potential for sparkling wine.

That includes quite a lot of Victoria – and in fact quite a lot of sites all over Australia's wine regions. Tasmania makes good sparkling; so does South Australia. In Victoria the Yarra Valley makes some; so does Henty, so does Grampians. Tumbarumba in New South Wales is a high-altitude region of major importance too. And as you might expect, there are almost as many styles as there are winemakers.

The Champagne method is now pretty universal for top-quality sparklers, though other methods like *cuve close* may be employed for cheaper brands. But even within the parameters of the Champagne method, you have choices. You can make bready, biscuity wines that are in the mould of Champagne itself, or you can make fruit-driven wines that are purely Australian in style. (Champagne houses have invested in wineries in Australia, just as they have in California; no prizes for guessing which style they make.) But the wackiest of all Australian sparklers is the sparkling Shiraz.

Sparkling Shiraz: yes, that's right. Sparkling red wine. It's dry, but brimming with dark fruits – mulberry, plum, redcurrants, blackcurrants – plus cream and chocolate and coconut. Feel like trying it? Go on – I dare you!

ABOVE **Salinger sparkling wine lying 'sur lattes' in the underground cellars, built in the traditional European style, of Australian bubbly producer Seppelt.**

A superb example of the fortified style for which Rutherglen is famous. This Old Premium Liqueur Muscat has intense raisiny aromas and complex flavour; it's sweet with evident age yet balanced with a long, dry finish.

Mornington Peninsula, right down on the strip of land that all but encloses Port Phillip Bay, is even cooler but frost-free. A lot of vineyards here are hobbies for Melbourne weekenders, but if you're serious about it there is very good wine to be made here, light but well structured. Pinot Noir shows promise; while Cabernet Sauvignon and, more suprisingly, Shiraz can both be ripened adequately. **Macedon's** wines are elegant and concentrated; **Henty** (formerly known as Drumborg**)** and **Gippsland**, two more coastal areas, are also cool; Henty specializes in sparkling wines and sometimes has difficulty ripening even these. Gippsland is an area of scattered, diverse wineries, mostly tiny but with great potential. Pinot Noir from here looks exciting. North of Melbourne, the **Goulburn Valley** produces deeper, richer flavours. The whites are intensely flavoured and well structured with Marsanne being a speciality of the region. Reds are complex and mouthfilling.

The further north you go, the warmer it gets and the more you have to seek high altitudes to find cool climates. Or, of course, you can settle for greater heat and the bigger, more solid reds it

produces. **Ballarat**, the **Pyrenees** and much of **Grampians** are quite high, but they make marvellous Shiraz, all spice and pepper. Cabernet Sauvignon is minty and eucalyptus-scented, and there's good Chardonnay as well. The **King Valley** manages to have so many climates, depending on where you plant, that it can make anything from rich reds to pale, elegant whites. It also supplies grapes to an large number of leading wineries across not just Victoria, but South Australia and New South Wales as well.

Up by the Murray river the vineyards pour out a steady flow of wine; mostly everyday stuff, but perfectly attractive. But it's south of here, at **Glenrowan**, **Rutherglen** and **Milawa**, that some of Victoria's most remarkable wines are made. The grapes are a dark-skinned strain of Muscat Blanc à Petits Grains (known locally as Brown Muscat) and Muscadelle, and they're turned into sweet, perfumed fortifieds that seem to live forever (see box below). New in Rutherglen, is a classification of Muscats into Rutherglen Muscat, the freshest style; Classic Rutherglen Muscat, older and richer; Grand Rutherglen Muscat, still more intense; and Rare Rutherglen Muscat, the very finest.

VICTORIA'S FORTIFIEDS

Australia used to make an awful lot of fortifieds – in fact it's only in the last three decades that the search has been on for cool-climate regions for lighter table wines. Until the 1950s and 1960s it seemed that fortifieds were Australia's natural vocation.

Now the pendulum has swung so far the other way that it's easy to forget that Australia still does make some fortifieds – and very good they are, too. There are delicious port-style tawny wines that Australia is ceasing to call port, and refreshing fino-style wines that Australia is ceasing to call sherry; but most of all there are the fortified Muscats and Tokays of North-East Victoria.

These are sweet, dark wines of almost shocking intensity. The grapes are left on the vines until they are shrivelled and full of sweetness; then the fermentation is stopped with a shot of alcohol and the wines are left to age for anything from a year upwards in hot warehouses; the principle is not unlike that of the warm aging of Madeira, although the similarity is almost certainly coincidental. The resulting wines are thick and stickily luscious, and the Tokays in particular (from the Muscadelle grape) have a tealeaf-like tang.

LEFT **Ancient casks and barrels at Morris, Rutherglen. Stocks of their heavyweight style of wine here date back to the 1890s.**

South Australia

This is the powerhouse of Australian wine, the source of more than half of the country's total production and home to most of its biggest wine companies. Yet if you looked on a map for the vineyards that are responsible for all this, you'd have to search pretty hard. Most of South Australia has no vineyards at all. It's only when you get to the bottom right-hand corner that you find them, tucked into the south, north and east of Adelaide. There are a couple more areas further south-east, near the border with Victoria, and a couple more, just as small on the map, on the Murray river. It doesn't, on the face of it, add up to a lot.

Add to this the hot, dry climate of South Australia and the lack of water in many regions – regions around Adelaide are especially restricted in their growth by the lack of available water – and you might begin to wonder how the state manages to make so much wine. Well, its secret weapon, the factor that ups the quantity dramatically, is the Murray river.

The state of Victoria, too, has its share of Riverland vineyards. Every spring a flood of melting snow runs off the Great Dividing Range, and is channelled into reservoirs to be turned, via generously yielding vines, into cheap everyday wine. It's rarely great wine, but it's perfectly attractive stuff for glugging. If you want great wine, you have to look elsewhere.

Most of the rest of South Australia is capable of producing great wine. Some of Australia's most famous wine regions are here – Coonawarra, Padthaway, McLaren Vale, the Clare and Eden Valleys and, perhaps most famous of all, the Barossa Valley.

The Wine Regions

It's quite easy, when you first visit the **Barossa Valley**, to forget that you're in a valley. The valley floor is so broad that the hills seem somehow unrelated to it; and yet they are crucial because they afford cooler sites where most of the light cool-climate whites and many of the finer red table wines are now grown.

That's not the only paradox in the Barossa. Until a decade ago people were saying that it was finished as a wine-producing region; that the odd vineyard might remain for sentimental value or to show to tourists, but that basically the Barossa had no future in grape growing. It was going to be a blending and winemaking centre only: most of the big companies had vast wineries there and used them to process much of the fruit they grew in other regions, in particular, the Riverland. It was a good spot for tourists: the Barossa had been settled by Silesian immigrants who had built Lutheran churches in the local grey stone and established a local taste for *wurst* and brass bands (drive round there on a Sunday and you'll see

The view westwards over the Barossa Valley. Skeletons of trees are a familiar feature of the Australian landscape, as are vivid patches of vines in the middle of parched earth.

signs offering *wurst* and cream teas, which might not be your dream combination). But the vineyards they had planted on the hot valley floor had been of red varieties, in particular Shiraz. Nobody wanted Shiraz any more: the fashion was for much lighter wines. The Shiraz was being progressively uprooted. The Barossa's main white grape was Riesling, and nobody wanted Riesling either. Chardonnay was flavour of the month. As far as growing vines was concerned, the focus had moved off the Barossa to the Riverland.

You know those stories you read in the papers sometimes about somebody being told that the bowl they'd been using for dog food for 15 years was actually Ming and worth a fortune? It was a bit like that. A few British journalists and shippers tasted the wines from these unirrigated, 40- or 50- or 60-year-old Shiraz vines and loved them. The Aussies said to themselves, 'Hold on a minute. Perhaps we've got something here after all.' Now they're bottling every drop of old vine Shiraz, Grenache or Mourvèdre they can lay their hands on, and it's acknowledged as being one of Australia's great styles. The Barossa, too, is recognized once more as a great growing area. I love a happy ending.

But what about Riesling, the Barossa's main white grape? There's not as much of that, because Riesling still isn't as fashionable as it should be. Riesling tends to be planted in the hills along the eastern side of the valley these days, where it attains a steeliness equal to that of the best German regions. Go far enough into the hills and the Barossa merges into the Eden Valley; and here, and in the Clare Valley to the north, is where much of Australia's best Riesling, Riesling to rival that of almost anywhere in the world, is produced.

Eden Valley Riesling is more austere than that of Clare, though both age brilliantly to a lime-and-toast maturity. The high, cool-climate Eden Valley vineyards produce first-class Pinot Noir and Chardonnay as well. **Clare** is warmer and also more complicated, because instead of being a single valley or range of hills it's actually three valley systems which between them offer

The Grapes

The main areas produce a relatively small range of wines, but in a wide variety of styles.

SHIRAZ from Barossa is one of Australia's great success stories: the best comes from old vines (and will usually say so on the label), has great depth of leathery, rich fruit and will age for years. It's equally good too in McLaren Vale, and sometimes softer and juicier.

CABERNET SAUVIGNON makes wines of good complexity and concentration in Coonawarra, and creamy, blackcurranty ones in McLaren Vale. Higher-altitude vineyards in the Clare or Eden Valley give leaner, age-worthy wines.

PINOT NOIR is grown in small quantities but can be perfumed and good in cool hillside sites around Adelaide.

Riesling

Cabernet Sauvignon   *Shiraz*

Wolf Blass has mastered the art of creating wines of high quality which are nonetheless easy to enjoy. Gold Label Riesling from the Eden and Clare Valleys is impressively intense.

1998
RHINE RIESLING
EDEN/CLARE VALLEYS
Gold Label
750ML WINE. PRODUCT OF AUSTRALIA

RIESLING reaches great heights of quality in the Eden and Clare Valleys and the hills to the east of the Barossa; these lime-and-toast-flavoured wines age superbly. Softer wines come from Padthaway and Coonawarra.

CHARDONNAY is at its best in the cool vineyards of the Adelaide Hills and the Eden and Clare Valleys, or in warmer Padthaway. Coonawarra also makes some rich versions.

SAUVIGNON BLANC is most pungent in cool regions like the hills around Adelaide. Padthaway also makes some tasty Sauvignon.

just about every possible combination of heat and altitude. So as well as producing terrific, long-lived limey Riesling (which needs a cool climate) Clare can also make big brawny Shiraz (which needs a hot climate). It's just as well that Australia doesn't have a European-style appellation system that controls which vines can be planted where, because the twists and folds of the hills of the Clare Valley would keep an army of bureaucrats busy until eternity, trying to decide what was what.

But these aren't the only vineyards near Adelaide. In the hills to the east of the city, in a region not surprisingly known as **Adelaide Hills**, there are more cool-climate vineyards making steely Chardonnay, tangy Sauvignon Blanc

OPPOSITE New vineyards of Leasingham in the Clare Valley. The mild climate here is good for spring flowers and vines alike.

Two big names from Coonawarra. In peak years Wynns releases the cream of its Shiraz as Michael. Petaluma's Coonawarra is an outstanding Cabernet/Merlot blend.

and perfumed Pinot Noir. Sparkling wines are very successful up here, too. It's quite damp in these hills, but dampness is only relative in South Australia and the vines still need irrigation to survive. That puts them in competition with the swimming pools of voters in suburban Adelaide, and means that there are never going to be all that many vineyards up here; there just isn't enough water.

There's not an awful lot of water in **McLaren Vale** either. Here they dry-farm a lot of their old vineyards to produce small amounts of blackcurrant-and-cream Cabernets and thick, luscious Shirazes. **Langhorne Creek**, on the Fleurieu Peninsula, is cooler and there is good tangy Sauvignon Blanc here, and toasty Chardonnay and Semillon.

In **Coonawarra**, however, water is not only abundant, but rather too abundant. Coonawarra is a long, narrow strip of land that is supposed to be higher than the surrounding boggy plain. Well, it may be a few inches higher, but to the eye the only thing that distinguishes the top-class vineyard land from land that really isn't all that good is the colour: the red soil is good, the black clay surrounding it isn't. And that's all. It's only when you dig down that you discover that there's more to it. That red soil covers a limestone ridge that provides ideal drainage; there's frequently no limestone under the surrounding black clay. The difference shows in the quality of the wine: Coonawarra Cabernets (and Cabernet seems to be the grape that Coonawarra does best) have a wonderful intense brightness of flavour, with mint and eucalyptus all mixed in. Wines from the black clay soil are far duller.

The bad news is that the best soil of Coonawarra is effectively all planted; and since it's mostly held by big companies, some of whom seem intent only on maximizing their yields, it may not be realizing its full potential for quality. The good news is that other areas to the west and north are being busily planted as alternatives to Coonawarra and these are beginning to yield excellent wines – **Mount Benson** and **Robe** on the coast and **Wrattonbully** between Coonawarra and Padthaway. **Padthaway** is warmer than cool Coonawarra yet produces stunning whites as well as sumptuous reds, which just goes to show how unpredictable climate can be.

WINE DOCTORS

Max Lake started Lake's Folly in the Lower Hunter Valley in 1963. In 1971 John Middleton started Mount Mary in the Yarra Valley. Pendarves Estate was founded in the Hunter Valley in 1986 by Philip Norrie; Peter Pratten started Capel Vale in Western Australia in 1975. What do all these men have in common? Answer: they're all doctors.

There are others, too: it was Dr John Gladstones who in 1965 recommended planting vines in the Margaret River in Western Australia; Dr Tom Cullity founded Vasse Felix there two years later, and was followed by Dr Bill Pannell of Moss Wood, and Dr Kevin Cullen of Cullen's. Wineries have been founded by people from every field of life, but doctors seem to have done far more than their share.

The medical role in Australian wine started early. When the First Fleet set sail from England in 1788, the doctor in charge, surgeon John White, made sure that there was enough wine aboard to be used as a medicine and to help prevent malnutrition. This helped to ensure the survival of 751 of the 775 convicts on board.

In 1801, the man known as the father of Australian wine, Dr William Redfern, arrived in the country. Unlike the other doctors mentioned here, he was a convict. He had been a naval surgeon who had supported the mutineers on the fleet at the Nore in 1797, and was transported. New South Wales needed his medical skills, and he was not only a very good doctor but an idealist who fought to improve conditions on convict ships and who gave as much

time to his convict patients as to the rich of Sydney. And he, too, planted vines. The list of doctors goes on: Dr Henry Lindeman was a Royal Navy surgeon who in 1842 settled in the Hunter Valley and established vineyards there. Dr Christopher Rawson Penfold arrived in Adelaide in 1844; his purpose in planting vine cuttings was to treat anaemia in his patients. Angove's, too, was founded by a doctor, Dr William Thomas Angove, who planted its first vines at Tea Tree Gully, near Adelaide in 1886; Houghton in the Swan Valley, Western Australia, was established by Dr John Ferguson in 1859.

Ironically it has only become widely accepted very recently that wine in moderation is good for you. These doctors clearly knew it a long time ago.

Western Australia

The first thing you notice about Western Australia is how far it is from anywhere. The second thing is how hot it is.

The first of these meant that if the early settlers wanted wine, they had to grow it themselves; and since the spot chosen for the settlement was the mouth of the Swan river where it opens to form a natural harbour, it made sense to plant the vines just a little way upriver. If it was hot, well, what of it? The fashion for cool-climate wines was far in the future; neither the early settlers nor the gold prospectors who followed later in the century were too worried about the lack of elegance or finesse in their wines.

The Wine Regions

In theory, the **Swan District's** hot climate – it's one of the hottest vineyard regions in the world – should put it out of court as far as modern wine styles are concerned. And certainly it's not the big producer it once was: attention has moved southwards, and the Swan is no longer Western Australia's prime area. But one of the standard-bearers for Australian wine back in the 1970s and before was **Houghton** with its White Burgundy, a rich, overripe, deep wine made from Chenin Blanc and Muscadelle. It wasn't modern in style; but it was good.

The curious thing about the hot Swan Valley is that it's actually white grapes that do best here. Only certain white grapes, to be sure: Semillon is successful, which is not that surprising when you consider how well it does in the hot Hunter Valley in New South Wales. Verdelho, a grape also at home in subtropical Madeira, is good, and so is Chenin Blanc. Because Chenin Blanc performs so brilliantly in France's cool Loire Valley one's apt to forget that it has the knack of keeping its acidity however hot the temperature, and that makes it very useful indeed in a place like the Swan Valley. There's good Shiraz and Cabernet grown here as well, but the reds can taste a bit baked if you're not terribly careful.

The Grapes

Western Australia's extremes of climate allow for a multitude of styles.

CABERNET SAUVIGNON seems to flourish in most of Western Australia, with its greatest successes coming from Margaret River and Great Southern. The latter wines are leaner than the former.

MERLOT, grassy and toffeeish, is mostly grown for blending with Cabernet, particularly in Margaret River.

SHIRAZ does well in the Swan Valley where it likes the heat and gives good leathery, berried flavours. Elsewhere it's rare but good and peppery.

PINOT NOIR is an obvious grape to try in cool spots like Great Southern, and it is showing promise here.

CHARDONNAY is found everywhere, from the Swan Valley right down to Great Southern. In warmer spots it gets fat and rich, in cooler ones more elegant and nutty.

RIESLING does best in Great Southern, where it is nicely elegant, with intense fruit.

SAUVIGNON BLANC seems happiest in Margaret River where it is ripe and tropical although it's also good in Great Southern.

SEMILLON flourishes in Swan River and in cooler Great Southern; in the latter it makes crisper, more zesty wines.

CHENIN BLANC'S high acidity makes it suitable for the hot climate of the Swan Valley.

VERDELHO is grown in the Swan Valley for the sake of its rich, nutty flavours and its tolerance of heat.

MUSCADELLE makes ripe, rather heavy wines in the Swan Valley. It's not really grown elsewhere.

Vasse Felix was one of the original wineries responsible for Margaret River's meteoric rise to fame. Oaky, buttery Heytersbury Chardonnay is a flagship wine. Cape Mentelle is another leading winery, with sister company Cloudy Bay in New Zealand. Superb, full-throttle Cabernet is its trademark.

Just because you're based in the Swan doesn't mean you have to get all your grapes from there. Houghton now sources a lot of its grapes from cooler regions to the north, or from Western Australia's other two main regions, Margaret River and Great Southern, and these are where the action is these days.

Margaret River is considerably cooler: the idea was that it would be like Bordeaux only better, without the spring frosts and rainy vintages that can drive growers to distraction in the Médoc. It was local doctors who got the whole thing going in the 1960s – Dr Tom Cullity of Vasse Felix, Dr Bill Pannell of Moss Wood and Dr Kevin Cullen of Cullens were all pioneers, following the observation of viticulturalist Dr John Gladstones that the climate had similarities to that of Bordeaux. In fact it's a bit warmer than Bordeaux but it is drier, and the breezes off the Indian Ocean keep the temperature within bounds. The trouble is that the winds themselves can be a problem when they turn gale-force during flowering – but, after all, it would not be a proper vineyard area unless it had some problems.

It's pretty good at producing a wide range of wines: Cabernet here has structure and backbone plus juicy, curranty fruit, and Merlot keeps the grassy plumminess that makes it such an ideal partner for Cabernet. Sauvignon Blanc is ripe and pungent, Semillon is intense and lemony, and Chardonnay is elegant and can sometimes even age well.

Standards are pretty high in all Western Australia's wine regions. There's no equivalent here of the hugely irrigated Riverland or Riverina vineyards of the south-eastern corner of the country; and further south, in the **Great Southern** area, it's too cold for that sort of thing anyway. It looks a relatively large area on the map, but the vineyards are scattered and isolated – some up in the Porongurup Hills, some along the coast, some inland by the Frankland river. Accordingly the right climate can be found for lots of grapes, from taut and lean Riesling to Shiraz that is surprisingly rich and peppery. Chardonnay and Cabernet turn out well structured.

There are a couple of other wine regions that are still in their infancy: Geographe (formerly known as South-West Coastal Plain) and Perth Hills. **Perth Hills** is self-explanatory: it's the hills to the east of Perth. Because the vineyards are quite high up on the slopes of the Darling

Margaret River high-flier Leeuwin produce this pricy Chardonnay – it could be Australia's nearest thing to Burgundian Montrachet.

WINE SHOWS

Wine shows are held all over the world: in almost any wine shop you can find labels plastered with gold medals from obscure corners of the earth. Ignore them: they're usually completely meaningless. Australia, however, has a wine show system that really does reward quality,

LEFT A prize certificate which was awarded to Yeringberg, a winery based in Victoria's Yarra Valley, in 1895. These days awards from Australian wine shows carry more weight than those from anywhere else.

even if at the same time it tends to impose a uniform style. Award-winning wines sell better, so companies determined to win awards make wines in the precise style that they know the judges like. The result is an excellent basic level of quality, with varietal character, balance and structure all as they should be; but also a lack of quirkiness. Eccentric winemakers making quirky wines (and the finest and most interesting wines in the world come into this bracket) tend not to get involved in the Australian show system because they know they'll get marked down for the very qualities that make their wines stand out from textbook examples.

That being said, the judges at Australian shows are of very high calibre, and it takes considerable experience as an apprentice judge before you're properly accepted on the circuit.

One of the greatest pests Australia's grape growers have to contend with is the kangaroo. They are virtually impossible to keep out of the vineyards and can cause havoc once they're in.

Range they're cooler, and growers no doubt have the success of the Adelaide Hills in mind when they start planting in these valleys.

The **Geographe** is barely a coherent wine region at all; really it's just a name given to a few scattered vineyards along the coast, from just north of Perth to just north of Margaret River. But they do have one thing in common: Tuart sand, which takes its name from the local Tuart gum trees, is the predominant soil. It drains like a colander, so you have to be able to irrigate. Because these vineyards are so close to the ocean they don't have extremes of heat and cold, but obviously the ones near Perth are hotter than those further south. It's a region that is showing promise: there are full-flavoured whites and some good Zinfandels appearing.

Another new region showing potential is **Pemberton**. The last few years have seen rapid planting with the first vineyards already showing good results. The climate here is relatively cool and some vineyards can even do without irrigation. There's also much room for expansion – native forest still covers much of the region. Chardonnay and Pinot Noir seem to do especially well in the area around Pemberton; the area around **Manjimup** seems to be particularly suited to the Bordeaux varieties of Cabernet Sauvignon and Merlot.

The Food of Australia

AUSTRALIA HAS A huge variety of good ingredients; in fact, one of the biggest and best in the world. These ingredients are remarkably well suited to simple cooking, barbie-style, and to the spices and flavours brought in by the influx of immigrants from the Far East and Mediterranean. The combination makes Australia's cuisine unique. Its prevailing style is one of intense, clear flavours that mix and match east and west and provide a perfect foil for the generous fruit flavours and robustness of the country's wines.

Added to the flavours of Europe and the Far East are an abundance of native fruits. Lillypilly sauce is sometimes served with trout: it has a plummy, slightly spicy flavour. There are small green plums that are the richest source of vitamin C in the world; roasted wattle seeds make particularly good ice-cream.

Fresh fish is everywhere, sold in astonishing variety in the markets. Crabs (mud crabs or blue swimmers) are simply steamed, and crustaceans like yabbies or freshwater crayfish are eaten ultra-fresh for the best flavour. Small, sweet rock oysters, too, are available even inland. Fish include barramundi, Tasmanian ocean trout and a host of others.

Meat can be beef, lamb or kangaroo which is delicious. It's gamier than beef, with a lean, tender texture.

Eating outdoors of course comes naturally in Australia and is now more sophisticated than ever. It makes full use of the lemongrass and lime leaves of oriental cooking. But it's still hard to beat a really good steak thrown on a barbecue, with a glass of old vine Shiraz to accompany it.

The only thing Australia lacks is really good cheese. Certainly cheese companies have sprung up, but they seem to focus on imitating popular European styles like Brie, and pasteurization is unfortunately the rule – so far.

Other Australian Regions

Outside the main wine regions, Australia can offer extremes of heat and cold – and, winemakers being what they are, if a spot is really difficult you can bet somebody will start planting vines on it.

Tasmania

Tasmania is a case in point. Logically, it should be the best spot in all Australia to grow vines, if cool-climate sites are what you seek. The trouble is that most of Tasmania is just too cool. Even when the temperature looks about right (about the same as Burgundy, that is) the wind can make life impossible. When Tasmania has a good

The tiny Freycinet vineyard, near Bicheno, on the east coast of Tasmania is in a suntrap location – even Cabernet Sauvignon will ripen here.

vintage it can be very good indeed, and produce superb perfumed Pinot Noir, Tasmania's finest red, and elegant, lean Chardonnay; but vintages can be wildly irregular here. Just as they are, of course, in Burgundy. Some Cabernet is grown for lighter reds but in less good years these can have a distinct green-pepper flavour. Riesling is well suited to certain parts of Tasmania too.

Most of Tasmania's vineyards grow grapes for sparkling wine, and they seem ideally suited to this: several top sparkling wine houses on the mainland take grapes from here. For still reds and whites the only answer is to get out of the wind. North of Launceston it is both sheltered enough and warm enough to be successful; near **Freycinet** on the east coast it is also warm and sheltered, and the **Coal River** area in the south can also ripen red grapes fairly reliably.

Queensland and the Northern Territory

Queensland goes to the other extreme. Here, in the vineyards of the **Granite Belt** region, the growers plant high up in the hills of the Great Dividing Range – but on the dry inland side, not the humid coastal side. It's still not exactly what you'd call cool here; in fact it's hotter than it is in Rutherglen in Victoria, but they make table wines which aren't bad considering. Shiraz is quite successful, varying from solid to jammy, and Semillon can be good too. Other Queensland vineyards are even further north in the **Burnett Valley** and at **Roma**, although there are fewer here than there used to be.

And things can get even hotter. Fancy growing grapes in the middle of the desert at **Alice Springs**? No? Well, there's a vineyard there. The winery is built underground to keep the temperature down a bit, and the survival of the vines is a miracle of irrigation; but wine is made there, year after year. It's actually the first wine made every year in Australia: the owner starts picking his grapes on New Year's Day. It's not, as you might have realized, the longest ripening season in the world.

NEW ZEALAND

The astonishing thing about New Zealand wine is how young it all is. It's become so much of a fixture that it's easy to forget that there was a time before New Zealand Sauvignon Blanc; and that time wasn't so very long ago. Only after 1960 were restaurants in New Zealand allowed to sell wine; only after 1969 could you get a drink in a theatre there; only after 1976 were wineries allowed to sell a glass of their own produce, and only in 1979 was the first wine bar established. It was 1990 before you could buy wine from a supermarket.

You might infer from this that New Zealand has no wine tradition, and yet it has – just. Missionaries planted the first vines in 1819. It's true that the English settlers mostly preferred beer, but the first British resident, James Busby, made wine in the north of the North Island to sell to soldiers – not, perhaps, the most discriminating of markets.

By the end of the century phylloxera had arrived, and the common solution was not, as elsewhere, to plant on American rootstocks, but to plant hybrid vines. Again, it wasn't a move designed to improve the national taste, which was mostly for cheap fortifieds. In 1919 it was only the votes of returning servicemen which prevented Prohibition – though given the quality of most of the wine, Prohibition might not have been so terrible.

THE BIRTH OF THE MODERN WINE INDUSTRY

In the 1960s the growers took a deep breath and decided to do something about the state of their industry. They called in foreign advice, which was a great idea, but they called it in from Germany, which wasn't. New Zealand, of course, has a climate that is extremely promising for Rhine Riesling – but that climate is found in the South Island, and the industry was concentrated in the North Island. In addition, the person who came from Germany to advise was Dr Helmut Becker, whose mission in Germany consisted of

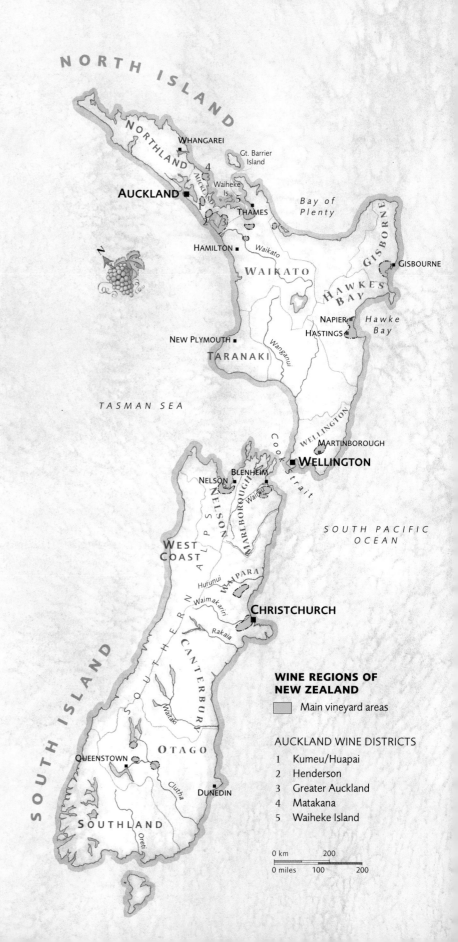

WINE REGIONS OF NEW ZEALAND

Main vineyard areas

AUCKLAND WINE DISTRICTS
1 Kumeu/Huapai
2 Henderson
3 Greater Auckland
4 Matakana
5 Waiheke Island

0 km   200
0 miles   100   200

Wairau Valley,
Marlborough, South
Island. It could only be
New Zealand – all those
sheep, all those vines.

Montana's Sauvignon
Blanc and Chardonnay
wines are largely to thank
for putting New Zealand
on the international wine
map.

trying to breed new vine varieties that could equal the quality of Riesling without the problems – an aim, it has to be said, that he never attained. Was he likely to recommend Riesling to the New Zealanders? No, he was not. He recommended Müller-Thurgau – a perfectly nice grape, but never an exciting one. Never one to set the world on fire, or build a national reputation. New Zealand planted lots of Müller-Thurgau and probably made the best in the world – but, so what?

Well, winemakers tend to be a curious lot, so it wasn't that long before they started to travel around and see what the rest of the world was doing. Come the 1970s a few visionaries started to set up new wineries and plant Chardonnay, Sauvignon Blanc and Cabernet; and in 1973 the first vines were planted at Marlborough on the South Island.

Planting vines became a craze. And since worldwide demand for New Zealand wines was not exactly overwhelming, there was such a glut of grapes that in 1986 the government ordered a vine-pull scheme. Twenty-five per cent of the national vineyard went; and that, together with closer economic ties with Australia in the 1980s that brought New Zealand wine into direct competition with Australian wine on its home turf, forced the industry to take a serious look at where it was going.

It was now that the first Sauvignon Blancs began to make an impact abroad. They were astonishing: more pungently gooseberryish than anything the Loire could produce; more zesty, more incisive, more intense. In 1985 Cloudy Bay (see box on p.251) produced its first vintage, and was an instant hit; now it's a cult wine, on allocation wherever it's sold.

So New Zealand wine really is very young indeed; and like most young industries, it's still finding its feet. The country is fortunate in having such a huge range of climates and soils at its disposal – if you transposed it to the northern hemisphere it would stretch from Paris to North Africa (only upside down, of course) – but that means, too, that it has a lot of exploring and experimenting to do. In those early years, when we were all raving about these brand new Sauvignon Blancs, we were not raving at all about the red wines, which seemed green and mean; well, at last the Cabernet is getting riper, thanks to better canopy management (see box opposite); and New Zealand Pinot Noir is proving to be some of the best in the southern hemisphere now that it's being planted in the south of the North Island, at Martinborough and near Christchurch in the South Island. The cool climates that are constantly being sought in Australia are here in abundance, but they bring their own problems.

The majority of vineyards are planted on flat land, mostly because there's no shortage of land and flat vineyards, with their potential for mechanization, are far cheaper to work. We're just seeing the beginnings of a shift of growers to hillside sites but this is more to do with pressure on land in more popular areas. The distinction between flat and sloping vineyards is less important here. Sophisticated canopy management can go some way to replicating slopes as far as exposure to sun and so on goes.

CLASSIFICATION

A system of **Certified Origin** guaranteeing the origin of all New Zealand wines has been planned for some time but has not as yet come into effect. It will not, however, go as far as regulating grape varieties and wine styles, as in many European appellation systems but it will ensure that 85 per cent of the grapes will come from the region, the vintage and the grape variety named on the label. A Geographical Indications Act came into force in 1994 and, in general terms, this provides for the protection of geographical indications from any misleading use.

New Zealand Pinot Noir is really causing a stir. This powerful, fruit-focused example from Ata Rangi is one of the best the country has to offer.

The early 1980s saw the start of winemaking on Waiheke Island, Auckland. Hot, dry ripening conditions have made high-quality Cabernet-Sauvignon-based reds that sell for high prices. Stonyridge is the leading winery.

CANOPY MANAGEMENT

The canopy of a vine is its foliage. In high summer it can form a lush canopy that shades the grapes from the sun. This is not always a bad thing – sometimes you want to protect the grapes from burning – but in New Zealand the extremely fertile soils produce immense amounts of foliage. This results in a very dense canopy that shades the grapes too much and encourages the sort of humid atmosphere around the bunches in which mildew and rot can flourish. The result, as well as less healthy grapes, is unripe, green-tasting wine.

It was Dr Richard Smart, government viticulturalist from 1982-90, who stressed the need for better canopy management in New Zealand, and it is largely due to his work that the wines (particularly the reds) are so much better and riper than they were. The techniques being practised range from the simple, like leaf and shoot trimming to reduce the amount of foliage, to different trellising systems that reduce shade and expose both leaves and grapes to more sun. The less vigorous vines of the classic European wine regions don't need such drastic treatment and over the centuries grape growers have devised trellising systems to suit their conditions. The New World, faced with different problems, has had to find different solutions.

ABOVE **Pruning vines at Collard Brothers in Auckland. Pruning and trellising systems both play an important part in canopy management.**

North Island

This is the heart of New Zealand wine: it's where it all began, and it's where most of the vineyards still are, even if they've moved around a bit since the first vines were planted north of Auckland.

In every country of the New World, vines were first planted where people happened to be, rather than in the best spots for viticulture. In the case of New Zealand, Auckland proved to be one of the trickiest parts of the country. Vines will grow here, certainly, and they'll ripen a crop, but the climate is warm and humid and rain and rot are a problem. So is quality: vines grow like weeds, if you let them. For making cheap, second-rate fortifieds Auckland and Northland were okay; for making high-quality table wines they proved less good, and the main growing areas moved to Gisborne and Hawkes Bay. Lately there's been a lot of interest much further south around the town of Martinborough (the area was formerly known as Wairarapa and is now called Wellington); and curiously enough new canopy management techniques (see box on p.245), and the exploration of new parts of Auckland, have led to new plantings on Waiheke Island and at Matakana. Cabernet gets good and ripe here, and Pinot Noir is rich; so some of New Zealand's best reds are now appearing from Auckland. If you wait long enough in wine, things always come round again, albeit in a different form.

The Wine Regions

There are lots of wineries still in **Auckland**, often founded by immigrants from Dalmatia, but most of the grapes they process these days come from elsewhere. But those wineries that do grow grapes in Auckland can make some pretty impressive and individual wines, both reds and whites.

When growers started to plant Müller-Thurgau by the acre, **Gisborne** was one of the places they planted it. It's a sensible spot to choose if you want to produce large quantities of gently fruity wine: the soil is terrifically fertile, there's lots of sunshine and the climate is reasonably dry

except (unfortunate timing, this) during the vintage. Müller-Thurgau will produce litre after litre of easy-going, mildly aromatic wine in these conditions. And even though nobody really rates Müller-Thurgau any more, it's still useful as a component of wine cask blends, and it's still the most widely planted grape in Gisborne, even though Chardonnay and others are hard on its tail.

Gisborne prefers to emphasize its Chardonnay, rather than its Müller-Thurgau. It even calls itself the Chardonnay capital of New Zealand, which is perhaps going a bit far. It's quite nice Chardonnay, with a gently tropical peach flavour, but it doesn't have the class of Chardonnay from, say, Hawkes Bay. Gewürztraminer can be good, too, but reds find it hard to ripen in the wet autumns.

OPPOSITE **New vineyards on the tiny but highly fashionable Waiheke Island in Auckland; so new, in fact, that the vines have just been placed on the ground rather than properly planted yet.**

The Grapes

This is where New Zealand finds it easiest to ripen red grapes, but there's scope for aromatic whites as well.

CABERNET SAUVIGNON is the most popular red grape, though it's often most successful when blended with something else, usually Merlot. Cabernet from Waiheke Island and Hawkes Bay gives ripe blackcurrant flavours in good years.

MERLOT is a minority grape, usually blended with Cabernet but it has good grassy, plummy fruit and may well turn out to be a top variety here.

PINOT NOIR is the star red grape of Wellington, where the cool climate gives nicely perfumed wines.

CHARDONNAY is found pretty well everywhere. A style of rich, almost syrupy, nutty flavours has developed in Hawkes Bay, Gisborne and Wellington, tempered by good acidity.

SAUVIGNON BLANC from Marlborough in the South Island created New Zealand's international reputation with shocking, tangy flavours of gooseberry, green capsicum and lime zest. Hawkes Bay also

grows Sauvignon in a softer manner and frequently ages it in oak to add complexity.

MÜLLER-THURGAU produces gently perfumed wine in all the older-established areas.

RIESLING shows promise in the cooler regions, particularly Wellington. Dry wines are floral and intense; sweet, late-harvest wines are rich, with balancing acidity.

GEWÜRZTRAMINER also makes well-structured wines in cooler spots.

Pinot Noir

Cabernet Sauvignon

Reds do much better in **Hawkes Bay**. It's a big, diverse area, but the best bits are the gravel beds along the rivers flowing into the bay. The best for reds, anyway: this is infertile, free-draining soil like that of the Haut-Médoc in Bordeaux, only more so, and Cabernet and Merlot thrive here, producing intense blackcurrant flavours. The **Bay View** and **Esk Valley** areas north of the town of Napier are also warm, and have the right sort of infertile soils.

Chardonnay does well in Hawkes Bay; it's notable for its elegance and firm, citrus character; Sauvignon Blanc is also good, more peachy than that of South Island Marlborough. There's still a lot of Müller-Thurgau grown here, but it's no longer the biggest variety and Hawkes Bay's reputation is pretty firmly one of quality these days. Its wine credentials are increased by being the place where New Zealand's first wine bar was opened, in 1979. One day, I suppose, it will be a place of pilgrimage.

Hawkes Bay is far from being a homogenous region as winemakers look ever more closely at its soils and climate. It is becoming clear that some parts make appreciably bigger, richer wines than others.

Which brings us to **Wellington** (formerly known as Wairarapa), around the town of Martinborough in the south of the island. It's much cooler here, but long, dry autumns and poor, gravelly soil are proving ideal for Pinot Noir. Here they show that New Zealand can make some of the best Pinots in the New World; not yet quite on a par with the best that California can produce, but seriously fragrant, silky wines that can be pure pleasure to drink. Quality can still be a little erratic, but after all, we're talking about one of the world's most erratic grapes, and Wellington is a new region. The potential is huge.

Another wine style that is making a name for itself is botrytized Riesling. Not everywhere; those dry autumns are not what is usually thought of as being ideal botrytis weather. But when they're good, they're very, very good.

Te Mata is the glamour winery of Hawkes Bay and this Chardonnay is a superbly crafted, toasty, spicy wine. Pinot Noir from Martinborough Vineyard is some of the country's finest. This Reserve is intense and complex and only made in exceptional vintages.

The Food of New Zealand

A COUNTRY WITH such a long coastline ought to have an abundance of seafood; and so it does. There is hoki, kingfish, snapper, yellow fin tuna, blue nose, blue cod, gurnard, tiger fish, deepsea dory and big, tasty green-lipped mussels, all waiting to be steamed, baked or sautéed, perhaps with locally grown garlic and local olive oil, perhaps with chilli, perhaps with coriander.

Culinary influences are being garnered from all over the world: New Zealand is part of the Pacific Rim culture and happily mixes Cajun and Mediterranean, Far Eastern and northern European traditions.

Expect to find the local lamb served with polenta, rabbit with olives, duck with wild rice or native cervena venison with *kumara*, the 'Maori potato'.

A country with such a range of climates can grow every sort of vegetable and fruit, from peaches and apricots to cool-climate apples and plums and (of course) kiwi fruit.

There is good dairy produce too, although as in Australia, the cheese has yet to reach the stunning quality of the rest of New Zealand's ingredients since pasteurization, sadly, is still very much the order of the day.

It's lucky that New Zealand red wines are much better than they used to be. Imagine having all that lamb and nothing to drink with it. A good Cabernet blend will fit the bill perfectly, just as Sauvignon Blanc is ideal both with New Zealand's huge variety of fish and the wide range of Far Eastern flavours in which so many New Zealand cooks revel. With delicious local game, Pinot Noir is a must.

South Island

Wine regions on the South Island are like mushrooms: they pop up out of nowhere, seemingly overnight, and in no time they're established. But there the analogy ends, because mushrooms have a rather short life, and South Island wine looks all set to be here as long as there are people around to grow the grapes and make the wine.

The Wine Regions

The crucial year was 1973. Montana, the biggest wine company in New Zealand, wanted to expand its holdings but didn't want to pay too much for the land. Land in Hawkes Bay was very expensive which ruled it out. So, instead, Montana bought 1620 hectares (4000 acres) of land in the north of the South Island, paid between a quarter and an eighth of what it would have had to have paid in Hawkes Bay, and planted it mostly with Müller-Thurgau. This was pretty adventurous: there wasn't a single vine here, and the land was completely untried. Even more adventurously, Montana set aside a corner, just 24 hectares (60 acres), and planted Sauvignon Blanc.

Talk about an inspired decision. From these 24 hectares **Marlborough** Sauvignon Blanc was born, and the world immediately sat up and took notice. Nobody had produced Sauvignon with such incisive, assertive, snappy fruit, all gooseberries and asparagus. It made Loire versions look lame; it made Sauvignon from anywhere else look dull. It made the Müller-Thurgau planted on the rest of the land look very old-fashioned indeed. And Sauvignon Blanc isn't as easy a grape to get right. Plant it somewhere too chilly and it will respond with lean, tinned-bean fruit that isn't terribly attractive – and yet give it too much warmth and it goes flabby and out of balance. Marlborough turned out to be just right.

Müller-Thurgau, quite rightly, is now on the decline. Not surprisingly, land in Marlborough is rather more expensive than it was; and not surprisingly a lot of other companies have moved in.

Marlborough is now New Zealand's largest area under vine; these vineyards are in the Brancott Valley.

Efforts to prove Marlborough's value as an all-round region have been less successful, though, which is almost a relief. Nobody else in the world can make Sauvignon like Marlborough; great Chardonnays come from a lot of places. That being said, there are some excellent buttery Chardonnays from Marlborough and there'll be more in the future, but at the moment a lot of Marlborough Chardonnay goes into sparkling wine. As far as reds go, Merlot is pretty good, but Cabernet Sauvignon will only ripen in good years in the warmest spots. Pinot

Stoneleigh Riesling, made with Marlborough fruit, perfectly captures the regional style.

Noir, which you'd think would be happy here, doesn't produce good results; what is very successful is Riesling. Most is dry, with the sort of taut balance that marks the grape at its best, but there is some sweet botrytized Riesling most years, and it's sensational, with a piercing acidity which balances the concentrated fruit and honeyed sweetness.

As to what makes Marlborough so good – well, partly it's climate and partly it's soil. Summers are long and cool, and autumns are reliably dry, so the grape growers needn't worry about having to pick in a hurry before rain sets in. The soil is stony and poor, but the stones hold the heat well, which aids ripening. In the north of the region it's so stony that irrigation is essential. So far all the plantings are on more or less flat land which is easy to work.

In **Nelson**, a small region north-west of Marlborough, they plant on the hillsides. The region is made up of a series of small hills and valleys, with a wide range of mesoclimates. It's cooler here than in Marlborough, and lovely Chardonnay and Sauvignon Blanc can be made. Pinot Noir shows definite potential and late-ripening Riesling can also produce excellent quality here.

Go south and you get to **Canterbury**. You'd think it would be getting a bit cold for vines here, but those varieties that do well in Nelson – Chardonnay, Sauvignon Blanc, Riesling and Pinot Noir – also do well here. Canterbury's growing number of small wineries are found either scattered on the exposed plains north, west and south of Christchurch or some 40km (25 miles) further north of the city at **Waipara**. Waipara is making surprisingly rich Pinots that challenge the best of the North Island; there's some Sauvignon Blanc and Chardonnay here as well.

Go south some more, and it really must be getting too cold. They go skiing round here, for goodness sake! But no: **Central Otago** is the only wine region with a continental climate and Pinot Noir from the north of the region looks rather promising. Gewürztraminer and Riesling also work well. These, at the moment, are the world's most southerly vineyards. But at the rate New Zealand is developing, in ten years' time who knows what might have happened?

The Grapes

A range of cool-climate grapes with clear, intense flavours.

Sauvignon Blanc

Chardonnay

SAUVIGNON BLANC from Marlborough is one of the great wine styles of the world, full of lean, pungent fruit and flavours of gooseberries. It is grown in every other region, too.

CHARDONNAY is grown everywhere, of course, and is probably at its best in Marlborough, where it is elegant yet rich.

RIESLING does well in all regions for both dry and sweet wines of great style and balance.

GEWÜRZTRAMINER is grown in Central Otago, and elsewhere as a minority grape. The cool climates of the South Island give intense, clean, spicy flavours.

PINOT NOIR, of all the red varieties, seems best suited to what is primarily a white wine island. Waipara in Canterbury is the South Island's best spot for it so far, though it is grown in Marlborough for sparkling wine.

CABERNET SAUVIGNON will ripen in the warmest parts of Marlborough, but looks as though it will always be a minority grape here.

MERLOT does ripen well in Marlborough; most is blended with Cabernet Sauvignon.

St Helena achieved fame with New Zealand's first outstanding Pinot Noir in 1982. Three years later, Cloudy Bay achieved instant cult status with the first release of its zesty Sauvignon Blanc.

CLOUDY BAY

Fine wines normally take generations to evolve. Years of fine-tuning vines and winemaking, years of learning the quirks of weather and soil are normally needed. Not at Cloudy Bay. At Cloudy Bay it took just one vintage. The concrete was barely dry in the winery when the awards started rolling in.

Cloudy Bay was the brainchild of David Hohnen, who owned the Cape Mentelle winery in Western Australia. Hohnen wanted to make Sauvignon Blanc like the ones he'd tasted from New Zealand, so he hired Kevin Judd, winemaker at Selaks in Auckland, to help him in his quest. All they needed now were vineyards and a winery.

Marlborough at that time was largely owned by two big companies. One of these, Corbans, had no winery nearby and was having to truck its Marlborough grapes to Gisborne. They were happy to let Hohnen have some Sauvignon Blanc grapes in return for use of the winery that he planned to build. The winery went up; the first vintage of Cloudy Bay was made in 1985 from grapes bought from Corbans – and made by telephoned directions from Judd, who was making his final vintage at Selaks.

What makes Cloudy Bay so special? Finesse, complexity, a marvellous balance of ripeness and freshness. A small proportion is fermented and aged in new oak, and there's a dash of Semillon added, too.

Cloudy Bay's label draws its inspiration from the Richmond Ranges which form the backdrop to the vineyards.

SOUTH AFRICA

Welcome to the newest of the new: the latest recruit to the global wine market. Welcome to South Africa.

Actually, South Africa has been here before: back in the 18th century, sweet Constantia dessert wine was a familiar feature of wealthy dining tables in northern Europe. Throughout most of this century South African 'sherry' was a useful, good-value alternative to proper sherry from Spain in many British households. And yet South Africa is very much a new player in the modern wine world because during the 1980s, when the rest of the world was transforming its wine more thoroughly and faster than at any time in history, South Africa was isolated behind the wall of apartheid. International sanctions meant that its wine was increasingly unpopular in international markets, and while dialogue between winemakers in Europe, the United States, Chile and Australia became ever more widespread and more productive, South African winemakers were left out in the cold, unable to keep up with what the rest of the world was doing. Only a small handful of exceptionally determined producers managed to produce world-class wines under these conditions; but that small handful

was enough to make the rest of the world hope for great things from South Africa when at last apartheid was abolished.

THE CAPE'S FIRST WINES

Winemaking had been thoroughly established in South Africa for many years. In fact, it is probably the only country which can pinpoint the birth of its wine industry to a particular date. Jan van Riebeeck, the first European to settle in the Cape, arrived there in 1652, and planted vines in the hope of finding a cure for scurvy, and as part of setting up a supply station for Dutch East India Company ships sailing the spice routes to the Far East. But while the Dutch had long been great wine traders they had little experience of growing vines or making wine, and it is much to van Riebeeck's credit that seven years later, on 2nd February, 1659, he recorded in his diary: 'Today, God be praised, wine was pressed for the first time from Cape grapes.'

The first wines don't seem to have been particularly enjoyable – they were so acidic that they tended to 'irritate the bowels', according to one early commentator – but in 1685 Muscat vines were planted by the governor, Simon van der Stel, just south of Cape Town, on the Constantia estate. Constantia wines, sweet and rich, red and white, were just what northern Europeans wanted. They seem to have been late-picked but unfortified, though they might have been fortified for export. They remained popular in Britain until the late 19th century, although after 1861, when the prime minister, Gladstone, removed empire preferential tariffs, French wines became cheaper and more available in Britain and South African wines began to be seen less.

In 1886 phylloxera arrived in South Africa, and, once the crisis was over, rapid replanting of high-yielding varieties produced a disastrous glut. The wine industry badly needed regulation and organization; and in 1918 both arrived, in the form of the KWV (Cape Wine Growers' Co-operative, or Koöperatiewe Wynbouers Vereniging).

European vines are a more recent addition to a landscape that has one of the most varied flora in the world.

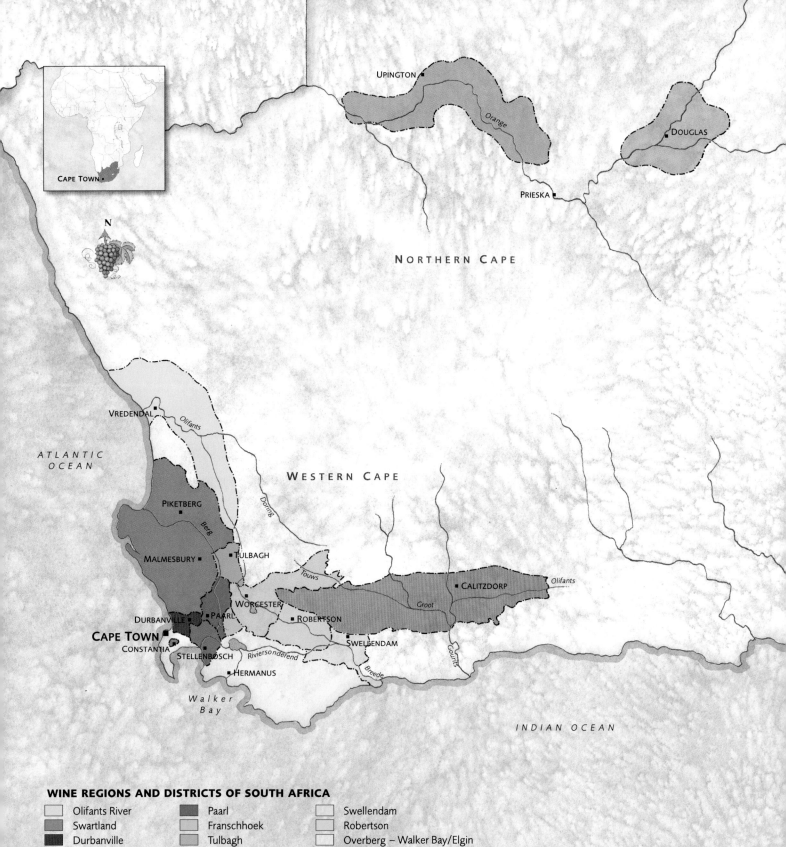

UPINGTON

Orange

DOUGLAS

PRIESKA

NORTHERN CAPE

CAPE TOWN

N

VREDENDAL

Olifants

ATLANTIC
OCEAN

WESTERN CAPE

Doring

PIKETBERG

Berg

TULBAGH

Touws

Olifants

MALMESBURY

CALITZDORP

Groot

WORCESTER

ROBERTSON

DURBANVILLE   PAARL

CAPE TOWN

SWELLENDAM

CONSTANTIA

Riviersonderend

STELLENBOSCH

Breede

HERMANUS

Gouritz

Walker
Bay

INDIAN OCEAN

WINE REGIONS AND DISTRICTS OF SOUTH AFRICA

- Olifants River
- Swartland
- Durbanville
- Constantia
- Stellenbosch
- Paarl
- Franschhoek
- Tulbagh
- Worcester
- Klein Karoo
- Swellendam
- Robertson
- Overberg – Walker Bay/Elgin
- Lower Orange River
- Douglas

0 km   100

0 miles   50   100

The Boschendal Estate in the Groot Drakenstein Valley, Franschhoek, is a fine example of Cape architecture with its Dutch-style gables and whitewashed exterior.

Beyers Truter at Kanonkop is arguably South Africa's leading Pinotage expert (see box on p.255). Charles Back at Fairview is a born innovator with a highly developed commercial perspective.

THE DEVELOPING WINE INDUSTRY

The KWV gradually acquired massive power over the industry. It fixed minimum prices and production quotas not just for its 4900 grower members but also for those producers who didn't belong to it. It handled marketing and acted as the official control board as well as being a producer, and while it did a great deal of good in the early days by stabilizing the industry, more recently it began to be seen as a dinosaur. The industry was organized for the benefit of the growers, for whom quantity was the aim, rather than for consumers or even small independent producers, some of whom tell stories of having had to fight the KWV at every turn. This situation prevailed until the 1990s, when the KWV began, little by little, to give up more and more of its powers.

Before then, however, by the mid-1980s, the regulations that made it well-nigh impossible for growers to get better clones of vines like Chardonnay were being eased; the dearth of decent vine stock had been a major drag on progress. Until then only a single clone of Chardonnay had been available, and it was infected with virus diseases. Good clones of Cabernet Sauvignon, Pinot Noir and other European classics were similarly hard to come by. Yet, it was only really in the mid-1990s that the first new vines began to come on stream; the improvement in flavours is already noticeable.

South Africa, then, has had a lot of catching up to do. It's not there yet: many wines are still unbalanced; others still show the marks of inexperienced winemaking. Only now are producers learning not to pick their red grapes too early; the hard green character and high acidity that marked most reds is only just starting to disappear.

There is still a tendency to play safe and make wines that are a bit dull, but that will change, too. Don't forget that for decades growers have been preoccupied with maximizing yields, and a lot of them still are. The good growers are leading the way with concentrated, ripe, exciting wines, often from cooler climates, many closer to the sea than the warmer traditional heartland of South African wine. They are producing delicate but well-structured Pinot Noir; Chardonnay of restraint and elegance that is somewhere between Australia and Burgundy in style; cedary Bordeaux blends, and chunky Pinotage.

This last is South Africa's speciality. It's a cross between Pinot Noir and Cinsaut, though without much of the finesse or perfume of the former. But when fully ripened and vinified in a modern manner, with or without oak, it has a most particular taste. As South Africa searches for more individuality of style, Pinotage is sure to come into its own.

What must bode well is the foreign investment that is increasingly a part of South African wine. Flying winemakers have the Cape on their schedules now; the first black winemakers are beginning to make their mark too. At Nelson's Creek, cellar assistant Mathewis Thabo was responsible for the first wines under the New Beginnings label while at the Fairview Estate in Paarl, Awie Adolf made a Chenin Blanc called Fair Valley. South Africa's progress is rapid by any standards.

CLASSIFICATION

A **Wine of Origin** system was originally introduced in 1973 and later adapted in 1993. Under this system, South Africa's winelands are divided into regions, districts and wards, and the origin is guaranteed by a paper seal on the bottle, if the producer has opted for participation in the Seal of Origin system which is not obligatory.

If the wine is labelled as a single grape variety, at least 75 per cent (and 85 per cent for export) must be of that variety; the same percentages also apply to a stated vintage year. If a producer has registered as an 'estate' then he or she may only use grapes grown on his or her property. Bear in mind, however, that not all the top South African wines are estate wines.

PINOTAGE

South Africa used to be embarrassed by Pinotage. It was a workhorse grape, never producing anything of interest; the best thing that could be done was to grub it up. By the early 1990s it was down to about two per cent of South African plantings – not much for the only grape South Africa could call its own.

It's a crossing of Pinot Noir and Cinsaut, and it was bred in 1925 at Stellenbosch University; Cinsaut was commonly called Hermitage at the time, which is why the offspring of these ill-matched parents was called Pinotage. Pinot Noir and Cinsaut. Well. You might as well match a dancer with a shot-putter and expect physically well-adjusted progeny.

Pinotage always had a bit of an identity problem. It could be coarse and pungent and smell of paint, but it could also be rich and deep-coloured and give you the feeling that it was intended for better things. But it wasn't until Beyers Truter started making serious Pinotage at the Kanonkop Estate that it became clear that Pinotage could give powerful, well-structured, long-lasting wine.

To be honest, it's taken a while for Truter's example to be widely followed. Lately many growers have been stuffing Pinotage into the ground as fast as they can, but until better clones become available the variety can tend to retain harsh acetone flavours. It's also taken a while to kill the conventional wisdom that stated that Pinotage should be fermented cold and drunk young; cold fermentation emphasizes its oddness whereas warmer fermentation and some French oak-aging give it polish and length. Some growers also take the view that where it is planted is crucial in determining whether it has these tricky acetone flavours.

When the turnaround happened, it happened fast. Nowadays Pinotage is seen – rightly – as South Africa's speciality, with deep berry flavours and a sweet-sour fruit that, when treated properly, is delicious. Some is made light and easy-drinking, some is bigger and more extracted, and quality is becoming more even. Like so many fashion changes, it was spurred on by interest from abroad: you'll find Pinotage in Zimbabwe these days, and occasionally in other parts of the New World.

Pinotage grapes, destined to make some splendidly deep-coloured wine.

ABOVE **Chardonnay vines growing in the Thelema Mountain vineyards in Stellenbosch. These slopes are proving ideal for a range of grapes.**

The Cape Winelands

The problem with South Africa is that there's just not enough of it. If it carried on for another 200km (125 miles) or so towards the Antarctic it would have cool climates galore, and it would be able to turn out lean, Burgundian Chardonnays and delicious Pinot Noirs by the bucketful.

But at least when the geographical goodies were handed out, South Africa did get the Benguela Current, flowing up from the ice cap of the South Pole and cooling the south-west tip of the country so that if growers hug the coast and go as far south as they can without actually falling into the sea, there are some pretty cool climates to be found.

Most of the country's vineyards are concentrated around this tip. Even so, those that go north and inland are decidedly warm, and the warmest spots of all concentrate on fortifieds and

brandy. Stellenbosch and Paarl are the heartland of the industry, and Elgin and Walker Bay are the newer, cooler regions. These, along with Constantia and parts of Robertson, are the main quality spots. Elsewhere there's a greater concentration on bulk wine from heavily irrigated vineyards.

Stellenbosch and Durbanville

Stellenbosch has long had a reputation for producing some of South Africa's best reds, even though a lot of land is planted with white Chenin Blanc. The potential for better quality is enormous. It's not that cool here, but by planting on the mountain slopes where there's more rain, where the temperature drops and where the drainage is good, quality can be pushed several notches. It can even be a good idea to plant vineyards facing away from the sun, which is heresy in most European regions. Here it's all part of cooling things down.

Durbanville is one of a number of smaller areas which are emerging with the new emphasis on quality. Others are **Helderberg**, **Devon Valley** and **Simonsberg** (these three are wards within the Stellenbosch District) – at the moment they're just names, but they're names with cool climates. Durbanville in particular, though it's mostly wheat country at the moment, makes attractive Sauvignon Blanc, and pockets of a particular soil here, Malmesbury shale, could mean that it has good potential for Cabernet Sauvignon.

Soil, you see. Soil matters in South Africa. It's interesting that the best of its wines are not particularly New World in style, suggesting that the country is already finding its own path rather than hanging on to the coat tails of Australia or Chile. A surprising number of the best producers are keen on the idea of terroir, and interested in reflecting it in their wines. Of course there are masses of fruit-driven wines in South Africa – but the growers at the forefront of the move to cooler climates and better grapes are taking (dare one say it) a slightly more European attitude. It's going to be fascinating to watch the development of regional styles here in the years to come.

Paarl

Paarl, further from the cooling effects of the sea at False Bay, is warmer, and like Stellenbosch it produces some good ripe reds. But it also makes rich Chardonnays and even Sauvignon Blanc with surprising pungency.

There is unexplored potential here, too. **Franschhoek**, where French Huguenots settled in the late 17th century after the Revocation of the Edict of Nantes in 1685 gave rise to persecution at

Stained glass from the Hartenberg Estate, Stellenbosch, shows the traditional method of treading grapes.

Two leaders of the field. Gyles Webb's success as a winegrower stems from his endless search for the perfect grape. He may have found it in Cabernet Sauvignon. Danie and Lesca de Wet have found theirs in Chardonnay, a variety they pioneered in Robertson.

The Grapes

The lack of good clones, for years a major problem, is now being solved.

CABERNET SAUVIGNON is currently producing most of the Cape's best reds, sometimes with an admixture of the other main red Bordeaux varieties. The most successful wines are of middle weight with good cedary fruit and firm structure, somewhere between Bordeaux and Australia in style.

CABERNET FRANC makes the occasional excellent red on its own, but is more usually part of a Bordeaux blend, where its fresh, grassy fruit works well.

MERLOT can be made as a varietal or blended with one or both Cabernets, where its plummy fruit acts as a softening influence.

SHIRAZ makes mostly soft wines, sometimes aged in new oak. However, some more challenging, smoky flavours are appearing.

PINOT NOIR at its best is perfumed, even silky, with a firm structure.

CINSAUT is not widely planted, but it can make fresh, redcurrant-flavoured wine that is either bottled as a varietal or blended.

PINOTAGE, the Cape's speciality red grape, makes both soft early-drinking wines and more structured, oak-aged ones.

CHENIN BLANC is South Africa's most planted white grape. It seldom reaches great heights of quality, but can make attractive everyday dry or off-dry white.

CHARDONNAY is the main focus in white wines of South Africa's drive for quality. So far, though, most are made in a safe, middle-of-the-road style.

SAUVIGNON BLANC from the best cool-climate producers is showing some of the most refreshing, tangy flavours in the New World. It is often soft and simple in warmer sites.

SEMILLON has ripe, soft, straightforward lemon flavours and is showing great affinity for new oak.

RIESLING can have good structure and a peachy, flowery character.

COLOMBARD makes everyday wine with soft, simple fruit.

MUSCADEL is usually made sweet; the most interesting are of middle weight, with some elegance.

Klein Constantia's vineyards were famous throughout Europe long before most of the present South African wineland was planted.

Dutch architecture. It's the Cape's most popular historic tourist attraction, helped no doubt by its close proximity to the city.

Worcester

Worcester is more of a mix, producing bulk wines that mostly get fortified or distilled as well as good-quality fortifieds and fresh, everyday whites. There are some indications of a move towards red varieties too. But it's a hot, dry inland region and irrigation is necessary.

Robertson

Robertson is hot, too, and relies on an intricate system of irrigation based on the Brandvlei Dam to keep its rose nurseries in flower and its race-horses (it's a great region for stud farms) happy. For a long time its wines were mere workhorses, from Chenin Blanc and Colombard. Robertson and Worcester produced cheap base wines for for-tification and for brandy; nothing more was expected of them. Yet in the past 20 years extra-ordinary transformations have been worked here – and, given the isolated nature of South African wine until this decade, worked very quietly. Robertson's limestone outcrops produced good roses and good grass for racehorses; why not good Chardonnay?

Such was the reasoning of a handful of pro-ducers, and it proved spot on. Limestone gives Chardonnay with good acidity in Champagne, and it performs the same trick here, streaking a citrus tang through wines that are otherwise big and lush. Sauvignon Blanc does well on the stonier soils, too, in spite of the heat. More and more growers have caught on, to the extent that there's even been a mini-boom in new bottling lines as growers have opted to leave the local co-op and set up on their own.

The next stage in Robertson seems to be a move from white to red, with Cabernet, Merlot, Pinotage, Shiraz and others being planted up the hillsides. The limestone soils in Robertson also seem to favour sparkling wines which are making a promising start here, with good Chardonnay and Pinot Noir.

home, is a particularly high-quality spot for wines, and there are other, similar side valleys in these mountains just crying out for quality-con-scious producers to plant them with vines. Just give it time, and an expanding market abroad.

Constantia

Constantia is close to where wine began in South Africa. The original Constantia estate has been divided, and there are now five producers in this small region of which one, Klein Constantia, has revived the dessert wine that made the old Con-stantia estate famous. All make table wines, red and white, as well, and the government-owned Groot Constantia is a splendid example of Cape

Other Regions

The newer, cooler regions are still hardly exploited, with just a few lone growers showing how good Chardonnay, Pinot Noir and other cool-climate varieties can be. **Elgin** and **Walker Bay** are next door neighbours in South Africa's most southerly vineyard area, with the former making zesty Sauvignon Blanc from high vineyards in country otherwise dominated by apple growers. Walker Bay is where the country's most impressive Pinot Noirs so far have come from, all perfume and restrained structure; there's even a Burgundian producer with a joint venture here, which is a sign of true faith. Pinotage is also being pursued successfully in warmer sites, mainly slightly inland.

Even the bulk producing regions are capable of producing some decent everyday stuff, though. (And why not? Australia's wine casks are filled from the irrigated Riverland and Riverina. Why shouldn't South Africa be able to do the same thing?) **Swartland** can make reasonable Chenin Blanc, Colombard and Pinotage but also some serious, well-made reds and good Sauvignon Blanc; **Olifants River** is the scene of some flying winemaking that is turning out fresh reds and whites. It's the most northerly of the Cape's winegrowing regions and most of the vineyards are stretched out along either side of the Olifants River where fertile soils result in high yields. **Orange River** (made up of Lower Orange River and Douglas) in the Northern Cape and **Klein Karoo** much further south are practically desert, soaking up vast quantities of irrigation that gets turned into bulk wine of little interest as yet, or into fortifieds. Good port-style wines come from Calitzdorp in the Klein Karoo and there's an annual Port Festival here too. Traditional Muscadels are also highly rated.

As well as looking for cooler spots, enterprising winemakers are also checking out higher ground. The mountains around Villiersdorp, just behind Elgin, look interesting, as does Ceres near Tulbagh, where cherries and apples also grow.

Hamilton Russell Vineyards and Bouchard Finlayson, both based in Walker Bay, are producers of leading South African Pinot Noirs in an elegant Burgundian mould.

The Food of South Africa

SOUTH AFRICA'S cuisine has evolved from various imported cultures – Malay, Dutch, French, German and Portuguese. Combined with South Africa's range of fresh ingredients and flavours, the results are unique.

Red meat consumption in South Africa is high. The *braai*, or barbeque, is a popular event where vast quantities of meat, sausages and baked vegetables are enjoyed.

You'll also come across the *bredie*, a pot roast of spiced meat and vegetables cooked slowly in a cast-iron pot. Waterblommetjies, a vegetable which grows wild or in dams, come into their own in this dish alongside succulent Karoo mutton. The sheep graze on wild herbs which gives the mutton a delicious flavour.

Wind-dried meats, or *biltong*, frankly don't look appetizing but are suprisingly tasty. The coiled *boerevors* or farmers' sausages can vary dramatically in quality. You'll find *bobotie*, a Cape-Malay dish made from minced meat flavoured with garlic, turmeric, cumin, lemon, pepper and herbs, on most menus. Pork and mutton are used for *sosaties* – wooden skewers of meat, marinated and grilled. Game is another speciality – venison, guinea-fowl and ostrich in particular. It's just as well South Africa has good sturdy Cabernet and Pinotage to wash it all down.

Seafood is also abundant. As well as shellfish, look out for fish like red roman, kingklip, snapper and Cape salmon.

Chicken pie, green beans and waterblommetjies

The Cape's orchards are full of fruit and vegetables squash, pumpkins and legumes in particular. Maize meal is also a staple crop.

If you've got room left after all this, *melktert* (Cape brandy pudding) and *koeksister*, sweet cakes, should fill the gap.

OTHER COUNTRIES

The areas we think of today as being the core of the wine world – Europe and certain parts of the New World – are not the whole wine story. Grape vines have been grown in Asia for millennia – the vine reached India from Persia as early as 3000 BC. China, as well as having its own indigenous varieties of vine, was importing Western wines by the 2nd century AD. Grapes have been cultivated in Japan for over a thousand years, and a taste for wine was brought over by Portuguese missionaries in the 16th century. Today India, China and Japan all have winemaking industries making wines based to a greater or lesser extent on the classic styles of Europe. North Africa's wine industry, while based on that of southern France some decades ago, is declining – and it seems there's little hope of revival.

India

In India one of the classic styles was port, which Portuguese colonists in Goa tried to imitate, with limited success. The Great Calcutta Exhibition of 1884 also had some Indian wines among its attractions, but there had never been a large market apart from the British (who were just as likely to drink spirits). A few aristocratic Indians drank wine, but the bulk of the population got its alcohol from various forms of grain. Phylloxera arrived at the end of the 19th century and destroyed the vineyards, and modern India takes an unsympathetic (though not always consistent) attitude to alcohol of all forms. The state of Gujarat is officially dry, though most other states make alcoholic drinks under government licence.

There are about 50,000 hectares (125,000 acres) of vineyards all told, mostly in **Western Maharashtra** – but before you start calculating how much wine that means, forget it. At least 95 per cent of the grapes never see the inside of a vat and are intended as table grapes. India's wine industry is not large.

It is also heavily dependent on irrigation. Planting at high altitude, where the temperature is manageable, was the answer in the 1980s,

India's best-known wine. Technology, with the help of Champagne consultants Piper-Heidsieck, generally produces a firm, fresh and chunky sparkler.

Colossal irrigation is needed to keep these vines in the vineyards of Champagne India, the producers of Omar Khayyam, happy and healthy.

when grapes like Ugni Blanc, Chardonnay, Colombard and Pinot Blanc were planted for sparkling wine as part of a joint venture with a Champagne house. The resulting wine, Omar Khayyam, is perfectly pleasant. Cabernet Sauvignon, Merlot, Syrah and Pinot Noir were also planted for still red wines. It has certainly proved that winemaking in India is feasible, and the quality of sparkling wine is reasonable. Whether it is a real competitor for the many excellent sparklers now coming from all corners of the earth is another matter; but at least it has curiosity value.

China

China's vinifera vines were imported at the end of the 19th century, mainly to cater for foreign communities living there. The Chinese themselves generally prefer rice wine, but if they're going to drink anything made from grapes they favour the most expensive kind of Cognac, which they drink with meals. Grape brandy will do at a pinch, but it has to be a serious pinch.

As for winegrowing, these days it looks as if the **Shandong Peninsula**, in the north-east of the country, has the greatest potential. The mountains there, the Dazashen, offer south-east- and south-west-facing slopes of poor, well-drained soil, but it is difficult to persuade local growers with no history of winegrowing that too much irrigation and overly high yields of underripe grapes are not what's wanted. Western know-how has entered the picture via several joint ventures and the best of these wines are clean and have some varietal character. Inevitably, such joint ventures focus on Chardonnay, though there are also some German and Russian (Rkatsiteli, for example) varieties; Chinese grapes have names like Dragon's Eye and Mare's Teat, which sound more like the contents of their pharmacies than anything you'd want to drink. But who knows?

Taiwan

Vines are also grown to a small extent in Taiwan, where experiments with European vines are proceeding under the advice of the University of California at Davis.

Huadong in China's Shandong province is a Sino-British/Hong Kong-backed operation with an Australian winemaker. An international operation but will the wines find favour in an international market?

Wine and Asian Food

MATCHING WESTERN wines with Eastern food can be tricky and the problems are compounded by the depressing nature of the wine lists in most Indian, Chinese, Thai and Japanese restaurants. But there are several reasons to be cheerful: for one thing, the best restaurants are gradually realizing that it's worth having a few good and suitable wines on their lists. For another, we're all eating much more Asian food at home these days.

Indian food is often characterized less by extreme heat than by rich and complex spiciness. It's true that if you do want to binge on the ultra-hot flavours of southern India then your best bet is *lassi* or lager, but with gentler dishes go for soft reds with little or no tannin, like Cru Beaujolais, young Spanish *joven* reds or soft young reds from the south of Italy, Australia or California. Whites are often more successful, particularly with vegetable dishes: try cool-climate New World Chardonnays with good acidity; Australian Semillons, Verdelhos or Marsannes.

Chinese food relies on balance for its effect: balance of textures, flavours and ingredients. It's not so much the flavours themselves that are tricky for wine to cope with: ginger, soy sauce, five-spice powder and oyster and *hoisin* sauce are not in themselves inimical to wine. It's the contrasts that present the problem, and the number of dishes (each with their own contrasts) presented at a time. Alsace wines are a good solution, provided they're fermented out dry, or nearly: Gewürztraminer is a particularly good match for ginger. Good Riesling (preferably from Germany, though Australian ones also work well) is the best all-round solution.

With Thai food, Sauvignon Blanc is the best bet. It has the right lightness and acidity to match lemon grass, coriander and coconut. Soft reds can work with beef dishes, but there's no point in trying a really fine red: it won't be flattered by the match.

Japanese food is the most difficult Asian cuisine for the wine lover. It's the startling intensity of dipping sauces and seasonings that can kill wine; *wasabi* is the worst of the lot. But a lot of the flavours are sharp, and acidic white wines are the ones to go for. Oak doesn't work; try instead Sauvignon Blanc or, with *sushi*, German Riesling. Fino sherry is the nearest Western equivalent to *sake*, but it's not as near as all that.

In Japanese vineyards vines are usually trained high to combat rot in the humid climate.

Japan

Japan has been growing grapes for over a millennium, but here, too, it was contact with Westerners that introduced a taste for wine. It's still a fairly minority taste, and some 90 per cent of Japan's grape harvest is of table grapes. There are few vineyards dedicated to wine vines, and the grapes that go to the fermenting vats are often those that didn't make the grade as table grapes. With table grapes fetching four or five times the price of wine grapes, it's not surprising that growers give low priority to the needs of the wineries.

It's also true that the wine producers have only quite recently begun to think in terms of better quality. Most wine from Japanese-grown grapes is light, sweetish and somewhat insipid; most, too, is bolstered by imported wine, or wine made from imported must or imported grapes. Only in the last few years have wine labels started to be more open about how much of the content of the bottle is imported and how much is made at home. That portion that is made at home, however, doesn't have to have come from Japanese grapes: merely to have been fermented in Japan is good enough.

There is some genuine Japanese wine, though. It costs more to buy, which means that the producers do have some incentive to improve quality. The most popular grape is the Koshu, a vinifera variety which is really better for the table than the glass. There's also a lot of a crossing called Neo-Muscat; there are some plantings of European varieties, but not many.

The main obstacle to a flourishing wine industry is the climate. Vines are grown in 46 of Japan's 47 provinces, but most wine comes from **Katsunuma** in the Yamanashi Prefecture where the weather is slightly more amenable; in most places it's too wet, too humid, too cold in winter, and the terrain is either too mountainous or too flat.

North Africa

There are still vineyards here, in Algeria, Morocco and Tunisia, but they're shrinking. The trouble is they're caught between the loss of their French market, which kept them going from the 1900s until the 1950s and 1960s, and the growth of Islamic fundamentalism at home. With little domestic market to speak of, there is no cash for investment and so vineyards continue to be uprooted.

Even those that exist don't produce anything particularly enjoyable. True, the vine varieties aren't designed to thrill: there's a lot of Carignan and Cinsaut among the reds, and Ugni Blanc and Clairette among the whites. But there's also some Syrah, Mourvèdre and Cabernet Sauvignon, and while it's hot and dry in North Africa, it's no hotter and drier than it is in parts of Australia – and we've seen what can be achieved there. A few flying winemakers could no doubt transform the wines of North Africa; but it's unlikely to happen.

All three countries have a structure of appellations d'origine put in place by the French. **Algeria's Coteaux de Mascara** is one of the more promising areas, and **Tunisia's** Muscats, both sweet and dry, aren't bad. **Morocco** does at least have a privately owned company, Celliers de Meknès, which is showing some interest in improving quality, but gains are so far small. Some of the pink *vin gris* can be pleasant, if a little tough, and the sweet Muscats have potential. But the general flavours of the North African reds are earthy, dry and tough, with somewhat battered overripe raspberry fruit; whites are mostly oxidized – a problem which could of course be solved relatively easily.

A Roman mosaic from the Museum of Tunisia. Viticulture was a part of life in Tunisia before the days of the Roman Empire. It was probably introduced by the Phoenicians when they established the city of Carthage, east of modern Tunis.

Glossary and Index

Glossary

ACID Naturally present in grapes and essential to wine, providing the refreshing tang in whites and the appetizing 'grip' in reds. Principal wine acids are acetic, carbonic, citric, malic, tannic and tartaric.

ALCOHOLIC CONTENT The alcoholic strength of wine, usually expressed as a percentage of the total wine.

ALCOHOLIC FERMENTATION The process whereby yeasts, natural or added, convert the grape sugars into alcohol and carbon dioxide. Normally stops either when all the sugar has been converted or when the alcohol level reaches about 15 per cent.

ANNATA Italian for 'vintage' date.

BARREL AGING Time spent maturing in wood, normally oak. The wine takes on flavours from the wood.

BARRIQUE Bordeaux barrel holding 225 litres (50 gallons).

BLENDING Mixing together wines of different origin, styles or age, often to balance out acidity, weight, etc.

BRUT French for 'unsweetened'. Used to describe the driest type of sparkling wines.

CARBONIC MACERATION Winemaking method where grapes are fermented whole in a closed vat; produces light, fruity red wine for drinking early.

CHAMPAGNE METHOD Traditional method of making wine sparkle by inducing a second fermentation in the bottle.

CLASSICO Italian term for the original central part within a DOC. Usually denotes superior quality.

CLONE Strain of grape species. Some grapes, Pinot Noir for example, have hundreds of clones.

COLD FERMENTATION Long, slow fermentation at low temperature to extract maximum freshness from the grapes. Crucial for white wines in hot climates.

COMMUNE French term for village. Often used in Burgundy, where each major commune has its own appellation.

COOL CLIMATE The areas at the coolest limits of grape-ripening, for example Germany, England and Washington State.

CRU French term literally meaning 'growth' that is used to describe a single vineyard, usually qualified with a quality reference such as 'Grand Cru', 'Premier Cru', etc.

CUVÉE Contents of a cuvée or vat. Also refers to a blended wine, often as in 'Cuvée de Luxe' implying a special quality.

DEMI-SEC Semi-dry, but more accurately translated as 'demi-sweet' in most cases.

DOMAINE French term for single vineyard.

ENOLOGIST Wine scientist or technician.

ESTATE A single property, though this may encompass several different vineyards.

FORTIFIED WINE Wine which has high-strength spirit added usually before the initial alcoholic fermentation is completed, thereby preserving sweetness.

HYBRID Grape variety bred from an American vine species and a European *Vitis vinifera*; contrary to a crossing, which is bred from two vinifera varieties.

LATE HARVEST The harvesting of grapes after the ordinary harvest date to increase alcoholic strength or sweetness.

LAYING DOWN The storing of wine which will improve with age.

LEES Initially a coarse sediment left in the bottom of the fermentation vessel consisting of dead yeast cells, grape pips (seeds), pulp and tartrates. A further finer sediment, the fine lees, may be left in contact with the wine in cask (*see also* 'Sur Lie').

LIEU-DIT Burgundian term for single vineyard below First Growth standard.

MALOLACTIC FERMENTATION Secondary fermentation which converts malic acid to the softer lactic acid. Normal in reds, though hot country whites may arrest it to keep the wine fresher and preserve acidity.

MATURATION Positive term for the beneficial aging of wine.

NON-VINTAGE A wine without a stated vintage year, usually a blend of more than one harvest.

OXIDATION Over-exposure of wine to air, causing loss of fruit and bacterial decay.

RACKING The clarification of quality wine by the transferral of wine off its lees to another barrel.

RESERVA Spanish term indicating wine has been aged for a specific number of years according to the DO regulations.

RISERVA Italian term indicating wine aged for a specific number of years according to DOC laws.

SEC 'Dry'. When applied to Champagne it actually means medium-dry.

SUR LIE French for 'on the lees', meaning wine bottled direct from the cask or fermentation vat to gain extra flavour from the lees.

SÜSSRESERVE German term for the unfermented grape juice sometimes added to wine to boost sweetness.

TANNIN The bitter, mouth-drying component in red wines, derived from skins, pips, stalks and sometimes wooden barrels, which is harsh when young but crucial to a wine's ability to age.

VARIETAL Wine made from, and named after, a single grape variety.

VINIFICATION The process of turning grapes into wine.

VINTAGE The year's grape harvest, also used to describe the wine of a single year.

VITICULTURE Vine-growing and vineyard management.

Index

Picture Credits

All photography is by Mick Rock/Cephas unless stated otherwise below. The publishers are grateful to the following for permission to reproduce copyright material:
p.2 Cephas/Ted Stefanski; p.6 Cephas/Kevin Judd; p.12 Lesley and Roy Adkins; p.13 The British Library; p.14 Special Collections, University of California, Davis; p.16 Cephas/Kevin Judd; pp.22, 35, 38, 40-1 Lyndon Parker; p.24 Cephas/Wine Magazine; p.28 (left) Cephas/Jerry Alexander; p.35 (grape backgrounds) Tig Sutton; p.48 The Anthony Blake Picture Library; p.61 Cephas/Kjell Karlsson; p.74 Cephas/Nigel Blythe; p.95 (top) Timothy Slade; p.98 Cephas/Top/Hervé Amiard; p.120 Cephas/Alain Proust; p.121 (bottom right) Cephas/Herbert Lehmann; p.130 (watercolour) Murray Zanoni; p.135 (bottom) Cephas/M J Kielty; p.146 Cephas/Roy Stedall-Humphryes; p.147 Cephas/Top/Pierre Hussenot; p.155 (main) Cephas/Nigel Blythe; pp.156, 157 Cephas/David Copeman; pp.160, 168, 169 Cephas/Nigel Blythe; p.175 Cephas/Walter Geiersperger; p.179 (bottom right) Hulton Getty; p.186 (centre) Patrick Eagar; p.187 Cephas/John Millwood; pp.188, 190, 192, 194 Cephas/Bruce Fleming; pp.195, 196 Cephas/Ted Stefanski; p.197 Cephas/Steve Elphick; p.198 (bottom) Cephas/Bruce Fleming; p.211 Cephas/Kevin Argue; p.212 David W Hamilton/Image Bank; p.213 Cephas/R & K Muschenetz; p.215 Cephas/Andy Christodolo; pp.216, 217 R & K Muschenetz; p.219 Cephas/Andy Christodolo; p.221 Cephas/R & K Muschenetz; p.223 Cephas/Louis de Rohan; pp.227, 228, 233, 236 Cephas/Andy Christodolo; p.245 (both) Cephas/Steven Morris; pp.246, 249, 251 Cephas/Kevin Judd; pp.252, 254, 255, 256 Cephas/Alain Proust; p.257 Cephas/Geraldine Norman; p.258 Cephas/Juan Espi; p.259 Cephas/Alain Proust; p.260 Cephas/Janet Price; p.262 (top) Cephas/Nigel Blythe; (bottom) Cephas/Mike Taylor.

Visiting Vinopolis

Where to find us
1 Bank End
London SE1 9BU
The main entrance to VINOPOLIS is at the
corner of Bank End and Clink Street. There is a
separate entrance for major evening events in
Stoney Street.
- Coach drop facility at Southwark Street, SE1
- Northern, Jubilee Lines to London Bridge
- Buses: 17, 21, 35, 40, 43, 48, 133, 149, 344,
  501, 521, P3, P11, N21, N35, N47, N70
- NCP parking on St Thomas Street and
  Newcomen Street

Facilities for disabled people
- Level access via the main entrance
- Adapted male and female toilets
Please call VINOPOLIS on 0171-645 3700 if
you have any special needs or queries.

Opening times
Open 7 days a week, from 10am.
Closed on Christmas Day.

How to book
Entrance tickets for visitors, priced at £10
and including the audio-guide, tastings and
entrance into the Gallery, can be booked in
advance through Ticketmaster by calling the
VINOPOLIS hotline on 0870 444 777 or by
using their fully transactional website,
www.ticketmaster.co.uk Ticketmaster is also
handling sales for groups, coach operators, leisure
operators and inbound tour operators.

Further information
For more information on VINOPOLIS,
City of Wine, please call 0171-645 3700.

If you are interested in obtaining further
information on wine tastings and wine education,
please contact Sophia Gilliatt on 0171-645 3707.

Alternatively, if you have any queries concerning
the banqueting and corporate hospitality facilities
available, please contact either Sue Reid, Events
Manager, or Delia Cottle, Banqueting Co-
ordinator on 0171-645 3705.

VINOPOLIS
CITY OF WINE